Blindness *for* Beginners

a renewed vision of the possible

Maribel Steel

Copyright © 2018 Maribel Steel

All rights are reserved.

The material contained within this book is protected by copyright law, no part may be copied, reproduced, presented, stored, communicated or transmitted in any form by any means without prior written permission by the author, with the exception of brief excerpts for review purposes. Thank you for respecting the work of the author and for not violating any copyright laws.

Published in Australia by BookPOD
Distributed by Heart Sight Press
Cover Creation by Bee Williamson of beesboutiquebooks.biz
Cover Photograph Copyright © Claire Farnham
Tech & Design Assistance by Harry Williamson
Edited by Brian Steel, Hazel Edwards and Lyndel Caffrey
Structural Editor/Proof Reader: Lyndel Caffrey

A catalogue record for this book is available from the National Library of Australia.

ISBN 978-0-9874461-2-1

To

Dad, Harry and Mike
for always helping me to achieve my dreams.

And, to my loving mother,
who passed away
before seeing how life can blossom after vision loss,
for her courageous spirit
that is the flame kindled deep within me.

What Readers Say...

'I am so excited about this book for those who really need to share Maribel's journey so that they can start their own on good footing with solid, heartfelt advice.'
Pris Rogers, *Aging and Vision specialist USA*

'In Blindness for Beginners, Maribel Steel takes us along her "journey of discovery where sight loss really can become a "renewed vision of the possible". From her early diagnosis and rejection of being labelled as "disabled" to her eventual acceptance of having to make changes in her life, Maribel's story will resonate with readers facing similar uncertainties. This book offers a creative approach for people facing challenges.
Peter and Nancy Torpey: *Hosts of Eyes on Success Podcast Show*

'I don't know where to begin! I enjoyed Maribel's stories so much I didn't want them to end. Her descriptive ability is so rich it makes her stories jump off the page.'
Leanne Gibson, *reader from Canada*

'The most uplifting self-help book I've read this year. And the autobiographical anecdotes from Maribel's life are the most inspiring part.'
Hazel Edwards OAM, *Author, Patron: Society of Women Writers VIC*

'A really superb writer. I'm sure this book will open another door for others.'
Stella de Genova, *Co-founder Vision Through Words*

CONTENTS

Foreword 1
Dear Reader 3
Introduction 5

PART ONE: MY SENSORY LIFE
Chapter 1   Touching to See 17
Chapter 2   Facing the Truth 31
Chapter 3   Beyond Expectations 46

PART TWO: HOW TO ADJUST TO VISION LOSS
Chapter 4   When Confronted by Change 61
Chapter 5   How to Really Handle Fear 74
Chapter 6   Tools for Progress 90
Chapter 7   Life-Savers to the Rescue 109
Chapter 8   Home Sweet Organised Home 126
Chapter 9   Cooking in a Tactile Kitchen 147
Chapter 10 Stepping Out 163

PART THREE: MYTHS AND TIPS FOR THE SIGHTED
Chapter 11 Open to Ingenuity 181
Chapter 12 Are You Too Polite to Ask? 192
Chapter 13 How Friends and Family Can Help 203
Chapter 14 Vision-Quest 216

References and Resources 222
Acknowledgements 227
About the Author 229

FOREWORD

A great title. Blindness for Beginners. This applies to those losing their sight and those who need insight into how to live or work effectively with a person who is blind. But this autobiographical book is also relevant to a broader audience of those wishing to solve problems more creatively. It offers strategies.

Superlatives are over-used when describing a person with a disability who has achieved anything. It would be patronising to do that for Maribel, who is a creative-problem-solver in any culture. She began to lose her sight at fifteen, a crucial age of self-awareness. Being quietly assertive and asking for the type of help needed, is a skill we all need. Being prepared to volunteer and try new challenges such as technology is a survival skill. So is challenging misconceptions about 'labels'. Even getting the terminology right is a challenge for those outside the culture. Do you say 'blind' or 'partially sighted' or 'disabled' or ....?

Maribel's writing strength is the day-to-day anecdotes of creative problem-solving and the humour with which it is shared. Bells on toddlers' socks so a blind mother can locate them. The fast-moving toddlers, not the socks. (Maribel has four adult children now). Being prepared to learn new technology like 'Where the Hell am I?' App or mastering JAWS, the digital device turning printed words into sound. And being willing to take on invitations such as speaking at an international conference and actually travelling there, complete with humorous images on a PowerPoint. All relevant to 'Blindness for Beginners'. And the chapter from the guide dog's viewpoint provides another insight.

Maribel's approach is to capitalise on her strengths. And we all need to do that. Her acute hearing, singing voice, musical understanding and trained memory have enabled her to devise new ways of participating both in work and social life. She's willing to ask for help, or to decline it because she has worked out the best way beforehand. Preparation meeting opportunity is an apt definition of success.

I first met Maribel about ten years ago at a Christmas drinks party for the Australian Society of Authors of which I was a director. Her organised approach to writing and even getting around with minimal fuss impressed me. Occasionally I gave her a lift and once I got lost, even using my GPS. Maribel got us to the event at the right location, and on time.

With the publication of 'Blindness for Beginners' Maribel has joined my Hazelnuts, the mentored group who each has produced a book on a significant subject. The significance of Maribel's book is not only that she has physically written it, despite visual challenges, but that the content is likely to inspire others to find their individual solutions to lifestyle challenges whether they are blind or sighted.

The most uplifting self-help book I've read this year. And the autobiographical anecdotes from Maribel's life are the most inspiring part. I've learnt a lot. Courage is about being prepared to try within the limitations you are given. And 'Blindness for Beginners' gives insight.

Hazel Edwards OAM, *Author, Patron: Society of Women Writers (VIC)*

DEAR READER

There are many challenges we face throughout our lives but perhaps none so confronting as the prospect of losing our sight. In my teenage years, I waged a silent rebellion of resistance at the time when vision loss first appeared. In hindsight, I should have reached out for much more support.

I rejected the label of 'disabled' for many years – it was an image I honestly could not accept. I am so glad to have come to my senses now. It's not that I see myself as a disabled person as such, but rather that I can accept my blindness is a part of me. My persona is both the light and the dark, the easy and the difficult, my capabilities and my visual limitations. It's a feeling of wholeness which had to be reconciled with my inner-self.

Going blind is a life-changing experience. If you or a loved one are facing a similar situation, my book will help you discover that to live with a degree of sight loss doesn't mean you have to stop enjoying a fulfilled life. I offer practical solutions which I have divided into three sections.

Part One is my personal story of my diagnosis, my struggle to hide my vision impairment, how I accepted the truth, and the appreciation and insight that acceptance brought.

Part Two presents practical ways in which a person new to vision loss can begin their journey of acceptance. It's followed by creative ways to overcome the daily challenges while retaining a sense of independence. Family and friends will learn strategies they can easily use to help organise a shared living space so that everyone benefits.

Part Three is for the reader who wants to gain knowledge of how they can assist a person with a visual disability; from revealing common myths to giving helpful tips on being an effective sighted guide. A list of references and further resources can be found at the end for anyone interested to learn more.

I hope my lived experience will take you on a journey of discovery, where sight loss really can become a renewed vision of the possible. As you find your own way to 'let go' of the many fears you will face, and accept that feeling vulnerable happens to each of us, you might just end up doing amazing things in your life, not yet imagined.

Maribel Steel

INTRODUCTION

I once asked a totally blind scientist during an interview, what came to his mind if I told him that the juice in his glass was orange? I was curious to hear his thoughts. He replied, 'I have no emotional attachment to colour.' I realised in that split second how seeing the colour spectrum was my connection to everything around me, to everything worthwhile.

When I began to lose my eyesight during my teen years, this was the confronting truth I faced. I felt caught between incompatible worlds. I was going blind despite my passion to become a visual artist. While sufficient sight lingered, so did my desire to cling to the light; yet I didn't know how I would be able to live in a world void of colour. If being in the fullness of light made my heart sing, I wondered if being in the depths of the dark would make me cry? I wanted to have the courage, like dear Thumbelina, my fairytale heroine, to face an uncertain future. She too had to accept her farewell to the sunlight.

The adolescent me wanted to stay camouflaged among my peers with our brown blazers and straw hats, nylon stockings and crooked smiles. But no one had warned me about the sneaky changes of adolescence; the way in which puberty could appear to disrupt the life of a perfectly normal teenager. Over a period of two years, my sight mysteriously began to fade. At first, it was easier to ignore the blurring of words on the classroom blackboard, passing it off as just another phase of adolescence. I was also painfully shy about the thought of being 'different' to the girls at school so I kept quiet about needing to wear glasses.

It was a new school year when the teacher noticed my squinting tendency.

'Did you bring your glasses to school today?'

I felt annoyed with my parents for conspiring with the teacher after the visit to the optometrist. He had concluded that I was short sighted. The adults in my life had no idea how foreign it felt to wear glasses, as silly as wearing swimming goggles on dry land. The teacher moved me from the back shadows where I was trying to hide, and placed me right in the front of the classroom.

One girl in the front row didn't seem to mind my paranoia of being different. Her comical seven-syllable name, Antoinetta Di Petta, gave me hope that her parents had played a mean trick on her too.

'What are you doing?' asked Antoinetta, amused as she watched me fumble under the desk.

'Be quiet,' I snapped back, trying to disguise the navy blue glass case.

'Show me?'

Her toffee-coloured eyes softened but I still felt ridiculous. I slipped the new pair of glasses onto my nose and pulled an ugly face.

'Oh cool! Those glasses suit you.'

I pinched her leg but I was mightily relieved she approved of my new glasses, and was even more grateful that she still liked me. Antoinette (as she preferred to be called) was a kind and studious girl who ignored the antics of immature drama queens and achieved high standards in her school work. A slightly timid creature, like the fieldmouse in Thumbelina, she was friendly, funny and anxious about the phases of puberty too. Sitting at the desk next to each other, our shoulders leaned together warm and close, so close her black hair, scented with the aroma of friendship, brushed across my cheek.

In the early weeks of having to wear prescription glasses, seeing was a little easier and the girls didn't tease me as I had feared. On some days, fuzzy writing at the far edges of the chalk board still eluded my vision so I began copying Antoinette's neat handwriting. Watching her craft precise strokes to form words and sentences was like being mesmerised by a magician producing something magical out of a blank space. One minute, an empty page, the next, a pattern of beautiful letters. She crafted an army of black ink-soldiers standing with military precision on faint lines. As I waited for the new line of biro figures to emerge, I was captivated by Antoinette's artistic flair. She often interrupted the private show by tugging at thin strands of her hair, sighing,

'I'm going bald, you know?'

'You are not!'

'See?' She held out a long strand of fine hair, as if I could see it. Then she studied it closely before parting with it, watching it drift to the floor.

'Just stop pulling it out,' I said, poking her thigh.

Two peas in a paranoid pod – Antoinette critical of her hair, my discomfort with bodily changes and blurred vision – we became inseparable confidantes for one another. We laughed when I bumped into a desk or knocked over a glass beaker during science class, but at home, my clumsiness was noticed with growing concern. In my parents' eagerness to glean any insight into my odd behaviour, they often peered from around corners to see how I was managing visual tasks. If they asked me direct questions about what I could see, it annoyed me to think there might be anything different to report since the last time they asked. The more they probed with questions I found hard to answer, the safer it felt to pull shut the door of uncertainty.

I didn't agree with my parents' view that there was anything to be concerned about. Wasn't my blurred vision simply the passage of change, a time of uncontrollable hormones and weird surprises? My eyes were still a clear sparkling blue, seeing well on bright sunny days and not so well on overcast ones. I looked and felt normal in every other way, but the truth lurking behind my eyes was a different story. Within the thin layers of my retinas, diseased cells were forming and spreading along the nerve tunic of the eye. These light-sensitive cells were slowly dying, losing signal to the brain, obstructing nutritional information vital for determining colour and visual details.

My strong desire at that time was to separate my insecurities from my parents' fears for my future. I craved to discover who I was becoming as I stared at the foreign image emerging in the bathroom mirror. I saw a girl who clung to being a visual learner. A girl who enjoyed light and colour. A young artist who looked for dazzling reflections. A stubborn teenager who refused to accept any shades of grey.

I had high standards of my own but as my sight faded, it became harder to achieve them, no matter how much I tried. Some days I thought that if I just blinked hard enough, the blurriness would clear, like wiping patches of mist off a windscreen on a frosty morning. It never did.

Months went by and sight diminished rapidly. My parents took me on a crusade, seeking out the professional opinions of fifteen ophthalmologists and other specialists. Time after time, we sat together in dimly lit waiting rooms full of elderly people. I felt so out of place, dabbing at dilated pupils, disguising my silent tears. The gap between the normal girl and this new creature sitting in the company of the visually impaired elderly grew wider, forcing me further and further away from the comfort of being who I wanted to be.

My family's search to understand my sight loss led to a two week stay in hospital. There, I lay dreaming of the day when my life would return to normal. Under stiff white sheets, all I could see in my mind's eye was Antoinette, catching the school bus without me. In the ward, nurses walked past my room with trays of medicated drops and little pills. My teeth clenched tight; *Don't you dare move*, my thoughts instructed waking muscles, *Let them think you're still asleep.*

I lay quiet for as long as I could, and wished my father were here to ask his annoying question, 'What can you see?' I'd be happy to tell him now. I could only see the vast washed-out sea of white nothingness. I was adrift on the ocean of loneliness, and felt pulled along in an acidic-white wave that frothed with fear. For the first time in my artist's life, I couldn't bear this shade of white. It wasn't the toasty almond-white of my mother's coconut macaroons or the warm winter-white of Antoinette's jumper. Nor was it the proud ivory-white pages of my father's first published manuscript. This was a new strain of hospital-strength white: strong enough to kill germs and zap the life-force from my dreams.

Maybe I should have been grateful to the white-clad specialists looking for answers among the uncertainty of my family's fears. Maybe I should have welcomed the medicine men who came and went at any hour of the day, prising open my eyelids as if diving for hidden treasures within the depths of my dilated pupils, and the processions of white-robed deities and their smorgasbord of medical students who breathed too closely in my personal space. Peering into my eyes, one doctor said,

'Hold still, please.'

He guided my chin into the metal stirrup of yet another alien contraption. I tried to cooperate, I truly *wanted* to be good, but my eyes were working independently from my will. They had developed a fighting personality of their own, having endured two weeks of invasive bright lights, injections and countless tests. Salty tears streamed down my cheeks, rushing in defensively to bar the path and obscure the doctor's vision.

'It would really help if you could stop blinking and hold still.'

My foot twitched, resisting the urge to lash out and kick this man on the shin. I wanted to comfort my eyes: *Hang in there, it won't be much longer.* The poking, the probing, the prodding, the pain. And all for what purpose? To learn *two new words*. We learned two words that changed our lives forever. Two words that made my mother weep, my father fall silent. Two foreign words I could hardly pronounce – Retinitis Pigmentosa. The doctors gave us their diagnosis and my life was branded forever.

Following the diagnosis, I was pensioned off as legally blind and had to learn how to accept this garment of change. It felt like being inducted into the 'disabled' club, a club with terms and conditions and a life-long membership I didn't want to accept. My imagination saw an exclusive offer presented to our household by an invisible salesperson.

'Welcome. You have an incurable eye condition. Whether you like it or not, you can spend the rest of your life indulging in any of the labels we proudly stock in our specialty store. Take your time to browse and choose carefully from our range of richly textured stigmas. This is your new image – now, sign on the dotted line.'

I didn't want a new image, or one of their differently designed garments exclusive to brands like Mademoiselle Blind, Itza Shame, X-Clude, Miss Understood, Lady Lack and Inferior Designs. I liked the image I already had, the 'me' I was growing into. I didn't want to wear any unfashionable labels. So I made a pledge to my future. No matter what anyone else thought was possible or not, I would place a shield of hope around my dreams. I wouldn't let the *disabled* label disqualify me from living a normal life.

With the new prognosis, my parents focused on finding ways to help me keep up with my school work. The short stay in hospital had put me behind with several assignments. I began to use a hand-held magnifying glass to peer at school text books in an attempt to catch up. In the evenings, I spent hours meticulously re-writing the homework as neatly as possible for the teacher. Sometimes, my mother sat by my side and coloured in those parts of my work I couldn't see. Her artistic talent caught my imagination and I aspired to develop skills in fine art drawing too. But my parents were keen to find an easier alternative to reading and ease my eye-strain. Braille seemed a good solution – to *them*.

Sitting in the kitchen after school, my mother placed a large artists sketch pad down in front of me.

'Look inside, darling,' she smiled, 'I've been busy all day creating a surprise for you.'

Her excitement was infectious and I thought she must have etched more drawings for me to admire. Turning the first page as cautiously as if opening a precious archive, I was surprised to see a series of rectangular boxes with purple circles instead.

'It's the Braille alphabet,' my mother said proudly. 'I've copied out all the letters in large format so you can see to learn them.'

For a few moments, I was taken by the beautiful symmetry of her work, the precise lines, the exact gaps between the boxes, the fullness of the circles in their correct formations, and then her intention hit me, my mother was asking me to learn Braille?

'Mum. I'm not blind. Why would I want to learn Braille?'

'Darling, you don't have to decide now,' she said with a hint of disappointment. 'Maybe just keep it in your room and look at it after dinner?'

My father was sitting at the kitchen table, half listening as he flicked through the newspaper. He saw me still staring at Mum's artwork while she scooted over to the stove, and broke the silence in an attempt to be helpful.

'Do you want me to read the employment section to get an idea of some of the career options you could consider?'

I knew he had not said 'now that you are vision-impaired' because it was a touchy subject. My mother turned down the heat on the stove and took a step closer to peer over my father's shoulder. He ironed out the crease obscuring the print with a flattened palm and with the other hand, took a swig of tea. Skimming the lines, he said, 'What about becoming a nurse?' Then he thought for a moment. 'Perhaps not. How about, er, airhostess?'

Mum shook her head.

'Here's one. Secretary?'

'That's a bit hard with a magnifying glass, don't you think?' I said, arching an eyebrow.

'OK. Well, what about becoming a teacher? An art teacher? That might suit you better?'

Silence from all three. My heart sank as it was obvious that being vision-impaired, my chances were getting slimmer by the day. Where was my future in among all these career options? Rather than learning Braille, I chose to take up a typewriting class at school, believing it to be a skill I could use later in life. Having shunned the Braille option, my parents investigated in an alternative method of reading. The one expensive device they did lash out and buy as a pre-cursor to digital technology was one of the first models of a CCTV which came to take up residence in my room and improved my life considerably.

The closed circuit video camera that was strapped to the side of a portable black and white television set could magnify anything that was placed under the camera and then projected onto the TV monitor. I loved it! I didn't have to learn Braille and I continued to catch up on school work. My bedroom became a sanctuary where I listened to records and doodled with Derwent pencils and watched my artwork appear on the black and white screen.

These were the early years of adjusting to my vision loss. But it took many more to actually *accept* the label of disabled that became firmly attached to the fabric of my life. With self-acceptance, awareness, kind support from others and practical adaptations, I gradually learned there are ways to master the skills for comfortable living with low vision.

When we face and accept the 'garment of change', we also discover the gifts hiding within its deep pockets that enable us to manage the changes with less fear and with much more skill. It may not have been what we thought we would be able to 'wear' at first, but with a willing heart and a practical approach to adaptation, we discover the real gift blindness can bring. Understanding ourselves as we truly are that connects us to a richly textured life.

PART ONE

MY SENSORY LIFE

*The best and most beautiful things in the world
cannot be seen or even touched
– they must be felt with the heart.*

~ Helen Keller

Chapter 1

Touching to See

Little snuffles and unfamiliar gurgles filled our dimly lit bedroom. It had all happened so quickly, not even our homebirth doctor had made it in time. I slumped back into soft pillows, relieved to hear our baby's first unaided breaths. Several moments after the natural delivery, I was holding my infant close, wondering what she looked like, who she looked like. My eyes couldn't see her in the ambient lamplight; seeing my baby for the first time took another twelve hours when the sun rose the following morning.

'She's beautiful, she's so beautiful,' my husband said, choking on tears of fatherly pride.

Our hands touched as he presented me with the whimpering bundle and gently placed her onto my chest. He moved so carefully, it was as if he were handing me precious porcelain. We were completely awestruck, having witnessed the miracle of our first born child. He covered us both with a warm blanket, and our sweet little daughter snuggled close to my heart as he said softly with a kiss to my hair,

'Well done.'

I was unable to speak. My hands traced over my baby's tiny body, feeling for every little bump and wrinkle. Her features felt so perfect; such tiny fingers, such cute toes, such weeny buttocks! While we waited for the doctor and midwife to arrive, I hummed the soft sounds of 'Amazing Grace'. The touch and smell of my infant's skin was the sweetest moment of my life. At twenty-one, I breathed in the scent of motherhood.

Parenting. How was I going to care for my child when I couldn't see? I learned with every sound and nuance to interpret my baby's subtle body language. I relished a deeper sensory communication with her and I tuned in, coming to know her needs intimately. My husband grew in confidence too and together we managed visual tasks and soon got into a routine. I also learned that one of the keys to parenting 'blind' was to adjust to a more creative approach to motherhood.

In the beginning phase, nursing my first baby did make me feel much more 'in the dark' than sighted mothers but from the moment my child was born, so too my other senses sprang to life. Invisible eyes at the back of my head appeared in the form of hearing-antennae linked to motherly intuition. I relied on different talents and became creative in solving visual tasks others considered impossible.

Like everyone else, my skills as an attentive mother developed each time my child entered a different phase of her own growth. Being vision-impaired did make my motherly role hugely challenging, with three more children eventually joining our brood. Of course, I suffered from normal parental anxiety but I grew in confidence by learning to listen, to intuit, to smell and to touch when deciding on the best ways to care for my children.

Naturally, my friends voiced their concerns: 'Aren't you afraid your daughter will fall off the play equipment? What if your son runs out onto the road or needs you to remove a splinter? How can you clean a wound from their grazed knee? How do you manage?' I did it with the collective help of my husband, close relatives, friends and the wider community who all pitched in.

One of my earliest mistakes happened when my daughter was eight months old. We were dining out on a rare occasion, feeling brave as relatively new parents with little Claire sitting between her mummy and daddy. I was feeding her small portions from my plate, discreetly using my little finger to guide the spoon to her mouth. Everything was going well, or so I thought, until my husband leaned in closer towards me and said,

'You know you are putting the potato salad in her ear?'

'What?' I shot him a horrified look, and blushed red. 'Don't be stupid. Why would I do that?'

He said nothing more but I could tell he was grinning behind his glass of beer as he reclined back into his chair. I checked my daughter's face and wanted to die with shame – it was true!

'You do it, then,' I said, throwing the spoon across the table. It seemed my daughter had turned her head to look around the room just at the crucial moment of inserting the spoonful of salad; I had mistaken her little ear for her small mouth. That was one moment when I wished the ground had swallowed me up whole. I was sure everyone in the restaurant had seen my mistake. All I could do was to secretly vow to avoid doing it again.

Our next set of challenges came when our baby developed into a toddler and was physically mobile. No longer was my child content to be by my side all day long – she was off and away to explore new things in interesting places. At this young age, Claire learned that I watched over her by using a combination of tactile methods as well as keeping up a constant chatter to know what she was doing. Little Claire was only too happy to have this interaction with her mother, and I had a child helping me with visual tasks and making my life easier – most of the time.

It was an unexpected gift to view life through my child's eyes, as a whole new world opened up, expanding my confidence as a capable vision-impaired mother, learning to adapt to life with a sighted family. With Claire's eagerness to run up and down the house on countless missions, her life was never dull. I encouraged my daughter to come to me at regular intervals, and tried to turn my dependence on her visual assistance into a game of hide and seek. We were like detectives, working everything out together. It didn't matter to my child that her mother couldn't see. Sometimes this was an added bonus for her: sticky handprints on walls, crayons on clothing, cereal under her chair, were scenes that were only brought to my attention by family or friends. I felt embarrassed by my messy house but at least I had an excuse and could conveniently 'turn a blind eye' to the stains just as my daughter did.

I encouraged her innate sense of curiosity, and later my other children were also 'trained' to carry out sighted jobs for short bursts of time. When baby number two was born, Claire took on her big sister role very seriously. Little brother Russell could not get away with anything. Dibber-dobber Claire kept a close eye on his every move, calling out when he was doing something she thought needed my attention. I will admit it was extremely helpful to know I could rely on her hawk-eyed observations. Knowing he had dropped food on the floor, or was putting something strange into his mouth, or was trying to climb out of his cot – Warden Claire was always on his case.

Young Russell wasn't too perturbed by his sister's bossiness and as he grew into toddlerhood he followed her everywhere, copying her behaviour. My children loved to be 'Mummy's eyes' and would run to help me find a missing sock, a misplaced earring or inform me on the activities of their siblings – except on some days when they were more inclined to disregard my requests in favour of their natural need to play.

One day the three of us entered a large department store. Claire and Russell scampered out of my view. With typical excitement, they wanted to play hide and seek, as if this expansive space was an indoor playground. I searched for them in vain, wandering around in circles; I could sense that people's heads were turned to watch me in a pathetic attempt to find them.

At this point in my life, I was not ready to pick up a white cane so no one knew I couldn't see. I could hear my children, but where were they? Desperation filled my heart. I needed them to stay by my side. Together we were supposed to read price tags and clothing sizes. This was not the time for play. Their giggles sounded so close but I couldn't see them. Then Claire suddenly sprinted past and I launched after her, grabbing her cardigan sleeve.

'Stop running around!' I growled. 'Come with me. What does this price sticker say?'

Holding out a garment and hoping the silly game she and her brother were playing was over, I waited for a discreet reply. But I cringed the moment she burst out in a loud voice for the entire shop to hear,

'DOLLAR SIGN. ONE. THREE. FULL STOP. NINE-FIVE.'

She managed to wriggle free from my grip and hid once more with her partner in crime under another rack of clothing somewhere. I called for them both to come back, pushing an empty stroller and spending most of my shopping time as a super-sleuth, tracking their giggles coming first from under racks of lady's lingerie, then over at men's winter shirts. It was the best hide and seek paradise for my children – with a vision-impaired mother doing the impossible seeking. I wasn't sure whether to laugh or to cry; little devils. I started my search by circling the aisles, narrowing it down to the spot where I heard conniving whispers.

'If you come out now, I'll buy you both a lolly.'

Bribery always worked. Russell was first to come out from his hiding place, darting back into the waiting stroller like a joey kangaroo scrambling into an empty pouch. Claire followed suit, crawling out from underneath a rack of dressing gowns and resuming her angelic chaperone position by my side. Obliged to fulfil my promise, we headed back to where we had come in.

'What well-behaved children,' said a woman, opening the door for us.

My little cherubs grinned at her, their sticky lollipops in hand as we paraded past, a serene picture of happiness, my empty shopping basket dangling on the handles of the pusher.

Part of developing a more sensory life was being aware of where my children were at all times. I am sure as parents or child-carers, we have all experienced that familiar realisation when a child is up to something due to an unusual silence. The absence of the noise of childish play is like an alarm bell alerting you to check out the situation.

Sighted parents can naturally take a casual glance at the child to satisfy themselves as to whether the activity is harmless or needs swift intervention. But I had to be more direct; I had to walk straight in, touch, smell, and badger my youngster with a myriad of questions to make sure everything was OK.

A friend of mine who saw this constant interaction with my children gave us an unusual gift one day. She presented us with two pairs of little red socks, complete with tiny bells attached.

'Now you can keep an ear on their every move through the house.'

It worked beautifully. But a word of advice; a toddler eventually grows into a teenager who is not so keen to entertain the thought of allowing such an inventive tracking method – pity.

I noticed also how a sighted parent may ask their child to hand over a toy which is most probably about to be confiscated for some reason and the child is likely to resist. Tears, argument or a tantrum may follow. But when a vision-impaired parent makes the same request, the child learns that the parent's need to feel the toy is likely to be a disruption to their play and not a total surrender of the fun activity. Needless to say, I was happiest when my children were making some sort of noise or we were sharing quiet time with books.

When it came to reading, although I used a magnifying glass to peer at print, we actually had a lot of storytelling time. At a library or bookshop, my children and I went in search of tactile books: anything with a soft fluffy tail, shiny snake skin, prickly whiskers – any book that had a touchy-feely element to help tell the story. The children were also fortunate to have the regular input from my father and stepmother. Dadan and Nana often popped in to see the children to have a vibrant play and they were especially keen to foster a love of reading. They went to great lengths to record the children's favourite books onto cassettes.

Having their own personalised tapes meant that my children knew when to turn the page from their grandparents' voice cue. After they had gone home, the children and I snuggled in at bedtime and 'read' along with the picture book and audio tape. Dadan acted out the different characters with animated voices. We all loved this special way of sharing story time.

It was during their early years that I began to type up our own bedtime stories. With my children's' fertile imagination, our pets became the heroes or villains of our tall tales. Our tortoiseshell tabby cat upset a birthday party in which the naughty kitten ate all the food, creating mayhem. Story after story, we devised our own adventures. If we didn't like the ending the following night, we changed it. Once the children had gone to bed, I spent many a happy hour typing up the latest dramas using an old fashioned typewriter, hoping that my manuscripts might also capture the imagination of a children's publisher. I came close to an offer of a contract on one occasion but the publisher dropped my story of hot cross bunnies and so it was back to being the family bard once more.

As my children grew older, I often attended general assembly at their school. With the other parents, we watched students receive awards or give a concert. I was happy to be part of the audience even though I wasn't seeing a thing. The excited vibes of the other mothers made me feel as eager as them to witness our children's glowing achievements. I pretended to see and I tried to take in the scene on stage but, in actual fact, the stage was a blur and the children on it all appeared like dancing blobs.

I had no way of recognising a single face or body shape. I knew my children were out there somewhere. It was frustrating at times to miss all the visual activity, but other parents kindly described the unfolding scene, allowing for my imagination to picture the rest. On one particular day, an elderly woman sitting directly in front of me swung around with great excitement and said,

'See that girl over there, the one on the end? That's my grand-daughter.' The grey-haired lady was just about falling sideways off her chair. 'See her?' she asked me, 'the one in red?'

She had no idea I couldn't see and I didn't want to disappoint her. Of all the parents she could have asked, why me? I thought she would just let it go when I replied, 'No. Sorry.'

Not wanting to leave it there, the old woman offered other clues, turning around again to add, 'The little blonde one, on the end.'

'Nope.'

The woman was astonished. 'You can't miss her.' She sounded agitated.

Oh yes I can, I thought.

'No, honestly, I can't see her. But that's fine.'

The grandmother pointed her finger at the stage again, as if giving me one last chance. 'LOOK.' She spoke through gritted teeth. 'Over THERE, in the front row! Are you blind or something?'

'Actually, yes, I am.'

The old woman stared at me, contemplating whether I was being rude. As she gave out a huff, and swung around to face the stage, I heard her mutter under her breath, 'Blind as a bat, if you ask me.'

I didn't take Granny's comment to heart. It wasn't her fault that I had been trying to disguise my visual impairment. It didn't seem necessary at the time to announce my visual limitations to her or to the world.

Fast forward eleven years and my fourth child appeared on the scene. I still hadn't picked up a white cane even though my eyesight had deteriorated, because the stigma still felt too great. While my children were keen to help, I conveniently excused myself from having to learn mobility training. The toddler's pusher worked beautifully to barge our way through shopping centres with my young driver in the seat calling out directions. The wheels of the stroller shuddered over rough pavements, the vibrations acting as an indicator of store entrances.

My son's little 'vehicle' and his observations were my guiding eyes with him safely strapped inside. To my way of thinking, I retained a useful amount of vision and didn't feel I needed to change anything. I certainly wasn't ready to surrender to using a white cane since the stroller worked as a nifty mobility aid; it was my way of trying to be a 'normal' mother. I got away with bumping into things just as if I were another sleep-deprived parent distracted by her child.

Michael always enjoyed our shopping jaunts. I feared them with a passion. Yet I was determined to carry out normal activities for my family. Parking my son's stroller to one side, I replaced it with a shopping trolley, and tucked little Michael into the front seat where he could see and be navigator. We surged forward into the unpredictable trolley-traffic, Michael oblivious to my stress as I took a deep breath and quietly chanted, 'I can do this...I can do this.'

I clung fiercely to the handle while wandering in a daze. Thousands of similar looking boxes, tins and packages: Oh my, how was I going to find anything? But, having used the same store on many visits, I learned certain areas by the strong odours of laundry liquids or the smell of freshly baked bread, hot cooked chicken and smoked bacon wafting from the deli. Shopping in the same stores every week gave me a sense of familiarity which made it possible to locate some of our favourite foods without requesting extra help. Michael also gave me clues as we navigated our way down each aisle.

'Chippies, Mum?'

Big clue – we were in the junk food aisle; funny how he could name all the items in this section.

'Lollies!'

I reached out to find something to keep him occupied as we sped away. My son's comments were like audible beacons for me. 'Juice. Cheese. Apples. Ice-cream.'

Every now and then, my hands reached out to touch the items we were passing in order to narrow down the selection with logical precision. Knowing I was standing somewhere near the tins of green peas, the canned tomatoes had to be close by.

'Darling, can you see the tin of tomatoes?'

My son looked around, then pointed. I followed his outstretched finger as an arrow to the target.

'Clever boy,' I said, kissing his sticky cheek, bulging with a lollipop.

Over repeated visits, I learned to identify our shopping preferences by the shape of the container, the colourful label, a bright picture or a large bold word that jumped out clearly when peering at items using a magnifying glass. Diving into the frozen food cabinets was also a game of pot luck, as the food was enclosed behind glass doors. I could neither feel nor smell them so when I had held open a fridge door for several minutes, the chilly air froze my hands. I'd quickly make a decision to remove what I thought to be the right package, only to later discover I'd made a completely unexpected choice.

On occasions, I'd accost a nearby shop assistant packing shelves, luring them away from their work to follow me up and down the aisles in search of different products. Some assistants were on the ball and alert to my low vision needs while others were completely unaware, pointing to things I couldn't see. I never used the term 'vision-impaired' to describe my eye condition but preferred to say to people that I was either 'partially sighted' or had a 'sight' problem; to which one person inquired, 'You have a slight problem?' *Yes, I wanted to say, your hearing!*

Dadan accompanied us at times, but this was more like a shopping raid as he always vowed to his grandson that he'd get us in and out of the store as quickly as possible. I produced the list and my dad scooted around with the trolley, Michael sitting upright and laughing as his grandfather whirled around the store, making the trolley sway and swerve as he grabbed items from the shelves and fridges, diligently following the list, nothing more, nothing less. As the three of us left the store, attached to various parts of the trolley, my father danced a merry jig all the way across the car park to load us into his car, proudly telling me of the exact time we had taken to achieve such a heroic feat.

Looking out for my child in the local playground could be challenging too. My 4-year-old son scrambled from one activity to the next. He knew I couldn't see him properly – my vision had faded years before he was born - but he still called out,

'Watch me, Mummy. I'm over here.'

I turned my head in the direction of his voice.

'OK, Mummy. Don't move your head. You're looking straight at me.'

I praised Michael's climbing ability, listening intently while praying, *Please don't fall off.* The hands on my Braille watch told me it was time to move on, and I was relieved from blind patrol duty. My son skipped beside me and we walked towards the Kindergarten.

'Can we play I spy with my little eye?' he asked.

I loved his passion for play and the way he could ignore my vision impairment.

'Sure. You first,' I said, hiding my feelings of visual inadequacy.

'I spy with my little eye,' Michael trilled, 'something that is...green.'

After a few wild guesses, we had arrived at our destination. He helped me to locate the handle to open the child-security gate and then he bounced away into the playground. But I felt a pang of anxiety as I tried to follow his disappearing trail. It was impossible to distinguish my son from the other children running past. Which fair-haired child was mine? Was that his voice calling, 'Mum, come and push me on the swing'.

Some of the other parents knew I was 'partially sighted' and watched Michael on my behalf, keeping me informed with a running commentary on his changing activities. I appreciated their thoughtfulness, but my motherly identity was challenged by a sense of guilt at not being able to watch out for my own child.

To compensate for this lack of sight, I devised other ways to 'see' by dressing my son in bright contrasting clothing. Sometimes I could look out for him in his green and white striped T-shirt and dark navy shorts, and at other times, it was a red top and grey trousers that stood out for me. My eyes roved the yard to spot his bobbing yellow cap or flashing white shoes. These things I did see. At other times, Michael sprang up from behind a tree to touch my hand.

'I'm going over there now. OK?'

Inside Michael's kindergarten, we would sit at a small round table on tiny wooden chairs doing visual activities together. On one occasion, the children were following the teacher's creative instructions as she showed the little people how to fold and bend paper to make a paper plane. Michael asked me for sighted guidance but I had no idea how to advise him. We persevered, turning the paper this way and that.

'Now, just fold along this line, then turn the paper over this way and then...' the teacher held up her paper plane. The children sounded impressed. I felt like a failure.

'This way?' Michael asked. 'Mummy, Is this right?'

I replied, hiding my frustration. 'What do you think, darling? Does it look like your teacher's plane?'

He seemed happy enough to persevere with the folding of paper unaware of my shame. The teacher came over to guide him through the process. She gently touched my shoulder in a reassuring way, as she kindly said to my son,

'Clever boy. That's nearly right.'

Back in the comfort of our home, and away from scrutinising eyes, I was more confident in helping Michael with his education. We collected cards of every type and cut out magazine pictures, chatting about the images, pasting them into our own scrapbooks while I remembered the scenes on each page. I sang playful songs and told stories and made up rhymes to spark his imagination. We shared a tactile communication – through puzzle play, clay moulding, Lego building, and baking cookies. Michael, like his older siblings, learned to bypass my lack of sight by tracing shapes onto my open palm, knowing that when he did, mummy could 'see' the object by drawing it. His little fingers often tickled my skin and I held back tears of love for his thoughtfulness.

Later one evening, as I struggled to read one of his favourite Mr Men books, I put down the magnifying glass and sighed,

'Oh dear, this is very slow, isn't it, sweetheart?'

Michael sprang up from under the blanket, and threw his warm arms around my neck. With his sweet blue eyes bright, and with the wisdom of a 4-year-old, he said,

'That's OK, Mummy. Don't ever give up. You can tell me one of your stories.'

Michael's words were so comforting, it was touching to feel the essence of unconditional love from a young soul who seemed to be more in tune with the truth than I had been willing to accept and face myself.

Chapter 2

Facing the Truth

When you walk to the edge of all the light you have and take that first step into the darkness of the unknown, you must believe that one of two things will happen. There will be something solid for you to stand upon or you will be taught to fly."
~ Patrick Overton, The Leaning Tree

After the divorce from my marriage of seventeen years, I began life again with my children in a new town in the state of Victoria. Mornington was like a city metropolis compared to the small seaside town on the far south coast of New South Wales we had left, and it took a while for me to feel well orientated in unfamiliar surroundings.

Still refusing to consider that I may have needed any extra mobility aids other than my children's eyes and a determined spirit, I was caught off guard on one particular day while out on my own running some simple errands. On this one single day, my world completely changed. I walked straight into my own mirror of truth; and it shattered my reality.

For nearly twenty years, I had been so proud of wearing a mask that hid my shame of being vision-impaired. If I admitted my defects to the world, I'd be considered a 'disabled' person. This was not who I believed myself to be so I bluffed my way around it as much as I could, pretending to be as normal as the next person on the street. I craved discretion at all times and did what I could to maintain this image.

That day, I walked into the bank and stopped dead in my tracks. A few feet inside the automatic doors I couldn't see where to go next. I simply couldn't see. It took ages before my eyes adjusted to the light and, even then, I still couldn't step confidently into the dark void to make my way to the counter. The voice of truth spoke louder than my feelings of panic: 'You just can't do this anymore. You really can't see.'

Why was I shocked to learn this about myself? Hadn't I been managing for decades to function relatively independently to the best of my visual limitations? I turned right around and went to the post office to pay the account and carry out the task there instead. A few steps inside, I came to a halt. I couldn't see with enough confidence to move forward. That inner voice spoke, a little more insistently: 'You have to stop bluffing, Maribel. You really can't see enough to get around on your own.'

I felt so defeated, I went home churning over what had just happened. As I searched for an answer and faced up to admitting the truth, what I saw for the first time was a woman who had been walking with false pride when it came to managing her mobility in public. All my life I had tried to fit in with the crowd, not wanting to be different, not wanting to appear disabled – and now, here I was, completely exposed to my real situation. The truth was confronting in a way I had never felt before. Who had I been kidding all these years? Only *myself*, by thinking I could hide my visual disability in public. Until I could accept my true limitations without feeling any shame, I'd remain in fear of being discovered to be a fraud.

The situation challenged my entire belief system. I was confronted with a disabled image of the real me; *Oh my God, I WAS one of them now.* I had to admit the truth. Lying on my bed, with tears subsiding, I wondered what a blind person would have done in the bank. How would they have managed it and kept their dignity? Then I remembered being impressed by Jonathon, a blind man I had met recently. A couple of months after arriving in Mornington, I had made an appointment with a social worker at a local Government office to discuss my career options. But I had no idea that the social worker himself was totally blind.

'Hi,' said the man dressed in a smart business suit as he held out his hand. 'I'm Jonathon, the Disability Officer.'

I struggled to spot his hand and we both fumbled to make physical contact. Feeling terribly self-conscious, I blurted out, 'Sorry, I can't see your hand.'

'Me neither!' He laughed as we found each other's hands in mid air like two clumsy fish colliding out of water. He took up the harness of his guide dog.

'Forward, Sam. Find the way.' With a slight turn of his head, he addressed me, 'This way, please.'

As Jonathon's guide dog led us both to a quiet office, I was impressed by the ease and the elegance with which he moved without bumping into anything. It was a truly inspiring moment filled with humour and dignity, and it was so unexpected. I had planned to ask his advice on how to set up a new business in town, but instead, we spent the hour candidly talking about blindness and guide dogs and his experiences as a 'blind' man.

I listened with complete awe. Jonathon was so honest as he shared his philosophy of dealing with vision loss. His words moved me deeply. He related his blindness story and how he had made the decision to work with a guide dog several years previously. As I listened to Jonathon's recollections of some of his 'funny' moments, the embarrassing times and the sad times dealing with his own issues, I felt complete admiration for his courage. He spoke with genuine confidence, and, later, it was his story that came flooding back to me as I lay wondering what I was going to do next after my bank fiasco.

The following day, I plucked up the courage to make a phone call to Guide Dogs Victoria. Thinking I'd make a few simple inquiries with a member of staff, I was surprised to be put straight through to the client manager. John Gosling's voice was gentle, and so empathetic, and I felt he personally cared for my issues of independence and understood my new realisations. By the end of our conversation I had made an appointment to visit the Guide Dog premises the following week. It all happened so quickly – I felt swept along in a fast moving current swirling with excitement and trepidation.

After the first meeting with the client manager, the next step in the process was to have a guide dog trainer come to visit me at home to conduct a more in-depth assessment of my mobility skills. In such a short time, I had convinced myself that working with a guide dog was my only option, no little white stick for me – even though I had once been given a long white cane, it was well tucked away and out of use.

I admired the grace with which Jonathon and his dog Sam moved independently and I wanted some of this assuredness in public too. There was a huge amount of emotional uncertainty resting on this next meeting. Would the trainer consider me eligible to have a dog and would I fulfil the assessment criteria?

The day before the trainer's visit, I thought I should at least know how to hold the white cane. I dragged it out from the back of a cupboard, and made a quick trip around the block. I felt stupid and awkward, swinging the foreign object like a pendulum randomly sideways to and fro. It felt like a lead weight in my hand. An internal dialogue argued with every step: 'Not like that. You're hopeless. Like this. Alright. At least I'm using it. The trainer will know you're a rookie. That's why I'm putting some scuff marks on the tip of the cane. Why is it so short? Who knows, who cares? Just keep tapping.' Later I was to learn that this stick was not the traditional long white cane to help me find my way, but a simple identification cane for alerting the public.

Exactly on time, the doorbell rang. But at the front door was not one, but TWO mobility instructors to interview me. Gulp! Peter had brought along a new trainer and together, they would complete this part of the process. After a preliminary discussion over a cup of tea, and having satisfied their inquiries about my reasons for getting a guide dog, Peter said,

'Let's go for a walk around your neighbourhood. You can show us how you normally get around on your own.'

Picking up my 'cane', I smiled to hide my dread and led the way. I hadn't realised that the trainers had to walk a few metres behind me to observe my walking pace and take note of how I approached kerbs and oncoming objects. It was like being followed by two stalkers. I hoped that no one would view them as suspicious and report them to the police. At every step while wielding the cane, I felt terribly self-conscious. I had to pretend they were not there and cross roads exactly as if I was on my own. I swung the cane out in front and continued around the block, down the street to the local shops. Eventually, as we stood at a set of lights, Peter asked,

'Know a good cafe around here? Feel like a coffee?'

Relief. 'Yes, please.'

Sipping on a hot cappuccino, I was burning to ask, 'Well? Will I get a guide dog?' The trainers gave nothing away. We headed home, with them performing the same ritual of following my every move. Then, out of the blue, an intuitive 'voice' spoke to me. 'Relax. You're going to get a guide dog'. In *that* moment, my heart knew this to be true. The trainers hadn't given me any sign but I just knew. I breathed a big sigh of relief and marched home with certainty and a feeling of contained joy, the trainers still a few metres behind my brisk pace. Once home, Peter said with a broad smile,

'Neither of us can see why you can't have a dog. We're happy to match you with a guide dog, if that is what you still want?'

'You bet!' I offered each trainer in turn a big high five! I had passed the test and was ecstatic – I was on the waiting list for my very own guide dog.

Ten days after my session with the trainers, the Guide Dog Centre rang. Peter's voice greeted my ears,

'Well, Maribel, it is most unusual to contact you so soon after your assessment but we have a dog for you. Are you able to start training next month?'

'Next *month*? 'I echoed in surprise. 'What if I can't?' My thoughts went into overdrive, just like the time when I had *not* been expecting my next baby: So soon? Was I ready? Did I really want to go through with this? Could I manage another mouth to feed? 'Um-err...'

'You'll stay on the list', he said, 'but we can't guarantee when you'll get another dog as well matched to your needs and personality as this one.'

I wanted more time to consider my options but Peter needed an answer. Then a fearful realisation struck: How would I train eight hours a day for a month when I had a young son needing my care? Who would look after Michael? The thought of having to wait possibly months and months for this same opportunity to arise was just as challenging. My heart gave a quick nudge to trust the process and make a decision.

'OK. I'll do the training.'

'Great!' Peter said. 'And don't forget, we can help you organise a local child care centre to look after your son on your training days.'

Plans swung well and truly into gear and so did my anxiety levels. I felt guilty about leaving my son in the care of people he had never met. Would he feel abandoned; would he adapt to the changes; would he play up and be difficult; would I be able to settle him at night; and how would he react to the new member of our family? Goodness – I was also leaving two teenagers to look after the house in my absence – how was that going to work? My father reassured me; he would call in on the teenagers every few days and make sure that the house was in good order on our return.

It had only been a few months since I had met Jonathon and his guide dog, and had made the milestone decision to apply for one myself. Even more amazingly, Jonathon and I were going to be in the same training group! As it so happened, his dog was retiring from long service which meant that Jonathon was scheduled to train with a new guide dog. It seemed serendipitous, as if all the doors were not just sliding open gently, but were being flung wide open by a force greater than my own.

Over the course of our training, I gained so much wise advice from my new 'blind' comrade. His often candid comments were both insightful and reassuring, but the one observation Jonathon made over and over again as if it was Rule Number 1 in his guide dog manual was: 'Just remember, you treat your dog like your own kid. Say what you mean and mean what you say. Follow this rule and you'll work fine together.'

It became obvious that Jonathon did not have a young child in tow. I tried out his principle on the first day Michael and I arrived to settle into our accommodation. My son had spotted the empty dog bed in the corner of our room and began to merrily jump up and down on its springy mattress as if it were his indoor trampoline.

'That's for our new dog,' I explained. 'Your bed is over here. See? This is where you sleep. Now hop off.'

'OK, Mummy,' Michael said, and continued to bounce on and off the mattress.

It was then that I realised I was in for a *real* challenge. In less than twenty-four hours, he'd have to move over for the guide dog and this would be like sharing the space with twins.

Bright and early the next day, I took Michael to his child care centre to settle him in. Once back at the guide dog centre, I waited in my room for Peter to bring the dog to meet me for the first time. It felt like the clichéd first blind date. What did he look like? Was he a kind character? Would he really care enough about me to be my guiding eyes? Could he love my children as his own? All I had been told the previous day was that my four-legged companion was a golden Labrador who went by the name of Nev.

'NEV?' I queried. 'Short for Neville?'

'No,' Peter said. 'Just Nev.'

'Nev? What sort of a name is that?' I asked, staring back at my amused trainer, 'my teenagers won't think much of that name.'

'They'll get used to it.' Peter replied, unfazed. 'And when you meet him, I think you'll find the name really suits him. He's a real character.'

I wasn't sure whether to take his comment as a compliment to the dog's personality or as a warning about the 'perfect match' having been made on my behalf. Who was this mysterious Nev character? Time to meet him yourself and read this extract from *his memoir* recalling our first meeting.

MEMOIR OF A GUIDE DOG
My Lady Love

That morning, I overheard the trainers talking about my new family. *Aha!* She was vision-impaired and she had a small boy child. Great, except – he'd better not pull my fur with his sticky fingers. Paws crossed. I can only hope he is as well trained as me. I felt excitement in the air as my trainer groomed me from head to tail.

'Hey Nev, you're going to a new home soon. Have to make you look smart for your lady friend.'

I was so excited. I had a quick drink from the silver bowl outside the kennels and tried my hardest not to run around in circles. I felt like a puppy again, with the fresh morning air tickling my whiskers. Four Labrador colleagues were also being taken to meet their handlers for the first time. I sniffed the ground looking for clues, I puffed and panted, in need of another drink. My trainer stopped just outside her door.

'Ready, Nev?'

My tail wagged furiously.

'Steady, boy.'

The door opened slowly – and there she was, waiting to greet me as she sat crossed-legged on the floor. I tossed my head proudly as I walked by my trainer's side, moving closer, my paws skidding over terracotta tiles. Her fragrance was like the smell of the sweet white flowers we had passed on our way. I got a whiff of doggy treats and my hopes soared.

'Steady.' My trainer pulled on my leash. 'S-T-E-A-D-Y.'

'Hello, Nev.' Her voice was sweet and kind.

I trotted right up to her face and gave her a polite lick on the cheek, forgetting in my excitement that she didn't see how close we were. She made a sudden movement and laughed. 'OH! There you are!'

My trainer put the leash in her hands.

'He's very excited. Why not get him to sit with you for a few minutes and calm him down? When you've had some time together, you can come and join us in the lounge room.' He smiled, turned briskly around and went out of the door, closing it quietly behind him.

He's gone? I looked around. *We're alone? Where's the boy child? Where are those treats?*

'Helloo,' she said again. 'I've got a little surprise for you, Nev. Sit down, boy.'

I settled down next to her and gave her hand a polite lick. She unclipped my leash, and tickled my chin. Then she held out her hand, right up to my nose if you please, her palm dotted with small biscuits. *AHA!* That's where they were! It was impossible to fool my retriever instincts. My taste buds went wild and I sprang up and failed my first test. Taking a quick dive under her bed, I tried to hunt down her stash.

Maybe over here, under the chair? Or over there, under the dresser, or...

'NEV. SIT!' Her sudden harsh tone startled me and I froze. 'You're a guide dog, stop circling my room like a monster shark. Come here, SIT.'

Slinking back to her side, I sat down still sniffing the air. *Okay, no need to growl. Keep your fur on!* I felt her fingers gently run through my warm fur, over my back and forehead, and she toyed with my velvety ears. With my legs stretched out in front, her hands moved gently all the way down my legs to my paws. I licked her hand again, offering an apology for being food-challenged, and all was forgiven. We peered into each other's eyes for a few moments and, even though I knew she couldn't see as well as me, I must confess that her blue eyes did have me wondering, *Love, are you sure you're blind?*

JOINING THE PACK

The first two weeks of training with a guide dog were like an emotional roller-coaster – I was high as a kite with anticipation one minute only to be reduced to a pool of tears the next. It was hard work, learning the skills required to handle a guide dog correctly; where to stand, how to hold the harness, when to praise the dog, when to correct him, what tone to use for each command, which specific words to use that the dog understood, how to set the walking pace and so much more. Gradually, over the course of the training, I gained an understanding of my role as navigator for my canine pilot. Finally, the big day arrived – our first walk in public.

Five obedient dogs, five anxious handlers and two confident trainers set off in the mini-bus to carry out the mission. A burst of nervous giggles swept through the bus. Our loyal dogs lay quietly by our feet. The engine whirred down a few gears, bringing the bus to a complete halt. Dead silence. The trainers turned around and briefed us on what to expect next. I felt like someone waiting in the back of a sky divers' plane about to jump out into the vast unknown. How would we perform in public? My palms began to sweat with the thought of getting lost on an unfamiliar street.

The sliding door opened and Peter announced the first team.

'Jonathon and Rory.'

Phew! I sank back into the vinyl seat, my hands straying over Nev's soft coat. He looked up at me calmly as my fingers played with his ears, he was my comforting teddy bear. A few minutes later, the sliding door opened again.

'Maribel. Nev. Ready?'

Nev sprang to his feet, bouncing towards the door and guided me down the two steps of the bus. Once on the footpath, I tried to organise Nev to take up position on my left. He waited as I untangled the leash from around his front legs, a hot doggy-tongue licking my ear.

'Ready?' Peter smiled as I continued a nervous dance on the pavement. 'Sometime today would be good,' he said, amused by my delaying tactics.

I took a deep breath and nodded. 'Forward, Nev, find the way.'

Nev lunged forward, skipping first gear. I felt his body swerve to the left and I followed suit. We cruised past curious stares and passers by admiring my guide dog as a hushed silence fell on the street. A rush of heat burned into my palm as I kept a firm grip on the harness and we stayed in perfect step. We were in full view of morning walkers and it felt empowering. We moved effortlessly past every obstacle and I was impressed with Nev's decision to detour around a child on a tricycle. Oh, my goodness. I was following his guiding eyes.

'Good boy. Find the way.'

I kept verbal commands clear as a smile broke free. Everything seemed lighter, and so much easier as I stayed close on the heels of my guide dog. An unexpected feeling of playfulness put a lighter spring in my step. He showed such grace and skill that my emotions swelled, and I could hardly believe we were walking together in relaxed harmony. As Nev pulled up by the end of the kerb, I bent down on one knee, buried my quivering lips into his soft coat and let my tears flow.

'Nev. We did it. You beautiful boy.'

Peter came sprinting to our side, thinking something had gone amiss.

'What's wrong – what's happened?'

I stood up and faced my trainer, wiping away the moisture from my eyes. 'Nothing.'

'Why are you crying, then?'

With a sniffle, I said, 'I can't believe Nev just did all that for me. I'm so proud of him.'

Peter's voice lightened, and he smiled. 'Good grief, Maribel. Is that all? I told you to trust him. He's your guide dog, that's what he's trained to do.'

At the end of that day, my blind companions and I celebrated with a bottle of champagne as we shared a meal together, laughing with real tears of joy. It was not our dogs who faltered, but their new handlers all learning the rules of pairing up as well coordinated navigators with their canine pilots. In the final days of training, I mastered one challenge after another, my confidence grew steadily and I was able to walk with Nev on my left and my young son on my right.

Somehow, I survived the four weeks of intensive training, Michael survived his long days of child care, my trainers survived my emotional outbursts and Nev survived it all. The time had come to go home and to establish the new hierarchy with my teenagers and make room for Nev as the new male in our 'pack'.

MEMOIR OF A GUIDE DOG
Off to Work We Go

My handler stood at the door. 'Where are you, Nev?'
I buried my bone and dashed to her side.
'We're going out.'
I did a quick mental check. Harness, check. Leash, check. Boychild – not checked, he was already at school. She gave me a big hug, sweeping a thick brush over my golden fur and placed the harness over my head, ready for work. Every time that leather contraption went on, something strange happened to me. My entire focus switched from being a dog to sighted-guide as if my brain became wired to her voice.
'Let's go. Find the way, Nev.'
I gave her a fleeting glance upwards – *gotcha*. These magical moments when we worked in harmony made my paws prance with happiness. Half an hour later, we trotted through the front door of the college. People watched our every move, fascinated by our team work. The second we entered the classroom, eyes travelled over me.
Yes, I'm a guide dog. That's right, I am very cute. Sniffing the air, I noticed the smell of a hidden salami sandwich.
'Nev. Sit down. D-o-w-n.'
Drats! She knew me too well. She was on to me like a hawk, and then assigned a student to make sure I didn't make a dive into anyone's bag – not even during the break. Circling five times under the desk to get comfortable, I let out a pained groan as all four legs collapsed like a deck of cards by her feet. The students laughed.
'Don't mind my guide dog. He always does that. I'll talk about him later, but first...'
Yes. And I'll be listening. I crossed my right paw over my left and yawned.
I'd heard this talk before. She was an ambassador for her breed too. She had come to tell the students about her life,

about some of the tricks of the trade with low vision, about our first blind date, about all the things she did without sight. I was so proud of her. My girl was a clever cookie – for a human. An hour later, I was awoken by her students' applause. Good, time to go home and back to my bone. I guided her to the taxi and we drove off to pick up the boy child from school.

'Hi, Mum,' the boy child said as he greeted his mother at the taxi window. He noticed me curled up by her feet and wrinkled up his nose.

Ha-ha, you'll have to get in the back seat. I ignored his frown. He was a switched-on kid, and I often thought he could read my mind. He climbed into the taxi, asking his mother why he had to sit in the back.

'Oh, you two,' she sighed. 'it's like having twins.'

The boy child poked out his tongue at me.

Jeepers, kid. You've still got a grubby face from breakfast. You're lucky your mother can't see – she'd be horrified. I could also tell by the way he was sucking his bottom lip that he was sure planning something for us. *I'm not playing your tug of war game today. I've got a bone waiting for me.*

We arrived home and she took off my harness. I was free to run around the back yard with the boy child. A little while later, I heard her call out to us, 'Dinner time!'

Race you to the back door.

He and I sprinted there in five seconds flat but the boy child closed the door behind him and I whined, *Hey, that's not fair. I like food more than you do. Let me in!*

After several howls, she appeared with my silver bowl.

'It's OK, Nev. Here's your dinner.'

Devouring my meal like a true Labrador, I licked the bowl clean in less than a minute. Bet you the boy child hadn't even picked up his fork – he was such a fussy eater. *Mmm,* my tummy felt full and life was good. My bone was safely tucked away, and with the sun setting on my golden coat, I felt warm all over.

'Nevie?' The boy child called sweetly. He must have had a full tummy too.

Truce. I'm coming. I made my way towards the house where the boy child stood, holding open the back door. Like cheerful twins, we nudged in close as we walked towards the living room. He tugged me firmly onto his foam sofa to curl up together in front of the TV. He plonked his little body on top of my fur coat as if I was his royal cushion, and to tell you the truth, on a full tummy, I didn't mind anything. My handler came to sit next to us on the floor.

'Good boy, Nev. Well done today.' She rubbed my velvety ears the way she had on the first day we had met. 'Tomorrow we're going into the city. Won't that be fun?'

'Can I come too?' asked the boy child.

She rubbed his tummy, 'Sure. We can have a picnic in the park.'

'Can we take some biscuits for Nevie?'

'Hmm. What do you think, Nev?' she said, teasing me.

Wagging my tail, I licked the boy child's ear. He fidgeted until he found a warm spot and leaned into my curved back, our breathing rising and falling together like floppy puppies. He tickled the hairs under my chin and whispered softly,

'Love you, Nevie.'

Ditto, kid. And I licked his sticky face clean.

Chapter 3

Beyond Expectations

As we rise to meet the challenges that are a natural part of living, we awaken to our many undiscovered gifts, to our inner power and our purpose.
~ Susan L. Taylor

With Nev by my side, I reached for new goals. The Millennium had dawned and with it came opportunities that might once have been beyond my expectations. The time had come for me to explore more than my neighbourhood; I entered the World Wide Web.

It intrigued me to hear family and friends talking about a craze called 'surfing the net' and it sounded so remarkable I realised I was seriously missing out on an entire world of possibility. But how could I operate a computer without being able to see the screen? How would I move around in Cyberspace where my guide dog couldn't guide me? I soon learned that people who were blind or vision-impaired were mastering this skill in different ways. Instead of using the 'mouse' as a cursor to manoeuvre around a computer screen, the sensory method was to adapt the keyboard and be guided by sound. In order to gain independence with digital technology, the computer buddy waiting to assist me was a verbose 'parrot' called JAWS.

As I had absolutely no knowledge of computers with their software, hard drives and floppy disks, JAWS was added to the list of foreign terms I'd need to learn. The way forward was to go back to school! Each week for several months, I took the train with my guide dog to complete three courses in assistive technology. On the first day at Vision Australia, I said to the trainer,

'I've never used a computer. I can only touch-type on a typewriter.'

His face lit up. 'That's fantastic.' The trainer took me to a computer. 'You can skip the lesson on keyboard basics and jump straight into using JAWS.' He handed me a set of headphones and switched on the computer. It was then that I discovered JAWS – a robotic sounding voice welcoming me to the world of assistive technology.

JAWS is the acronym for Job Access With Speech, and not the infamous white pointer shark movie buffs were terrified by from the film with the same name. The JAWS I was introduced to was a verbose screen-reading software program for blind computer users which spoke *non-stop* from start up to shut down. My challenge was not only learning the skills in keyboard commands designed to move around the screen without using a mouse curser but also trying to keep one ear on JAWS and the other on my trainer. It was overwhelming at times, having a computer buddy prattle on with each press of a key.

'Menus, leaving menus. File, edit file, leaving file. Not connected, wireless networks are available. Windows Explorer. Enter. Library documents. Items. View. List box. Edit. Do you want to save your changes?'

I learned to let JAWS guide me verbally through the computer maze but he had a tendency to dart around inside open files and I had to work out which one he had disappeared into. I also discovered that I could push 'his' buttons without upsetting him – unless it was the one key accidentally pressed to shut him down. In a surprised tone, the synthesised voice inquired, 'Are you SURE you want to quit JAWS?'

Oops. Sorry. No.

It was the beginning of a co-dependent relationship, keeping up with each other's demands, moving through Cyberspace together and compromising on our shortcomings: JAWS with his phobia of being silenced and me with my impatience to fast track through the foreign tech-terrain. It took patience, a commitment to problem solving, and a determination to gain web accessibility. After a year or so, the process became easier and more logical. My steady progress from beginners to intermediate and on to the advanced course was achieved with the help of headache tablets and warm aromatherapy baths at the end of a long training day.

Being paired up with a chatterbox may not be for everyone but the screen-reading software enabled me to expand my skills as a writer and educator. I took on other courses and became a guest presenter for Guide Dogs Victoria, as well as speaking to students at secondary and tertiary colleges. There was no stopping me. The skills of independence learned by having a guide dog and using assistive technology allowed me to step confidently into everyday life. Accepting my public persona as a vision-impaired woman had finally come to fruition.

One 'gift' that helped me, and still does to this day, is having an acute sense of hearing. Listening for tiny details within sounds became a way of seeing. Not only did I join a choir, a drumming circle and began to compose my own musical, but my love of music also led me quite by 'chance' to a new life-partner and a career in sound.

Looking back, the combination of intuitive feelings and perceptive hearing has replaced my need to see. Without trying, my listening is always on high alert. For example, when I meet a person for the first time, all my senses jump to attention. With a calm exterior and a sense of slight anxiety, my ears begin tracking clues in search of verbal body language. My eyes pretend to offer eye contact but what I am secretly trying to achieve is a sensory feeling to bring me any insights into their character.

I often dive in and instigate a hand-shake, to both men and women, which strikes others as a little eager on my part; but I am looking for a hint that tells me if a person is giving off a genuine vibe or a guarded one. The voice appears friendly but is that nervous giggle hiding something? Could that acid-remark be masking prejudice? Many things can be hidden behind a polite smile if you are only relying on visual clues.

I may not make a personal judgement of people's appearances, their fashion statement, their preference for make-up and hair style or the colour of their skin – but my listening deepens in order to discern the timbre, quality and inflection of a person's voice. What a person says, or more truthfully, how they say it, is my main clue to their body language – along with a possible initial hand-shake. We may have only said 'Hello' in this exchange, but my hearing is patrolling the tonal quality of this one word. How it is spoken reveals much more than you might think.

We all have our own verbal-signature, rich with qualities unique to each person. If a sense of heat creeps into my ears or an internal cautionary bell rings, I get the feeling all is not what it seems, making me guard my own body language while fast calculations try to sum up the person's mixed sensory messages.

When recognising people the next time we meet, the first and most powerful clue is any accent in their voice. The thicker the style of inflection and pronunciation, the more obvious is their verbal-signature. This often stirs up my hearing, and I become keen to track more clues about their country of origin. I delight in the melodic lilt of the Irish, the humorous phrases of a New Zealander, the seductive verbal caress of the French, the cautious monotone of a Russian, the passionate excitability of the Spanish – each of us has a little something special captured by vocal expression.

Apart from listening to the delivery of a voice which may be soft, strident, kind, impatient, nervous or playful, I am continuously gathering clues for any other obvious feature from the person I am standing near. Does he have a beard? Does he have a thin or bulky silhouette? Does she have dark or light hair? Is her hair long and wavy or short and trim? Was that a glint of light from a pair of glasses? As much detail as possible flashes through the internal brain computer to store for easier recognition next time.

It is very natural for me to be listening to several sound-images at once. On entering a room, my hearing instantly scans the space, and so does my sense of intuition. What am I hearing? What do I feel? What can I 'see' from invisible wires of sound? Audio antennae leap out of my head to pick up instant information within seconds of being in the enclosed space such as an office, a train carriage, a rest room, or even a police station – which by the way, is an obvious place where people appear calm while waiting to address the law, yet the air in a place like this can feel thick with apprehension.

The most challenging places are in crowded venues. The barrage of sound floods my senses. I strive to filter out all the things I don't need to hear: the conversation on my left and conversation on my right, the coffee machine frothing with hot cappuccino, the CD player raging with disco music, the bursts of loud laughter from people in the far corner, a chair scraping over the wooden floor, the clinking of glasses and cutlery, the orders being given to the waiter at the next table, the jingling mass of coins at the counter. That is when I have to harness my hearing and request, 'Ears, please, I feel like the clown in the middle. Just listen to the person opposite me.'

'Hello. I'm Harry' were his introductory words that serendipitous night fourteen years ago, when I first met my second life-partner. Three little words, nothing flash about them – ah, but it was the way he said them.

His tone carried intrigue, and was like a warm and fullbody claret with a hint of good humour. His soft delivery of an English accent made me pay closer attention to other words and their inflection because I too was born in England and was curious to know more about him, his music and his possible role in my life as a music producer. The musical I was composing needed a collaborator – could this Harry character be the man for the job? It was his kind, yet playful giggle as we exchanged business cards that stirred something more than professional interest. I felt excitement and uncertainty as well as awakened female intuition.

During our early days of collaboration, Harry and I listened to tracks in his music studio, the skilled producer configuring graphs and analysing coloured dots on the computer screen. It soon became apparent that my skill for listening was an asset to the recording process. While Harry weaved his magic with the music tracks, sliding levers up and down to make minuscule changes in the mix, I was sitting quietly and listening intently. Every now and then, he turned to ask,

'Does that sound better or worse to you – Big Ears?'

I felt both privileged and nervous to be included in the mixing process. What did I know about CD mastering? Harry had been doing this for over thirty years. He was a brave man to ask such a novice assistant but the one thing I did know about myself was what I could hear exceptionally well and I claimed that as my certificate of competency!

Working with Harry was a real joy. When I closed my eyes, I could hear the smallest of details: an odd note, a vocal tone out of place, a subtle tap of a foot caught on the recording. The harder, or more carefully I listened, the deeper I was able to go and pick up on even finer detail. As Harry watched a kaleidoscope of colours, dots, wavy lines and complex patterns on the screen, we both listened to subtle changes on studio speakers.

If a click or some other unwanted sound caught our attention simultaneously, we knew there was an error to correct. But sometimes we heard the same thing and at other times, possibly due to auditory exhaustion on Harry's part, my big ears heard things that were far less obvious and I sat up straight to pinpoint the glitches.

At times these mistakes in the recording were so subtle to a sighted listener that I felt it best to ignore them. But at other quality control times, I was so insistent that he find the tiny error on the screen that it slowed down the mixing process.

'I can't see it,' Harry would say, searching for visual clues, going slightly crazy.

'It's there. I can hear it.'

After much searching, he'd locate the faint prickle to my hyper-sensitive ears. With harmony restored between us in the studio, the listening went on – as did our discovery of each other as life partners through our mutual love for creativity.

The musical didn't win the financial grant we applied for but we had more than money could buy – a future to carve together. Life was on the move again. My youngest son and guide dog came with me, and together we settled into Harry's studio-home.

Walking to Michael's school, I often tapped out a rhythm with my white cane. Nev had been retired from guide dog service and I had been freed from all my inhibitions. I felt liberated like a butterfly, ready to take on new colours.

My son's school didn't have a music program. As I couldn't offer to help with reading, as a singer and songwriter, I suggested to the teachers that I run a weekly music appreciation program, another way to enhance the students' literacy through music. The teachers were delighted.

Each morning, I walked with my eight-year-old son down quiet lane-ways, the cane tapping out a jolly rhythm; a bouncing pattern that echoed off our footsteps. Michael was used to me bursting into song. On one particular morning, as I moved to avoid a bin, a step, a pole and then a car – the words blended in sync with the tapping rhythm of the cane. A new song was born! 'Bin – step – pole – car. Bin – step – pole – car...'

'Hey, Mike, listen to this.' I repeated the words, tapping the cane, and asked him to continue the chant. I ignored what I imagined to be the rolling of his eyes. 'Please? The kids will love it.'

With the promise of a bribe, he indulged my songwriting fantasy. Lyrics for the verse came easily. 'There are too many things in the way; too many things to avoid; all I want to do, is get safely, to school. Bin. Step. Pole. Car. Bin. Step. Pole. Car...'

As I taught the various grades songs from around the world, it was a challenge to keep them engaged. Some students, particularly the boys in the senior grades, were too cool to fully participate in group activities. So, I brought in a variety of percussion instruments from Harry's studio which posed another challenge – how to keep the students quiet long enough to listen to my instruction?

The boys were thrilled to have a legitimate excuse for banging on drums and djembes, shaking the living daylights out of wooden maracas, and deafening us with cymbals and bells until the class teacher shouted them back into order. Some days the students were so hyperactive, I prayed for the bell to ring before the next uprising. Even though classes were often noisy, it was deeply satisfying to be contributing to my son's school community.

Several months later, another opportunity came my way. I applied for the job of Teaching Artist with the Song Room – and I landed the position! This not-for-profit organisation employed musicians and performing artists to run creative programs in under-privileged primary schools around Victoria. The children I taught were new arrivals to Australia and came from refugee homes with little knowledge of English. My job description included having to teach literacy through inventing a repertoire of songs and musical games.

On my first day at the new school, I counted thirteen steps to the front door. Tap, tap, tap – I walked down twelve steps and on through a dark corridor, my cane scattering children left and right. I noted that it took sixteen paces to the music room. I felt for a door handle and was relieved to open the right door. Making my way to the wall of windows, I opened the blinds to let the sun stream in and folded up the white cane, hiding it under the desk and away from curious little hands. I danced around the room, familiarising myself with any low desks at perfect shin-bruising height.

Excited voices trickled down the corridor. A teacher hushed giggles just outside my door, and I thought to myself, *any minute now it will be like the running of the bulls at Pamplona.*

Some children entered quietly in pairs, while the daredevils made a mad dash to clang on the percussion instruments. I asked them to climb down off the shelves and sit in a group on the floor. Once settled, I explained my role as the teaching artist who would create weekly music sessions with games and songs. Twenty-five small bodies sat huddled in a semi-circle on the floor around me. All I could see were little blobs with dark smiling faces, their shining white teeth beaming. As far as they knew, I was just another teacher, until I brought out my special gadgets; in an instant, my white cane and talking watch had them spellbound.

It was a time of questions and puzzlement on their part. They had never met a 'blind' person before, a blind person with clear eyes who seemed to be looking into their amazed faces. Questions toppled over one another in their haste to make contact with the blind teacher.

'Can you see me...over here, can you see me?' came a chorus of calls. 'Can you see *me*? *How* can you see me?'

I responded individually to acknowledge them, and those I could vaguely see in the front row sat smugly as if I had given them a prize. To be seen by the 'blind teacher' turned into an award-giving ceremony. One seven-year old girl held a white piece of paper and tucked it under her chin. In a quiet voice she asked,

'Excuse me, teacher? Can you see my face?'

Indeed I could. I marvelled at her ingenuity. The bright contrast of white paper tucked under her dark Samoan skin stood out a mile. She beamed when she knew I had really noticed her.

The more I spoke about needing to be up close to things to see them, the more the children edged closer to my chair until they were almost sitting on top of my feet. The younger students were fascinated by my talking watch. Total silence could be achieved in five seconds flat when I asked for quiet to hear the speaking voice announce the time – with one child asking me, 'Who lives inside your watch?'

I was thrilled to know I could control an unruly grade during the chaos. An entire class would stop dead in their tracks, squeezing closer to my side as if in a game of gridiron football, to listen to the voice announcing the time. Some of the teachers asked where they could invest in such a wonderful silencing device.

The rest of the week was consumed by preparing for the next sessions, a job I adored. I scouted out new songs for the younger students, and wrote original lyrics for the older ones. Creativity flowed in my life, and Harry added his skills as a sound engineer, composer and musician. In his music studio, we recorded soundtracks for the students and wrote compositions and lyrics to enhance English literacy. As the weeks went by, dozens of song lyrics filled our folders. CDs were piled high on my desk while I worked with assistive technology to write up lyrics on my computer.

Within a few months, we had produced two songbooks, complete with lyrics and accompanying CD for the teachers. I felt so well equipped to teach my choirs that my anxiety to find my way independently with a white cane to and from the school was somewhat eased by being so well prepared and emotionally supported.

A highlight for the senior choir was an invitation to sing as part of a 300-voice choir. *The Big Sensation Concert* culminated with seven primary school choirs from around the state of Victoria sharing the limelight in one colourful performance. We had ten weeks to learn a repertoire of six songs chosen by the choir director. She arranged the tunes into two-part harmonies, providing the teaching artists with a practice CD to follow when teaching the various choirs their respective parts.

The aspect I liked best was being given free rein to choose one song to showcase our individual choirs. I presented an upbeat pop song and my choir was hooked. We were soon rockin' and boppin' to the lively tune. The lyrics reverberated around my mind well after the session had ended; as I grooved all the way home, my white cane tapped in time with my singing, a gentle rhythm echoing off pavements and cobblestones.

During weekly choir rehearsals, my group and I jived to the swinging melodies, all eyes watching my theatrical hand gestures and body movements. I was impressed with my choir's ability to follow their vision-impaired teacher and had to trust they were paying full attention. I moved around with over-accentuated body gestures while mouthing the lyrics, giving clear visual instructions. They had to know when to sing softly, when to raise their voices, and when to finish on a clear single note. Above all, I encouraged my choir to dazzle the audience with their flashing smiles.

Performance day arrived and the Melbourne Town Hall was a hive of activity. Over three hundred excited child-protégés were buzzing with anticipation.

Supervising teachers droned like worker bees, placing groups of choristers under colourful banners to form a hexagonal shape on stage. I waited in the foyer until my choir arrived and was grateful to be led by the students as we pushed through the crowd and took up our spot, avoiding the swarm of volunteers fussing with last minute preparations. Lights on – wave those rainbow-coloured flags; we're on!

For the first few songs, I rocked and swayed with my choir, feeling the adrenalin of live musicians pumping from the band to a thrilled audience. A hush. Then the spotlight fell onto our group. I stepped out with one of my Grade 6 singers who led me to take centre stage in front of the choir. Panic struck momentarily; *What if I'm not facing the right group? What if I bounce around so much during the performance, I don't notice I'm going off stage?*

The band rocked to our tune and adrenalin pumped once more. Arms swung wildly and my face lit up to encourage the girls to sing their best for our début performance. They gave it all they had and by the end of our song we were almost flying into the air with sheer happiness. Proud parents and teachers applauded their appreciation. The spotlight swiveled around the massive hall to highlight the next choir while I moved back to be closer to my group, hearing their giggles of delight. A reassuring touch on my arm from the class teacher tingled with appreciation.

'You were great. Well done.'

The girls huddled for a quick group hug, with the best moment yet to come. One of the young singers tugged at my sleeve and I turned to face her beaming smile.

'Wow! Teacher. Does all that applause mean we are famous now?'

I gave her a big hug, and said, 'Anything is possible.'

These are the many threads I have weaved into my garment of change to create an attractive life my young self could never have imagined. The girl who longed to play with colour is the woman who today paints with words. My blindness has brought much kindness, both from others and in my learning to accept experiencing a 'different' *and* loveable life.

Now we will go on a journey of discovery to find the hidden gifts waiting to empower your life too. First, comes an adjustment phase but, be reassured, there are strategies in moving through them, one step at a time. Face the changes with acceptance and know that as the beginner to blindness, this is a challenge you can rise above. What is waiting to be revealed is *your own* story of overcoming.

PART TWO

HOW TO ADJUST TO VISION LOSS

All the art of living lies in a fine mingling of letting go and holding on.

~ Havelock Ellis

Chapter 4

When Confronted by Change

You have most probably dealt with many changes throughout your life but maybe nothing as challenging as the prospect of losing your sight, or living with a loved one who is facing this situation. It is difficult not to feel overwhelmed. These chapters offer hope and a way to forge ahead. Trust that you will find the courage, support and resilience to enter this new phase of your life. There are many aspects of this 'going blind' scenario you really do have some control over.

The main challenge when dealing with the prospect of losing your eyesight is keeping the balance right, still enjoying life even as sight fades and maintaining emotional stability. I want to reassure you that with a positive approach, and a willingness to take one small step at a time, the fear becomes more manageable. You can conquer fear when you are ready to move forward again. You can learn to approach the challenges you face in a way that makes coping a natural part of living.

I have often given a presentation, 'Living with Possibility: How to See Beyond Our Limitations', which is a talk based on my lived experience of a disability. It helps the audience gain an understanding of the benefits of accepting a life challenge when it arises, and highlights the best ways to approach a major hurdle that seems insurmountable.

Adjusting to a major challenge, whether it be a loss of sight or something just as difficult, we suffer or adapt according to our internal thoughts and attitudes. We can feel like a victim of circumstance or become the victor over the challenge, depending on our attitude. This is the first hurdle to overcome within our personal way of thinking. Our priority then, is to attend to the inner-work that must come first in order for any of us to be at peace with our situation.

Let's begin with a few questions for you to consider. How do you react when you are faced with sudden change? Are you able to go with the flow or do you fly into panic? Do you like to control an outcome or can you adapt fairly easily to a new set of demands? Are you more likely to hold on to the old or let go and embrace the new?

These are general questions, and your answers will depend on your situation and the perceived 'threat' vision loss poses to your current life circumstances. If you're ready to face your deepest feelings, try completing this thought: I fear the prospect of going blind and I feel....

Sit with your thoughts for a moment.

You may feel terrified. Devastated. Upset. Confused. Numb. Out of control. These are natural responses and ones that could keep you feeling stuck for years. The thought of going blind is the second most feared prospect for people next to being diagnosed with a terminal illness. It's a true shock to the system and can make you feel like you've been dealt the worse blow you could have ever imagined.

Let me take your hand here. If you are feeling crushed with fear, I do need to point out a harsh truth in the most gentle way I can. For any of us who have been given the diagnosis of an eye condition that can rob us of sight, here is the key to letting go of fear – you are not dying from a terminal illness. Your life will go on in a different way. This may be the hardest truth for you to accept in the midst of change.

Whether you are ready to face this truth or not, it will help to be realistic. Vision loss is an unbearable minefield to navigate at first, until you realise that you CAN actually have some control over the situation. Physically, you are not able to avoid bodily changes, but emotionally and mentally, you can take a helpful reality check by looking at the attitudes you are holding on to and think about perspectives that would serve you better if you could begin to let your fears go.

One empowering technique is to replace fearful thoughts with the understanding that your life is not ending but has placed you on a different path, one you hadn't chosen to take. Life is never fully certain and situations can suddenly change: a close relationship ends; an unplanned pregnancy is announced; an employer wants you to move to a different location; a person slams into your car and causes much havoc; a company you invested in goes bankrupt. What do these changes have in common? Life goes on. You manage the 'detour' in the most practical way you can and find other ways to get over the obstacle. This is also an effective approach when dealing with the confronting prospect of going blind.

Imagine your future as a detour rather than a dead end, a situation where you will learn about other choices instead of feeling you have just hit the wall. The detour is neither a better nor a worse route; it's just different. Don't turn around and head straight back home. Follow the new signs and adapt to a different direction, even though it can be annoying. Being annoyed or frustrated only makes you suffer more. The solution is taking some sort of action, even if it means going the long way around. This is a better option than staying stuck or withdrawing.

The 'long way around' in this case is to assess your needs and concerns and find the best supports that already exist, and will help you get to where you want to be in your life. This analogy may seem simplistic but when you have to face a change, you are forced to reconsider your options. When dealing with a life-changing situation, there is a natural passage of acceptance to navigate through, explained here as 'The Phases of Adjustment'.

THE PHASES OF ADJUSTMENT

According to research, no matter what the 'crisis' may be, we all go through a psychological pattern of reactions. These are well described in the landmark text by Dr Dean W. Tuttle and Naomi R. Tuttle, whose research on the impact of going blind outlines an adjustment process of seven phases. Their co-authored book, *Self-esteem and Adjusting with Blindness: The Process of Responding to Life's Demands,* is considered invaluable reading in the United States for professionals studying in the field of vision loss.

Through his many writings, Dr Dean Tuttle, who is a blind professional in Educational Psychology and Special Education, clarifies the psycho-social relationship that can impact an individual's life and their family who are trying to cope with a disability. He describes the process that occurs when developing a new sense of self as people face rebuilding their self-esteem in what he calls the 7 phases of adjustment:

1. The Trauma
2. Shock and Denial
3. Mourning and Withdrawal
4. Succumbing and Depression
5. Reassessment and Reaffirmation
6. Coping and Mobilisation
7. Self-acceptance and Self-esteem.

Take a closer look at these phases and see where you are on the spectrum of adjustment. Be aware that this is a process we all go through. You might feel relieved to know you are actually where you are meant to be right now. Coming to terms with each stage (or whatever you may need to go through to allow for the following stages) can help you to reassess your new situation. How long this process will take depends on many factors, including the setback itself and the impact it creates on your life.

Even the changes you DO see coming require a certain amount of courage and flexibility if you are to work through these cycles of emotional adjustment. It is possible to begin with a degree of control over your life. You are still the same person, with unique gifts and talents. You have the ability to make decisions and good life choices. As you adjust to living with an eye condition that creates sight loss, you learn to become more resourceful in problem-solving, more often.

What I do know and encourage people to realise is that accepting an unpleasant situation doesn't mean you have to like it before you can fully enjoy your life again. To accept the situation it helps to come to terms with the facts that this uncomfortable reality has to be faced, and that only you can really turn the situation around, and only when you are ready to do so. When you truly understand this, it is not so much about trying to overcome the difficulties as about making a personal reconciliation to your situation in order to alleviate your emotional pain and mental suffering. Making a conscious effort to do what you can in accepting the situation is the moment where small shifts in attitude and action turn many things around – in your favour.

To 'begin again' is to take stock of reality. As you change your personal focus, realise it is possible as a person with low vision to develop skills in managing daily living tasks, and maintaining your independence. Adapting the home and work environments is possible and practical, as is completing your studies, fulfilling professional goals and attaining personal aspirations. This section of the book is your treasure trove of tips and strategies which we will explore in more detail soon. For now, the following list of insights are my own reflections which I have often included in my presentations. You can take them with you on your 'detour' as a beginner to blindness.

HELPFUL INSIGHTS

INSIGHT #1 Be mindful of your self-talk.

Our self-talk is the internal dialogue that translates whether we choose to see things as 'good' or 'bad'. It is like a computer program running non-stop inside our mind, and this is why it is important to catch these thoughts as much as possible but not to get stuck on them, especially if they create feelings of great anxiety.

Being an observer of our thoughts allows them to be, and then pass, without dragging us deeper into their terrified interpretation of a situation. Know that it is YOUR thoughts that influence your sense of well-being on a deep level, and that these thoughts govern how you view everything that happens to you. The way you think and process the situation at hand can either keep you stuck in a continual loop of gloom or help you to look for hopeful clues, depending on the meaning you attach to life events and your current 'story'. Becoming fully aware of your thought patterns is an effective method in remaining calm while considering your options.

As the popular saying goes, what you focus on, grows; so master your thoughts before they corrode your inner peace of mind. Develop healthier ways of coping and find refuge from difficult thought patterns by actively doing things to influence your internal dialogue in a positive way. Include self-soothing techniques such as listening to calm music, practising meditation, being out in the garden, going for a stroll in nature or taking a warm bath. You will have your own relaxation methods that help you unwind from anxious scenarios that insist on playing out in your mind. Sometimes, I simply retreat to my bed with a hot cup of tea to give myself a short time of nurtured rest. Going gently is the key.

Collect and verbalise quotations or reassuring affirmations that really speak to you. Placing your mind's focus on something more positive than your current worries allows you to take a step back and become present to your thoughts. In this way you can create feelings of hope and realise that you can thrive amidst the change. A friend of mine wears a t-shirt that reads, 'It is what it is' as a reminder for him to go with the flow of unforeseen challenges.

INSIGHT #2 Verbalise your fears.
Ever shared your deepest thoughts with a close friend who has helped you through a crisis? If so, you know how comforting it is to be heard. Now is the time to bravely reveal your inner turmoil, if you can, to a close friend or counsellor.

How you are feeling and what you are thinking are likely common fears for people in your situation. Sharing helps you to feel less alone in your struggle to readjust to sight loss. If you are willing to express your concerns, no matter how big or small they seem, you are opening a channel for the communication to ebb and flow, and you will find that the right person gladly gives you their listening ear and may be able to offer another way to view the situation.

What can often happen during a time of honest sharing between two people is that a clearer picture emerges, giving you other ideas to explore. Try not to shy away from reaching out to those people, both within and outside your family circle who are capable of supporting you with genuine empathy.

INSIGHT #3 Commit to trying again.
One of the hardest things to face is the feeling we have failed at something. When we fall short of achieving a goal, or feel we are unable to change a situation, we can find our self-confidence deeply bruised, and listen to our internal critic say, 'You're not doing that again.'

But what if 'failing' at something is the perfect opportunity to try again? If you are new to vision loss, this is a challenging thought. Your sense of confidence can be so damaged in the initial phase of a diagnosis that trying again is not on your agenda – yet. Let me reassure you, that when you can muster even a small amount of courage, whether you relearn a new way of doing something you enjoy, or you seek out services that can really aid your progress, once you do commit to try again, you begin to rebuild the self-confidence that is necessary to bring you a genuine sense of accomplishment.

INSIGHT #4 Balance between progress and rest.

As you consider your options in the midst of great change, Mother Nature will give you a clue about how to move forward. A year is made up of four seasons, with their different rhythms that support growth and rest. Each of us has our own natural cycles too. It is important to grow and develop new skills in living with low vision, and is vital to reflect and plan the next steps that nurture your growth.

It is seasons of perseverance and effort, balanced with patience and self-awareness that lead each of us, in time, through our personal cycles of adjustment. Each 'season' helps to keep your cycles in balance, physically, emotionally, mentally and spiritually. Being in tune and aware of the 'right timing' involves being patient and achieving a balance between taking action and accepting rest.

Another approach to the cycles of life is to let go of the old to make way for the new. Healing takes time. It's a natural process. Looking to healthy alternatives will bring a renewed sense of self which is crucial to boost your self-esteem. Taking on new skills, for example, and giving yourself time to rest so the new knowledge can sink in, allows you to respond more effectively to the situation at hand.

Life will bring you occasions over which you have no control but as you take your time to put ideas into form, you will begin to get a sense of achievement while working steadily towards your goals; if Mother Nature is resilient, then so are you!

INSIGHT #5 Freedom to choose.

At the heart of everything you do, you are constantly making life decisions and personal choices. But what constitutes the difference between making a decision and making a choice? Is there such a difference? The answer lies in the meaning of these two words: a decision is the act or the need to make up one's mind whereas a choice is selecting a course of action, with a sense of having the opportunity to do so.

The origins of these two words in the English language help to clarify their subtle meaning; 'decision' means 'to cut off' whereas 'choice' means 'to perceive'. Choices are powerful, a tool of the will, whereas a decision is a result of deliberation and is always subject to revision and opinion.

In short, choices are the steps you perceive as the best way to meet your needs. But what if having too many options becomes overwhelming? Instead of being liberated, you may feel trapped in indecision, which creates even more stress. You can also feel obliged to come to the 'right' decision. Procrastination, depression and inaction may be the result. How are you supposed to choose your best options? Let's use choosing a smart phone as an example.

You most probably know how difficult a task this can be. You want to make the 'right' choice, to find a phone that meets all your needs at a price you can afford. The solution comes when you DO select one above the other, the proactive part of the process, and then you begin to choose all the apps you require. Sure, it can be anxiety inducing at first, but the freedom to choose exactly what suits your needs soon follows on from your decision. To summarise, you can be a proactive decision maker with the ability to weigh up your options to choose the ones that suit your needs best.

INSIGHT #6 Change is a catalyst for new directions.

We all face many detours in our lives, and often it is our acceptance of 'what is' that helps us progress emotionally. But what you might fail to recognise when the unexpected occurs in your life and you jump to all sorts of impossible conclusions due to having to change your ways is that perhaps this new direction will serve you best if you can see it as a timely catalyst for good. You won't realise it at first but with a measure of TRUST, you edge your way into the bigger picture of your own story.

Being willing to take one small step, when you have no idea what you are doing, or where you are going, is a positive sign which will allow greater things to come into focus as you set off on this new journey. Be the spiritual warrior, not worrier, of your future.

AFFIRMATION

I trust that

even though I can't see the next challenge,
I am choosing a mindset to deal with the 'bigger picture' as it comes into focus.

I am taking bold steps
to realign my lifestyle with low vision
and redefine my reality.

I find the right people and services
who are there to support me on my life's journey,
and I place myself on a better path towards my future.

♥ From Cataracts to Accomplishment

Setting off in a new direction happened many years ago, taking me on a journey of self-discovery. My role back then was as a wife and mother, a caregiver to my elderly mother-in-law, a midwife to a menagerie of farm animals and the secretary to our family business.

I noticed the cloudiness of my eyesight had become more disturbing than usual, and although my eye condition had been a natural part of my life, something made me take notice of the extra blurred vision. It seemed best to pay a visit to the ophthalmologist. Even though I knew he couldn't do anything for my condition, at least we could discuss my new concerns.

The ophthalmologist probed my eyes with a special torch and said,

'I'm not surprised you're having difficulties. You have advanced cataracts in both eyes.'

The specialist went on to explain how a painless operation to remove cataracts was relatively simple. As he described the intricate procedure, fear pulsed through my veins. He seemed unperturbed by the fact that the patient remained conscious during the surgical operation. I couldn't share his optimism that the operation would be a pain-free experience and worried for several weeks how I would allow my body to surrender to the process. The more I imagined the surgery, the less I slept at night.

The day arrived and as I entered the corridors of the hospital, the antiseptic tang rose to greet my hyper-sensitive sense of dread. My husband took a seat next to me and we gazed around the waiting room. My vision-impaired eyes roamed the walls as I tried to find an object of distraction. On the opposite side of the room, an array of perfectly spaced frames caught my attention. Edging closer to view them in more detail, I peered at the white pieces of paper under glass.

The embossed red seals carried the proud stamp of my surgeon's history of success. The deep red circle on each certificate conveyed such a story of determined effort, of persistence and of triumph that it had a profound effect on me, as I thought: One day, I would like to have an official certificate with a red seal of competency too.

When called to speak with the eye surgeon briefly before the operation, I couldn't help but tell him how seeing his certificates of accomplishment had inspired me to hope I could one day obtain one of my own. His kind words, 'I'm sure you will,' brought a touching moment of encouragement and validation.

Half an hour later, I was reclined on a trolley and being wheeled into surgery. I took out a miniature radio from my pocket, and unwound a set of headphones. The surgeon moved closer to my side and smiled,

'Are we quite comfortable?'

I nodded, gripping the portable radio and turning up the volume to drown out my fears. Any minute now and I'd be dying with pain. Breathing deeply for a few seconds, I had to let go and trust in my surgeon's capabilities. One tiny little prick from a needle and then, nothing. No pain. It was incredible. I was awake for the entire operation and all my eyes could see were very dim shadows coming and going from view.

During the following months, a series of serendipitous events led me to undertake a professional course in Aromatherapy and Remedial Massage. With much determination and passion, I set my sights on completing the two year study course and set time aside each day in between my home duties for my family. Once the children were at school, I was free to study. The bigger picture seemed daunting, at times, even impossible. There was so much to learn and using a magnifying machine to see the text books was exhausting. One reference book on anatomy was at least three inches thick, and it was slow going, as each page I read had to be held carefully under the screen of the reader so that word after word was magnified to a level I could see.

Line by line, paragraph by paragraph I combed through the medical terms. In order to write notes for the assignments, I had to remove the book from view and place it on my lap so I wouldn't lose the page. Then, I put my writing paper under the screen to write a few notes and traded the space all over again for the text book to go back under the screen. Slowly but surely, I worked my way through the huge amount of text and found I was growing with knowledge and passion. My heart yearned to finish the task I had set to qualify for a career I could do from home, by completing one assignment at a time. The goal was in sight and I was determined to get there.

Eventually, a large envelope from Health Schools Australia arrived in the post. I knew it meant only one thing – I had achieved my credentials as an Aromatherapist and Masseur. There in my hands, my fingertips traced over two embossed red seals on white paper as tears of pride broke free – my dream had become a reality. Inspired, I set out on a new professional path, creating a healing room at home for clients in our seaside town.

Chapter 5

How to Really Handle Fear

*Our dilemma is that we hate change
and love it at the same time;
what we really want is for things to remain the same
but get better.*
~ Sydney J. Harris

Moving from a sense of dread you might feel on a daily basis due to having vision loss to one of creating a life of self-confidence can seem like an impossible task. For the beginner to blindness, it is like trying to walk on a tightrope when you know you can't handle heights. The feeling of loss that disturbs your sense of equilibrium and affects your identity could make you fall victim to your deepest fears. Unstable thoughts may rush in to throw you off balance, making you feel uncertain about everything. It is natural for thoughts and doubts to haunt you: Who am I now? How will I manage...? What will I do if...? How can I continue to...? What will become of me if I can't...? It's so unfair, why ME?

    I understand these fears; it's natural to feel vulnerable and highly uncomfortable in the midst of great uncertainty. It is for this reason that I'd like to bring to your attention the philosophy of acclaimed author, Susan Jeffers, known for her best-selling book, *Feel the Fear and Do It Anyway*. This book is a must-read for the beginner with a degree of sight loss. It is also an insightful text to develop coping methods when dealing with life issues in general. Jeffers' profoundly simple philosophy has helped to change the lives of millions of people around the world. Feel the fear and do it anyway can become your personal mantra to assist you in taking that first shaky step towards acceptance. Jeffers writes, 'Self-awareness is the first step toward positive change'. Let's explore the universality of her core message to help begin a journey of self-discovery. Jeffer's book describes the common fears that occur on three distinct levels.

3 LEVELS OF FEAR

Level 1 – The 'life-happens' fear.
These are the type of fears we all tend to have at some point: 'situation-oriented' fears. They are caused by normal situations, such as applying for a job, making new friends, raising a family, changing careers, speaking to an audience, losing a loved one, ailments of ageing, contemplating financial insecurity, ending an intimate relationship or dealing with health issues. They are impossible to avoid because it is an essential part of being human.

Level 2 – The 'ego-based' fear.
These fears are related to our inner world and the 'story' we invent around our experiences. For example, when we are rejected, or feel failure and lose positive self–image, or when we are criticised or feel vulnerable or inferior, we are creating internal states produced entirely by our ego. These secret feelings are invisible to our friends and others.
When we live in the ego-based realm we are most likely to close off our feelings and shut out the world, causing further pain that impacts on our life and hurts relationships.

Level 3 – The 'I-can't-handle-it' fear.
This particular internal belief will crush a person's ability to get back in the saddle after a fall – every time. In order to

have another go, Jeffers poses this question to the reader; 'If you knew you could handle anything that came your way, what would you possibly have to fear?'

Any guesses?

Her answer is, 'Nothing'.

As you read these distinctions, you may find them too simplistic for such a complex life-challenge. Being told you 'have nothing to fear' when you are afraid of going blind sounds completely insensitive and absurd. What Jeffers goes on to say is that although the fear may never go away completely you can develop a way of living with it. This is the essential key to handling fear. As long as you are seeking solutions and are willing to trust in your ability to handle a difficult situation, you are more likely to go ahead and 'feel the fear and do it anyway'.

When you identify your fear, you are more able to adapt, adjust and accept what needs to be done next. Use one of THE most beneficial 3-letter words in the English language, I CAN, which will gently begin releasing the fear that will otherwise keep you feeling unhappy and helpless for years. When uttered with strong conviction, saying I CAN is a powerful affirmation for success. We learn it as children and use it over and over again. Often its power fades as we get older because our ego-based fears creep in as we experience rejection, disappointment and other emotionally painful, and sometimes imaginary 'failures'.

Think about this; what do children say when they want to do something adults consider impossible? Their positive mantra is 'YES I CAN!' and they don't give up easily on this thought, even if it seems totally unreasonable. They are not governed by reason, but by determination to get what they want. Often, what stops them from achieving their plan is the adult's firm reply, 'No, you can't.' Of course, there are valid reasons for adults to say this, several times a day in fact, but following on from our childhood experiences, our self-talk learns to identify feelings of success as good, and feelings of failure as bad. As we grow, we avoid encounters with hurtful situations and so we give up on many activities, just in case they fail. Our confidence is undermined, seriously limiting our lives as we grow older.

Consider how much certain words influence you on a deep level; they can guide you towards opportunity or make you shrink away and retreat in fear. Your thoughts govern how you view relationships, life situations and challenges, and career options. Examine how you are choosing to interpret what being blind means in your life, and you can create a completely different perspective. Naturally, this does take time but when you are able to go within your thoughts to affirm that, I CAN manage this new change, I CAN learn new skills – a powerful mental shift occurs; hopelessness transforms to hopefulness. It is as if the thoughts you hold on to most become your balancing pole on the tightrope of life. With a certain amount of self-control, a sense of courage will not be too far away.

♥ Courage on a Mission

I will never forget a conversation one night with an old friend. Jim had been a test pilot in England during World War II and was recounting some of his terrifying missions while flying Spitfires. His job involved pushing the plane to breaking point, testing the plane until engine failure caused thick black oil to spew out and cover his face and goggles.

If this happened, he had to be ready with an 'I CAN' plan. Jim plotted a strategic landing site every few minutes which gave him a feeling he was still in control, even if he was forced to make an emergency landing. For Jim, it was just what he had to do, and with unwavering confidence he carried out his missions time and time again.

Imagine my surprise when he raised a glass to toast what he saw was my 'bravery': my positive attitude to going blind. Silencing the other friends at the table, he said,

'This woman is incredible. She is so brave.'

'No, no, Jim,' I protested. 'You risked your life every day. I am not that brave.'

He leaned over to put his arm across my shoulder and said, 'I'm losing my sight and I'm in awe of your courage. Believe me, you are brave.'

I was deeply moved by his praise. Here was a WWII test pilot who had risked his life countless times, yet the thought of going blind in his eighties had diminished his sense of courage. Both of us acknowledged the brave face we saw in each other's life situation, yet it was apparent to me how we didn't recognise our own heroic spirits. The conversation with Jim helped me realise that to remain confident is to walk the 'tightrope of life' and the gift of courage is our balancing pole. Each of us is capable of achieving many things when we trust we can handle anything that comes our way.

RESILIENCE IS THE NEW NORMAL

At the onset of any life challenge, it helps to know you are more resilient than you think. Audrey Demmitt, peer advisor for VisionAware (USA) wrote a great piece entitled, 'Resilient People Live Well with Vision Loss'. She reminds the reader that many people have more ability to cope with a life-challenge than they give themselves credit for.

Audrey writes of attending an event in her community, happily mingling with the crowd, with her guide dog at her side, when a gentleman approaches and says,

'Wow! I am so impressed that you are here. How do you do it, I mean, I don't think I could do it.'

Audrey goes on to write, 'I have had many similar encounters with people who fear blindness and don't believe they could deal with it. My response is always the same, 'Oh yes, you could if you had to. You already have within you what it takes to adjust to something like this – you just don't know it.'

Audrey too had to learn this about herself. 'There was a certain something already in me that made it possible to adapt to my disability. Of course, I still had to go through the painful process of grief and find a new normal in life, but I made it through.'

I often have these types of discussions with the people *I* meet. They say it is inspiring to see a person who is blind or vision-impaired getting around and taking life in their stride. But we are merely displaying a resilient nature; for us, there is only one way out of a difficult situation and that is to get through it. I really don't mind if my life inspires others because I feel I am continually dispelling the myths surrounding my disability. As Audrey says, 'It is not that extraordinary.' From our perspective, we have both learned to say 'I CAN try again' and focus on the part of life we want to continue enjoying regardless of our vision loss.

You can do this too.

Remember how children approach life with their wonderful dreams, schemes and ideas? They don't stop for a moment to talk themselves out of their grand desires. If we can all do the same as adults, we would gain confidence and pay less attention to our debilitating fears.

One way I confront my fears when I am sensing a measure of doubt or anxiety is to use my mental butterfly net to catch the negative emotion, sit with it for a few minutes and see it for what it is: a fearful thought, weighing down my heart with deep concern. Then I let it go. Once I am aware of how the thought is making me feel, I can create a different viewpoint. I accept that I am human and mistakes are made. Life happens. I heed the voice of resilience. I really do believe that each day is granted to us as a new opportunity to try again, to give strong support to our aspirations. As a person on the journey towards blindness, you will be pleasantly surprised to discover that a willing heart gains strength each and every time it confirms 'I CAN' always try again'.

♥ When Destiny Calls

Being the mother of a young family, I often found I had to squeeze in time to pursue my love of singing. Once a week, I attended the local choir rehearsals in our seaside town and returned home to resume motherly duties. Then one day, destiny called.

'I know this is very short notice,' said the choir director over the phone, 'but do you think you could learn the lyrics of a song by tomorrow night? The lass who was supposed to sing a duet in our concert has succumbed to laryngitis.'

My mind buzzed with the thought; *learn an entire song by tomorrow night?*

The director sounded panicky. 'Do you think it's possible? I don't want to put you under pressure.'

I was delighted to have been asked, yet terrified to commit. It was my first duet performance in public. The thought took me to the edge of my comfort zone, arousing a sudden mixture of exhilaration and fear.

'What's the song?'

'Perhaps Love, by John Denver. Do you know it?'

I knew the tune but didn't know the lyrics. I silenced the voice of fear and replied, 'Sure. I'll do it.'

The choir director thanked me profusely and began to recite the verses over the phone while I scribbled frantically. It was only after the call that my fearful voice returned: 'You idiot! What have you promised?' I argued back, 'It's only *one* song!'

All the next day, while cleaning the house, hanging out washing and cooking for the family, I sang the verses over and over again. In the evening, I arrived for Opening night to prepare backstage and to be fitted out in a cobalt-blue gown and long white gloves. Choristers fussed about. I heard the sound of audience clapping. My hands sweated in the heat of the excitement – what if I forgot my lines? I tried to compose my thoughts and ignored the terrible dryness creeping into my throat. *I'm going to stuff up, I never should have said yes.*

My singing partner stepped closer and smiled at me. 'We're on.' He gestured to hold my white gloved hand. As we moved towards the stage, some of the choristers wished us the good luck chant, 'break a leg'. We strolled to the spotlight on centre stage and began our duet. We appeared relaxed and engaged, even though the sound of my heart-beat was thumping wildly in my ears. My male companion held my hand throughout our ballad, giving it a reassuring squeeze every now and then that encouraged genuine smiles between us.

As I let go of my fear, I relaxed into the performance and began to feel light and happy – I was actually enjoying the experience. Our ballad was over in a flash, just as I was beginning to get comfortable and could stay to sing a second song. My partner bowed, I gave a demure curtsey and off we sauntered. Backstage, praises and hugs were showered on us by the other choristers. I blushed with happiness and was proud to tell them that I didn't even break a leg. I had triumphed over my fears and I knew, if asked to sing centre-stage, I would say 'yes' and welcome the hand of destiny again.

TRANSFORMING THE OBSTACLE

To have some control over our lives that gives us a sense of personal empowerment, I've learned that it is not so much being vision-impaired that will bar the way forward but how we react to oncoming obstacles. If frustration, anxiety and negative attitudes are holding you back, then identifying them is one way to push past your perceived barriers.

It will help the beginner to blindness to realise that a lot of what you imagine or might fear is not necessarily going to come true. Your unsettled mind may be trying to retain control, but in second guessing every scenario possible, it is creating even more barriers. Consider the following attitudes that can impede your ability to move ahead. Do any of these ring true for you?

I Tend to Think the Worst

Your reaction to a situation has you mulling over frightening scenarios. You are digging yourself deeper into a hole and can't help it. Your feelings turn to despair and you can't see the way out. Here is the good news! It is totally possible to learn other skills that will strengthen your resolve to manage life with any physical limitations you face.

You'll soon discover other ways to help your mindset work for you, not against you, and ways to self-manage with real strategies that will help achieve personal fulfilment.

I'm Too Scared to Tell Anyone

Perhaps you're getting away with keeping your fears of going blind to yourself and doing an amazing job of bluffing your way through each day. It can often seem less complicated to hide your vision loss, especially if you are the shy and private type. Whose business is it anyway? You've managed so far, and survived all the embarrassing moments of clumsiness.

But putting off dealing with the reality of your situation can be detrimental to your long term relationships, and dangerous to your safety. If the public are not aware of your low vision, you will experience more episodes of being verbally abused, and you run the risk of causing unnecessary accidents. Come out of hiding and you will discover the world really cares about you.

Asking For Help Makes Me Appear Weak
Where does this attitude come from? Possibly from childhood when you were told to 'get over it' or 'don't be such a baby' or 'boys don't cry'. Comments like these can ruin your personal outlook if you continue to let that story run your adult life.

Being able to express your feelings and let go of self-pride is a true mark of strength. You show great courage when you are willing to take this first major step towards asking for the support you need and deserve.

I Don't Want the Stigma of a Disability
Few of us want to be labelled, or branded or feel stigmatised due to a disability – but like it or not, society places people into broad categories as a means to govern a population with diverse needs. Often the stigma you feel attached to your personality by others is a perceived stigma: it can't stick to you unless you let it.

There is no doubt that it does take a certain amount of courage to ignore the misguided attitudes you will come across, but what you receive in return for your boldness is good wishes from others who want to support, not judge you. Communicating your truth is liberating in so many ways.

I'm Too Old to Learn New Skills
Contrary to this belief, no matter how old you are, it is never too late to learn new information. According to an article on

the BBC website by David Robson entitled, 'There is an Effortless Way to Improve Your Memory', informing the reader that young students, or patients with Alzheimer's, can use a simple technique to boost their memory.

It involves minimising distractions after taking in new information. Sitting quietly for fifteen minutes allows the knowledge to enter the memory-bank. We can all manage to find some down-time to give our brain the chance to recharge with fewer distractions. New research suggests this to be an effective way to enhance our memory skills.

I Don't Want to Be a Burden to Anyone

If we turn this thought right around, we reveal a completely different attitude. When you let go of assuming you are a burden to your family and friends, a new 'gift' is given to those who care for you.

Not only do your family and closest friends want to help you, but they are also given the opportunity to share their compassionate nature by assisting you in visual tasks. I'm sure if roles were reversed, you wouldn't think it a burden to collaborate.

What's the Point? I'm Going Blind Anyway

If you fear you will have to put your passions to one side, I'm stepping into the role of your life-coach: being blind or vision-impaired is not an excuse to quit the game of life.

It's normal to feel lost with an eye-condition affecting your prospects in the beginning phase of emotional adjustment but giving up before you have begun to try another way is not the solution. For example, if you are a keen cyclist, why not become a member of a tandem bike club where you can be involved with social events with other bike enthusiasts?

There are many social groups, recreational and professional circles where people meet to support each other in mutual hobbies and interests. Hiking, kayaking, sailing, bowling, goalball, cricket, tandem skiing are only a few sports to consider.

It is not sight loss that stops us following our aspirations but a lack of imagination and motivation. Try to be proactive and say YES to opportunity – NO to limitation.

STEPPING STONES TO SUCCESS

Having outlined some of the limiting attitudes that block progress, it's time to uncover ways in which you can transform an obstacle (a physical limitation or a mental belief) into your stepping stone to better things.

Try to reclaim your influence over a situation with a different attitude. By doing so, you will experience a transformation in the way you handle your vision loss.

I Can Practice Response-Ability

In any situation, you can either react or respond. This means you are response-able for how you 'react' to your challenges. You cannot control the prognosis of an eye condition, but you do have some control over your reactions to it.

When you are able to take Response-Ability for your thoughts, attitudes and actions, you begin to take charge and make 'executive' decisions about your life's business. Life can be less challenging when you observe your reactions and then learn to respond more positively the next time you are confronted by frustration or disappointment.

I Can Get Support

You can do way more than just survive life with sight loss, you can thrive and know people are there to help you at every turn. Their love and support are available to encourage you to fulfil your potential. You shift from being 'blind' to being 'boss' – the one who knows what you want and the one who can organise your team of helpers.

You have the option to delegate visual tasks to others when the need arises. As Travis Bell, a motivational speaker, says, 'concentrate on your strengths and strategically outsource your weaknesses.' Think of it as 'delegating powerfully' as you discover how teamwork will help to achieve your personal and professional goals.

I Can Adapt and Be Flexible

Think of all the times you have had to adapt to learning a new skill at work, a new method of helping a child understand their school work or even how you organised the move to a different home – perhaps in another state or country. Wasn't it your ability to be resourceful and determined to see it through that got you to your goal?

Many times you may have wanted to give up, but being persistent and adjusting to change created positive results. To live well with low vision means being able to bend and flex – to sway with change without it breaking your spirit. If you need training to gain skills in assistive technology or work on retaining your independence, ask for it and do it. Whatever it takes, be adaptable; learn new skills and you won't regret it. Take one day at a time and know it is possible to recalibrate your life with new options.

I Can Persevere with Confidence

Life can get tough at times. But when life gets tough, you have to get even tougher. If you can diligently chip away at an obstacle that is barring the path forward, you will shift the massive block of resistance little by little. Whether it is a case of a negative attitude or loss of self-confidence, a measure of determination will help you get beyond such challenges.

I Can Be More Resourceful
Join a support group. In order to develop more resourcefulness, you can also draw on the knowledge and experience of others who are dealing with the same challenges and obstacles. Practical solutions to everyday living when you are blind or vision-impaired can be met in ways you may not have considered yet.

A friendly group, either in person or online, can offer emotional support and valuable information to keep you feeling connected and empowered.

I Can See Beyond My Sight Loss
Whenever the obstacle of blindness threatens to block your path, see its potential instead. Something out of your control is pushing you to take a different course of action; don't let it beat you. Never give up.

You may need to talk with a friend or counsellor. Rest and reflect to find your inner wisdom. Renew your focus and give yourself credit for taking things at your own pace, one achievement at a time.

I Am a Diamond in Hard Rock
Any time you can take some form of action to help you move forward, it is like exposing a little diamond hiding in hard rock. Like a difficult situation, a diamond continues to be just a hard stone until it is polished to bring out its hidden brilliance.

Your new life-challenge becomes a unique opportunity to help you shine when you are ready to come out and experience unexpected pleasures with new sensitivity.

♥ Heart of Spontaneity

It hadn't been in my plans to go into the city, it was going to be a quiet day off at home. As a writer, I am accustomed to allotting the hours to various tasks: time for writing, time for sorting, time to spend with friends, time for whatever is on my 'to-do' list.

So, when an appointment was changed and I had to quickly make a trip into the city on my day off, I was challenged by the need for spontaneous action. Luckily, my partner is a master in the art of being spontaneous. He has shown me that sometimes we have to let go of our magnificently organised plans and jump into the world of uncertainty to experience the true magic of the moment.

As we both worked from home, I invited him to come into Melbourne for the day.

'Sure,' he said. 'We can do whatever you like.'

With a spontaneous spring in our step, we set off for the city. What I learned from our unplanned adventure was to experience the beauty in the moment. As a result, we stumbled across a psychedelic art exhibition I could actually see. In the heart of the National Gallery of Victoria, giant fluoro-coloured polar bears were poised in the centre of Federation Court. These eight life-size sculptures by a contemporary Italian artist were a stunning installation, inviting the visitor to edge closer and interact with these flamboyant creatures made of urethane foam.

I hardly ever get the opportunity to SEE artwork under bright lights in such high contrast, so I was giggling like a little girl and had to say Hello to each polar bear in turn. The next unexpected treat came when my partner managed to coax me away from my new psychedelic friends and led me to the gallery shop.

It was as if the exhibition inside the NGV, with its quirky collection of Italian and Japanese hand-made trinkets, miniature ceramic sculptured bowls and dainty Eames chairs in metal and leather had been put on display especially for inquisitive art-loving hands like mine. We spent the next hour exploring the shelves of beautiful pieces of textured art that I could touch.

Sharing the artwork with Harry was like a graceful Tai-Chi dance between our hands. Harry slowly lowered each object into my open palms, releasing his grip the moment my fingers closed in to grasp it. Waiting patiently, he offered more verbal clues until, fully satisfied that I'd 'seen' the artwork, I returned the piece to him, our hands touching in an exchange of graceful movements.

'Want to see something else?' he asked.

'Of course!' My face glowed.

By being able to embrace uncertainty, I gained another insight. At the heart of spontaneity, life can take us on an amazing adventure; it's all in the letting go of expectations and in staying open to new experiences.

Chapter 6

Tools for Progress

It wasn't until the light sensation completely vanished and I knew there was no way back that I said, I've got to try to understand blindness otherwise it will destroy my life.
~ John M. Hull, Touching the Rock

Professor John Hull, theologian and academic realised in 1983 that he was losing his last remaining sliver of light perception and began to keep an audio diary. Over a three year period, Hull recorded his experiences as he struggled to come to terms with his life-changing situation: He noted, 'I began to feel as if I didn't exist.'

Even though his family were used to him being legally blind (he had developed cataracts in his teen years, and later lost a substantial amount of sight due to Retinal Detachment brought on by numerous surgical operations), as the final dim shadows disappeared altogether, Hull was alarmed to find himself unprepared and grieving his loss.

Not wanting to burden his wife and children, Hull began speaking into a cassette recorder. He delved deeper to untangle his inner turmoil of thoughts and dreams in an attempt to understand blindness. He found it disturbing in this readjustment phase to be a stranger in his own life: 'I had taken up residence in another world.'

Seven years later, Hull's autobiographical recordings on cassette tapes were compiled into a best-selling book, *Touching the Rock: An Experience of Blindness*. In the book,

Hull openly explored the impact his sight loss had on his closest relationships and on his professional career. Initially, his diary entries were merely a way to help him reach an understanding of his new struggles – 'So full of challenges, making a cup of tea, putting on a tie' – but broadened in depth and scope to reveal his deepest thoughts and subconscious dreams as he explored what it meant to him to be blind.

Touching the Rock is his honest journey from personal loss to an adjustment that opened up an entirely new field for Professor Hull, writing and lecturing around the world on blindness and living with a disability. In 2012, the UK's Royal National Institute for the Blind (RNIB) honoured John Hull with a Lifetime Achievement Award for Services to the Literature of Blindness.

Like John Hull, I've experienced the transforming benefits of keeping journals to untangle mixed emotions and thoughts when I have been upset or confused by the surprises that are a part of not being able to see. My first typed reflections began at seventeen, capturing my random thoughts on white pages tucked into an electric typewriter. The whirring sound thrilled my sense of hearing and the keys tapped urgent messages reflecting on my latest experiences. It often surprised me to discover the real feelings underlying my reactions. Later I took to writing in a lined notebook using a CCTV, an enlarging machine with a camera that could raise the print on a page by up to 40 times magnification. I watched my handwriting appear on faint lines, filling my journals with thoughts. Today, my diaries are crammed into files on my personal computer and read back to me by a synthesised screen reader.

The mystery of the transition from self-reflection to self-revelation has never ceased to amaze me. It is with this in mind, that I encourage the beginner to blindness to consider using a journal as a pathway to emotional wellbeing. By taking time to delve deeper into the issues you face and by asking yourself soul-searching questions. In time, the voice within you has a chance to reveal aspects of life which you can view with more clarity.

EXPRESSIVE WRITING

Perhaps you already keep a personal journal – in which case, I urge you to go even deeper during this time of uncertainty. However, for the reader who would like to learn more about expressive writing, I'm delighted to introduce you to the technique. Expressive Writing is a method of recording your thoughts to help relieve stress. In some circles, it is also known as therapeutic writing where you tap into your true feelings; ones hidden deeply in the subconscious until probed.

Keeping a private journal, whether handwritten, typed, or spoken into a device, where you ramble freely to express all sorts of emotions is especially effective for people who find talking about personal issues to another person too painful or too burdensome to repeat. Taking up Expressive Writing (or recording the voice) is worth considering as a way to manage your stress because there really are so many benefits to reflecting and voicing your thoughts. During the process, the person is able to express anger safely; to gain insights that help to push past feeling stigmatised; to strengthen emotional fragility by choosing to feel the pain and then reframe it in a less painful way; to reflect on new ideas and design a plan of action; and to allow the heart and mind to release negative thoughts to realign the self with a renewed sense of purpose.

Those able to sit quietly and be honest with themselves in contemplating a challenging situation, recording and reflecting on their thoughts, are more likely to feel strengthened emotionally by moving through the pain. Confessing to a torrent of fears is not meant to make you relive them over again but to bring a sense of relief and meaning to something that seemed insurmountable. By taking time to process what you are feeling during a difficult phase, you create a safe haven in which to retreat for a little while. The advantage of using expressive writing or audio journalling as a method for self-healing is that you don't have to be a good writer. No one else need read your work.

Using a creative approach like expressive writing as a tool for improving a person's recovery after experiencing trauma has led to hundreds of studies worldwide. Researcher and author, Dr James W. Pennebaker, in his book, *The Secret Life of Pronouns: What Our Words Say About Us*, writes, 'The mere act of translating emotional upheavals into words is consistently associated with improvements in physical and mental health.'

In order to gain the most benefit from recording our life 'sufferings', Dr Pennebaker believes that it is helpful to fully acknowledge the negative aspects of a situation and face them so we can move into a more positive frame of mind. He conducted a series of experiments where people were asked to write freely for fifteen to twenty minutes a day for four days to reflect on their experience of trauma. 'Compared to people who were told to write about non-emotional topics, those who wrote about trauma evidenced improved physical health. Later studies found that emotional writing boosted immune function, reduced blood pressure and feelings of depression while elevating daily moods.'

During the writing of this book, I used expressive writing several times while going through a difficult situation. I jotted down my random thoughts into a computer journal, describing disempowering feelings that kept me stuck, seeing everything as hopeless. Through this journalling, I was able to observe the turmoil of my thoughts and question them. Before long, I found my focus shifted to finding brighter solutions, and it felt comforting – like self-induced therapy. I began an internal dialogue, and that inner, wiser part of me was inspired to offer tangible solutions. I then realised I had strategies to use the next time fear threatened to take hold. By changing my pattern of thinking, a different approach became possible and the situation shifted in a positive way.

I've learned that reflection and brainstorming with oneself is like taking a walk with the mind. At the end of the walk, I feel rejuvenated by my increasing insight and understanding my own thoughts and reactions. I can even emerge feeling ecstatic with a totally new sense of direction.

STEPS TO JOURNALLING

When beginning your own journal of expressive writing, the following steps may inspire you to work through the many elusive and challenging aspects life brings to the beginner to blindness.

Step 1 – Begin with where you are now.

Choose a quiet space where you won't be disturbed for at least half an hour. Get comfortable as you record your feelings and thoughts about your current situation, being as honest as you can. No one is going to read your journal, or listen back to your recordings, so dive right in. Don't be afraid to bring up all your doubts and phobias – they are all valid.

The key is to express your inner world without judging what you write or say. Perhaps ask yourself, what do I fear most in this new situation? What do I feel I can't share with anyone right now? Jot down anything: your troubled thoughts, doubts, indecision, loathings, or fragments of fear as they crop up. Any dark or bullying thoughts will be forced out into the openness of your mind. Keep going if you can because there will be many layers to uncover.

Step 2 – Don't edit the thought process.
Writing as therapy works best when you don't correct your private dialogue. It's all about enabling you to heal and to progress rather than to be perfect in your current expression. In time you may seek rehabilitation services to help you cope with your life challenge but for now, in the newness of the prognosis, just speak or write frankly and get in touch with true feelings.

Step 3 – Be your best friend.
Think of your journalling as pouring out your heart to a good friend – who just happens to be you: a friend who is there to listen, to allow you to express how you truly feel; a friend who really cares about your well-being. By revealing your thoughts, you are paying full attention to the stirrings of both heart and mind.

Just as when you are addressing a dear, supportive friend, you can open up more and more. Are there any other questions he or she would ask? If so, answer these questions without editing. Try to notice the advice your 'best friend' would give you in this situation. Often this is where your *Aha!* moments can occur.

Step 4 – Reframe your outlook.
There is no wrong or right way to handle a life-challenge but there are definitely positive ways to help you progress. One method on those days when you feel you are going nowhere or even falling backwards is to try and reframe the situation.

For example, think about or write into your journal five things you can be grateful for. During a time of angst, this is the last thing you might want to do but it will create a total shift in your perspective. Asking your mind to consider the positive in a time of distress can flick an internal switch. If you feel grateful for one simple mercy, your heart is briefly strengthened by this. Continue to dwell on five simple mercies and before you know it, your perspective starts to change.

Keeping a 'gratitude journal' as part of your expressive writing diary is a way of taking notice of the good things you tend to forget about during times of stress. Writing about the positive; your hopes as well as your fears can boost self-esteem and renew confidence. Recollect your successes, no matter how small they might seem. A thoughtful realisation, a commitment to making progress, a willingness to try again, or anything you feel to be a personal achievement, are all worth noting.

Step 5 – Commit to reflecting.

To reap the benefits of expressive writing, it is advisable to commit to writing (or recording) regularly in a private nook where you can cry, laugh or just think. Give it a go every day for a minimum of ten days to see how this form of self-care really works. Regular practice will help you to form the habit of journalling, enabling you to stay on top of your emotions with a technique that brings you renewed inner strength, as well as giving you a focus on how to plan your next action steps – or quiet retreat.

In the words of Dr Pennebaker, 'When we encounter adversity, we react by thinking about it. Our thoughts rapidly congeal into beliefs. These beliefs may become so habitual we don't even realise we have them unless we stop to focus on them.' By making a commitment to observe your random thoughts in order to reflect and reframe, you create insightful moments that can nurture your emotional life.

♥ Legacy in First Draft

In 2010 I felt a nagging urgency to create a legacy for my family. I wasn't planning to leave the planet but I knew that the past history of my life would never be known in full to my children unless I began my autobiography. How could they understand the bizarre things that had occurred with the onset of blindness, or the events that shaped our lives as a family and my spiritual perspective on life if I didn't write them down?

I took to writing everything as it came flooding back. The good, the bad and the unexpected. One year later, the stories I had compiled in my computer added up to over 200 print pages of autobiographical writings. Chuffed with my achievement, I asked a writing mentor to read through the manuscript to give me her honest feedback before I went in search of a publisher. Her reply made me sit back and rethink my plan.

'It's alright. For a first draft.'

First draft? I thought I had finished it. Disappointed at first, I had to admit that there was a lot more to learn about the craft of writing an engaging book for another reader. Even for the family, I had to go back to the drawing board. I am so glad that I did. Devoting just about every evening to the craft of writing for the next two years, I devoured article after article on the craft of writing; advice on writing nonfiction and fiction, strategies for building characters, plotting a narrative arc, constructing dialogue and the art of memoir writing. I became even more passionate about writing. It hooked me completely.

Yet, my family had not yet seen a scrap of my work and I felt like a fraud not having one single story published anywhere even though I was calling myself an 'emerging' writer. It occurred to me that if I took some of my autobiographical stories from my unpublished manuscript and polished them up as short stories, using the knowledge gleaned from my internet studies, I could not only submit them to a writing contest but also create my very own blog and publish them myself. This revelation launched my online writing career as a blogger, *At the Gateway to Blindness*. My second blog, *Touching Landscapes*, followed two years later.

There, in view of the world, my short stories of family life, travel and living with blindness emerged. I was so surprised to receive emails from people I didn't even know, who left kind comments about how much my words were encouraging them. Writing for my blogs was more than a passion, it became an addiction but I still didn't have a book to call my own.

In 2012, with the availability of self-publishing becoming a real avenue for writers to explore, I went with an impulsive idea – to create my first book as a surprise present for my family. Thanks to the encouraging words from an artist friend and book designer, Bee Williamson, who said when I inquired if she could help me, 'Let's do it, girlfriend'.

I set out on a whirlwind adventure to publish my first book within a three month deadline. Bee hit the 'PUBLISH NOW' button while we held hands and squealed, 'We've done it!' Two weeks later, *My Mother's Harvest: A Collection of Family Recipes & Short Stories* arrived in a box holding the first 100 copies. Voila! What a surprise for all of us.

Personally, the experience was a great success. What I gained professionally by self-publishing a book was an unexpected increase in opportunities to publish elsewhere as a freelance writer. All this began with keeping a diary, internalising issues as they arose, listening to the wise small voice within, following my muse to play with new ideas and using the *Aha!* moments experienced along the way as the seed-thoughts for my creative writings.

Using Expressive Writing could become a life-changing tool in your hand too. Where will *you* begin *your* story?

IMPROVING THE WIRES TO MEMORY

If your sight is compromised by a loss of vision, it is important to strengthen cognitive activity. One skill people fear losing as they get older is the ability to rely on their memory. We can all fall victim to believing in the old saying, 'you can't teach an old dog new tricks', but is this really true or could it merely be an excuse not to improve the function of memory?

Scientists and neurobiologists agree that we can all boost our long or short term memory. They have also discovered that neuroplasticity – which is the human brain's ability to reorganise new neural connections (nerve cells) after an injury or illness – can respond by adjusting to the new situation.

I find that being blind or vision-impaired requires me to be extra observant – like a Sherlock Holmes type of character who has to detect not only minuscule details of the changes going on around me but must also build on my capacity for recall. As sight fades, I am aware of how much I am gathering clues from listening, touching, smelling, tasting, intuiting and observing as best my eyes can. Above all, there is one undeniable device working overtime in helping me to adapt to change. It's called my MEMORY. I consider it to be a personalised computer app wired to my brain. And you have one too!

When you lose the ability to scan with your eyes and have to rely on memory to update, store and retrieve data you need to remember, the essential skill to develop is to train the multi-sensory operating system inside your head. Every time you intellectually challenge your brain, the activity stimulates dendrite growth, and the brain accommodates the growth of these new networking neurons that connect and proliferate, regardless of your age.

As a beginner to blindness who has to switch from scanning with your eyes to relying on your other senses in order to strengthen the function of memory, you have a vast resource inside your head that can be trained to retrieve details in ways you may not have tapped into yet. The human brain is surprisingly malleable in creating new neural pathways to accomplish new skills. Being able to recall details is about developing good habits and effective techniques by not limiting your cognitive abilities. In other words, your brain's capacity for storing information is virtually limitless.

Each time you learn a different skill, complete with all its challenges, you are stimulating the mind and improving the mechanism of recall while creating 'files' inside your memory filing system. I hope you will be encouraged to know that it is possible to become a whiz at remembering things no matter how old you are as your sight fades. Memory is acquired, not retired.

Consider the findings of a researcher at the University of North Carolina, Dayna Touron, who conducted a series of experiments with adults over the age of 60, which found that they often underestimated their ability to use their memory as a reliable tool for retrieving information, and were not using their function of recall to its full capability.

'We do see some adults who come into the lab who never shift to using their memory,' Touron said. 'They say they know the information, they just prefer not to rely on it.'

This sounds plausible because I have noticed how sighted people on the whole override their ability for recall and use their sight as a more reliable informant. For example, they write down a phone number rather than remember it, they use their eyes to read a person's name tag at a conference rather than commit it to memory, and they can scan their eyes over a menu as many times as they like. As a person who is blind or vision-impaired, you must use a different technique to store similar information.

Blind People Have Superior Memory Skills, an article on the LiveScience website reveals some findings that may be of interest. A neurobiologist by the name of Ehud Zohary of Hebrew University (Jerusalem) and his colleagues conducted two memory tests with 38 people. Half of the volunteers were sighted and the other half were blind from birth. The first test involved hearing a list of 20 words which the volunteers were asked to recall. In the second test, the volunteers were asked not only to recall as many words in the list as possible but also to remember them in the correct sequence. (Hands up those who are glad not to be doing this test!)

The tests revealed that the volunteers who were blind were able to remember 20 to 35 percent more words than did the sighted volunteers. But perhaps more impressive was the fact that the blind volunteers were able to remember twice as many more words in the right sequence. This suggested to Zohary and his colleagues that with the absence of sight, people who are blind are constantly using other cognitive strategies, giving them 'superior' memory skills. Zohary concluded that, 'congenitally blind people appeared to be using the visual cortex for other needs, and now we may be seeing part of how this area is getting used for other functions, to maybe be more involved in memory and language processes.'

One cognitive strategy I have developed over time to deal with the absence of sight is to remember details in a sequence or in a pattern that makes sense to me. It's like having a jigsaw puzzle inside my mind that takes information in by repeating the details in such a way that it fills a missing part of the puzzle piece by piece. This creates a mind-map inside the brain that with practice becomes a reliable method of retrieving information. Sighted people regard this as an admirable talent.

The more you can repeat words, even putting words to popular tunes (as I did when studying the top 20 elements in Chemistry by using an ABBA song), the easier recalling important information will be. Use a creative pattern to jog your memory. Look for anything that can become a mental landmark and file it with focus and repetition. This is an effective strategy and an essential tool you most definitely already have within your reach.

♥ Hallelujah for Mind Maps

Singing has always been one of my passions, especially because I don't need to see in order to sing; a good listening ear, an awareness of pitch and a method of remembering lyrics is all that is required.

When I listen carefully to the verses of a song I have been asked to perform at a concert, I notice words that jump out first. These words form the structure my mind builds on. As I repeat the verse, random words are snatched up by memory, which is on the prowl in search of the next keywords to cement together, until the song is built like a mental scaffolding with the lyrics firmly in place and in the correct order. I'm aware of my mind looking for words it can either group together or use as a prompt to remember the rest of a verse. As long as I don't get too anxious about keeping up with sighted singers, and relax into the mind-mapping process, I can sing with confidence with my eyes closed. Other singers are sight-reading but not necessarily putting the words into their memory.

If you have ever tried to remember the verses of Handel's choral arrangement, The Messiah's Hallelujah Chorus, you will most probably want to cling to the song book for visual guidance through the complex layers of harmonies. The first time I performed the choral work was with the Montague Choristers. The choir consisted mainly of retired people and I turned up one rehearsal night as their youngest soprano.

They welcomed this new choir chickie to the brood and warmly ushered me towards the protective wings of the mature hens between the sopranos and the altos. It was a prime position and I soon felt right at home, allowing the clucky-musical hens to place me in their pecking order. Their admiration for my ability to retain lyrics puffed up my pride and increased my singing confidence.

Several months later, we were preparing for a Christmas concert. The choir were struck by a dilemma: would they take their music books on stage or could they sing from memory?

'What about Maribel? She doesn't have a book like us, won't that look a bit odd on stage?' asked the soprano who was sitting next to me.

'She doesn't need one,' joked one of the men from the bass section, sending a chuckle rippling around the room.

'That's right,' said the soprano more soberly. 'If she doesn't need a songbook, why do we? If she can remember all the words, why can't we?'

The banter in the bass section stopped. For a group who relied on sheet music, this was a frightening thought. No one wanted to abandon their beloved books. I sat smugly on the border listening to their comments flying across the room. Finally, the choir director took charge.

'It's OK,' she calmed the group. 'You can take your songbooks on stage. I have an idea that will keep everyone happy.'

At the next rehearsal, I was presented with a book that looked exactly like everyone else's brown-covered songbook – except that mine was a gardening calendar full of glossy photographs of spring flowers. The audience would never know. On performance night, I held my 'Messiah Songbook' just like the other choristers, and sang together with them, counting the bars on my hidden fingers. Every now and then, I pretended to be reading when I would feel a nudge from a soprano on my left or my right to indicate 'Turn the page now'.

While flicking over the pages with the others, colourful blooms caught my attention. Bright yellow daffodils, red and hot pink tulips, and deep purple hyacinths held my gaze momentarily until a jolt from Memory reminded me of the words in my head waiting to be sung. At interval, when all the choristers had left their songbooks on their seats, I impulsively swapped my brown-clad gardening calendar with a real song book sitting on the abandoned seat on my right. That very chorister came over with a cup of tea (and her brother) to make casual conversation.

'Why don't you show Howard your music book?' she suggested with a grin, expecting to reveal the secret of the spring flower calendar.

'Sure.' I smiled back. I flicked open the book and showed Howard.

'Hmm?' he remarked with a slightly arched eyebrow. 'Black music dots, quavers and lyrics in neat rows.'

With a straight face I turned to my fellow chorister, who was now looking confused. 'Why not show Howard your songbook?'

She opened the song book and burst into laughter. 'OH! The flowers that bloom in the spring!'

A MEMORY SKILL

As mentioned before, working to improve your memory is like being your own super-sleuth. You have to take notice of details and then place mental notes to self into a filing system inside the brain. This process is called 'encoding the memory' and there are two other follow-up procedures that make it highly efficient in recalling any stimulus the mind considers to be important information to retrieve later, like being able to remember a person's correct name and a host of routine daily tasks.

When memorising something, visual or auditory stimuli are converted into an electrical message that is transferred from neurons to the brain and kept in a complex storage system. The memory can then go into that space to retrieve the facts or information that passed through this memory-formation encoding system. All this is happening without any of us really understanding how powerful our capacity to remember can be. The facts may slip easily from our minds but Memory is ever ready to assist.

A highly effective way to enhance your memory if you are experiencing vision loss is by being alert to other sensory information waiting to give you vital clues. Sensory cues and landmarks are everywhere but are you aware of them?

The way in which I have adapted to a more sensory recall is to 'converse' with 'Ms Memory' everywhere we go. On walks around my neighbourhood, for example, I am fully aware of an internal dialogue that basically goes on for the entire outing. Ms Memory assists by reminding me of the crucial points of reference that will keep me moving confidently and safely through my local environment.

'Remember this kerb is usually flanked by a large puddle on rainy days. Move a few inches to the right, just after the bright red post box. Walk around that tree, you don't want its overhanging branch to smack you in the face again. Don't forget the council workers recently installed a telegraph pole in the middle of the laneway. What day is it? Rubbish collection day. OK, avoid those large things scattered to the right. You're coming up to the house with the barking dog who likes to frighten the living daylights out of everyone – but not you today because you've remembered to move onto the nature strip. You're approaching the spot where you will have to walk around the white vehicle that is always parked on the pavement. Shouldn't you place a little card in their letterbox to request the path be kept clear? (Ms Memory jots down this brief thought.) Just a little further, that's right, past the large clump of bushes on the corner, not too close. Turn left NOW. Road crossing in a few metres. Listen for the audible beeps and traffic flow. Here you go – sounds like your tram is fast approaching.'

On we go, Blind Sherlock and Ms Memory in a constant search for clues, sometimes scolding each other for missing an important detail that has changed. Ms Memory promptly makes a mental note for next time.

This constant banter with oneself might sound exhausting but it is a technique that will develop over time as you become proficient in retrieving important information you can no longer see. Don't worry too much if details slip your mind at first, because sometimes our short term memory has limited capacity for storage.

Our short term memory is occupied with current thoughts that only last about a minute before moving on to other thoughts. On the whole, it limits our storage capacity to around seven items at a time. Learning this helped me understand why I can suffer brain-fatigue as a vision-impaired shopper in a supermarket. My aim might be to buy orange juice. I home in on my choice, but sometimes a sighted helper will tell me the other fifty varieties of juice. I find so much information overwhelming to store in my head. If this were to occur with every item on my mental shopping list, I would literally feel brain-dead by the end of the shopping trip.

My senses are in overdrive just concentrating on staying out of people's way and taking in other sensory information. This means that I often decide to stick to my original choice of orange juice, simply to keep the lines to my short term memory clear and avoid overloading my system. In this situation, multi-tasking is not so helpful because it interrupts one task to focus on another.

On the other hand, our long term memory has the ability to remember anything from a previous time (even from days or years ago) and has an unlimited storage capacity. Here, the brain can retrieve details of past events, factual data and general knowledge we have acquired through study and mental focus. With such an amazing neural super-computer inside our brain, do any of us really have an excuse to neglect the power of memory?

One technique for improving memory I recently came across is apparently so effective you hardly have to do anything at all. Freelance science writer, David Robson, who specialises in writing in-depth articles on medicine, psychology and neuroscience, published 'An Effortless Way to Improve Your Memory' online at BBC Future. Robson's article suggests that simply taking some time out to rest after digesting new information, minimising distractions of any kind, has proven to be a powerful way of retrieving this information for students and the elderly alike.

By sitting quietly for 10 to 15 minutes after taking in new information, it has been proven in many scientific tests that one can boost the ability of memory to retain the data a person wants to remember much more effectively than if they had continued with other tasks. This means that multi-tasking is not so efficient if we want to enhance and improve our power of recall.

Robson writes that 'The remarkable memory-boosting benefits of undisturbed rest were first documented in 1900 by the German psychologist Georg Elias Muller and his student Alfons Pilzecker. In one of their many experiments on memory consolidation, Muller and Pilzecker first asked their participants to learn a list of meaningless syllables. Following a short study period, half the group were immediately given a second list to learn – while the rest were given a six-minute break before continuing.

When tested one-and-a-half-hours later, the two groups showed strikingly different patterns of recall. The participants given the break remembered nearly 50% of their list, compared to an average of 28% for the group who had been given no time to recharge their mental batteries. The finding suggested that our memory for new information is especially fragile just after it has first been encoded, making it more susceptible to interference from new information.'

It appears that the best way to memorise new information is to avoid rushing to stack more facts on top of what you have just learned, and to allow the brain a small amount of time to recharge its internal battery as a matter of procedure. This technique requires you to deliberately avoid activities, such as going on your smart phone to check for messages, or starting up the computer to surf the internet, or getting involved with any task that may hinder the initial encoding process the brain is performing for memory formation. Minimal interference is the key. More rest and less mental clutter may be just the solution for all of us.

♥ Have You Seen My...?

I am forever touching things wherever I go. Blind Sherlock, with Ms Memory close at hand, tracks clues as we patrol the domestic precinct. I often come across misplaced objects, mostly my partner's, which Ms Memory is quick to jot it down: one wallet in the washing basket, one guitar capo by the kettle, one set of keys on the bookshelf, one pair of glasses perched by the bathroom mirror. When he asks,

'Darling, have you seen my...?' he knows full well the blind super-sleuth most probably has.

Shoes – glasses – car keys – wallet – laptop. This 'game' is usually played in haste on the way out of the door to an important meeting or before a weekend getaway. His request *sometimes* amuses me – and I forgive him, for he is the artistic type, a right brain sort of guy, spontaneous, a risk taker, a creative inventor, who complements my left-brain approach to life, which is practical, reality-based and highly organised.

Chapter 7

Life-Savers to the Rescue

When you want something, all the universe conspires in helping you to achieve it.
~ Paulo Coelho, The Alchemist

Having covered the importance of being more aware of cognitive abilities, there are also two other natural human traits we all have waiting to serve us well. These are our sense of intuition and our sense of humour.

Some of us are able to tap into them more often than others but we all have the ability to connect to these inner resources of the human spirit, and I can't emphasise enough how precious they are as lifesavers in times of stress and uncertainty. In order to do more than just survive a challenging situation, your capacity to trust in these two innate senses are as essential to your way of being as are breathing, eating and sleeping.

What humour and intuition both have in common is the way they can relax a tense situation, and allow for something to take its natural course, rather than forcing an outcome as you tune into your authentic feelings. I'm sure you can recall a time when you allowed your wiser self to steer you towards a better response or reaction, where you followed your intuition, or let a lighthearted approach gloss over an embarrassing moment.

On the other hand, there can be many times when ignoring or doubting your gut instincts leads you into unpleasant situations. Developing your senses of intuition and humour is as precious as gold when you are out of your comfort zone. For the beginner to blindness, they can be your allies and lifesavers. Let's look at them both in turn.

INTUITION

Intuition is an instinctual awareness in the core of everyone. You will have heard the expressions 'having a sixth sense' or 'going with your 'gut' feelings'. Intuition is known by many names in different cultures. Some believe it to be the gateway to higher knowledge. Phrases such as, 'Follow your heart' – 'Speak from your heart' – 'Connect to the heart and tap into what it is telling you', all describe the act of intuitive thinking.

For some of us, this feeling of instinctive and hard to articulate certainty is what we experience when we stand at the crossroads of indecision. It helps us to take our next step. This sensory perception is experienced in unique ways for each one of us. You may already be well acquainted with how your gut feelings or 'small voice' works in alerting you to pay attention to bodily sensations and other signs which can so easily be ignored.

Personally, I call intuition my 'heart-sight', an internal vision securely linked to deep feelings that guide me in all sorts of ways. As my eyesight has diminished over the years, it is not so much that I know intuition exists as my internal guidance system – it is my 'internal vision' that helps me to observe from a clearer perspective. My heart-sight enables me to fully trust in unexpected feelings that, when pursued, often turn out to be a reliable source for better outcomes. I take notice of my heart-sight with complete trust.

I distinguish an intuitive feeling from a conscious thought by the fleeting 'message' that makes itself known to my mind AND heart at exactly the same time, like a cord connecting and synchronising the two parts of my being. This is a silent but firm feeling in a split second of time. After the feeling, my mind can sometimes think of a reason why this feeling isn't logical, but my heart stays faithful to the feeling and pushes away any other thought; I trust in the unseen until it becomes visible. When I am able to trust my intuition and disregard the mind's logical reactions, I am freed from conflict between rational thinking and insightful guidance.

It's natural to want to make the 'right' decision when confronted by the need to choose a plan of action. So how do you allow intuition to guide you in such a way that you feel confident with your internal GPS system? First, you need to trust that you know more than you think you do on a subconscious level. Next, you follow your gut feelings even if you can't explain them. Disengage from logical argument when the heart wants to rule. Then act from the clarity of inner vision. By trusting your sensory impressions, choices become easier. Your creativity is awakened and you are inspired to take the 'right' steps, with confidence, achieving your aspirations through the guidance of your heart-sight.

I recently learned of the fascinating research by scientists over the past thirty years in the field of neurocardiology. This is the interdisciplinary fields of neurology and cardiology. They have discovered another level of communication between the heart and the brain which researchers are calling 'Heart Intelligence'.

Scientists at the HeartMath Institute based in California, USA, have shown that through the connection of the nervous system, the heart sends more information to the brain than the brain sends to the heart. In this way, your Heart Intelligence, which is also known as Heart IQ, governs your awareness and connection to every aspect of your being; physically, mentally, emotionally and, for many, spiritually.

It seems that the heart is doing much more than pumping blood around the body to each cell in every part of us. It is also keeping a synergy of intuitive communication alive inside the mysterious workings of the body and mind –

which are in complete harmony. It's fascinating to know that we can learn how to trust the natural driver inside our Heart's Intelligence.

The next time you feel your mind is trying to override your intuitive awareness of a situation, you might like to read up on the work of the HeartMath Institute. A co-authored book by Doc Childre and Howard Martin, called *The HeartMath Solution (1999)*, is considered to be the definitive research work on the intelligence of the heart.

By understanding the workings of your heart, and how your mind and emotions are aligned through the powerful sense of intuitive awareness, you will be able to access and activate a deeper communication with your internal vision as you progress on the journey into the world unseen. Being blind or vision-impaired can guide you to discover other career options too.

♥ Making Scents

As an Aromatherapist, I loved my sensory work. It often deepened my ability to trust in my intuition especially when choosing therapeutic oils for my clients. Before each treatment, I prepared a nurturing space where I reflected on my client in order to be in tune with their emotional-heart.

I placed fresh towels on the massage table and chose a suitable CD. I circled the room and lightly sprayed the air with scented oils, and took a few moments to make a relaxing massage oil blend. For my self-conscious clients, my visual impairment was an added bonus to them. On retreating under the waiting towels, they expressed their relief that I couldn't cast my eyes over their physical imperfections – forgetting that my hands were like all-seeing eyes.

With my client taking a few deep breaths to begin the relaxation process, I'd close my eyes and allow my hands to lightly hover over their body, not making physical contact at first but standing quietly with an open intuitive heart. As my client went deeper into a relaxed state, I waited for clear guidance to direct my hands to the areas of their body most in pain.

I knew with some of my clients who had mentioned a physical area of tension that often, there were other, deeper, emotional issues to clear. Sometimes images came into my awareness that held a 'story of hurt' they were holding onto, and I would mention what I was 'seeing' with eyes still closed. The effects of being in touch physically and emotionally with my clients through aromatherapy massage clearly had a profound effect on their intuitive-heart too. The person confirmed the 'story' to be true and by the end of the treatment, they emerged relaxed and transformed, feeling peaceful and cheerful.

I also had to guard myself from negative emotional 'fall-out' from deeply troubled clients which I did by being still within my own mind. By embracing this practice, I felt intuitively protected and the natural oils on my hands were also helping to keep me immune to my client's anxieties. Oils like rose-geranium, lavender, mandarin or sandalwood soothed restless emotions; rosemary, eucalyptus, lemongrass or peppermint revived aching muscles; and frankincense, rose and jasmine scented the heart with feelings of joy – for client and therapist.

Since I worked from home, my teenagers were expected to keep their death-metal music to an inaudible level. But my toddler had a tendency to wander into the massage room to check out the stranger lying beneath blue towels. I knew he was peeking when I heard the quiet turning of the door handle, a pause, a soft click as the door shut again and then the sound of feet running all the way down the hall. Thankfully, my clients often didn't notice as they were drifting away into a healing state of relaxation.

My policy was to only treat male clients who were related to a friend or an existing client but there were the odd times when I received very strange phone calls from men who were looking for more than just an aromatherapy massage. Their sheepish tone was a dead give-away and the conversation didn't last long.

I only got caught off guard on one occasion when a male caller asked if I did 'hand-relief massage'. Thinking it to be a new form of therapy I had not yet heard of, I asked naively,

'What sort of massage is that?'

The male voice fell silent. His thoughts hit me loud and clear. The suggestive penny dropped.

'Definitely not!' I said as if a bolt of lightning had passed down the phone. Before hanging up, I added, 'I suggest you look elsewhere in the Classifieds.'

After the call, I reminded myself to be more alert to my sense of intuition next time.

HUMOUR

How valuable it is to have a good sense of humour as another essential skill for coping with sight loss. As I've grown into my feminine skin as a woman with a visual disability, Humour has rescued me on many occasions. My skin has not necessarily become tougher, but I've developed a stronger connection to my funny bone.

Like the time when a girlfriend and I sat talking in a wine bar and two men came over to chat us up. As we introduced ourselves, one of the guys offered to shake my hand – but, having no useful sight in the dimly lit venue, I didn't notice his friendly gesture. My girlfriend burst into peals of laughter.

'That's not going to help much; she can't see you, she's blind.'

Oh great. Thanks for being as subtle as a battleship. I wanted to sink under the table to hide my blushing face.

'OH?' he replied. Then, leaning in a little closer towards me and gently taking my hand in his, he joked, 'Don't worry, love. After a few drinks and in a couple of hours, I'll be just as blind as you are.'

When laughing at an awkward situation, whether it is me or the other person instigating the comment, I know we are not laughing at my inability to see but, rather, we are joined in an attempt to see the funny side of the silly situation that has suddenly propelled us closer. Actually, laughter is the medicine we all need at times to keep life in perspective.

I've noticed how people tend to lean on humour when they feel relieved from a health scare that is soon resolved and danger has passed. If you have ever sat waiting in an emergency room of a hospital, have you noticed how people use humour to combat their fears? Once a patient has been seen by the medical staff and they feel a measure of relief that the situation is not as bad as they imagined, an ironic banter sometimes breaks out. I've heard the good humour of staff to patients as they have been stitching up their wounds and all is thankfully under control.

'Well, at least you have your other four fingers intact... Just as well you are right-handed... An overnight stay will give you a break from the kids at least.'

Laugh and the world laughs with you, not at you. If you can adapt to living with a disability by focusing on a positive outlook to defuse stress, seeing the brighter side of life brings out a sense of fun which helps to cope with the unexpected hurdles of adversity. When you can accept your vision loss even a little, you are able to master your lifestyle rather than feel like a victim.

It becomes much easier to face awkward moments when you can let go of feeling like the butt of a joke and turn it around with a witty retort. In an instant, what stood in your way as a possible insult is transformed into an ironic comment and the other person is left feeling somewhat embarrassed with themselves. Because you can't see them, they often shudder with the clumsiness of their words or actions and regret not being more observant.

When you begin to relax about the reality of your visual impairment, something extraordinary happens. If you use language as a so-called weapon to foil ridiculous comments, you are seen as an attractive person in the eyes of others. Seriously, it's true. Sighted people stand with you in solidarity for having the courage to show your spirit. It's another way humour works to help us overcome the constant need to be politically correct in modern society.

The moment any of us openly share the hidden advantages of being blind – with tongue in cheek – others begin to let go of stereotypical beliefs they may have had until that moment. You've given them permission to see the funny side too. Humour has the unique capacity to place us all on an even footing where we can relax into the conversation.

'How much can you see?' is a question that often starts it all.

When I meet a sighted man for the first time, either at a social gathering or professionally, I can guarantee that after having asked me this question, and I have replied, 'Not much. I can't see your face', he is going to respond in one of two typical ways.

I smile at him, knowing what is coming next. The witty ones will say, 'That's a pity. You can't see how good-looking I am', while the more sensitive types will reply, 'Don't worry. You're not missing much.'

When we can smile at the many ways being blind or vision-impaired lands us in awkward situations, we let our funny bone support us. We leave behind preconceived ideas of what it means to live with a so called dis-ability, and find novel ways to live life with a playful heart.

♥ Where are All the Nice Guys?

Many, many moons ago, when I found myself back on the singles shelf, a divorced mother sharing a home with my toddler and teenagers, life was so full it was hard to imagine ever needing to be part of a loving relationship again.

I stopped looking at the barometer of love which only seemed to forecast stormy new relationships. Where were all the nice guys anyway? None on my radar. I got on with life, making friends with other women and going out on fun outings with my Dad and my young son. Every now and then, purely for my own entertainment, I would peer with a magnifying glass at the classifieds in the local newspaper to read the section, 'Male Seeking Female'. Some of the entries were hilarious, others shamefully honest, others boring, but a few were interesting. I told myself I wouldn't go so far as to answer any of the ads; no, no, that was not my style. But on one occasion, I answered an intriguing ad.

Several pleasant phone conversations later, it was time to meet this new man. The relationship barometer was signalling Sunny for a change. I was nervous, how would I see if he looked as nice as he sounded? Did it matter? What was good-looking, anyway? I asked a female friend who managed a local cafe in my home town if she would help me out. As a vision-impaired single, this was the perfect place to meet my new male friend.

Sue and I talked about how she could be my eyes and look out for any dodgy body language radiating from this unsuspecting male. Our plan was to talk about the weather in his presence to steer me either closer towards him or further apart, depending on his 'performance' in the café. If she thought he looked like a pleasant guy, she would say, 'The weather has been particularly lovely this week'. But, if he displayed odd body language, her steer-clear message would be obvious: 'It's a pity the weather hasn't been all that great recently.'

On the day we met in the cafe, the guy took his seat as Sue wiped down our table. She smiled at me.

'Not bad weather today, eh?'

The guy agreed and I winked at her as we ordered lunch. By the end of our date, I could tell by our conversation he was a kind man but there was no heart-felt connection or magnetic attraction. In the end, I listened to my own instincts and put the experience down to another adventure in the life of a vision-impaired single female.

FRUSTRATION

Apart from being in touch with your intuition and leaning on your sense of humour, dealing with frustration needs a strategic approach too. This is a very difficult emotion to appease but if you can develop ways to make peace with frustration, you will find this a vital skill for your wellbeing.

Feeling frustrated when a situation goes right out of your control is one of the most challenging emotions to 'make friends' with, but I have learned that it is absolutely essential in managing the extra stresses that occur with vision loss. It is natural to get angry or annoyed when you find your limited amount of sight preventing you from doing tasks you used to do easily and independently.

In the beginning phase, you may experience unbearable frustration. I truly empathise with feeling agitated and aggressive towards life when it has nothing better to do than throw you challenge after challenge. What I can offer the beginner to blindness is this: at those times when you begin to feel bothered and frustrated for whatever reason, know the situation can also be the impetus you need to accept a different outcome. Maybe it is not a time to find a solution, maybe you can stop obsessing for a result, and maybe, just maybe, you are meant to pay less attention to frustration and put your energy into developing other skills.

It may be helpful to let you know that I am still learning the art of being patient, after all these years with a visual disability. It hasn't helped at times as my Taurean nature (the zodiac sign with the not-so-adorable attributes of being feisty when provoked and stubborn when single-minded) can take charge when frustration waves life's little red flag of torment.

Not only can I feel totally depleted of energy but I also get more upset when I focus on my shortcomings. Guess what the voice of patience tells me to do at times like these?

'Don't waste your energy fighting frustration; you won't win.'

If I am able to heed my inner voice, a sense of patience is welcomed into my heart and takes over the situation. Instead of asking, 'Why is this happening?' I am reminded that 'life is what it is'. Letting go of a desired outcome is the way of the peaceful warrior.

The following story of the real-life frustration we all experience from time to time was written by Jeff Flodin, a cyberspace-friend living in Chicago, USA.

His blog, 'Jalapeños in the oatmeal: Digesting vision loss' has a treasure trove of anecdotes about his experience of going blind. Jeff's deeply honest and sometimes painful accounts can make me cry, cringe or break into a broad smile. I know just how he feels on those days when frustration gets the better of him.

Jeff's story was published in 'Behind Our Eyes 3: a Literary Sunburst' and is reproduced here by kind permission of the publisher.

It's one of Jeff's best reflections that shows how even planting a pretty punnet of spring flowers taught him a valuable lesson in anger management.

Springtime means gardening. My wife prunes the peony bush while I plant pansies.

"Oh, dear," says my wife, "you're planting the pansies upside-down."

I throw down my trowel. "That's it! I can't take this blindness anymore! I'm out of here."

"Where are you going?" asks my wife.

"To the garage, to find that wood handle I broke off the broom. To carry it into the alley and smash it to smithereens."

"Go get 'em, tiger," says my wife.

It takes me a while but I find the broom handle. I tap my way to the alley. I'm just about to bash it against the asphalt when I think, What if a splinter flies up and sticks in my eye? I storm through the back yard. My wife asks me where I'm headed this time.

"To get my sunglasses," I say. She tells me it's overcast. I tell her it's not the sun I need to protect my eyes from. Upstairs, I fish around my dresser drawer. I find my Swiss Army knife and my baseball cap. Finally, I find my sunglasses. I storm across the back yard again.

"Go get 'em, Mr Cub!" calls my wife.

Back in the alley, I can't find where I left that broom handle. "All right, who stole my stick?" I holler to no one in particular. And no one answers. I grope here and there but come up empty-handed. Then I think maybe I'll go ask my wife to help me find the stick so I can smash it. But then I ask myself, How ridiculous am I willing to appear here? Besides, I've pretty much simmered down. The urge to kill has been removed, so I mosey into the back yard.

My wife says, "I didn't hear the crack of the bat out there, Slugger."

"I'm back," says I. "I want to plant pansies, the ones that say, Plant Other End."

~ Jeff Flodin

COLLABORATION

A friend once said to me: 'You can't make an omelette without scrambling the eggs first.' How annoying to have friends like that! But she is right. We do have to let things become scrambled up and be at peace with the process. Frustration becomes our friend when we allow the voice of patience to be heard, rather than reacting in negative ways.

It isn't easy to surrender to patience in a time of great frustration but there is one gift awaiting the person willing to quit thinking about how unfair everything is. That is to enrol others who are more than happy to assist you. The gift hiding within frustration is the possibility of teamwork and collaboration.

Visual tasks become so much easier when you accept asking for help as a strength and not a personal weakness. You can waste your time beating yourself up with hurtful thoughts and allow frustration to thwart your efforts in trying to live a 'normal' life; or, like me, you can choose to enrol another person as your sighted assistant. The best response to frustration is to hone your ability to calmly delegate.

Use a friendly voice and people are more than happy to give you their time and attention. Working out who you can delegate in helping you reach an amicable arrangement is better than being alone with your frustration. The more you can delegate, the more resourceful, composed and positive you become. So, when you find yourself in need of visual assistance, how do you enrol others to collaborate?

Look upon it as having your own personal assistant at those times when you could really use their help. Being able to delegate sighted tasks is sensible, time saving and satisfying – for both of you. If you approach it correctly and focus on seeing through a different lens, the lens that focuses on teamwork and cooperation, you'll discover another gift of being blind or vision-impaired.

It is so much easier to invite a sighted person to become your personal assistant from time to time. It means you get tasks done with far less stress. We can all enrol others when we know how to ask and the results are amazing. Turn to a loving spouse or partner, a mature child, a best friend or kind neighbour, a reliable colleague or school buddy – anyone in your life who understands you will need a dependable assistant at times.

Be totally honest with yourself by acknowledging your personal strengths and limitations. When a visual task has become too difficult to carry out on your own, or could be better achieved with the aid of your sighted assistant, this is the time to graciously accept help, knowing that there is no shame in being limited by your vision loss. It opens the door to a wonderful act of creative collaboration, and your helper may also benefit in ways you can't imagine.

As an example from my own life, I am keenly independent when it comes to managing my writing career, yet I can't see my computer screen. I have trained in adaptive software for the blind and work very contentedly on my own, up to the stage where I need to publish articles online for a sighted audience.

This is when I request the crucial help of two special sighted people: my father who is my editor/proof-reader; and my life-partner who is my webmaster and tech-wizard. My collaborative team has produced far more possibilities in my career than I could have achieved on my own, and I know it brings a sense of personal fulfilment into their lives too.

Imagine how much more you can enjoy life in spite of any vision loss by seeing the hidden hand of patience waiting to help you out of frustration. But a word of advice: When you are preparing for a visual task you think will require extra time and added skills from your sighted assistant, be sure to give them plenty of notice if you can. Timing matters.

An impromptu approach may not produce the desired outcome and could create tension between the two of you, which may leave you to work out the final steps on your own. Open communication is the key to partnership success.

If you find it annoying and are not sure why your helper is taking so long, understand that being vision-impaired means that you can misjudge what others are doing, especially if they are not giving you a verbal commentary on their silent (and unseen) activities.

Your sighted helper might have been reading an email, or be deeply lost in thought, or was perhaps about to make a phone call when you asked for help. It could be that your timing that was off, and not the request for help itself. Once you've asked for assistance, check in frequently to avoid misunderstandings. And, if all your attempts fail, let frustration spur you on to try another way around the problem.

♥ Dear Diary

I have to tell you about another one of my 'funny' adventures today. I made my way by tram into the city for my appointment with the dentist. I know that going out sounds like a simple task, but as I rely on my white cane, I feel somewhat nervous trying to find new places by myself. I have to expect the unexpected all the time.

Thankfully, I got off at the right tram stop just outside the dental hospital. To save myself from unnecessary stress, I turned to ask a fast moving person for help to locate the entrance. Chris was his name and my helpful guide led me to the front door and disappeared.

'Hey?' I wanted to call out. 'Don't go so fast? Where do I go now?' Taking a few steps gingerly forward and sweeping the cane from side to cautious side, my foot bumped into something large. The inquiry desk. Bingo.

I proceeded to enlist more help, this time from the obliging security guard who must have seen me coming. He offered to walk with me through the maze of corridors, stairs and elevators, with people darting madly about. At this point I felt grateful for his cordial good-nature and close guidance. Arriving on Level 4, he showed me to the waiting room where everyone was holding a numbered ticket. The queue was horrendous. Seeing my dilemma – that a blind person could wait all day here – the security guard went over to get me a ticket too. Twenty minutes later, I heard, 'Number twelve.' 'That's me!

The security guard, who was still standing in a corner, came over to lead me to the counter. I gave my name to the woman behind the glass window but to my surprise, my appointment was not noted in the system. My dentist was not expecting me today and was with someone else for the rest of the afternoon.

'You've got to be kidding? 'I protested. 'He wrote the appointment on a piece of paper and said he would let the secretary know'.

She was not impressed and asked that I return to the waiting room. From my seat I was briefly distracted from feelings of frustration by the sounds of organised chaos around me. Nurses opening doors left, right and centre, calling out names at random.

A couple arguing with the receptionist about their bill and how they were being chased by a debt collector. A man (who made it clear to everyone he was fed up with having to wait so long) even took umbrage with the security guard, threatening to leave the building. I felt like saying to him, 'Get a life, buddy, at least you've GOT an appointment.'

Restlessness kicked in as I realised I was facing the prospect of sitting around for hours. To make my presence known again to the receptionist, I plonked myself in the chair by her window. My plan was to reschedule another appointment. Horrified by my boldness in approaching her without being summoned by my numbered ticket, she called the security guard.

'What is this woman doing here? She doesn't have an appointment.'

Hmm. Why doesn't she talk to me directly? I'm only vision-impaired, not deaf.

'Maybe the system got it wrong for a change?' I said with a wry smile.

Apparently not. My appointment was rescheduled for another day. Making my way home by tram and sitting quietly by a window, a 'kind' woman swiftly scooped up my cane that I had folded up behind my seat. She was about to hand it to the driver.

'Hey, that's mine!'

'Oh. I'm so sorry,' she said. 'I thought a blind person must have left it behind.'

Really? 'It's not something a blind person would forget,' I said. 'How else would they find their way off the tram?'

Oh Dear Diary, some people are just too kind!

Chapter 8

Home Sweet Organised Home

> *Good management is the art of making problems so interesting and their solutions so constructive that everyone wants to get to work and deal with them.*
> ~ Paul Hawken

The popular saying warns that familiarity breeds contempt, but when it comes to organising your home, familiarity breeds contentment. As you can imagine, being able to move around confidently and function independently when you live with a sighted family requires problem solving on a daily basis.

It is vital to maintain an organised way of living. Putting everything back in a specific place is not proof that a control-freak is in residence – it's an efficient way of staying safe around shifting hazards. It's also a matter of survival. The more sight fades, the more you are forced to problem solve. A sense of familiarity is everything, from home to work and all the places in between.

This chapter focuses on problem solving strategies around the home to help you in your quest to retain independence with vision loss. A few simple modifications, an organised approach to living, and an awareness of high and low-tech gadgets made specifically to help people who are blind or vision-impaired, along with your willingness to give it a go, will help the beginner to blindness master daily living challenges. Depending on how much sight you are using, some of these suggestions will help those who can still see a little colour, while others will help you even with eyes closed! Preparing your personal space is the first basic step: Choose a place for everything so everything has a place.

I practised this vital strategy as a mother, making it my mantra for the family. It was a daily challenge to keep items in their place with my kiddies running around randomly leaving toys in my pathway. It took a lot of mental and physical energy to maintain a relatively clear space so that I could tread lightly through our living areas. Unfortunately, some of their toys did get accidentally trampled underfoot as I whirled about the house from room to room on a tidying up mission, the poor kids watching on in horror as a fragment of their ruined toy was tossed into the bin. It broke my heart to unintentionally destroy their play things but they knew the rule: pick up your toys or they might get broken.

One solution that helped at times was putting a large blanket on the floor. That was their play pontoon, out of bounds from mother's feet. Every evening just before bedtime the children packed away their things in large baskets, boxes and overcrowded shelves to preserve their belongings for another day's play.

Looking after children from dawn to dusk demands great management skills for any parent but if you are relying on non-visual methods to keep order in the home as sight fades, it is absolutely crucial to develop an easy set of house rules you can teach the little people. Whether you are living with children or not, you will still need any sighted persons sharing your home to be involved in your 'keep things tidy' system. This basically means that you have an expectation for your shared space to have everything put back in its proper spot. If this sounds totally unrealistic, well, it may be at times. We are all human, and people live busy lives. But the more you practise your system and insist on it being observed by your family and house visitors, the more it becomes second nature to everyone and the better you are able to meet the challenge of finding your way around.

Keeping your belongings in order becomes a vital technique for everyone as they realise it helps to minimise stress for all involved. Good old familiarity brings you the comfort of knowing that nothing has moved from where you last put it. Even more importantly, it decreases the number of times you collide with objects left in your way. Your home is your sanctuary, a safe haven shared with loved ones and perhaps a menagerie of pets, which is why it is necessary to keep clutter under control as much as you can. Otherwise it can end up under your feet.

Before I went to live in a house that had the lounge room set up as part of my partner's recording studio, visiting musicians didn't have to be concerned with where they put down their gear: drums, bass guitars, violins, bags and masses of electric leads were strewn over every chair and floor space. But with a vision-impaired singer turning up for rehearsals, their patterns of behaviour had to change – for my safety and to keep their gear intact too.

My partner reminded them on arrival, 'Can everyone please pick up your things and put them over in the corner. Maribel is vision-impaired and she could trip over your instruments.'

Suddenly, everyone became acutely aware of where they were putting their belongings – welcome to my world. It felt wonderful, but my self-confidence vanished in a flash the moment the system was forgotten. At times like these, when I had a minor accident or collision, I had to remind myself that people can't always remember my needs and that I had to move around more cautiously with visitors in the house.

Like me, I am sure you will soon discover that if you allow chaos to creep into your system, not only will you accumulate a collection of physical bruises but your self-confidence can dive dramatically. Managing potential chaos like this in the home before it happens not only helps you function independently, but it also provides you with the confidence you need to negotiate the obstacles in every room of your home.

When you are sharing a living space, collaboration is vital. If your house rules are met with resistance, you might like to remind your family that knowing where things live can help save them time and frustration as well.

Insist that all cupboard doors are kept closed. Dining chairs should automatically be tucked away the moment a person leaves the table. Agree that all internal doors should either be left fully open or fully shut. With fragile glassware, it is best to wash it up immediately and put it away. There are many practical issues to consider and what is at stake is your ability to move around independently.

When this is understood by everyone, and they make your rules their own, try not to take it for granted. There will be many times when you will have to forgive their forgetfulness. Life is not always as predictable as we'd like to make it: someone has forgotten to close a kitchen drawer, a child has left a bike in the middle of the path, a person has shifted the TV remote, a guest has 'kindly' put away the vegetable peeler in the wrong place, another well-meaning person has moved important paperwork to a safe place – so safe that you can't find it.

At moments like these, it is easy to feel distressed and flare up like a fire cracker loaded with anger and frustration. When this happens, catch yourself and breathe through the anxiety. All can be smoothed over if you can forgive imperfections and reinstate your agreements. It's not easy for others to live by someone else's house rules. The more you remind them of your tidy-up rituals, the more ingrained they become.

Your confidence will grow as you discover that to relax with low vision is to develop skills in micro-management. This means that you are conscious of how you store personal items (as in keys, a purse or wallet) as well as other items in the home; from cupboards and drawers in every room to bookshelves and filing cabinets – it all requires your meticulous attention to detail. Bothersome, you say? Maybe – for your family! For you, it is a 'life-saving' skill worth developing.

Remember, your memory has a vast capacity to assist you; it might sound like overloading your mind right now but if you regularly stop for a brief moment to jot your actions down in your memory, it becomes a habit. If you stick to repetitive procedures and consistent storage solutions, you naturally become proficient in locating items again with much less stress and without having to depend on sighted eyes.

One area to begin with is storing personal belongings in specific places. I am so methodical when it comes to organising my handbag that I never get flustered trying to find it in a hurry on the way out of the house, if a taxi happens to arrive early, for instance. I always keep it on the same sturdy hook on the shelf in my writing room. Without fail, I place it back there, ready for my next outing, with everything inside checked before I leave the house again. Of course, I have a collection of handbags in my wardrobe, but only one bag hangs on the hook. When I want to use another bag, everything I need is transferred to it; on returning home, a quick reshuffle replaces these items back in the 'mother' bag and all is in order again.

These few minutes of micro-management are my means of knowing exactly where my purse and keys are all the time. I try not to tempt fate by being absent-minded. I never plonk my keys down on a surface with a bag of shopping and think, I'll put that away later. The anxiety this can cause when looking for it again is not worth it.

Another helpful technique to keep things together (including your sanity) is to use a tactile storage method. This involves using mini-baskets, textural cloth bags, small trays, sturdy shoeboxes or other recognisable containers with obvious differences. These will help you to locate a group of items quickly in every area of your home. If you have a small dresser or table near the front door, this is the perfect place to keep your cane, umbrella, or anything else you need to grab on the way out in a hurry. This level of order sets you up for being calm from the moment you leave the house; there are enough challenges to deal with out in the big, wide world without creating extra ones inside your home. By being methodical, the potential for chaos is replaced with comfortable living.

USING COLOUR CONTRASTS

Another easy modification to improve your comfort level with low vision is to use bright colours that work in contrast to each other. Depending on your eye condition, you are most probably still relying on a residual amount of sight, so being able to use a range of bold colours to distinguish different items can help enormously.

Colour contrasting is a common technique often suggested by Vision Rehabilitation Therapists. These professionals are qualified in teaching adaptive methods for people who want to retain independence at home or at work, and you can reach out for their services for more one-on-one ideas. They can suggest simple modifications that help a person new to sight loss retain skills in managing every aspect of daily living. You will find some helpful tips coming up next in Bathroom Etiquette, Gadgets Galore and in Chapter 9, Cooking in a Tactile Kitchen. For now, the focus is on incorporating colour for maximum effect.

Even though you may be experiencing a decrease in colour perception, it is still possible to retain your independence and safe mobility by using colour contrasting techniques. Placing contrasting items close to one another gives each item higher visibility. This is an effective way to enhance your ability to see items and objects even with low vision.

There are a few strategies to consider when using colour contrasts as you reassess how safe and accessible your home needs to be. These strategies are not expensive and can be highly effective. For instance, choose bright colours: anything that helps to highlight other items to make them stand out gives you more confidence in making your way around the home. This could be as simple as placing a royal blue mat by the back door that contrasts with a light tiled floor, or a cherry red throw rug placed on a lounge chair that helps define light-coloured furniture against light painted walls. Strategically defining areas of your home with bright colours will enable you to 'see' areas you want to walk around. This helps you avoid bumping your shin on the edge of a coffee table, and enables you to find your way out of a door rather than walking straight into a glass panel.

Colours known to be difficult to distinguish if you have low vision include combinations of blue, purple and green; brown, maroon and black; and yellow, light green and pink. An interesting observation from my perspective is the way my brain can interpret colours incorrectly when I am shopping alone. As I take a piece of fabric, whether it be a cushion or a set of sheets, and place it under direct lighting, my eyes may see it as being orange. But when I confirm the colour with the shop assistant, they tell me 'It's green.' Only *then* do I see it as green. I find this happens all the time. Blue can be interpreted as purple; pink can be seen to be pale green; red can be brown. If I do choose that item, my memory makes a mental note of its actual colour to help me coordinate our bedding and other soft furnishings.

My suggestion for you is to get a free colour swatch from a material store or upholsterers so that you can determine at a quick glance which colour combinations you prefer. Be aware, however, that lighting plays an important part in influencing the appearance of colours – in a dimly lit room, for instance, you may find it difficult to see any colour, whereas in a well-lit area, bright colours are intensified and may be too fluorescent on the eyes. That is where colour swatches may be a great help. Take swatches of the colours you can see best along with you when choosing home furnishings. This may also be one solution when helping an elderly person decorate their home with the colours they can see, without having to inconvenience them by taking them out to the shops, especially if they have a mobility issue along with a visual disability.

Create a strong visual edge between floors and doorways. Just be careful with rugs that have a 'busy' pattern if placed near stairs as this can make it difficult to define the edge of the steps. Equally importantly, avoid having a patterned carpet on stairs as there is little chance of being able to distinguish one step from the next with a random patterned design, especially when going down stairs.

Another practical reason for bringing bright colours into your home is that you can take full advantage of the way they reflect more light on dark surfaces. Let me give you a perfect example of setting a dining table using colour contrasting as a high-viz method. If you use white crockery, it is naturally more visible when placed on top of a dark placemat or table cloth. I know this sounds glaringly obvious but often, we don't stop to implement such a simple method even though it really does make dining with sighted friends less stressful, both for you and them, as they slip a casual glance over your plate to see how you are managing.

The comment, 'shall I cut that for you?' is a dead giveaway that 'big sister' is watching. So, choose the colour contrasts that work especially well for you. Having crockery and place settings that you can define easily with low vision and by touch is not only an effective solution with minimal expense; it gives you more independence and will add another housekeeping skill to boost your confidence.

Glassware: Some people will advise you to limit your use of glassware for obvious reasons but who wants to drink out of a plastic cup at the dining table – especially if a glass of wine is on offer? The simple solution is to ask a sighted friend to place your glass on the table and to describe its exact spot as you would read an analogue clock that is facing you.

'Your glass is sitting at 1 o'clock.'

This is a precise method of indicating the position of glassware on a table. Over time, your hands will become masterful in locating fragile items by simply running them slowly along a surface rather than waving them around in the air – I'll toast to that!

As a vision-impaired person, I am also a collector of blue glassware and simply love to explore galleries with coloured glass with my partner. In our home, my blue glass collection is positioned on window ledges that allow for natural sunlight to stream through glass bottles and trinkets to reveal the deep hues I am still able to see. In this way, I continue to enjoy the delicate ornaments scattered around my home and use a careful sense of touch to look after them.

Lighting: Another sight-enhancing technique. When it comes to having sufficient lighting as a way to manage your vision loss, you can't go wrong when installing more lamps in strategic places. I love lamps of all kinds and keep a few switched on all the time, especially in the evenings.

You might like to try using an LED lamp on a kitchen bench or side table as it makes a great beacon when placed in areas that can help you navigate safely around obstacles in a poorly lit room. The extra light assists in guiding you in the direction of a doorway. The added bonus in using an LED lamp over a conventional one that uses bulbs, is that LED lighting doesn't get hot to the touch which means it is a safer option and can be left on for longer periods of time.

A novel way I use a string of little LED lights, known as fairy lights, is to place them in a tall clear glass vase that sits on our dining table. It is arranged in such a way that the tiny stars of light cascade from the top of the vase to spill over a small area of the table – attractive and effective. During evening meals, my family enjoys the added soft lighting instead of using a candle with an open flame which can be dangerous. Placing fairy lights around the home works wonderfully for a dinner party too. It adds ambience for your guests, directional beacons of light for you!

BATHROOM ETIQUETTE

Sharing a bathroom with your sighted family can pose the first challenge of the day. You need to devise an organised system in this room too. You may not even have given it a second thought – until now.

For instance, without full sight, how will you detect the difference between shampoo and conditioner bottles? Are you confident that you can find your own toothbrush in a jar with several brushes, especially when your brush is moved by someone else? Ladies, have you resigned yourself to the fact that applying make-up will be impossible when you can no longer see into a mirror –even a magnified one? And for the men, no, you won't need to grow a beard and neglect your facial appearance unless, of course, sporting a beard is your style.

Let's take a look at these specific new challenges and find a workable solution. Like every other room in your home, living with a measure of sight loss calls for micro-management in the bathroom too. Even when you do have specific techniques that work effectively, your beloved family will forget the rules at times, mostly when they are running late for work or an appointment or for the simple reason that they too are concentrating on dealing with their own personal needs.

That is fine and totally understandable. But if they accidentally forget to leave the bathroom in the same order as they found it, you can be left with a real dilemma. Mutual strategies maintain consistency and are vital to retain the harmony within family relationships. Apart from being mindful and vigilant, it is important to establish the family's bathroom etiquette: everything must have its place and must not stray.

It is very upsetting if you are left to grope around in the bathroom trying to find things that have been moved, especially if you end up with shaving cream on your toothbrush. EEK! It really doesn't taste nice at all and the flavour lingers even after using strong mouth wash. This is why I am keen to save you from common bathroom disasters by suggesting simple ways to avoid unnecessary drama (and steer you clear of discovering the disgusting taste of shaving cream!)

You can begin defining your personal items by using a range of simple and affordable tactile markers, sticky bumps and rubber bands. What is a tactile marker? A tactile marker is a type of adhesive Velcro, felt or other soft material which you can place on the top lid of a cosmetic jar or your favourite hand cream to quickly identify it from other jars and creams. These little helpers are invaluable to have around and are readily available in haberdashery shops or organisations such as Vision Australia who can show you a range of the most useful bumps and stickers other people with low vision use throughout their homes.

One of my other favourite quick solutions is to reach for a rubber band or a hair tie to help identify a bottle in the bathroom that is shaped like other containers. True, I could store it on a different shelf but it is safer to put a band around it in case someone who shall remain nameless happens to move it; it's like life insurance (for him). It's better to be safe than sorry.

A handy little rubber band is one of the most versatile solutions in solving another very common problem: how to tell the difference between identical-looking hair care products such as shampoo and conditioner bottles as you fumble around under the shower trying to tell them apart?

There are a couple of easy solutions to consider: the first is to wrap a strong rubber band around the shampoo, with another two bands on the conditioner. Do this ahead of time, just after bringing them home from the store. Another smart approach is to purchase these items from different manufacturers as the shape will vary, which makes it much easier to detect, even with eyes closed in the shower.

If you purchase some inexpensive hair ties, these can be placed around personal items, one being your toothbrush. This is readily recognisable to the touch in a jar of brushes but even more practical would be to keep your toothbrush in its own separate container along with a tube of toothpaste (and relegate the shaving cream to a bottom drawer).

Small baskets are great to keep things together, for instance, facial cleanser, toner and moisturiser. You can use mini-trays for other items. In our bathroom, I have a ceramic bowl that holds some of my 'girlie' things which keeps the males well away. I have also designated the yellow towels as mine for personal use as I can partially see this bright colour – woe betide the men in the house if I find my towel has been moved. This is one of life's little red flag moments that again, calls for good life insurance!

Another helpful solution if you want to store vitamins or medications without getting them mixed up is to try using a combination of sticky bumps and tactile markers, and keep them in a special shelf or cupboard in alphabetical order. If the labels are difficult to read, have a sighted person go through this with you initially. Once every item has been easily marked in a tactile way, be vigilant in retrieving and replacing the packets and bottles for next time.

You will become highly inventive as you work out your own system to avoid any confusion or unpleasant mishaps. Just be sure to remember to store antiseptic creams and other powerful products on different shelves to your personal cosmetics as you don't really want to discover a bottle of peroxide is not mouthwash after all – been there, done that too.

FEMININE FLAIR

Moving on to feminine matters such as applying makeup, people have asked me: 'Why would anyone bother to put on make-up if they can't see it anyway?' My response to such a question is simple. Being vision-impaired doesn't mean you have to give up enjoying feminine pleasures like using make-up and being fashionable.

There are problem solving strategies for the visually impaired in this aspect of life, too. Besides, sighted people are able to see me. Why wouldn't I want to make my own fashion statement like other women do? I have a few secrets to share with you.

When it comes to applying make-up, it's simply a matter of practice to develop light touch techniques and, of course, the confidence to persist. One short cut I use on occasions that can save time and stress is to book an appointment with a beautician. Having your eyelashes tinted, eyebrows neatly waxed and nails on fingers and toes painted by a professional is not only a wonderful treat but it also makes colours and tints last longer. Relax and let others admire your beauty regime without having to reveal your top secrets.

I do have one more beauty tip that helps me to keep track of my favourite cosmetics. It is quite a challenge to know the different shades of lipsticks in a collection of colours so I use a couple of quick tricks to manage this visual task. One method is to wrap a thin hair-tie around my favourite shade of pink lipstick, while a rubber band is placed on my favourite copper tone. I also keep lipsticks stored apart by grouping similar colours together in different cosmetic bags which means I can reach for a pink or copper shade confidently when in a rush to leave the house.

From time to time, if my system gets mixed up, I ask a sighted person to confirm the shades in my cosmetic bags, and prefer to ask a female friend to a male one. Not because I have noticed my male friends are less fussy about the correct shades of lipstick – apparently, men in general are more prone to be colour blind than women are. *AHA!* Maybe this can be your justification if you are a male reading this to your female better half with low vision; you may be just as colour-challenged as she!

♥ Why be Fashionable if You Can't See?

When I give presentations to interested groups on what it is like to be vision-impaired, I can guarantee one question will ALWAYS be asked: 'How do you know what you are wearing?'

Women especially, are surprised that I can be colour-coordinated from top to toe. There is no great mystery involved. There is no other person dressing me in the morning (although I do ask sighted family from time to time to check a garment for cleanliness). I manage my own dress sense with a few techniques I have developed over time. Choosing an outfit is more of a tactile decision than a visual one. My good memory is supported by my consistent storage system.

Every item is stored in a regimented order within cupboards and drawers. I hang clothing in groups so that matching, colour co-ordinated items are placed together to save time and stress. I'm what you could call a 'touch-aholic', so going in search of matching dresses, shoes, handbag and accessories is an enjoyable experience as long as I also allow plenty of time to work out my options.

When I go clothes shopping, browsing with my hands is a joyful experience. I feel the textures of soft materials or glide my hands over jewellery, not always because I want to buy the item, but to satisfy my curiosity about that season's fashion and to know what other women are wearing. To visualise the world of ever-changing trends is enjoyable even if I can't see. It includes me in a visual world.

I think it's a 'girlie' thing – taking delight in touching garments; soft fabrics, satin trims, things with buttons and bows. Lingerie in particular is one of my touchy-feely delights as it is worn close to the skin, and naturally makes a woman feel sexy. My view is that when a woman begins the first layer of clothing feeling feminine, she will wear her outfit with upright poise and be admired for her attractive dress sense.

Apart from seeking comfort and prettiness of garment, even in casual wear, I am fussy about colour and design. When shopping on my own, I take my time to scout out an item. I examine the texture carefully and the cut by feeling around it. I know what styles suit me by past experience. Many times, a garment has fallen literally into my hands, and turns out to be a serendipitous find.

I often quiz the shop assistant for the colour and price and if it passes my feel-right-straight-away principle, I purchase it with confidence. Another technique I find useful is to visit the same clothing stores because it is easier to get around the shop without feeling overwhelmed. I have my favourite shopping precinct where the store assistants know me and are quick to offer visual descriptions. Even though it might be more expensive, the price of being looked after is well worth it.

But I do have to be in the right mood as it takes a lot of concentration to keep track of my movement around the store, to avoid prams and other obstacles. Sometimes bumping from one object to another can feel like being inside a live pinball machine. On some days, when I am less confident to handle the challenge, I reduce my shopping list to the groceries and go back on another day.

Naturally, I also like to shop with friends or my partner on an expedition to help me find something more specific, like an outfit for a presentation or a dinner party. I often end up buying things I never knew existed because my companions point out items on special I wouldn't have seen otherwise. My friends know that I have a particular fancy for feeling shoes. As I have no idea what people wear on their feet, a shoe shop is a lovely place to wander. I get to understand the different types of heels and the shape of this season's shoes, and find great pleasure in simply touching my way around a store.

It is so easy to enjoy fashion just as much as my sighted friends, and when it comes to smelling fragrances at perfume counters – I am in scent-heaven.

As we leave bathroom etiquette and personal organisation for now, remember that each area of your home will require attention to detail in some way. Unique challenges will obviously emerge but please be reassured; a practical solution is often not far away.

A valuable resource which gives an in-depth approach to managing your home, room by room, is the book: *Making Life More Liveable: Simple Adaptations for Living at Home after Vision Loss* by author and Low Vision specialist, Maureen A. Duffy (M.S., CVRT). This book offers the reader an abundance of practical living solutions I can highly recommend. And, *The Bold, Blind, Beauty'* blog by talented fashionista, Stephanae McCoy is another great resource, providing tangible solutions in the application of make-up and other fashion-related techniques.

If you would prefer a more personal connection for assisted living strategies, it's best to contact an organisation working in the low vision industry. They will be more than happy to arrange a home visit to discuss workable solutions, no matter your degree of vision loss. Think of it as bringing the mountain to Mohammed rather than Mohammed having to face the mountain alone – it's just another practical way to approach life with a renewed sense of the possible.

GADGETS GALORE!

Now we come to the fun part, with gadgets galore to explore! The beginner to blindness can be reassured in knowing that for every visual task there is a workable solution – the challenge may not necessarily be so much losing the ability to see as lacking the confidence to find the perfect gadget to help master specific tasks.

There is a wealth of devices known in the trade as 'low' or 'high' assistive technology, and the following pages may pique your curiosity. A low tech-aid can be as simple as using a plastic template designed to help you sign on a dotted line of a document; high tech-aids are those devices that require a more concentrated level of skill to operate.

It is a quandary at first for most of us to imagine how to continue reading our favourite books, or how to stay engaged in sports and hobbies, or how to operate a computer without sight. Impossible? No, not when we are motivated to find the types of assistive technology that best meet our different needs. The main aim in exploring these low vision alternatives is to bring to your attention that it is possible to find practical solutions to achieve many of your goals. To succeed with less sight means we have to keep trying to solve our life-puzzle.

Not only do people who are blind or vision-impaired learn to develop a resilient nature in problem solving, they also learn to hunt out devices that will assist in achieving their goal for independent living. For instance, learning how to work a computer without being able to see the screen was a challenge for me at first, but over time, it has become my lifeline to so many opportunities as a writer, networker and lover of all things educational.

When it comes to sharing books with children or grandchildren, there are some fantastic resources online these days. One highly innovative website is called 'Storyline Online'. It is an American website that offers free children's books that are beautifully read by actors from the Screen Actors Guild Foundation. When you select a title from a varied list, a video shows the actor reading the book so that your sighted child will see the colourful pages come to life while you follow the voice. In this way, both of you can be immersed in story-time together.

My favourite book in the collection is an Australian book called 'Stellaluna' by Janell Cannon, read by Pamela Reed. It is the story of a little night creature who asks, 'How can we be so different but feel so much alike?' when it realises it is not a bird, but a bat. You can cuddle up close and enjoy being read to by your own personal narrator who might even be Al Gore reading the children's book, 'Brave Irene'.

Maybe the following suggestions from my friends and colleagues who have little or no sight will get you thinking of gadgets to fit your life-puzzle. In this section, my intention is not to help market specific products but to simply point out a few solutions that may inspire you to investigate options for your specific needs.

My friend Julie is a woman on a mission, determined to solve all her blindness issues. One of her favourite gadgets is a device called Pen Friend. This is a hand held portable unit that can record her voice onto adhesive labels that can be secured to a wide range of items.

Julie uses a speaking label-reader to read the small stickers she has prepared to distinguish similar objects in her cosmetic bag, where the stickers placed individually on each item helps her to identify different shades of eye-shadow. In other areas of her home she uses the Pen Friend recorded stickers on spice jars in the kitchen and food containers in the freezer.

'I mostly use the stickers to tell me what the item is in the freezer and its use-by date, helping me feel more independent in my home.'

The Pen Friend stickers are re-usable, and can be used in many other ways, for instance to help identify function buttons on a washing machine, a dishwasher, an oven or microwave.

Another of Julie's gadgets is a set of talking kitchen scales. She has a fussy pet dog and has to cook up his food so he gets the right amount of protein each mealtime. By listening to the audible voice, Julie is able to weigh out the dog's food exactly and is reassured he is getting his dietary needs met. She does have another audible set of scales.

'But don't ask me about my talking bathroom scales,' said Julie. 'I wish it had a volume control so no one else can hear it speaking.'

My friend Frank makes his own Braille labels with a Braille machine to mark specific items in his kitchen. He makes one label for beef or another for chicken meals and reuses the labels year round because they are durable. Frank admits he has had to become inventive.

'I use laminated plastic with words marked in Braille because they are non-perishable and especially effective on freezer goods.'

My colleague Robby is a businessman and speaker who also values his independence. He has adapted to becoming tech-wise after losing his sight, and found in his early training days that the 'Talking Typer' was a useful tech-aid to help him brush up on his computer typing skills. Over time and with practice, Robby picked up other ways to boost his confidence in personal and professional activities.

One adaptation he uses on his smart phone is an App called 'Where the hell am I?' (I should look into this one myself). This particular phone App informs the user of their current location from an internal GPS.

'It's much easier to find a place, especially if I get lost, because my wife's phone is set up to know where I am and together, we can work out where I *should* be.'

My friend Alex is a keen marathon runner, but never gets lost, even though he is totally blind. He swears by his Apple-watch to keep him on track to achieve his athletic goals.

'This device has streamlined my life. I utilise it every day to calculate speed, time and distance on the track and when at home, I can text, email or take notes, all on the one device.'

The other tech-gadget Alex finds useful is a 'Bar Code Reader'. Being so involved in sport, he likes to fuel his body correctly. He uses the Summit Bar Code Reader to locate specific foods in a supermarket so that he can stay healthy in his body building program. The lightweight, hand-held device tells Alex the exact item he is looking for.

On the subject of smart phone Apps, there is an array of choices designed to help people who are blind or vision-impaired. A visit to an App store or an online forum discussing the usefulness of tried and tested options is a good place to start. One popular phone App as an example is called the KNFB Reader. This App has several useful functions that can take a picture of anything you want to read, for instance, a restaurant menu, and immediately read the text out loud. Many options exist on the market, so once again, it is a matter of personal choice to locate a reader that fits your needs and budget.

A device called 'Braille Sense' helps my travel agent Kirsty to carry out her work duties for a tourist company. This device is a Braille input and output device designed for people who can read and type in Braille. She uses it to keep notes, to plan staff rosters, to email clients and to fill in schedules. Kirsty also relies on the Braille device to make appointments, browse the internet and read her favourite books. Other features include: an address book, a dictionary and an in-built GPS with Google maps. Now that sounds like a great puzzle-solver.

A final word on the top end scale of technology; some companies have begun to market glasses for the blind. With a lightweight camera and small computer device that fits in the person's pocket, the interactive features attached to the glasses make it possible for the person to 'see'. Relying on audio feedback to relay visual information, the computer uses speech via a small ear piece to help the wearer to read text, look at products and to recognise a person's face as they approach.

I have had the opportunity to test one of these devices at a conference for the blind and was astonished by its sophisticated technology. I wanted to take it home on the spot! But, in my view, it does have one downside – the exorbitant cost. Like many high-tech devices designed for people with a visual disability, most of us will have to wait several years for the prices to become more reasonable, which is disheartening when the technology could be making a significant difference in the lives of those who really need it *today* but can't afford it.

My aim in writing about the highs and lows of assistive technology is not to overwhelm you but to inspire you. I hope this brief summary is enough to motivate you to consider how you could benefit from and navigate the wide range of assistive technology available today. The best advice I can offer is to visit a blindness organisation or an assistive technology company that can demonstrate some of the devices in person.

Whether it be talking scales, speaking phones, GPS devices or assistive computer software, there really is a gadget to put together the missing pieces of your vision loss puzzle. As you narrow down your choices, even your most tech-nerdy friend will be envious of your ability to adapt by using new and fascinating gadgets not even *they* have heard of.

Chapter 9

Cooking in a Tactile Kitchen

*It's so beautifully arranged on the plate
– you know someone's fingers have been all over it.*
~ Julia Child

When people see me out and about with my white cane at the grocery store, and we are waiting together in a line, they sometimes interact with me.

'Excuse me. I hope you don't mind me asking, but does someone cook for you at home?'

'Sometimes,' I reply with a smile, 'but mostly I do or my family would starve.'

'Really? But how do you cook for them if you can't see?'

The person standing next to me can't imagine cooking without sight. They recoil in horror just imagining how it must be for a 'blind cook' to pour boiling liquids into small containers, deal with hot oil in a sizzling pan or reach into the depths of a scorching oven to check on a batch of cookies – all with vision-impaired eyes.

'Well, I don't know how you do it,' they comment, expressing a mix of surprise and admiration.

If I had time, I'd explain exactly how I do it. It's a matter of being highly organised and adapting the kitchen to suit the chef with low vision. If only they knew about my first baking failures. I quickly glide over the memory.

'You always learn from your mishaps. You just have to find other ways.'

Beginner to blindness, don't fret; if cooking is your passion you won't have to give it up – unless you'd like to pretend it is an impossible task for you and make your family cook for themselves. I'm assuming you'd rather grow in confidence and incorporate a few simple modifications into your kitchen space. This is the first phase of setting up a tactile kitchen.

The following tips and tricks of the 'blind master chef' are based on practicality and are not expensive adjustments. As you read through, you may be inspired to sort out your kitchen space in other ways that will work better for you. To begin with, I reiterate one basic philosophy you have come across before: everything has a place. To this, we now add a measure of tenacity into the mix.

THE TENACIOUS APPROACH

TIP #1 – Making Space

Preparing the kitchen for the person with low vision really makes all the difference to their ability to manage it successfully. If you set up a system by organising items on shelves, and store food in cupboards in a methodical way, including fridge compartments, you are able to prepare and serve meal after meal with confidence.

It makes sense to store tins of food by category: tins of soup on one shelf, cans of pet food far away on a different shelf. The same goes for organising your fridge shelves. Once you are happy with a workable system, show it to your family so they can help you to manage it daily. Remind them, too, that they must put things back properly. If they are not sure where things go, they should ask you, or leave the item out on the bench in full tactile view of your hands. That way you are less likely to open the wrong tins and packets, and day old leftovers for the dog won't end up on their plate by mistake.

TIP #2 – Using Tactile Containers

An easy way to know what food is in which packet is to use a variety of different sizes and shapes of containers. Have storage containers of varying designs, from heavy-duty glass jars to fabric or wire baskets to group foods together so you can identify them with confidence.

I use tactile containers to store spice jars so I can pick the correct basket and only rummage around in that one rather than move everything out of place on a shelf while searching for the correct jar. A wicker basket can be removed easily from the pantry and placed on the bench for extra lighting, and I can then lay the jars out on the bench top until I find the one I want. By the way, sweet spices live in one basket, savoury spices in another.

If you really want to keep to using identical containers, you can attach a tactile marker, like the ones mentioned previously in Bathroom Etiquette, or simply use an elastic rubber band around your most used herbs to distinguish the jars from the others. Ultimately though, go with what your nose knows.

TIP #3 – Label Touch-Sensitive Controls

If you are wondering which button to press on a microwave or how far to turn a dial on the stove, this too can be achieved by placing tactile markers that can stick to a smooth surface at the most used temperature points on your cooker. These self-adhesive fabric dots and rubber bumps are handy to place on all sorts of things to help guide your fingers to the correct spot; on a microwave or on an electric oven or, if leaving the kitchen briefly, on a TV remote to identify the on/off button.

The small adhesive bumps work well on so many items around the home and office. Their use is only limited by your imagination. Even your gym equipment such as an exercise bike can be dotted with markers to help you independently work the digital controls.

TIP #4 – Bring in Extra Lighting

The kitchen is definitely an area of the home where you will benefit by setting up extra lighting to define work surfaces. A couple of small lamps that can throw a spotlight on your preparation space if you are readjusting to low vision may be all you need to do in modifying your space.

High-intensity lighting (with an LED light) goes a long way to boost your cooking confidence, as does learning to work with contrasts. Incorporating items with strong colours in the kitchen will help to define the edges of bench tops and cooking trays. An effective approach is to use a dark-coloured chopping board if you have a light-coloured kitchen bench top, or work with a white cutting board placed on a dark surface.

When it comes to extra lighting in my kitchen, I have two 'spotlights' strategically placed near the food preparation space. One spotlight swivels to shine over the gas stove, and the other one lives permanently beside a wooden chopping board. I can't fully see the food being chopped up under my knife but at least I can confirm that the food is going into the right pots and bowls.

TIP #5 – Invest in Kitchen Gadgets

We all have our favourite gadgets in our kitchen. But did you know that there is a range of audible kitchen devices for the 'blind' chef? You can get a talking meat thermometer, an audible set of kitchen scales, and a liquid-level indicator that beeps when pouring hot water into a coffee cup, just to name a few. Your only problem may be in keeping the little people in your household from removing the gadgets to put in their play kitchens.

TIP #6 – Safety is Priority

A kitchen can be a place of many hazards, so you do need to consider your safety options. You can invest in extra-long kitchen gloves to use when placing hot trays and dishes in and out of the oven. Another safety tip is to wear shoes, not slippers or open sandals because you will be handling hot liquids like soups and casseroles. If you do happen to knock over a glass container that shatters to the floor, at least your feet will still be protected as you carefully step away and seek sighted help to clean up the mess.

If you live on your own and an accident like this happens, a friend of mine who is totally blind offered me her safety tip: use slices of bread to mop up any spilt liquid (of course, you are going to throw away the bread). The fragments of glass will also stick to the bread for you to place carefully into the bin at the same time. This sounds like an innovative solution, but I'd still be super-careful.

Another cautionary warning is to take particular notice of the stove when you move into a new home. Check it well for evenness to ensure that large pots can be boiled safely without gradually vibrating off the trivets. You may not see the pot beginning to fall until it is too late and causes severe burns. This did unfortunately happen to me. An alternative solution to being able to cook safely is to invest in an electric frying pan or slow cooker as they are much friendlier to use.

As you become more confident in 'baking blind', you might even end up being a guest on 'A Taste of the World' which is a popular YouTube channel hosted by Penny Melville-Brown – blind chef extraordinaire.

♥ Two Blind Cooks in My Kitchen

I first heard about Penny Melville-Brown on the VisionAware (USA) website. Penny is a UK chef who was selected as one of three winners of the Holman Prize. The Holman Prize is an initiative of the Lighthouse Foundation for the Blind and Visually Impaired based in San Francisco, which funds three blind or vision-impaired individuals from anywhere in the world to pursue their most ambitious projects.

For the inaugural award in 2017, the judges of the Holman prize had selected three entrants with ambitious dreams: Ahmet Ustunel, who planned to kayak Turkey's Bosporus Strait solo; Ojok Simon, who wanted to teach his fellow Ugandans how to become self-sustaining beekeepers; and Penny Melville-Brown who planned to tour her YouTube baking show to six continents.

The Lighthouse wrote about Penny's project that she would, 'travel to Costa Rica, Malawi, Australia, China and the United States, all over the course of a year. Along the way, she will meet chefs, teach blind people and community leaders the techniques and panache of blind baking, and film these encounters to ensure that people change their assumptions about the capabilities of blind chefs.'

When I learned that Penny was going to be cooking in my home city of Melbourne, I had to make contact. I found her 'Baking Blind' website and took a confident leap across the World Wide Web, inviting Penny to cook with me in my kitchen. Within 24 hours, Penny and I were sending emails back and forth and connecting on many creative levels. Penny instantly accepted my offer for her to cook with me in my home kitchen and tour plans went into gear.

Imagine my excitement to host Penny in my kitchen! Our plan, as two 'blind' cooks involved demonstrating one of my family's favourite dishes, often cooked by my mother, Spanish Eggs a la Flamenca. Penny was burning to try it out. She had five days set aside for the Melbourne leg of her baking tour and needed to find a few more cooks to create culinary delights for a global audience. She planned to 'vlog' each cooking demonstration for her YouTube channel, 'A Taste of the World'.

We were both amazed by the quick response we received when I contacted a hub of local sighted chefs who were keen to work with Penny in their professional kitchens. She also had a cooking demonstration lined up with the young recruits from HMAS Cerberus (a training branch of the Royal Australian Navy).

The day arrived to meet Penny, and it was an incredible feeling having forged a friendship through our email correspondence – to share our passion for cooking and to organise how we would make it all work on the day. I had prepared the kitchen space to allow for filming by removing the clutter on the bench top. I placed a vase of flowers casually in the background, and pre-cut the ingredients to save us time.

When Penny arrived in a taxi, I raced to the front door to greet her and her sighted companions. Toby, her nephew, filmed the entire day and her partner, Alan, was on the tour to lend a hand. I squealed with delight as Penny and I exchanged a hug, and then I noticed – both of us had chosen to wear a red dress.

After Penny had a feel around my kitchen and we had discussed how filming would be done, we spent the next two hours enjoying the space together, sharing a conversation about being blind, her tour so far, cooking family favourites and the multi-culinary scene in Melbourne. We even had time to visit an exquisite spice shop after the filming. I had a bottle of champagne to celebrate the occasion and it was a fun challenge to find each other's glass and elegantly toast to the project – on camera.

We chopped, chatted and cooked, and then enjoyed the dish we had prepared with our sighted crew. I hadn't noticed my partner bring out his ukulele and before I knew it, we were singing an improvised song to give Toby a tune for the video clip. But the biggest surprise of all was when Penny presented me with a special honour. She gave me a pewter medallion in the shape of an apron, which she had personally made back home in the UK. The medallion was attached to a long red ribbon, and I felt like an athlete who had won a gold medal. Penny had brought along several 'Baking Blind' medals to give to each chef she cooked with on the tour as her token of thanks for supporting the project. It is a day I will treasure, and I agree with Penny's sentiments.

'When we have the same enthusiasms, whether it is food, work, music, sport or anything else, we can come together as equals. If we can manage to cook like everyone else, there's no limit to what else we can do too.'

SENSORY LOGIC

You may not fully realise it yet but having low vision gives you a cutting-edge advantage in the kitchen. That is because there is much more enjoyment to food than seeing it displayed on a plate.

For a sighted person, it is a mystery to work out how to accomplish what they assume to be a visual task. They can't imagine cooking without being able to see. But surely, the real pleasure in cooking anything comes from our other senses, sometimes even from closing our eyes to savour an explosion of delights as they burst forth from every taste bud.

In retaining your joy for cooking, or even preparing your family's evening meals, when you have less sight than before, the secret is not to give up altogether but to adopt new methods in your kitchen. Cooking is one such activity where you can let go of sighted techniques and gain new sensory skills.

If you enjoy cooking, you have likely already explored many ways to create your favourite dishes. Practising and tasting has taught you what works and what doesn't. I'm happy to say that the art of cooking doesn't rely solely on seeing, and the preparation of favourite dishes can be a tantalising sensory affair.

From one vision-impaired cook to another, it's not as difficult as you may imagine. In my home, there was no other choice but for me to adapt my cooking skills. My young family would have gone hungry many times if I hadn't been able to trust in my other senses in the kitchen. Keeping your zest for cooking alive as it gets harder to see is about being more in tune with your other physical senses.

Sense of Touch

Your hands are one of the most useful 'tools' for any kind of cook, sighted or blind. It is how you use them that makes the difference. Trust your hands to feel and pat, turn and roll foods. Your awareness is right at the edges of your fingertips. It's delightful. Sensing the readiness of many dishes is a matter of gently touching your way around baking trays and other pans.

You can still use sharp knives to chop and cut as long as you stay focused. For instance, using a short knife gives better control than longer blades. Chopping requires rehearsal so that you develop the technique of keeping fingers neatly tucked away from the sharp blade. Never be tempted to rush this process or allow distractions to take your mind off your fingers.

Sense of Smell

Cooks often rely on the nose to smell everything from the freshness of ingredients to the progression of a cooked dish. The person who is vision-impaired is at an advantage here. Sight doesn't have a look in when it comes to appreciating the aromas of cooking.

The nose simply knows how to gauge the complex scents of well-cooked meat, the ripe smell of fresh fruit and vegetables, the subtleties of bread and pastry, and the fragrance of a finished dish. Trust your sense of smell and you will gain the enviable reputation as the 'aroma authority' in your kitchen.

Sense of Hearing

Listen carefully while you are cooking because you can actually hear when food is ready. Being more alert through the sense of hearing tells you when to take the next step. The audible bubbling and squeaking emerging from deep pans and mixing bowls are your clues.

With attentive listening, you'll hear sounds in your kitchen you never noticed before as you create 'music' with spice shakers, tins, pots and pans, timers and audible gadgets. Before you know it, you'll be conducting a symphony of sound in the kitchen.

Sense of Taste

One of the advantages of not seeing is that you can delight your taste buds more often by dipping into your dishes in the preparation phase. You have the perfect excuse, right? Sip and taste as you go.

No matter how well a dish is visually presented for sighted dinner guests, ultimately our enjoyment of food and its success is based on the fine balance of flavours and aromas created by the delicate spices and textures all cleverly mixed together. Not by sight but by sense.

One other important skill to partner your cooking ability is to weigh everything up with a measure of logic. The addition of some good old-fashioned logic when working in a kitchen will be more helpful to you than how much you can see.

One Task at a Time

Don't try to carry too many things at once from bench to stove or from bench to table. Focusing on one task at a time helps you to stay safe, calm and organised. You may need to set aside extra time for certain dishes, or ask for assistance for specific tasks such as grilling meat, where heat and a gas flame can complicate the judgement process.

Be Efficient

Every skilled chef has a system when preparing food. In the case of cutting up vegetables, work from left to right. On the left, you can easily feel for the unprepared vegetables, in the middle you have a bowl for the discarded pieces and on the right, the prepared vegetables await their destiny. Professional chefs often use several bowls for prepared ingredients and you can do this too as it adds efficiency to the process.

Use Deep Cooking Pans

If you have very low vision, the safest way to cook with hot oil when frying food is to use a deep saucepan rather than using a shallow frying pan. This method reduces the chances of hot oil spitting up at you and can save on washing up if you continue to use the pot to complete your recipe.

It also helps to pay attention to how you place your pots onto a hot stove. Keep the handle of a pan to one side and use this side every time so it becomes second nature to your way of cooking. This means you avoid accidentally bumping into a handle sticking out on the stove.

Time Everything

You may be used to seeing when baked dishes are ready to come out of the oven but now you can simply use an audible timer to save opening the oven door too many times. Your sense of smell will guide you; so remember to keep your ears on the time and your olfactory senses on the aromas in your kitchen.

By building your confidence little by little, you will retain your zest for cooking. Add tenacity, logic and sensory flair into the mix and creating your culinary favourites can be enjoyed for years to come.

Be Sneaky

When throwing a party, people tend to gather in the kitchen. Naturally, this is where food and good conversation are bubbling away in the heart of the home. I have noticed that sighted friends are curious to watch their vision-impaired host chop with a sharp knife or dive into a hot oven and, of course, they want to offer their sighted assistance; they would hate it if something went wrong in front of them.

If you are like me and would prefer they left you to your own devices, set them another task – like serving the other guests with bowls of nibbles or garlic bread. This gives you that little extra time to dish up in private, where no one needs to see your hands moving swiftly over the food to arrange it neatly for their visual enjoyment.

But, more importantly, I tell my guests that I work better if I am not watched as I need the freedom to move from oven to bench-top without any bodyguards in the way. At the moment of dishing up, my advice to any cook with low vision is to avoid the hilarious gesture of unseen help caused by someone moving plates around as you are dishing up – you can imagine the outcome. I've plonked mashed potato down onto what I thought was a plate but it had been 'kindly' moved closer towards me without me realising it until I heard the food hit not a plate, but the kitchen bench. *Oops!*

PRESERVES FROM ME TO YOU

Before we leave the topic of cooking, I'll share two of my favourite preserve recipes to demonstrate how easy it can be to make the most delicious spread which doesn't require the ability to see. I have often made a batch of my mother's Lemon Butter or other jams packed with fresh fruit from our garden as gifts to my family and friends – now they are my gift to you too.

MUM'S LEMON BUTTER

INGREDIENTS
8 lemons
500g sugar
250g butter
6 eggs, beaten

Method:
1. Wipe the lemons clean and grate the rind.
2. Squeeze lemons and retain the juice, discarding any pips.
3. In a saucepan melt butter over a low heat and add sugar, stirring gently until smooth.
4. Add the lemon zest and juice. Stir then add in beaten eggs.
5. Stir until thickened (approx 20 minutes).
6. Pour into hot sterilised jars and seal.
The lemon butter will thicken upon cooling.

TARKA APPLE & RHUBARB JAM

I created this jam recipe in celebration of my partner's World Premiere performance in Melbourne 2010 for his symphonic music of Tarka; but that is another story.

INGREDIENTS
6 cups diced apples
6 cups diced rhubarb
4 cups raw sugar
Rind of 1 large lemon
1 cup of water (include lemon juice)

2 tablespoons ground cinnamon

Method:
1. Place all diced fruit into a heavy-base saucepan.
2. Stir in the sugar and mix thoroughly.
3. Add all other ingredients and bring to the boil.
4. Simmer on medium heat with the lid off for 35 minutes, stirring occasionally to make sure the fruit is not sticking to the pan.
5. Cook until the fruit is soft, turn off the heat. Leave for 10 minutes.
6. Carefully pour into clean sterilised jam jars (makes approx. 6 medium jars).
Bon Appétit!

♥ Jamming in Too Many Jobs

At the beginning of each year, I like to look ahead. I 'dwell in possibility' as January dawns, allowing a theme for the year to emerge. In a quiet place, I sit with my thoughts and ask, 'what would I really like to achieve this year?' With a non-rushed focus, I feel my heart and mind working out the possibilities. It often doesn't take very long for a flash of inspiration to clarify my goals.

At the beginning of 2018, a number of exciting opportunities began to present themselves. It was a 'lucky' windfall and I found myself cramming in a whole lot more jobs than I had anticipated. I was preparing for a speaking tour in California but other distractions were taking me off task. It was summertime and fruit mania was in full swing on our bush block outside of the city.

Each January, Harry and I like to spend some tranquil time tending to our small orchard of fruit trees nestled in a blue gum and eucalyptus forest. This summer the apples, pears, plums, peaches, quince and apricots had somehow managed to ripen without being eaten first by the local wildlife – king parrots and other native birds - as well as possums, wallabies and wombats.

As Harry and I cruised around the garden, we were astounded by the cornucopia of fruit. Two days later, our car was fully laden with the bountiful harvest. On the way home, it groaned with the extra weight.

'What do you want to do with all the fruit?' Harry asked, as we carried the huge containers into the cool storage space back in our city home.

'Give away as much as possible!'

The thought of processing all the fruit while preparing for an international presentation overwhelmed me. What could I do with 80 lemons, 15 bags of apples, pears and plums and another large bag of wild grapes? If it had been 60 kilos of grapes, I might have been tempted to try a little wine making. But I had to stay focused on creating a PowerPoint presentation for my talk, so I asked for a little help from my friends.

While I whipped up jars of lemon butter, Harry created a vast quantity of apple sauce. While he sorted out the grapes, I washed damson plums and together we made dozens of jars of organic Damson plum jam, grape and ginger jam and stewed larger plums to make plum ice-cream. Any of our friends who called by were handed a jar or two from our harvest. I found our preserves worked as a barter in exchange for other things. When an author friend called in with her latest publication, we happily traded a signed copy of her book for a jar of Lemon Butter and Ginger-Grape jam. Smiles all round.

Later that week, a girlfriend came over for a serious day of preserving, as we still had so much to process, and my flight deadline was fast approaching. Richenda was only too happy to pitch in with the peeling and mixing of apples. She tossed in cups of raisins and watched both Harry and me in a lively discussion about how much muscovado sugar should be measured out and added to the vat of vinegar and hot spices. Harry took on head-stirrer role and a few hours later, Richenda left with a store of filled jars for her friends.

We made the flight and the conference but we still have a wonderful harvest to share. If you live in Melbourne and want to exchange your creative goods for our jars of jam – just give me a call!

Chapter 10

Stepping Out

*The real voyage of discovery
consists not in seeking new landscapes
but in having new eyes.*
~ Marcel Proust

Now that we have everything in its place inside the home, it's time to step out and discover how to travel well with low vision. Getting around safely and independently requires you to develop skills in Orientation and Mobility Training (O&M).

O&M training involves learning specific methods of mobility for the visually impaired, with either a long white cane or a guide dog. Many people are unsure of the difference between using a white cane or having a guide dog: simply put, a white cane helps you to identify objects and obstacles and then you move around them, whereas a guide dog walks you around obstacles and actively follows your verbal commands. Whichever option a person chooses is based on meeting their personal circumstances.

Let's explore the white cane option first. You have most probably seen the iconic image of a white figure on a black background holding a long white cane and recognise it as being the international symbol used to identify a person with a visual disability.

In the beginning phase of losing your sight, it can be emotionally challenging to identify yourself as a blind person. Getting around with a white cane when you have been sighted for most of your life may make you feel that you will be 'branded as blind', and can be a real psychological barrier to take up this option. Sadly, I know some people who feel that to accept the long white cane is like yelling out to the world, 'Danger! Blind person on the loose.' They may still see enough to get around, but not quite enough to be safe. Instead of feeling empowered by the prospect of a white cane, they feel vulnerable and in the spotlight of the general public.

Fearing the stigma of having a visual disability, they choose to shy away from using a white cane as their mobility aid. Some vision-impaired people have even been made to feel like a fraud when misguided individuals have confronted them and accused them of faking their blindness and taking advantage of social benefits, so they do their best to remain inconspicuous.

If you or a loved one are facing the fear of being judged by others due to that darn little white stick, reading the following pages will help. From experience, the key is to free yourself from feeling stigmatised and know it is possible to take hold of a white cane and transform it into a 'wand of power'.

The shift from vulnerability to empowerment grows steadily as you become more confident as a cane user, radiating a different message to the world. Accepting this mobility aid means you can also accept it is merely a device and not the insignia of a character defect. It is similar to looking at a plant and deciding whether it is a flower or a weed – it's a subjective opinion.

How would you feel right now if you had to take hold of a white cane? Does the thought upset or empower you? It is worth looking at your personal attitude because sometimes our own opinions are the barriers that block progress. I know, because once upon a time, I wouldn't have held a white cane to save my life – which it often does now. I felt embarrassed to let the world know I had a visual disability, and was afraid of being judged as a burden to my family or to my community.

It was pointed out to me in my early days of resistance that the cane isn't just for my benefit, but is a way of alerting other people so they can make allowances on my behalf to avoid collisions. What I have learned is that the moment anyone accepts the white cane as their mobility device in their determination to pursue an independent life, a positive shift in consciousness takes place.

By stepping forward with a measure of courage and purpose, that person accepts the cane as a highly practical mobility aid and discovers the joy of its many advantages. This confidence spreads like ripples in a pond, producing wider circles of positive reactions, changing the way people interact. Over the years, I have noticed the ways blindness can evoke kindness.

When I began using a cane, as if by magic, I began to receive kindness from people I had never met. They offered their assistance in all sorts of ways. An encounter with a total stranger on a bustling city street can still take me by surprise. I hear a kind voice offer assistance or feel a gentle hand reach out to touch my arm right at the moment when I am hesitating to move forward. Just when I am wondering, 'Where do I go next, how do I get out of here, which way to the...', a real life 'angel' in the form of a stranger appears.

Out of the shadows of a grey city street, a friendly voice enquires, 'Can I help you? Do you need any assistance?'

The offer can come from a young mother or a businessman, from a foreign tourist or a tram driver, from a waiter or a shopkeeper, and even from a homeless man – Pete the Russian, who walked with me each time our paths crossed to make sure I found the right tram stop in central Melbourne.

In our brief interactions, and no matter who it is offering their support, the conversation is direct and to the point. There is no time for mistrust. We are two people on a mission. In a fleeting moment, all barriers fall away and a common spirit of goodwill unites us. At times, we can even feel part of each other's lives as we share an open conversation until the mission is accomplished and we bid each other farewell.

Naturally, this is not always easy. It requires a measure of trust when dealing with people you have never met but who presumably approach you with the best of intentions. Being open to receiving help is an individual's choice. Maybe I have been extremely lucky to have had so many truly amazing encounters with 'strangers'. However, I do think that one has to trust to a certain degree if one wants to experience the goodwill of humanity. It seems to me that goodwill travels in a cycle; the more you are open to receiving, the quicker help from others will come. If you stay closed and distrust people's motives, it is less likely that help will show up when you need it.

All I can say from my own experience is that the more I am open to accepting help, the less vulnerable I feel. I try to ignore scrutinising stares during my 'performances' in public and take full advantage of my VIP status (which in the 'blind trade' is the acronym for Vision-Impaired Person), knowing that my cane offers me a wand of power to use with maximum effect. Sighted people from all walks of life will happily go out of their way to assist. I have engaged in so many fascinating conversations with friendly travel stewards, and even a co-pilot on one occasion, when we both exited the plane at the same time. With his travel bag on one arm and me on the other, we trotted across the tarmac, enjoying the novelty of our brief encounter.

When I carry a white cane, the public no longer view me as a threat to their safety. They see me as a person they can trust. They reach out in empathy and I either gladly accept their assistance or decline with a courteous thank you for their thoughtfulness. It truly moves me to be cared for by a community; when I can't rely on my sight, I trust that my blindness will bring kindness. On the odd occasion when I may have created an accidental moment of calamity, I thank those of you who were present for your generosity of spirit.

♥ Soft Patch of Forgiveness

It was a pleasant autumnal day, with a thick carpet of leaves covering the street. I swept a neat swathe through the leaf litter, tapping a path with my cane while humming a cheerful tune.

'Look out: bin. Move over: doggy. Watch out: pole'.

Suddenly, my foot stepped into a soft patch on the pavement. I glanced down.

I hadn't seen the small sign on the nearby grass that read WET CEMENT. Nor had I noticed the man crouched down over a patch of pavement, passing a trowel back and forth, smoothing out ripples in the concrete. With great flair, I had delivered a dainty footprint smack bang in the middle of his artwork. *Whoops!*

A few colourful expletives escaped the man's mouth. I braced myself, half expecting the worker to fly at me with his trowel. I stood there motionless, my foot sinking deeper into the wet cement. The man took a sideways glance, noticing the carbon-fibre cane poised by his knee.

'Oh sorry, love,' he apologised, dropping both the trowel and his annoyance.

I couldn't believe it. He was apologising to me?

'Wait. I'll guide you to the kerb.'

His readiness to forgive my mistake with a sense of good humour as he led me away from the soft patch of calamity, joking, 'it's all good, love' – when I knew I'd wrecked his finishing touches – relieved the embarrassment I felt and we parted with a smile.

MOBILITY MATTERS

Like most great inventions, the long white cane came about as a mobility aid due to a specific personal need to solve a problem. In 1921, James Biggs of the UK had been working as a photographer until he had an unfortunate accident which caused him to lose his sight. He retained his desire to be independent but was alarmed by the increasing amount of traffic around his neighbourhood that posed serious danger to his safety. Mr Biggs had the bright idea to paint his walking stick white and found it to be much more visible to drivers and pedestrians alike.

Then in 1930 in the United States, George A. Bonham witnessed a man who was blind attempting to cross a road using a black walking stick. Mr Bonham was horrified to observe that the dark cane was hardly visible to the traffic, and being a Lions Club member, he raised his concerns with other members.

Soon after this incident, Lions Clubs International not only painted the man's stick white but a year after this event, they also began a program for other people who were blind and vision-impaired, to promote the use of white canes as a safe and recognisable mobility tool.

Also in the early 1930s, on the other side of the Atlantic, Belgian-born Guilly d'Herbemont launched a national white stick movement. In a presentation witnessed by several French Ministers, Mademoiselle d'Herbemont gave the first symbolic white canes to two blind citizens. Shortly after, 5,000 white canes were issued to other World War 1 blinded civilians.

The humble beginnings of the little white stick advanced to worldwide recognition when on October 6th, 1964, President Lyndon Johnson of the United States made the first proclamation to declare October 15th 'White Cane Safety Day'. Each year people all around the world continue to observe the day as a celebration of independence and social inclusion.

The white cane has evolved in many ways to suit our modern lifestyle, and today can be fitted with a variety of tips, such as the Pencil Tip, the Ball Race-over Tip, the Rubber Support Cane Tip, the Pear Tip, the Rural Tip and the Jumbo Roller Tip – who would have thought there were so many options?

No matter which one is preferred, if you choose to use the white cane, it will soon play an integral role in maintaining your safe mobility. With a cane in hand, you will learn how to identify the depth of steps, know when you are approaching an escalator and discern many other changes on the ground.

It gives you a boost of confidence because it enables you to respond quickly to obstacles and maintain a sense of independence. You can learn these orientation skills from an O&M trainer. Organisations that assist people with a visual disability are the place to start.

The benefits are not only for people with low vision. Consider the role a cane plays in the lives of the sighted too. When accompanying a person using this mobility aid, often the sighted person is delighted with the 'magical' effect it has on other people. As they guide you, they will notice how quickly oncoming human traffic moves aside.

It can be challenging at the best of times to get through a crowded train station, a busy shopping centre or music venue, but on the whole, when the public do notice your cane, they take a wider berth around the two of you. This brings the sighted guide much relief and eases the pressure from other sighted pedestrians who become more helpful.

One of my author friends, Amy Bovaird, understands the challenge of accepting a long white cane. Her two books, *Mobility Matters: Stepping out in Faith* and *Cane Confessions: The Lighter Side to Mobility*, are written from her experience of losing her sight.

In Mobility Matters, Amy steps out in great faith to embrace her life as she moves between the worlds of being sighted to being partially blind. Confronted by the need to accept long white cane training to maintain her sense of independence, she meets a highly encouraging trainer, a totally blind man, who challenges Amy at every turn. She is determined to learn what it means to be blind and 'to get it right', always aiming for a 20/20 attitude. Amy faces every obstacle with inspiring honesty, upbeat focus and a lovely sense of humour. Her experiences are a wonderful testament of how we can rise above life's difficulties – especially when our mobility matters.

Those who accept this challenge as a normal part of living with a visual disability, and choose to use that little white stick with a realistic attitude are helping their sense of confidence grow each and every time they step out on a mission to improve their independence. Being open to exploring new pathways is the way for the courageous soul.

Another friend who doesn't let his vision loss stop his love for adventure is Maxwell Ivey Jr. He is a Texan who also happens to be blind. He is known as the 'blind blogger' and the 'blind entrepreneur' and it's not surprising he inspires people he meets or chats to on his podcast show. He loves to share how he approaches his life-challenges with huge optimism.

When Max read about a prestigious writing contest, he did what he always does: chased after his wildest dreams. Shortly after applying to the Amtraks Writers in Residency Program in the United States, he won an all-paid train adventure to New York City. His most recent book, *The Blind Blogger's Adventure to NYC*, chronicles his ensuing travel tales, during a Christmas and New Year holiday season.

Max ticked off many things he set his heart on experiencing when he arrived in New York. He rode on his first subway train, and took a ferry across to Staten Island. He went skating at Rockefeller Centre and was in the audience of 'Wicked' on Broadway – just to mention a few of the things he challenged himself to achieve. Even though he had been warned to be careful in New York City as a person on his own and with no sight, he found people to be friendly and extremely helpful.

'During the course of twelve days, a man bought my breakfast in a restaurant, a cabbie tried to give me his umbrella, two fellows from England put me in a pedal cab and paid the driver, and another taxi driver refused to charge me when my credit card wouldn't work. So many people offered me information, directions, or a shoulder to follow to wherever I was going next.'

Like Max, we can all use a sense of adventure and determination to make our bucket-list dreams come to life – with or without sight.

♥ Challenge the Challenge

I had heard glowing reports of the Woodford Folk Festival, an annual music event held each year in the sunshine state of Queensland, Australia. Many a musician had told me, 'It's an amazing event that music lovers should experience at least once in their lifetime.'

Imagine my excitement when my partner, Harry, booked for us to go to experience it for ourselves.

'It might be a challenge though,' he said, 'getting around with you and your white cane AND a hundred thousand other punters?'

'Nah. I'm up for the challenge. It will be fun!' I said to reassure us both.

Off we went by plane and made our way in the heat of summer – in high spirits, with adventure in our hearts and with plenty of sunscreen on our skin. For one whole week, we mingled with thousands of other music lovers, all eager to welcome in the New Year, listening to dozens of international and local music acts. The music was world class but the heat? It was so unbearably hot, even at 7am, that I thought I was going to die!

But the real challenge came in the evenings when we got caught up with a throng of people all plodding along the dusty track like cattle as we moved on to the next concert. Very few people could see my white cane in the dark and even though Harry was doing his best as my bodyguard to protect our walking space, we became absolutely fed up with being bumped and knocked around.

'There has to be a better way,' Harry said, scratching his head.

The next thing I knew, we were standing at a market stall that was selling a myriad of LED lights. Within ten minutes, Harry had strapped a string of small bright lights to the length of my cane – making it light up like a Christmas tree!

With this new invention, folk moved around us rather than on top of us and we steamed ahead with renewed pleasure. The added bonus was that if we happened to get separated, I could raise my dazzling stick in the air and he'd be able to see it glowing in the dark above the crowd.

Harry wasn't the only one with innovation in mind. Prior to leaving home, I had packed an unusual item that I knew would make life easier when having to identify our tent among nine hundred other identical looking canvas tents in Tent City.

On arrival, I unpacked the fake bouquet of flowers and planted it at the front of our tent, in an obvious position to define the entrance. All I had to do when trying to find my way to our tent was to look for the brilliant white blooms of plastic daisies. They worked exceptionally well and I heard other people comment as they passed by to find *their* tents.

'Turn left now, by the patch of white flowers.'

Being at Woodfordia was certainly a test of perseverance and resourcefulness but at the end of the day, the experience gave both Harry and me another heart-warming example of how innovative living makes all the difference in adapting to a life with less sight.

THE CANINE OPTION

The other favoured option used by people with a visual disability as a mobility aid is learning to work with a service animal called a Guide Dog or Seeing-Eye Dog.

In Australia, there are over 450,000 people who are blind or vision-impaired. This number is also predicted to rise due to an ageing population and the growing amount of people being diagnosed with diabetes.

Naturally, not everyone with a visual disability will choose the canine option, as various eye conditions require different approaches to living. For some people, however, learning the skills to handle a guide dog enables them to maintain independence and stay active within their community. As you have read from my own experience in Chapter 2, pairing up with a canine companion is a totally different experience of independent travel.

As the handler, you become the navigator while the dog adjusts to being the pilot – a formidable team indeed. Your pedigree pooch is much more than a good-looking specimen of its breed. A Guide Dog or Seeing-Eye Dog (known by the organisation breeding and training these service animals) is a fully-qualified dog that has gone through months of rigorous training and health checks from the moment it is born.

After six weeks of age and for the pup's first year, it is placed in the care of a person or family known as puppy raisers. These are volunteers who follow strict rules to help the pup to become well socialised by gaining skills in obedience training. The role of puppy raiser is hugely important and rewarding, although it must be challenging to give up the pup and hand it back to the training centre when the puppy has matured to twelve months of age.

Once well socialised, and with the basics of dog obedience learned, the 'adolescent dog' is assessed by a guide dog mobility instructor to begin the harness training program at the Guide Dog centre. It remains in the kennels cared for by staff during its training until matched up to its new handler.

It's interesting to know that the qualities required for any pup to become a recruit, no matter where they are being trained in the world, are to display a level of confidence and initiative and to be responsive and adaptable while having a calm and intelligent disposition.

Each dog is also critically assessed for a healthy physique and kind nature. The whole process, from adorable puppy to fully graduated guide dog, and then bonding emotionally with the handler takes around two years of the dog's life. By then, the dog is raring to take on the next phase of its working life.

It costs over AU$50,000 to breed, raise, train and match each working guide dog to its handler and to support them as a team throughout the dog's working life. The service is free to the client and the dogs really do work hard to earn their status as fully-fledged guide dogs and seeing-eye dogs.

For you as the handler the challenge begins here. During the first weeks of training, it is easy to become overwhelmed by the specific skills you have to learn and practise. The key is in developing good communication between you, as the handler and your guide dog, and in remaining relaxed. You both rely on trust as each day you learn to move smoothly through a world of obstacles. It takes a little while to settle into a routine but the feeling of independence most of us have looked forward to can be fully enjoyed with a highly trained canine companion.

The many things your guide dog learns to assist you in include being able to walk at your own pace while avoiding all obstacles and unpredictable human traffic en route. The dog is trained to stay focused on the job, ignoring distractions such as other dogs, cats, moving balls, and food – which can be especially challenging for a food-obsessed Labrador. A guide dog awaits your every command before carrying out your request and will slow down before a kerb and stop, or halt at the top or bottom of stairs and escalators to alert you to be mindful of your next step.

For the safety of the person who is blind or vision-impaired, a guide dog is also trained to refuse a command if the handler happens to make an ill-timed request. This could include asking the dog to cross the road at the wrong time or allowing the handler to move too close to a dangerous edge.

It never ceased to amaze me that my dog knew his left from his right when I gave him the command to turn in either of these directions. He was also trained to guide me away from overhanging branches and other hazards at head height, as well as ignore people who tried to distract him by talking to him.

Perhaps the 'funniest' encounter we experienced was when an elderly gentleman dressed in a tweed jacket and cap came over to where we stood waiting for a lift. The old man leaned down and began to pat my dog. I said nothing at first, knowing people are attracted to guide dogs, and although it is wise to inform them not to pat a working dog, I thought he would give Nev a quick pat and move on. But the elderly man ruffled up Nev's coat with great vigour, speaking to him and ignoring me.

'Excuse me. Please don't pat my guide dog. He's working,' I said firmly while shortening Nev's leash.

Still half bent over, the man stared up at me. 'Don't tell me what to do with dogs!'

Taken aback, I said, 'He's a guide dog. You don't pat a dog when it is working.'

With a final ruffle to Nev's coat, the man stood up straight and said, 'I know he's a guide dog. *I'm* not bloody blind!' – and he walked off without another word. Even Nev seemed surprised, but ignored my command to bite that man in tweed.

Ending this chapter on the many benefits of choosing either a white cane or a dog companion, it is worth noting that one added bonus to having a guide dog in your life is that he or she not only absolutely loves to work and play with you every single day, but your loyal friend adores you unconditionally. That is a special friendship indeed.

THE GIFTS

We have covered so many practical aspects of managing vision loss, but in order to keep a focus also on personal strengths, it also helps to know your 'gifts'. These aspects of your personality are integral to who you are, regardless of sight.

Are you aware of your gifts? When you are able to recognise your strengths, you can keep them front of mind on days when you need to put some balance back into your perspective. When you face a difficult situation, and can remember the gifts you share with others in your life, you are also able to gift them to yourself. Can you recognise any of your strengths in the list below?

'I have the gift of...'

The gift of Encouragement	The gift of Creativity
The gift of Knowledge	The gift of Endurance
The gift of Healing	The gift of Focus
The gift of Music	The gift of Friendship
The gift of Hospitality	The gift of Playfulness
The gift of Art	The gift of Parenting
The gift of Humour	The gift of Mediation
The gift of Wisdom	The gift of Service

The gift of Listening
The gift of Organisation
The gift of Speaking
The gift of Nurture
The gift of Conversation
The gift of Practicality
The gift of Hope
The gift of Leadership
The gift of Honesty
The gift of Reliability
The gift of Dreaming
The gift of Intuition
The gift of Spontaneity
The gift of Gentleness
The gift of Health
The gift of Giving
The gift of Sports
The gift of Curiosity
The gift of Generosity
The gift of Partnership
The gift of Adventure

The gift of Confidence
The gift of Cheerfulness
The gift of Languages
The gift of Cooperation
The gift of Teaching
The gift of Storytelling
The gift of Positivity
The gift of Perseverance
The gift of Advocacy
The gift of Writing
The gift of Fairness
The gift of Beauty
The gift of Singing
The gift of Empathy
The gift of Dance
The gift of Sensuality
The gift of Finance
The gift of Motivation
The gift of Flexibility
The gift of Love
The gift of Innovation

PART THREE

MYTHS AND TIPS FOR THE SIGHTED

*What the caterpillar calls the end of the world,
the Master calls a butterfly.*

~ Richard Bach

Chapter 11

Open to Ingenuity

I had my order ready, my Visa card handy, and waited on the phone to make my purchase. The sales person began the conversation.

'Can I have your driver's licence, please?'

I smiled, thinking, here we go. 'Sorry, I don't have one. I'm legally blind.'

After a moment, she said, 'Oh! You don't sound blind?'

'Really?' I was taken by surprise. How was I supposed to sound?

'Yes, you really don't sound blind at all,' the operator's voice trilled. 'You sound so, er, intelligent.'

'Gosh. Really?' Forgetting all about the purchase, I asked her another question. 'So, can you tell me, how do blind people sound?'

'Oh, well, you know, they can be a bit vague.' The operator replied as if she were revealing a deep insight.

'Vague?' I said, trying to sound vague.

'Yes. But you don't sound at all like that.'

After a few seconds, I persisted, cross-examining the salesperson like a defence lawyer, and hoped our conversation was being recorded for coaching purposes.

'Hmm. I'm curious. You say you have spoken to blind people before and they haven't sounded very intelligent? That's interesting.'

She let out a laugh.

'Well, you know, they can sort of be a bit vague at times, that's all.' Noticing my silence, the operator quickly added, 'But I'm so glad you're not vague. How may I help you today?'

When I am confronted by well-meaning people like the phone operator who have no idea of what it means to live with a visual impairment, it makes me wonder how I can help to change their misconceptions. Rather than taking offence I prefer to dispel the myths of being blind. In the case of the operator, I was bemused by her assumption that people with a loss of sight also have a cognitive impairment.

Although it was slightly comical at the time, it is a sad fact that little is understood about the ways 'the blind' can function as well as sighted people regardless of how little sight they have. At moments like these, I feel caught in an ancient shroud of mystery and wish to be freed from society's misconceptions of blindness. Perhaps it is traditional fables and folklore across cultures where blind characters in stories were depicted as either being supernatural or subhuman that has created mistruths that are still believed to this day.

Living with a degree of sight loss is not so mysterious when you can be open to the reality, dispel the mystery and welcome ingenuity in its place. Consider the following pages to be a new story waiting to be told. Many insights can be gleaned simply by taking a walk in my shoes as your 'blind' guide.

A couple of years ago, I was working for a social enterprise known worldwide as Dialogue in the Dark. As one of the blind tour guides, my job was to lead sighted people through an exhibition in total darkness. The tour was created to be an immersive experience where visitors gained a new appreciation of what it means to live with a visual disability by stepping into an unknown environment without the ability to see. I witnessed many reactions by sighted visitors and gladly answered a myriad of questions. I learned that to be a guide, we were not simply leading people through a darkened space.

'As tour guides, you also have to be highly creative and flexible, an ambassador for the blind, a counsellor who is aware of people's feelings and emotions, and educators of social inclusion,' said one of our head trainers from Germany, Daniela Dimitrova, Director of Dark Operations.

Picture this if you can: I am standing by a sliding door in the pitch black and hear a group of people walking towards me. Actually, it sounds more like a scared shuffle, with white canes swinging wildly, banging the walls. They grip a long handrail that leads them along a zig-zag corridor away from the light and into total darkness. My voice alerts them to the fact that at the end of the handrail, a person is in close proximity and they are not alone. I hear their voices express astonishment.

'It's so dark in here, I can't see anything!'

The Welcome host lets me know that everyone is standing with me in this dark space, and the dialogue begins. I reassure them that they are in good hands and pose the first question: 'In a word, can you tell me how you are feeling right now?'

A few people will say, 'curious' or others might comment, 'nervous' but most visitors used a synonym for terrified. This is the most frightening part of the experience; it is the fear of the unknown. Every sighted individual is confronted by the immediate challenge of trusting themselves in a world without sight: What will they be expected to do, will they get hurt, can they get out of here, how will they even take their first step into the challenge?

This is when I take a moment to explain our reversal of roles. I tell them I will guide them safely with my voice as they explore using their white cane, their hands and their other senses, to 'see' from a different perspective. In this way, the visitors begin the challenge of being in total darkness by letting go of fear and moving slowly and with trust. I open the sliding door and lead the group through the exhibition. For the next hour, we experience an open dialogue in the dark. We explore together some of the recreated iconic places of Melbourne by sounds, textures and city scents. Individuals gain a different perspective through the conversations that help each person to become more relaxed and confident. For me, the most rewarding part of being a tour guide was witnessing the transforming effect it had on people's assumptions in only one hour.

Near the end of each tour, we sat in the dark in a lounge area where the visitors could reflect on their experience. As their tour guide, I was open to answering any of their questions about life in the 'real' world. People shared their concerns and admiration, and emerged grateful to have spent a short time 'in the shoes' of a person without sight.

'It's opened my eyes – I'm not so scared – it's amazing!'

Stepping into the newness of a visual disability obviously was terrifying, but each visitor was rewarded by their willingness to be vulnerable to the challenge; they gained a deeper appreciation through being flexible to change. I liken it to the mysterious and beautiful transformational process that happens to a curled up chrysalis inside a dark cocoon. Before it can emerge as a creature with new colours, it first has to leave a part of an old life behind.

Only after an internal struggle to adapt, and by being in tune with what needs to come next, can it become the marvel Nature designed. So too, if we open to allow our own life to move in mysterious ways, albeit dark and strange in the beginning, the journey towards blindness can be another beautiful life story waiting to unfold.

Perhaps the 'cocoon' is not our own; but one society places us in. There is a delicate dance others can struggle with – between making a person with vision loss feel empowered or helpless. For instance, it is surprising how often a person has asked me; 'If I see someone who is blind and they look like they need help, should I approach them and offer my assistance?'

This question surprises me. I wonder why they would hesitate – surely we are no different than any other person who would benefit from assistance. My reply is always, 'Of course. Why wouldn't you?'

Instead of being relieved, they are even more confused. They go on to explain that their reluctance is not due to being uncharitable but because they fear they may hurt the person's feelings.

'I don't want to ask in case they think I am interfering or being patronising.'

This is a very common concern, and I appreciate the thought that the act of kindness offered to 'intervene' may imply the other person is not capable of doing the task for themselves. Rather than risk embarrassment, they hold back the natural urge to help, while feeling guilty about not having asked. But isn't this creating a lose-lose situation?

I explain that if it were me, I'd rather they asked than watch me fumble around or leave me stranded and looking lost, and encourage them to go ahead and offer help next time they feel drawn to do so. In my opinion, a genuine act of kindness is not patronising, it is a sign that people are willing to care for each other's wellbeing.

Every time any of us act out of a kind heart, we break through the barriers that may have once kept us apart and discover the myths we have believed in may not be true.

An article by Rosemary Mahoney, a teacher at a school for the blind, caught my attention one day while surfing the Web. She addressed the question, 'Why do we fear the blind?' The article, featured in the New York Times, mentioned how a sighted woman at a party once asked her, 'How do you talk to your students?'

Ms Mahony explained that her students were blind not deaf.

The woman, still confused, replied, 'Yes, I know they're not deaf. But what I really mean is, how do you actually talk to them?'

'I knew,' wrote Ms Mahoney, 'because I had been asked this question before by reasonably intelligent people, that the woman didn't realise exactly what she meant. All she knew was that in her mind there existed a substantial intellectual barrier between the blind and the sighted. The blind could hear – yes, but could they properly understand?'

Perhaps this explains my own curiosity to know why others are reluctant to help a person with low vision, as if we are a different species – the 'blind' versus the 'sighted'. Having a dis-ability does get in our way if we allow the so-called disability to stand out more than the person's natural capabilities as a fully functioning human being – who just so happens to be blind or vision-impaired.

Let me ask you a question. Would you know what to do if a person with a white cane appeared in need of help? Would you be the first to assist them? In theory, you may think so but in reality, as mentioned before, most people do hesitate. What makes all the difference is being able to shift your feeling of hesitation to one of assuredness.

When the person approaching me shows their confidence to ask, and I respond with the confidence to accept their offer, we both gain a sense of connection and deep satisfaction. What may have been a few moments of awkwardness is avoided when we remove imagined barriers – the sighted versus the blind – and begin to relate on an even ground, sharing more commonalities than differences.

Sometimes the beneficial feeling of 'common ground' can be difficult to establish if the sighted person swings into over-protective mode. On occasions when I have accepted an individual's kind offer, it can trigger a green light for them to take on a parental role. With all good intentions, they take over the situation completely, leaving me to feel as if all my liberties have been removed - like a teenager caught arriving home after curfew. This creates an internal annoyance on my part and is one reason why people who are blind or vision-impaired may reject help even if they do actually need it.

It's a delicate balance between making a person feel empowered or helpless. One example I can give you is in the way people smother my hand with their own while trying to assist me. They take hold of my white cane to guide me into a tight spot or grab me by the wrist. When this occurs, I stand my ground briefly and rearrange the person's hands to place them where they work best, as I am not keen on the sensation of being handcuffed.

'No. Let me take your arm so I can follow your movements.'

Some people stand surprised as if I've revealed a great mystery. All I have done, in fact, is to be open to allow understanding to flow. With these formalities over, the helper, now positioned as a sighted guide, is more comfortable, and probably relieved, knowing we can continue our visual quest in a less awkward way.

Misunderstandings do happen easily. It comes with the territory when you live with a disability. I've realised over the years that my ability to partially see some things but not others confuses those trying to assist me. It can be easily overlooked that a person with low vision may be able to see, even when they say they are legally blind. This is the complexity: there are many varying degrees of blindness.

Let's explore the term 'blind'. It seems a fair assumption to interpret being blind to mean a person lacks the ability to see. But this is not true. Most 'blind' people can actually see something, even if these images are vague and blurred. So many factors make each person's experience of blindness unique, depending on varying eye-conditions, personal health and external influences like natural or artificial light. Even people suffering similar eye conditions are not all affected in the same way. I have Retinitis Pigmentosa (RP), and I don't wear sunglasses as my eyes function best with as much natural light as is possible to distinguish objects; a friend with the same eye-condition can't stand outside glare and always uses sunglasses.

The simple truth about blindness is that only a small percentage of people in Western countries are *totally* blind. Others adjust to using whatever small amount of sight they have left by maximising their limited field of central or peripheral vision. Even being able to tell the difference between night from day sends the brain some form of visual information.

This presents a dilemma for the sighted community, and for the visually impaired, as it is difficult to explain the nature of a vision impairment, especially when a person's vision fluctuates on a daily basis. Some people who say they are blind may appear to look you straight in the eye or reach out to shake your hand. They may spot something small on the ground, yet promptly bump into large furniture or walk into a door.

People are frequently confused by the mixed messages coming from the body language of a person experiencing vision loss. How can the blind person wear perfectly applied make-up or be colour-coordinated or pull out their iPhone to give you directions? What is going on? They are not supposed to see through blind eyes. *That's* the grand misconception.

If we use my own eye-condition as an example, the word 'blind' may take on a different meaning. Apart from being almost blind in both eyes at night, my right eye is totally blind during the day, while my left eye, the 'good' eye, helps me to discern objects through a constant thick blur. The minimal amount of central sight that remains, along with my brain and memory, work together to make sense of visual clues by looking for high contrasts. I also use outlines of objects, bringing logical deduction into the equation.

This means I can pick out a white dinner plate when resting on a dark placemat or vaguely see the white lines of a zebra-crossing. I'm not necessarily seeing them but my eyes and brain are working out clues. When out and about, I notice steps going up much more, as sunlight casts a shadow on the underside of the step but looking down a flight of steps, I can't tell the depth of each step or whether there are steps at all. So, I am both blind and partially sighted, not seeing but also perceiving as a 'legally blind' person.

LEGAL BLINDNESS

What does it mean to be legally blind? Here is another good question often asked.

You may already know that in order to test a person's central vision, reading the letters on an eye chart allows an eye specialist to record their visual acuity using the familiar letter chart. Normal sight is known as seeing with 20/20 vision. The first number refers to the distance (measured in feet) that the person is tested from the chart. The second number is the distance from which a person with normal eyesight can clearly see the letters on the chart.

However, if a person is scored as having a visual acuity of 20/60, this indicates that they are seeing the letters at 20 feet which a person with normal sight can see at 60 feet. In short, the higher the second number in the visual acuity test, the worse the person's vision.

As stated by the American Academy of Ophthalmology, 'when your visual acuity with eyeglasses or corrective lenses is 20/200 or worse, or your side vision is 20 degrees or less, you are considered legally blind – even though you may still have some useful vision.'

With normal vision, our eyes also use two kinds of specialised cells for seeing called rods and cones. Millions of these cells within our retinas allow our eyes and brain to work together to detect the colour spectrum, movement and the shape and size of everything we look at. Rod-cells help us to adjust quickly to light and dark changes and work better in the dark; whereas Cone-cells are sensitive to colour, meaning they work best in bright light. If a person is colour-blind, they are lacking a particular type of cone in their retinas.

For me, my ailing eyes can only offer the brain vague information coming from faulty light-sensitive cells at the back of my retinas. Yet, as if an internal dialogue takes place between the eyes and the brain, I am acutely aware of a silent relay where a certain amount of brain logic is doing the seeing; my brain prods the eyes to send more information to clarify the scene ahead as if by constantly asking, 'What's that?'

♥ Imagining a Sunset Sky

I was looking upwards towards a cloudy sky, the sun setting like a painting. Obviously though, most of the six million cone-cells that are supposed to detect colour in my eyes were not conveying reliable messages to the organ of sight. I could sense the brain becoming impatient as signals via the optic nerve were not being transmitted quickly enough.

Brain asked my eyes, 'What colour is the sky?'

My eyes gazed at the sky more intensely, trying hard to guess the colour.

'Well, at this time of dusk, logically, it should be a shade of deepening blue, right?'

My brain likes logic, and in a few Nano-seconds, it scanned my childhood memory-bank to recall all the blue hues I had stored there. Like the painter Monet, I was eager to capture a sense of the light dancing across the vast canvas of the skyline. It was then that I asked, am I seeing through vision-impaired eyes or am I perhaps 'seeing' through the logical deductions of the brain? I came to the conclusion – it was a mixture of both.

The internal dialogue shifted to ponder what colour had begun to blanket the evening sky as it turned from a light something, to a darker something. I was content to be seeing the 'whatever' it was before my eyes – amused by the relaying of signals and mixing of colours in the brain.

My mind chose logical deduction from other body sensitivities too. If the current of air had travelled over my sun-warmed skin, the likelihood would be that a summer's day was shedding her glow, and my eyes could imagine warm shades of vivid pink, crimson yellow or orange chrome. But, the mildness of the day could have easily suggested that the sky was a mixture of cool-grey swirling with tinges of mauve-purple.

As I wondered, a much darker shadow caught my attention from skyline to fence-line. It was the deep green blob I knew to be the Australian Blackwood tree. I could see the tree's image as a tall and wide dark something, towering upward to the night sky, casting a majestic shadow over our garden. The distant sound of a light aircraft gliding across the sky distracted sensitive hearing. I tilted my head towards the sound, pointing my audio-antennae, like Hobbit-ears, to track the stereo effect: from far left, to the centre of the sky, and away to the far right. The staccato rhythms of the insect chorus reached a deafening crescendo and dominated the sounds in the night air.

The sky had shifted through many shades in a short time, and my brain asked my eyes one more question.

'Do you remember seeing the evening stars as a little girl?'

My internal dialogue between heart and eyes replied, 'Vaguely. But I'm happy to imagine them again. Brain, tell me, what does the night-sky look like?'

Chapter 12

Are You Too Polite to Ask?

*I've learned that people will forget what you said,
people will forget what you did,
but people will never forget how you made them feel.*
~ Maya Angelou

Throughout this book, my aim has been to clarify what it is like to live with a visual disability to empower my reader, whether you are sighted or going blind, to be less afraid of having low vision. The core of my message is to help you meet this life-challenge from a whole new perspective.

Another way to do this is to unravel the most common questions people are curious about when living with a degree of sight loss but are often too polite to ask. Perhaps you have been wondering some of the same things? Apart from the following 10 questions, I will give the young boy of twelve the prize for asking me THE most intriguing question I have ever been asked,

'Do they send blind people to war?'

What an interesting thought! Here are a few more.

Do blind people like to feel a person's face when meeting for the first time?
Not really. This is more likely to happen in a movie than in real life. When a person who is blind or vision-impaired meets someone, we are using different sensitivities to gauge a picture of the other person. Our blind eyes may be

impervious to visual clues but people give off certain 'vibes' that are felt without having to physically touch them.

I don't ask to feel a person's face and, in all honesty, it is more comfortable to interact with people using clear language. I'd rather greet someone with: 'Great to see you', rather than say, 'When will I feel you again?'

There is also much to be said for listening to the tonal quality of a voice. The subtle body language can be heard through nuances of a person's tone – as when I met my life partner: his interest to pursue a connection with me was clear through his open and playful tone which was more obvious than the words he used.

It does become a natural skill to observe life through all the senses when your eyesight is not able to help with visual cues. Throughout your journey, your other senses will become more heightened simply due to necessity.

Is it rude to use visual terms when speaking to a blind person?
Not at all. If you have to ask, 'How do I talk to a person who is blind or vision-impaired?' be reassured because the simple answer is: as you would address anyone else. People live in a visual world and we are used to hearing visual language terms like: 'Look out', 'Watch your step', 'See that over there?', 'Let me show you'.

There is no need to adjust your language unless you are acting as a sighted guide in which case you do need to be more careful to give clear directions.

A tip here: when sighted people can see the unintended humour in using words with visual connotations to those who can't see, we are all able to lighten up and get on with our lives without being afraid of saying the 'wrong' thing. I have a totally blind friend, Amir, who always greets me with a hug and says, 'Great to see you again,' which starts our conversation with a giggle.

Do people who are blind all know how to read Braille?
No. Braille is not always the means by which a 'blind' person reads print materials. It depends on a person's level of blindness and whether they want to use assistive technology or the tactile raised dots we know as Braille. Like learning a spoken language, people are driven by their desires, and it is this which creates the motivation to learn Braille or to choose a different tech-option.

As mentioned in Chapter 8 under the heading, Gadgets Galore! the reason why people are no longer obligated to learn Braille is due to significant advances in technology. An entire industry has sprung up to assist the blind and vision-impaired to vie with sighted technology users.

A wide range of devices enable people with a visual disability to perform tasks independently, especially if they use a smart phone with apps to help them read and see content. Devices which use audio (and sometimes Braille) to communicate are readily available in the market place.

However, some people with low vision still opt to learn a basic amount of Braille to enable them to read tactile signs, while others will take on learning Braille to a higher level of proficiency. Personally, even though I am legally blind, I have never felt the need to learn Braille in order to read precisely because of all the advanced tech choices I have at my fingertips. This comes as a surprise sometimes to those who assume I would like a print menu or brochure in Braille.

Can a person experience déjà vu if they are not able to see?
Yes. The fleeting sensation people call déjà vu (which literally in French means 'already seen') is not only triggered by eyesight. I am able to verify that through my other senses I have also experienced the phenomenon of déjà vu. The strong sensation that something seems to have happened before can also be triggered by a feeling, a smell or a particular sound.

How do people who are blind know what colour clothing they are wearing?
Another way this question has been expressed more bluntly is: 'Who dresses you?' I'm always tempted to say, 'My guide dog, of course.' But I know that what they mean is, 'How do you know what colours you are wearing?'

The process begins at the purchase stage, and often a sighted shop assistant or friend can help by describing the colour or style of a garment. The person with low vision can also shop on their own and may initially be attracted by the texture, style and comfort of the item. Once at home, storing clothing requires a methodical system and, equally vital, a way to remember that system.

Everyone has their preferred method. My own preference for keeping track of my clothes is to place them in military fashion in rows of co-ordinates. My casual gear goes to the left, smart clothes to the right and anything that suits either category lives in the middle space. Whatever I am looking for, it is easier to be feeling my way through only one side of the wardrobe.

Colours are grouped together, orange scarves in an orange bag, and my red scarves with my deep red satin bag. Another helpful trick I use is to store shoes in their original box which helps avoid being caught wearing odd coloured shoes. This did happen on one occasion and I pretended to the young boy who pointed it out on my way home that I was starting my own fashion.

Other popular techniques people use are either pin a Braille label to the back of a garment or sew a small button on the inside. For instance, a round button is sewn on to white clothing whereas a square button is sewn on to black garments. Basically, it gets back to organisation, memory and some sighted assistance along the way.

Why would a person who is blind go to an art gallery or a visual exhibition?

Dare I say because it is fun? Our eyes may not see fully but there is much pleasure and knowledge to be gained by spending time in a gallery, either doing an audio-tour or going with a friend who appreciates the fine details of art.

Many times, I have experienced so much pleasure in having the art or visual display explained to me in great detail by my partner. As his words paint an image for my mind to imagine, we both get a better understanding of the artwork. He helps me to find the best lighting to see a sculpture through its silhouette, and on occasions, we have asked the curator of an exhibition if it is possible to touch any of the exhibits. This special permission to delicately run my hands over an art piece has been a source of great joy and an added reward for my love of art.

♥ Bravo for Audio-Described Theatre

I have always had a particular fondness for going to live theatre shows and naturally rely on my sighted companion to keep me up to speed with the happenings on the stage. But sometimes our whispers can annoy people around us who haven't noticed my folded white cane and tell us off for what they think is unnecessary chatter.

You could ask, what's the point of going if I can't see anyway? I can tell you the answer in three words; audio-described theatre. When I experienced it for the first time, I was wonderfully surprised. The difference it made to my enjoyment of a live show was life-changing for this theatre lover.

I had heard of a free audio description service run by a group of volunteers from Vision Australia but had never experienced it personally. When an email alerted me to a musical performance coming to the Comedy Theatre in

Melbourne, I paid closer attention. The musical show was 'Flower Children, the story of the Mamas and Papas', and it was being audio-described. I loved their music and so it seemed a perfect opportunity to 'see' the live performance with this new service.

Within two hours after booking a ticket for my partner and me, the coordinator had sent a detailed description of the costumes and stage props before the screening of the show. Everything that a sighted person would see had been made available as a word document for the person to read with a screen reader. I listened to my computer as it read the text, and it was like having my own private 'viewing'. The notes painted a vivid picture.

'Papa John, played by Matt Hetherington, is a man in his early thirties. He is approximately 6 foot tall, and of medium build. He has brown eyes, short brown hair and sports a beard...' Each performer was described in a similar way.

On the night of the show, my partner and I arrived with great anticipation. Friendly volunteers greeted us and gave instructions on how to use the portable radio receiver. Off we went to find our seats. Using the device with ear-phones was simple, so, for the first time in my theatre-viewing life, I could keep up with the whole story.

The clear voices of the volunteers speaking through my ear-phones brought the show to life. I was laughing at the gestures being described, understood who was coming on and off the stage and imagined the colourful descriptions of the shifting props.

At one point, Harry leaned in close to describe a scene as he usually would. Before he could speak, I grinned, with eyes alight.

'I know. I just heard that!'

After the performance of the Flower Children, there was an added surprise. The coordinator had organised a tactile tour with the stage manager for a group of us as vision-impaired patrons. We stepped up onto the stage, feeling the props and some of the costumes worn in the show. While there, one of the stars, John Hetherington, came to join us with his guitar and invited us to sing a rendition of *California Dreaming*.

What a thrill. Talk about feeling like royalty. Encore!

Why do some people have a guide dog and others use a long white cane?
The reason is simply a matter of personal choice. A guide dog and a long white cane are both considered as mobility aids. Each come with a set of natural pros and cons depending on the situation of the person involved. Some people prefer to fold up a white cane having arrived at a destination, whereas a guide dog requires extra care like feeding, toileting, regular walks and health checks.

The guide dog option gives some people a feeling of extra protection and companionship. Using a white cane gives others a sense of personal freedom. One main difference between the two mobility options is that a guide dog helps its blind handler to move around obstacles, whereas the person using a white cane is more likely to encounter the obstacle, then move around it.

One option requires a life-long commitment to working together as a team while the other choice is a collapsible tool in one's hand. Both methods require different skills to achieve safe mobility and either of them will meet an individual's needs. I have worked with both methods – the extra joy my guide dog brought into my family's life (when he was off duty from guide work) was an added bonus for all of us.

Wouldn't you be afraid to live on your own if you were blind?
It may seem a better option to live with sighted people but, for whatever reason, people who are blind or have low vision can live quite happily on their own. Having a visual disability

makes a person seek other ways to adapt their skills in living independently.

A major challenge facing people with vision loss is convincing their families that they can live perfectly well on their own if they choose to. The most helpful thing other people can do to assist their loved one is to treat them normally and give them space to learn new skills. Be willing to assist if required and you'll be contributing to their sense of freedom as capable and independent adults.

How does a person who can't see find their way around a busy city?
Most of us with a degree of blindness take the time to plan a route, learn the safest way and commit to memory crucial points of reference in our neighborhoods so we can reach our destination safely and with confidence. More than others, those who are blind or vision-impaired need to know where they are going.

A person with vision loss who is using a white cane or a guide dog has trained in Orientation and Mobility (O&M) to develop specific techniques in moving independently through their environment. If you happen to find you are giving a lift to a person who has a visual disability, feel free to discuss options for the quickest route to your mutual destination. They have most probably already researched it and can 'lead the way'. Asking for directions from your passenger demonstrates that a sighted driver is open to trusting in the opinions of their blind navigator who can also use their Smart phone GPS – now what a ride that would be!

How do people who can't see identify money?
There are a few techniques that aid a person to identify money. In Australia, the Reserve Bank has rolled out tactile banknotes with the inclusion of a Braille-like bump at the top and bottom of each banknote that makes it easily recognisable to the touch. Each denomination has retained

its unique and contrasting colour along with being slightly longer in size than the next as they increase in monetary value.

In other countries, as in the United States, where banknotes are too similar to distinguish by touch, one technique is to fold the paper banknotes: a $5 note can be folded in half with the short ends together while a $10 note is folded in half lengthwise, and other notes are folded in more elaborate ways. Loose coins are best kept in a separate purse with dividers for accuracy and quicker counting.

I check my coins and notes before leaving the house, which gives me not only a reliable method of keeping track of cash but it also gives me the confidence of knowing what I am handing over in a cash transaction.

Another great example of how assistive technology can help is in the array of smart phone apps specifically designed to identify money. Those with a visual impairment who also like to travel and use smart phone technology may find the app, 'Look Tell Money Reader' invaluable as it can identify the different denominations of 21 countries.

Of course, the simplest way to carry out money transactions with ease is with the ever popular plastic bank card. The only problem is that the new exclusively touch screen ATMs being installed in retail and commercial outlets are not accessible for the blind and vision-impaired. This forces some of us to give our pin number to another person in order to complete the visual transaction. Advocates are working on solving this problem, raising the issue to enable banks to be more inclusive in electronic money transactions.

♥ Hands on the $5

The Reserve Bank of Australia first designed banknotes to incorporate large numerals in 1992 and gave each denomination a unique and contrasting colour for easier recognition for people with low vision. In 2016, they put into circulation a banknote with a difference.

It was the first accessible banknote of its kind, enabling easier recognition for people with a visual disability, as well as having security features which made it a world first. I was lucky to be one of a small group of vision impaired people at an information session in Melbourne to learn more about this advanced 'technology' as it rolled 'hot off the press' to begin its journey into daily circulation.

It was exciting to get my hands on one of the notes and check it out for myself. A representative of the Reserve Bank's design department gave us an eye-opening account of the life-cycle and life expectancy of the new accessible $5 banknote, printed on a shiny piece of plastic.

My ears pricked up at the word 'life-cycle' and my thoughts regressed briefly, imagining an old poster I had seen during a biology class, which depicted the phases of a tadpole becoming a little green frog. With each snippet of information we gleaned, the development of the new $5 banknote sounded just as transformative. It didn't take long into the presentation for the group to voice a unanimous desire to get our hands on the new currency. Like being given a special sweetie, we held our hands outstretched and examined the new banknote, with a few *oohs* and *amahs* during the handing out ceremony.

A few days later, I spoke with Michael Andersen, Head of Note Issue of the Reserve Bank of Australia who explained a few more details that went into producing the new currency. He pointed out two main objectives: to upgrade security features and to retain familiarity for the public. After much consultation with a variety of business groups and people from the blind and vision-impaired community, adding a tactile feature became a somewhat 'interesting and insightful experience'. What they intended to be a helpful feature, often took designers back to the drawing board.

The new generation banknotes require 13 processes to apply no less than 19 layers of security features, some only 1 micron thick, to ensure the architecture of each note is uniquely protected. It is the inclusion of a Braille-like bump at the top and bottom of the clear strip that gives it a quick recognisable feature for visually impaired users. Not only are the new series of banknotes tactile and accessible but they are also attractive: each denomination will feature an embossed wattle flower and native bird as part of a distinct Australian theme.

With the $5, $10 and $50 banknotes now in circulation, I'm looking forward to the rolling out of the $20 and $100 notes. This new generation of tactile banknotes is facilitating another type of exchange within my community.

Chapter 13

How Friends and Family Can Help

*Too often we underestimate the power of a touch, a smile,
a kind word, a listening ear, an honest compliment
or the smallest act of caring:
all of which have the potential to turn a life around.*
~ Leo Buscaglia

Have you noticed the key in every successful venture in life is a result of collaboration? An idea, a seed-thought, an initial plan comes from the individual but it is the power and effectiveness of teamwork and cooperation that prove to be one of the most efficient ways to reach any noble goal. This is where you, the sighted reader, come in.

Welcome to this final chapter aimed at the sighted reader. The following tips and strategies focus on effective guiding techniques for people to use when offering to assist a person with vision loss. Like my children and other family and friends, you may already have great guiding skills especially if you work within the blindness community or know someone with a visual impairment.

But did you know that in a report by the World Blind Union, it has been estimated that by 2020, the number of Australians over the age of 40 with a degree of low vision will be around 800,000 people. This is due to the increased life expectancy of our aging population, as well as a rise in diabetes. The probability of meeting a person with a visual disability, therefore, is growing each year.

With this fact in mind, it is important to have a certain amount of knowledge of safe guiding techniques to be sure you feel comfortable when you offer your assistance to a person with a degree of sight loss. As their guide, you are giving verbal descriptions that can empower the other person to make choices. You also take on the temporary role of steward to protect their safe mobility. Even if they simply have to sit down at a cafe table, there can still be many obstacles to manoeuvre around.

For the reader completely new to what it means to be a sighted guide, relax and learn some 'tricks of the trade'. For the experienced guide – maybe you will learn a few new things here too.

SIGHTED EYES, GUIDING HANDS

Before you reach out physically to assist a person who may require your help, there is a question to ask – how will you make contact? Naturally, this depends on the situation but in general, when you approach a person who can't see you coming, the best way to greet them is with your voice or a gentle touch of your hand to their forearm.

Be mindful however that by simply saying 'Hello' you may not get their attention immediately. On many occasions, I have replied to someone I thought was addressing me, only to realise a moment later that the friendly voice was answering a phone call on their way past me.

Be Obvious

If you want to approach a person with a visual disability, they most probably are not going to see you coming. So if you change your mind, now is the perfect time to turn around! No? You're up for the challenge? Great! Go ahead and make your introduction by being obvious and speak directly to the person so they are in no doubt it is them you are addressing.

If you have the advantage of knowing the person's name, please do use it – this makes the world of difference in how you will be greeted. I know that if a person approaches me as a stranger, I will be slightly more cautious in my tone than if I am greeting a friend; which helps me feel I am doing the right thing by them. It causes me a minor sadness if I neglect a friend without realising it was actually someone I knew.

You are now standing nearby. Do you offer a handshake or not? You most certainly can if this is a formal greeting, but you will need to announce to the person in a subtle way that you are offering an outstretched hand if they haven't noticed, otherwise you will feel quite silly with your hand hovering in mid-air. Once you have established you are there to offer assistance, how do you get physical when needing to guide?

Wait for Instructions

This is the interesting part. Every person with low vision has their own preference of how they like to take hold of their sighted guide. The best thing you can do is not to assume you know what they want but to let the person with low vision point out their preferred method. All it requires in this initial stage of establishing your role is to take a few brief moments to get their instructions. One, clarify the visual task, and two, confirm how they would like to take hold of you as their guide.

Some people like to hold their guide's arm, just above the elbow, while others will be happy to place a hand on your shoulder and walk slightly behind you to one side. I tend to wrap my arm through another's arm to feel comfortably attached.

A person using a guide dog will instruct the dog to follow you, so no body contact in this case is necessary. Be happy to lead the way and the guide dog will listen to its handler give the commands. Whatever you do, never try to talk directly to the guide dog or be tempted to take hold of any part of the harness. If you do, interacting with the dog interferes with its training and it will be its handler that will growl at you.

Avoid Novel Grabbing Techniques

If you knew all the many times I've been grabbed in novel ways by well-meaning sighted guides, you would think it was a comedy sketch. I've held hands with total strangers as if we were approaching a dance floor, our hands majestically held high in the air. At other times, people have taken hold of my cane and flourished it about as if it's a weapon and we are on a crusade or in a medieval jousting tournament forcing our way through a crowd.

But by far the worst way anyone can make contact is to clamp their hand around another person's wrist. Personally, I feel instantly locked into a vice and disempowered. Trapped like a wild cat, it makes me want to roar, 'Let go!' I don't think the sighted community take hold of each other by the wrist unless they are being arrested by the police; neither should you make contact in this way with a person who only wants to be guided, not shackled.

Once you have arranged yourselves comfortably, then you are off to a flying start. Just one other word of advice: it's a bit embarrassing if you take the trouble to find a seat, then gently push them onto it, or ask someone to vacate theirs, and then find your companion promptly springs up again. It's best not to assume that we always want to take a seat just because we are blind. There is nothing wrong with our ability to stand unless there is an added mobility consideration. I know that for me, it makes me feel less obvious as a 'disabled' person in a crowd of people when I take my place alongside them – standing up.

I realise it is easier for my sighted guide on occasions if I wait on a seat, but I'm not comfortable for that decision to be made on my behalf. I'd rather be asked than feel obliged.

Give Clear Verbal Directions

When you are both ready to step forward and have established your visual 'assignment' as well as their preferred side to stand, be mindful of your verbal directions. As the sighted guide, it is up to you to describe things clearly and in a relaxed way.

You can be creative and it is more fun for both of you when you paint the picture as much as possible of where you are going and what you are passing. You don't have to describe *everything*, but things of interest are helpful to know and perhaps you could mention some of the objects you are avoiding too. The person with low vision will be using their other senses as you walk together. It helps for your companion to know the general environment in which you are moving so they can adjust to shifts and changes of direction with ease, especially if they are planning to do the same route later without sighted help.

If you pay close attention to the spaces you are traversing, you will note subtle clues as to the size and layout of an area. This helps to add another dimension to your verbal descriptions. As you describe the path ahead, also remember to say left or right from the other person's standpoint. It is fine to use visual terms like 'Watch out for this pole' or, 'Look out, we are approaching a low tree branch,' without having to be politically correct with visual terms. We understand what you mean and are not easily offended by the use of sighted language.

Speaking of being polite, one area where social standards are challenged is in being a male guiding a female. What's the technique in this case?

Men Do Go First

For men acting as a sighted guide, especially in our Western culture, it can seem impolite to walk through a doorway or enter a lift first when you are guiding a woman, but you really need to stay slightly in front at all times.

To put it simply, to keep guiding his companion effectively through a narrow space, the male goes first and in single file if need be. As you move, your body gives many clues and these are very useful for your companion. The absolute no-no is to push the person you are guiding through a doorway or pull them through a gap or onto a moving escalator.

Being guided by a sighted male through narrow places can end up being quite 'interesting'; as when on one memorable afternoon I was literally yanked by my hair into a hot sauna as my male companion tried to guide me through the tiny door that had to keep out the cold air for the other sauna-buffs. I guess Tarzan hadn't had time yet to read my manual on best sighted guide practices.

Setting the Pace

Pacing how you walk together can be a minor challenge. It all depends on where you are, how many obstacles and people are in the way, and if there is a deadline to arrive somewhere. Some sighted guides are so cautious and 'thoughtful' for their 'blind cargo' that they happily lead at a snail's pace.

Others are so confident that they charge ahead, creating a minor tsunami, making the oncoming public dive for cover. Remember the story of Goldilocks and the Three Bears? Being a guide is a bit like this; don't walk too fast, and don't walk too slow so that, hey presto, you'll get it just right!

Another good reason not to be in haste which people tend to overlook is the simple fact that, together, you are twice as wide and can't necessarily squeeze through narrow spaces, especially in a store with fragile wares. A guide can forget about their companion's shoulder bag that can so easily become snagged on an object they hadn't allowed for in their determination to get through a gap.

Is guiding with sighted eyes beginning to sound like too much hard work? I hope not as I merely want to point out how it feels being attached to the guide. The skill to aim for is to move as a contained package at a comfortable pace – for both of you. How do you know what is a comfortable pace? Just ask, be relaxed and at ease. Your body language will convey this to your vision-impaired companion and they will feel more relaxed in being able to advise you. Together, the experience of gliding in and around obstacles, or getting through narrow doorways, or negotiating awkward spaces with shifting levels under foot will be less like a comedy act and more of a pleasant exchange for you too.

Another consideration is knowing what to do when you need to separate briefly from your companion to go to the bathroom or to pick up the tab after a meal. The solution is to say what you are doing and where they can wait for your return. Please don't just walk away, thinking it is obvious that you have gone. It is very embarrassing to chat to an invisible ghost not realising the sighted guide has just vanished into thin air. This is more likely to happen in a busy place like a café, restaurant or shopping mall, where the noise of clashing sounds interferes with hearing others clearly. Your friend with low vision can't rely on lip-sync, so make sure they have heard you correctly.

Be Accurate with Steps

It is common knowledge that one area in the environment that could cause a fall, whether it be indoors or outside, is the approach to steps and stairways. It's important to know how to safely guide your companion on and off steps.

To approach a set of concrete steps, or carpeted stairs or a moving track like in an escalator or airport travelator requires an accurate verbal description. This doesn't mean that, as the guide you have to count the exact number of stairs in a long staircase stretching out towards the distance but a quick estimate helps.

'Some steps ahead, maybe around eight' is useful to know.

Approach the steps squarely and never at an angle for obvious reasons. THE most vital piece of information the guide needs to remember to announce is whether the steps are going UP or DOWN. You may not realise but this is an area where words can be ambiguous and their meaning misleading. For example, 'We have some steps coming up', you say, but what might be more accurate is, 'We are approaching some steps and they are going *down*'.

If this crucial piece of information is unintentionally ambiguous, the person you are guiding may hesitate for a while, wondering what to do next. Do they prepare to step up or will they need extra support if going down? This important decision is often rushed because other people are in a hurry and may be pushing past as they haven't noticed the person's white cane. Then what seems to happen when you move as one is a natural counting of each step which your companion may store in their memory for another time. The act of being focused together does help to keep the two of you in sync and step with a safe rhythm.

A final suggestion on how to approach a set of moving stairs is very simple; as people with a white cane carry it in their dominant hand, you can direct the hand which is free to the moving handrail of the escalator *before* stepping on to it.

This alerts the person to the direction of the moving stairs and gives extra certainty, enabling them to take the leap forward. No one wants to experience being thrown off a walking conveyer belt backwards – I've been spat off from a treadmill in the gym and let's just say that I was relieved to be wearing sports leggings at the time, as it wasn't my most lady-like performance in public!

Part of the challenge as a sighted guide is knowing how much to say on behalf of your companion, and who is best situated to answer a question. You will find that the general public are inclined to ask you to be a spokesperson on behalf of your 'blind' friend as naturally, this approach is simply quicker and more convenient. When and where you are the spokesperson will depend on the situation. We understand this and will not be offended. But there is one clear instance that will create a feeling of indignation (and sometimes a scene) for the person with a visual impairment. That is when we are treated like a child dependent on the adult by our side.

'Would she like this?' says the shop assistant holding up a garment to the sighted guide. 'What is your friend's date of birth?' asks the desk clerk. 'Is she happy to take a seat over there?' smiles the medical assistant. 'What would your friend like for lunch?' asks the waiter. 'Is he able to sign this document?' asks the secretary. 'Can you tell your friend...'

Excuse me? We are standing right there, hearing all these questions. It is a common experience. As a well-informed guide, you can help by simply saying,

'Why not ask her/him yourself? I'm sure she/he can answer this question for you.'

This common situation arises from the issue I spoke of in a previous chapter where we explored the myth of *Why People Hesitate*; the public are not used to interacting with people who have a visual impairment so it is fairly easy for communication to become awkward or embarrassing.

Being our spokesperson at times, and our sighted guide as the need arises will be appreciated by those you assist and you'll walk away with an added awareness of what is involved. These are the basic techniques of being a sighted guide. For anyone who would like to view a series of well produced videos, the Canadian National Institute for the Blind (CNIB) has created a series for you to view on YouTube at your leisure. They are seriously worth watching, no matter your level of experience as a sighted guide.

YOUR CHALLANGE

It is natural for a person with a visual disability to sometimes rely on their sighted friends, family or carer for guided assistance. It makes sense to allow the visual person to take responsibility for travelling safely. But this is the challenge. Without knowing it, the caring sighted guide may be causing more anxiety for their companion than they realise.

In your enthusiasm to assist, you may not pick up on the one easy mistake that will upset everything. I may be hopping on to my soapbox briefly but I promise it is for a good cause. The one common aspect to being a guide you can fail to appreciate is to get both of you caught in a rush to a destination. Following the lead of a sighted guide is more challenging than you might imagine, even if your decisions are correct. One common scenario goes like this:

Imagine a sighted person guiding their friend down a busy street, chatting and working together to move around cafe tables and busy human traffic, and in general, having a good time. They come to an intersection on the street and, naturally, the person with sight announces when it is safe to cross and wants to do so promptly through the gap in traffic.

The person with low vision, who is usually adept at crossing roads, is paying attention to other sensory clues which may contradict their friend's judgement. The sound of traffic or the texture of the pavement is being assessed every second. The sighted friend says, 'Trust me, it's safe to cross now.'

The person who can't see may react in one of two ways. They may pull back and hesitate. To be advised when to cross doesn't suddenly over-ride their natural survival instincts to observe from their other senses. Instead of feeling assisted, they can feel compromised.

The other reaction is to follow their friend's guidance and feel extremely anxious without revealing that the visual decision has caught them off guard. Keeping up with their sighted guide can put them in a difficult situation. They are grateful for their assistance yet at the same time, it is too rushed, the pace is not comfortable and stepping out suddenly feels like launching into thin air. Make the wrong move and it's all over.

'Where is the kerb? How deep is the step? Will my cane get caught in the tram tracks? I'm not ready. Will I fall?' All these are reasonable concerns going through their mind in such situations.

This is why giving extra time, whether if it is just a few seconds or waiting till the next change of lights, is crucial to our emotional and physical wellbeing. In keeping up with a hurrying guide and being forced to make quick movements with unexpected changes, the person with low vision doesn't have enough time to allow for the micro-adjustments needed. Without getting enough time to translate a visual decision to cross a road or jump into a lift, your companion can experience anxiety and yet hide it from you.

There is nothing more frightening than to be asked by your sighted guide, 'Trust me' and then be expected to jump off a kerb and cross the road on a diagonal. It is less stressful and much safer to find a crossing with audible signals. People with a visual disability really do prefer to walk in straight lines because it helps to manage the chaos involved in navigating through unpredictable spaces.

Having low vision, a person does need to be more deliberate in most things. Moving around safely is definitely a conscious series of choices. It is stressful to dash for a closing door of a lift, or to be expected to dart out on a pedestrian crossing to catch the lights, or to gallop across a road to hail a taxi or departing bus. Perhaps there are justified reasons to launch into a smart pace but, at times like these, the VIP feels a bit like being a human ball swirled around inside a pinball machine.

'This way, whoops, not that far, yes, a bit to your left, sorry, I meant the other left, stairs coming up. Are you OK? I should have told you they were going down, not up. Oops, I thought you could see that door...'

If it reassures you, getting caught up in a rush happens to all of us. In honour of sighted guides everywhere, here's an adventure tale of my own. Hold on to your hats My father doesn't like to be late for any function, least of all for a special event on International Guide Dogs Day.

♥ Blind Bandits on the Run

'One hour should give us plenty of time to find a car park,' Dad chirped as we cruised the city streets of Melbourne in his silver Honda. 'We're way too early.'

I threw him a smile, keeping vision-impaired eyes peeled on the grey city streets as they zoomed by.

After forty-five minutes, he couldn't find a parking space anywhere. We drove round and round in the cavernous belly of two underground parking lots and then drove round in reverse gear, inhaling fumes of panic. We escaped a heated argument with the attendant at one boom gate which set off a screaming alarm. High-tailing it down a busy city street, my Dad did a U-turn, straight out of some movie car chase and sped off again.

With his options diminishing by the second, my father was preparing to sell his grandmother in exchange for a park anywhere in this concrete jungle. His foot hit the accelerator and then the brake pedal in syncopated rhythm with his heart beat. I was beginning to think that anyone seeking a 'fun' ride should forgo a rollercoaster ride and book a daredevil parking adventure with my father.

Minutes before the luncheon, he seized a spot in another parking lot. How to walk out of this underground maze posed a new set of blood pressure problems. We had five minutes to get to a building we had yet to locate. Fleeing on foot as fast as we could, like bandits on the run up the stairwell of the fire escape, my father and I spilled out onto a laneway.

'This way...no, this way...' he called in a blind panic.

I thrashed my white cane in front of me as I tried to keep up, hoping I wasn't about to collide with a brick wall or whack the shin of an unfortunate pedestrian. I felt like a human tsunami – chasing after my father's coat-tails that were billowing in the breeze as he raced ahead. In the foyer of the building, I finally got to latch onto his coat sleeve. Pulled along, I skimmed across white floors polished to a mirror finish. I took a running leap, cane first into the lift just as the steel doors were closing.

BING. 'Thirty-fifth floor', said the audio announcement as my father gave me a sharp nudge to step out of the lift. Guests and guide dog staff were mingling in the restaurant room, admiring the view. The long white table was still being fussed over, and remarkably, we had arrived on time.

'Care for a drink, Sir?' asked a waiter addressing my father.

'Why not,' he replied with a smile. Turning to give me a glass too, he said, 'Got to live dangerously, hey?'

'Cheers, Dad.' I sipped my drink with a grin, knowing this would go down as another story to tell.

Chapter 14

Vision-Quest

*You can't go back and change the beginning,
but you can start where you are
and change the ending.*
~ C.S. Lewis

Where blindness was once my 'disability', it has become integral to a fulfilled and happy life. I've learned that vision is not just for the sighted, it's a quest to see beyond a physical limitation, and to appreciate the many aspects this life-lesson has to teach.

As I've matured over the course of losing my sight, it's become easier to adapt and grow, to flex and bend, to laugh and especially to love this blind life. I wake up every morning hoping for similar things to you: to be happy and healthy, to feel a sense of purpose, to be at peace and in harmony with life, while contributing in positive ways to my family and community.

These similarities are all part of who we are and explain why, when living with a 'disability', people don't regard their weakest feature as the core essence of who they are.

For anyone who is losing their ability to see, this is particularly true. The key is in being able to find the courage to weave a meaningful life with threads of hope, trust, joy, tenacity, persistence and all the other qualities that will make *your* 'garment of change' beautiful in your own unique way.

When I was seventeen and trying to hide my vision loss, I never thought that I'd be leading my community on a journey of discovery. Not only did I find my voice as a writer and speaker decades later but I also designed a walking challenge called Vision-Quest, Melbourne. I wanted to create something special for my community. That was to set a challenge, and 'build a bridge' of understanding.

The challenge was for a sighted person to experience being comfortable in the company of a person with a visual disability while collaborating on a sensory walking trail. It took four months to design, with the support of friends, family and the wider community. The promotional material set the challenge: anyone game to see Melbourne through 'blind eyes' could register for the event.

Teams consisting of one sighted person, one 'blind' person and a coach were the perfect mix required to carry out the mission. Teams could interact in a fun and relaxed way, collaborating to stay on track within a two hour time frame. The twist was to pair people who had never met before.

To really see through 'blind eyes' meant to experience being a sighted guide, and to gain an understanding of how challenging it can be to navigate around a busy city. I had enrolled several of my friends and family to be the coaches so that, hopefully, no one would get lost!

To design the circuit for the walking trail, I researched an area of Melbourne with my partner and we plotted out a route, looking for sensory points of interest. A week before the event, Harry and I took the coaches over our course as a trial run to make sure timing was realistic. I even had donations as prizes to share at the end of the quest.

A sunny morning blessed our day. The people who had registered their interest were raring to go. Five teams, each with a vision-impaired person, a sighted guide and a coach, stood around chatting while I briefed the photographer. Andrew Follows had kindly volunteered to capture the event. Being vision-impaired, he and his guide dog joined the crew. Harry ran around with his video cameras, taking footage that later became our VisionQuest YouTube clip.

The team coaches were pumped up, and after my quick briefing, I handed over the printed map with cryptic clues. They gathered up their teams and set off. After so much preparation, it was like launching a balloon into the air as I released my attachment to how it would all pan out. Once up and away, it was everyone else who would make it happen and figure out what they wanted to achieve from the experience.

Check point number one – the Ian Potter Gallery, in the heart of Federation Square. Teams navigated steps and an escalator, and arrived at the first challenge for the sighted guides. This was to describe an abstract sculpture. The person with the visual impairment was able to touch it as well and during a brief discussion about the art piece, the coach noted their comments.

Moving on to the next exhibit inside the open-spaced gallery, the team came across a traditional Australian installation. The beauty in the carved and painted figures from Arnhem Land was expressed in their sacred designs, rich in texture and colour. Exploring deeper into the labyrinth, teams were drawn to the next checkpoint: an audio-visual installation with unusual sounds.

Everyone stood still for a few moments with their eyes closed, taking in the soundscape, appreciating their sense of hearing. Shortly afterwards, the sighted guides faced the challenge of guiding their companions to an unexpectedly low seat as part of the final exploration inside the gallery.

Moving outdoors, teams were taken by surprise. The corner of what was usually a city car park was transformed into the 'Pop up Patch' – several large boxed gardens brimming with herbs and vegetables. It so happened on that day that some food stalls had also popped up to celebrate a food festival, giving the teams an unexpected array of treats to taste.

On to the lower level of the car park and nearer to the Yarra River, teams ventured to locate the next tactile point.

The instructions read: 'Find the head of the Rainbow Serpent, marked by a carved tree stump. Feel the scales and follow her body set into the ground. At the tail, find the pole and there you will discover Bunjil, the wedge-tailed eagle, protector of Victoria, carved into a boulder.' Eager hands felt the stone carving before moving on.

Up a flight of steps, and out into a large flat area of grass where some of the sighted guides tried on goggles that represented different eye conditions. The cardboard glasses gave the wearer a brief experience of 'seeing' as if they had Glaucoma or Macular Degeneration, Cataracts or Retinitis Pigmentosa. It was so effective that one guide, whose wife was new to vision loss, felt unsettled by his instant understanding of her eye condition.

'I found that changing light has a significant disorientating effect,' he said, 'and I experienced a mild feeling of vertigo as we were coming out of the lift.'

We had a brief rest and a quick photo shoot with all team members, who gave the camera a Mexican wave before moving to the final surprise element of the walking trail. Crossing a wooden bridge, each team was deep in conversation and relaxing into the challenge as they took the final stroll to the Federation Bells.

This art installation of thirty-nine upturned bells is a unique instrument where the general public can get up close to play the bells from their Smart phones. It was the *pièce de résistance* and I had to include it. Not only could all team members interact with the bells but Harry (who is commissioned by the City of Melbourne to keep the Bells in tune) was able to demonstrate exactly how to play them live by touching icons on a phone or tablet device.

It was a beautiful and memorable day, and it touched my heart that people came together on a vision-quest, not knowing what to expect, simply trusting the process, and appreciating each other in new ways.

'It was amazing,' said a Team Coach. 'I learnt so much. I asked lots of questions and it was great for me to get into a vision-impaired world.'

And one of the sighted guides said, 'I took in my environment so much better because I was conscious of us going through it together and I was much more aware of the other senses. I really enjoyed the fact that we could talk about what we are capable of doing together.'

Vision-Quest was not a race, but a heart-connecting adventure for my community. It was a novel way of getting to know each other's capabilities, and an opportunity to make unexpected friendships – one person, one perspective, one story at a time.

If there is one thing to take away after having read this book, I hope you can see that we all have the potential to effect great change in our lives and within our relationships – when we have the courage to create a vision for our future. When we embrace this life-challenge, losing our sight is not the end of the world, but the door to a new way of being.

As the beginner to blindness, you can continue to look forward to being a part of your community, sharing your story, your challenges and victories and, above all, your own vision of what is possible – loving life with all your sense-abilities.

Embrace the journey, take the challenge, and celebrate what happens when your brave heart says 'YES, I can always try again.'

REFERENCES AND RESOURCES

The following list of references and resources are a collection of the books and web links mentioned in various chapters and appear here in alphabetical order. Some are also added as suggested further links.

Accessible Books Consortium (ABC)
Accessible Publishing
www.accessiblebooksconsortium.org/publishing/en

American Printing House for the Blind (APH)
www.aph.org

Arts Access Australia
Arts and Disability
https://artsaccessaustralia.org

Audible Australia
Audio-books Online
www.audible.com.au

Audio-Described Theatre
Vision Australia
www.visionaustralia.org/community/events/audio-description-services

Blind Sports Australia
www.blindsportsaustralia.com.au

Holly Bonner, Blind Motherhood
Never Losing Sight of Life, Love and Laughter
https://blindmotherhood.com

Amy L. Bovaird, Author
Mobility Matters: Stepping Out in Faith and
Cane Confessions: the Lighter Side to Mobility
https://amybovaird.com/

Canadian Institute for the Blind (CNIB)
Basic Sighted Guide Techniques Videos
https://cnib.ca

Stella De Genova and Jeff Flodin
Vision Through Words
Poetry and Essays by Visually-Impaired and Blind Writers
https://visionthroughwords.wordpress.com

Doc Childre and Howard Martin
The HeartMath Solution (1999)
www.amazon.com/Doc-Lew-Childre/e/B001IGLU7W

Audrey Demmitt
Resilient People Live Well with VisionLoss
https://www.visionaware.org/blog/visually-impaired-now-what/resilient-people-live-well-with-vision-loss/archive/125

Dialogue in the Dark, Melbourne
A Social Enterprise Worldwide
https://www.dialogueinthedark.com.au/

Maureen A. Duffy (M.S, CVRT)
Making Life More Liveable:
Simple Adaptations for Living at Home after Vision Loss
https://www.amazon.com/Making-Life-More-Livable-Adaptations/dp/0891283870

Hazel Edwards OAM, Author
Patron: Society of Women Writers Victoria
https://www.hazeledwards.com/

Eyes on Success – Weekly Podcasts with Peter and Nancy Torpey
https://eyesonsuccess.net/

Jeff Flodin, blog
Jalapeños in the oatmeal: Digesting vision loss.
https://jalapenosintheoatmeal.wordpress.com/

Andrew Follows
Blinkie Photography
https://andrewfollows.wordpress.com/

Freedom Scientific
Screen reading Software: JAWS
https://www.freedomscientific.com/jaws

Guide Dogs Australia
www.guidedogsaustralia.com

Hadley Institute for the Blind and Visually Impaired
Distance Education Worldwide
https://www.hadley.edu/

HeartMath Institute
https://www.heartmath.org

John M. Hull (1935-2015)
Touching the Rock: An Experience of Blindness (1990).
Reprinted in 1997 as
On Sight and Insight: A Journey into the World of Blindness.
https://www.amazon.com/John-M.-Hull/e/B001IU0FI8

Maxwell Ivey Jr, the Blind Blogger
Leading You Out of the Darkness Into the Light
A Blind Man's Inspirational Guide to Success
www.theblindblogger.net

Susan Jeffers (1938-2012)
Feel the Fear and Do It Anyway. 1987
www.susanjeffers.com

Susie Kahlich
Artipoeus – Art You Can Hear
https://soundcloud.com/artipoeus

Lighthouse for the Blind and Visually Impaired, San Francisco
The Holman Prize
www.lighthouse-sf.org/tag/holman-prize

Magnets and Ladders
Active Voices of Writers with Disabilities, online literary magazine
https://www.magnetsandladders.org/

Rosemary Mahoney
For the Benefit of Those Who See: Dispatches from the World of the Blind (Amazon)
https://www.amazon.com/Rosemary-Mahoney/e/B000APTOQG

Stephanae McCoy
Founder/CEO, Bold, Blind, Beauty
https://boldblindbeauty.com/stephanae-mccoy/

Penny Melville-Brown OBE
2017 Holman Prize Winner, Baking Blind
www.bakingblind.com

James W. Pennebaker
The Secret Life of Pronouns: What Our Words Say About Us
www.secretlifeofpronouns.com

David Robson, Journalist
An Effortless Way to Improve Your Memory
www.bbc.com/future/story/20180208-an-effortless-way-to-strengthen-your-memory

RNIB (UK)
Connect: Podcasts and Audio
https://www.rnib.org.uk/connect-podcasts-and-audio-0

StoryLine Online
Children's Books on Video
www.storylineonline.net

Toastmasters International
https://www.toastmasters.org

Touching Landscapes Travelling Blind Stories
https://touchinglandscapes.com/

Dean W. and Naomi R. Tuttle
Self-Esteem and Adjusting with Blindness:
The Process of Responding to Life's Demands
https://www.amazon.com/Self-Esteem-Adjusting-Blindness-Process-Responding/dp/0398075093

Vision Australia
Blindness and Low Vision Services
https://www.visionaustralia.org

VisionAware
For Independent Living with Vision Loss
www.visionaware.org

Vision-Quest 2015, Melbourne
YouTube
https://www.youtube.com/watch?v=OSfyWTXznsI

Harry Williamson
Audio Recording, Video Production, Sound Booths
www.springstudio.com.au

Women with Disabilities Australia (WWDA)
Gender and Disability Issues
www.wwda.org.au

World Blind Union (WBU)
www.worldblindunion.org

Write-Ability Victoria
www.writersvictoria.org.au/writeability

Ehud Zohary
Blind People Have Superior Memory Skills'
https://www.livescience.com/4503-blind-people-superior-memory-skills.blind

ACKNOWLEDGEMENTS

If I may roll out a red carpet for the special behind the scenes people who have supported me on the journey to create this book, here is the 'Who's-Who'.

I'd like to give thanks to my close friends for being so understanding in allowing me the space to retreat into a writer's den to forego the many outings we have missed (not to mention the glasses of champagne). So, Susanne, Richenda, Bee and Amir, it's time to pop those corks and celebrate my return to the flow of convivial life.

To dearest Eve, my 'earth-angel' and mentor, who has always encouraged me to complete my creative endeavours. To my children, Claire, Russ, Sharon and Mike, for their kindness in being my eyes, and giving me so many wonderful stories to write.

To my father, Brian Steel, for his constant support and dedication in everything I set out to achieve, and especially in seeing this project through to the very end. In caring for my manuscript, his inspired gift for language has been the wise voice guiding me through every line and paragraph, sprinkling his 'magic' into the text and making sure each story is properly polished.

To Harry Williamson, my talented life-partner, who has lovingly devoted so much of his own blood, sweat and tears to work beside me in making every aspect of creating this book (and my blogs) possible; and for understanding that when the creative muse takes hold, the pleasure in going down the 'rabbit hole' is much more fun when shared.

To Bee Williamson, my skilled book designer, for her patience in guiding me through the frustrating process of choosing fonts and colour designs, and for her willing heart to collaborate with a 'blind' friend.

To Hazel Edwards, for all her generous acts of support and kindness, keeping me well connected within the writing community; and for mentoring me as one of her 'hazelnuts' – for which I am deeply grateful. To Lyndel Caffrey, for being my attentive and supportive writing 'midwife' since the beginning of my writing career and for embracing many of my first drafts as if they were 'children' of her own. Thanks to her devotion to the written word, and to her friendship, she has helped my writing project come to fruition.

Then there are my dear friends in the USA, Amy Bovaird, Audrey Demmitt, Max Ivey, Steph McCoy, Jeff Flodin and others too numerous to mention here, who share the journey of going blind and inspire me with their courage and determination to make this world a better place to be. To Pris Rogers, my dear friend and colleague. Sharing the journey with you has been enriched by your encouragement to publish stories for a global audience on VisionAware – just look what you have created in me: a passionate writer keen to take on the world!

To my treasured Beta readers, Beryl Beaney, Nancy and Pete Torpey, for their enthusiasm to read my manuscript and for being the type of supportive friends every author needs. To Richenda and Christabel Millar, for spending so much of their time mulling over tag-lines and possible titles, going slightly crazy with me in the process, but we got there. To Beth and Linda at Jefferies book shop, Malvern, for giving me their honest advice on designing a book cover; their knowledge of the industry has been invaluable in helping me make my design choices. To Harriet Gaffney at Write-Ability, for the generous support of a grant for the proof-reading phase.

And finally, to you, my reader, to whom I am also thankful for your curiosity in choosing my book, and for giving me the best reason to persist as a writer, to share in the mutual appreciation for learning about other people's lived-experiences.

ABOUT THE AUTHOR

Maribel Steel is a highly creative person who encourages people to see the positive side to living with a visual impairment. She was diagnosed with Retinitis Pigmentosa (RP) in her teens, but went on to raise four children and trained as an Aromatherapist and Masseur.

She was a children's choir leader for two primary schools in Melbourne and continues to enjoy being a singer and lyricist with her life-partner, musician and CD producer, Harry Williamson.

Maribel launched into writing full-time in 2011 with her blogs, *At the Gateway to Blindness* followed by *Touching Landscapes*, and as the vision loss 'expert' for the about.com network in 2016. She has written over 200 non-fiction articles and short stories, personal essays and anecdotes that have been published online, in print journals, in anthologies and as audio podcasts.

Her career as an educator, an award-winning blogger and Toastmaster, a mentor and peer advisor for VisionAware (USA) have all helped to broaden her scope in reaching a global audience.

She is an international speaker, having presented at the American Foundation for the Blind Leadership Conference in 2018, and other events in California. In 2017, she was awarded a High Commendation in the WriteAbility Fellowships (Victoria) and received an 'Inspire' Award in the Lynette Rowe Best Achievement in Community Service.

For the past 4 years, Maribel has been invited to sit on the selection panel for the Accessible Books Consortium (UK) to judge the annual winners of the International Excellence Awards in Accessible Publishing, presented at the London Book Fair.

Maribel always welcomes collaboration!
To book Maribel's 'Living with Possibility' presentation,
or to get in touch with your feedback and ideas, please write to:

- E: maribel@springstudio.com.au

- W: www.maribelsteel.com

- B: www.touchinglandscapes.com

- T: www.twitter.com/maribelsteel

CPSIA information can be obtained
at www.ICGtesting.com
Printed in the USA
LVHW080524160522
718816LV00013B/1307

PRIVATE LICENSE

A SAM QUINTON MYSTERY

PRIVATE LICENSE

A SAM QUINTON MYSTERY

KEVIN R. DOYLE

CAVEL PRESS
Kenmore, WA

A Camel Press book published by Epicenter Press

Epicenter Press
6524 NE 181st St.
Suite 2
Kenmore, WA 98028

For more information go to:
www.Camelpress.com
www.Coffeetownpress.com
www.Epicenterpress.com
www.kevindoylefiction.com

All rights reserved. No part of this book may be reproduced or transmitted in any form or by any means, electronic or mechanical, including photocopying, recording, or any information storage and retrieval system, without permission in writing from the publisher.

This is a work of fiction. Names, characters, places, brands, media, and incidents are either the product of the author's imagination or are used fictitiously.

Cover design by Scott Book
Design by Melissa Vail Coffman

Private License
Copyright © 2024 by Kevin R. Doyle

Library of Congress Control Number: 2024933672

ISBN: 978-1-68492-304-5 (Trade Paper)
ISBN: 978-1-68492-305-2 (eBook)

PRIVATE LICENSE

A SAM QUINTON MYSTERY

KEVIN R. DOYLE

CAVEL PRESS
Kenmore, WA

A Camel Press book published by Epicenter Press

Epicenter Press
6524 NE 181st St.
Suite 2
Kenmore, WA 98028

For more information go to:
www.Camelpress.com
www.Coffeetownpress.com
www.Epicenterpress.com
www.kevindoylefiction.com

All rights reserved. No part of this book may be reproduced or transmitted in any form or by any means, electronic or mechanical, including photocopying, recording, or any information storage and retrieval system, without permission in writing from the publisher.

This is a work of fiction. Names, characters, places, brands, media, and incidents are either the product of the author's imagination or are used fictitiously.

Cover design by Scott Book
Design by Melissa Vail Coffman

Private License
Copyright © 2024 by Kevin R. Doyle

Library of Congress Control Number: 2024933672

ISBN: 978-1-68492-304-5 (Trade Paper)
ISBN: 978-1-68492-305-2 (eBook)

For my mother, who passed away this year after eighty-four years of life. And for the staff and management of the following entities, who made her last year, and mine, much easier and more comfortable than it may have been: Andover Court Assisted Living, Andover, KS; ClearPath Home Health and Hospice, Wichita, KS; Westview of Derby Rehabilitation and Health Care Services, Derby, KS; and Hampton Inn, Derby, KS. Deepest appreciation to all.

CHAPTER ONE

Even though I run my own gym, or at least run as much of it as my manager will allow me to, it's been a number of years since I've done a full-body pullup—not that I don't have the arm, chest and back strength for such a move. It's more like I've found over the years less stress-inducing ways of building up my upper body.

However, the night before Keri Eckland had shown me one of those dorky online challenge things where a bunch of young toughs struggled to see who could top who in number of pullups. It got me to wondering, as I creep closer to hitting the big five-oh, how many I could still do.

While I may look like an over-the-hill gym rat, complete with almost shoulder-length graying blond hair, I'm no dummy, and I do have something of a concern with my public image, such as it is. Besides, the good time of year was coming up.

It was the first day of May, and in a few weeks would come the glorious annual tradition where most of the local university students headed out of town and returned to wherever they called home.

Year-round residents of Providence, Missouri, look forward to this time every year. Much as we enjoy the economic benefits of the town's university and two colleges, it's always nice to get a break from the constant thrum of youth activity. In my case "youth" being defined as anyone under thirty-five, which included not only a large number of the students but a fair share of their professors as well. In a few weeks, we native geezers would start coming out from our holes, looking around and, seeing no signs of studenthood anywhere on the horizon, start enjoying our town again.

Among other things, I was looking forward to gorging myself at a local hole called Road Dog's Ice Cream Shop. It's a little storefront on one of our north/south streets that's been there for as long as anyone can remember, and while it doesn't have all the whoop/ bang/ razzle-dazzle of the big chain places, it serves some of the best ice cream in the central part of the state. It had been far too long since I'd indulged, and the last couple of times I'd sauntered by, student customers packed the place so much that someone my size wouldn't even have been able to fit through the door.

The Blaster, the gym I've owned for years now, is almost dead quiet on the weekdays between eleven thirty and noon. The suburban moms and trophy wives have already come and gone about their days, and the lunch-hour corporate climbers have yet to show up, leaving only a few senior citizens, most with even more gray hair than I have, quietly occupying the lone machine here and there.

Since Lisa Nolan, my manager, has relentlessly worked at turning the gym into a sparkling array of the latest high-tech gizmos for molding the body, some days I hardly recognize the place. However, off in a far corner, tucked away out of sight from the front door, is a lone pull-up bar Lisa had somehow managed to overlook in her unending cycles of "modernizing," where I was currently in the process of struggling through pullup number nine.

"Wow," said a familiar voice behind me, "I thought you were supposed to be an expert at this kind of stuff."

Without saying anything, I gritted my teeth, made it through number nine, then did one more for a nice, round number, and dropped to the floor.

Turning around, I grinned at the woman standing a few feet away.

"How you been, Karyn?" I asked.

Karyn Roberts grinned back. She looked as good as she had the last time I'd seen her, almost two years ago. She had kept her five-foot seven figure in good trim. Her blonde hair was cut shorter than the last time I'd seen her and styled a bit around the ends. About my age, Karyn also has a sprinkling of gray. While it was still there, I didn't see any more than the time before.

She was decked out in khaki slacks, blue short-sleeve polo shirt, and navy-blue sneakers.

A busy woman, at her full-time job she's a vice president for a public relations firm in Kansas City, Missouri. On the side, she's heavily involved in an advocacy group that works to free wrongfully-incarcerated people.

Despite her casual clothing, I had a feeling she wasn't in Providence for a vacation.

"I'm doing okay, Sam. How about you?"

I grabbed a sweat towel from the floor and mopped my face. "Good enough to do ten pullups nonstop."

"You were kind of grunting on those last two," Karyn pointed out.

"Not grunts," I said. "Manly whuffs of accomplishment."

"Got a little time to talk?" she asked.

"Of course. You in any trouble?"

Karyn shook her head as a look flickered in her green eyes. "I'm fine, but a friend of mine isn't."

I cocked an eyebrow at her. "An Amendment V friend?"

"No." Karyn shook her head. "A friend friend. She really needs help, Sam."

"Cops are generally good at helping people out," I said.

Karyn shook her head again. "Not with this kind of trouble. She needs real help, Sam."

I threw the sweat towel around my neck and, although she knew the way from previous times, ushered Karyn to my office. "After you," I said.

CHAPTER TWO

"Her name's Lorie Jones," Karyn said a couple of minutes later.

We'd made ourselves comfortable, and I'd poured coffee for both of us. As I handed her a cup, I'd taken a minute to look Karyn over a little more closely.

She was a vice president at Lewis and Cochran, a public relations firm on the Missouri side of the Kansas City metro area. She also did quite a bit of work on the side for Amendment V, one of several charitable projects that had sprung up in the last couple of decades devoted to providing legal representation for people convicted of major crimes.

When she and I had first met, Amendment V had secured the release of a woman who'd unjustly spent twenty years in prison for the murder of her husband.

I wasn't exactly sure of Karyn's age though she looked to be somewhere around her mid-forties. Up close, I saw a couple of crinkle lines around the eyes I'd never noticed before.

While I took a long sip of my cup, Karyn looked around the office. She'd seen it before, but there was something new since her last visit. I watched her focus on the corner of my desk, where I had an old-fashioned framed picture of Talia Sanderson.

"New friend?" she asked, her head inclined towards the picture.

"Bit more than a friend," I said.

Karyn nodded. "Good for you, Sam."

"So," I asked, "who and what is a Lorie Jones?"

Karyn grinned, though I didn't see a lot of humor in the gesture. "She's a department director at my firm."

"The PR firm," I clarified.

"Yes. Lewis and Cochran."

"Okay." I nodded, almost like a priest eliciting an awkward confession.

"She's going through a divorce," Karyn continued.

I shook my head. "I don't do divorce cases if I can avoid it."

Now it was her turn to shake. "No, Sam. Lorie lives in Overland Park, not here. Though you're half right."

"She hired a detective to help her out?" I asked.

"Correct. Her husband's an accountant for a firm in Kansas City. She felt she needed a little extra oomph when they go into court."

"He must be one hell of an accountant," I said.

"Why so?"

"Because your standard middle-management, paper pusher type usually can't afford to live in Overland Park."

Karyn grimaced at that. "Don't believe everything you hear. The whole town isn't all millionaires and above. There's actually quite a few middle-class people there. However, while I'm not really privy to it, I believe one of the problems in their marriage was a lack of financial restraint."

"That's the issue in a lot of marriages," I said. "Still, I don't see a problem here. If your friend's got it all set out there, what do you need with me?"

Karyn sat a little straighter. "When Lorie decided she needed some backup, she asked around and eventually ended up at Hobart and Howard."

Now I sat up. "Damn, PR people must make more than I thought."

"I assume you've heard of them."

"Karyn," I said, "anyone in my business within three or four states has heard of Hobart. Your friend Lorie's in good hands."

"You'd think so, wouldn't you?"

I frowned. "Didn't they take her on?"

"They did. Actually hooked her up with one of their top people, an executive vice president or something, and it was off to the races."

My frown probably deepened. "You sure about that? As far as I know, at large, major investigative firms, the executives tend not to do field work. They've kind of worked themselves beyond that."

Karyn tapped her fingernails on her coffee cup for a moment. "I never even thought of that, but it makes sense. Hobart and Howard have, what, a couple of hundred people on their staff?"

I shrugged. "I've obviously never dealt with them, though my guess would be more like three hundred or more. They'd need a couple hundred just to handle their business in KC, and they work in all the surrounding states."

"Maybe this person assigned to her likes to keep his hand in."

"You mean like a vice president in a PR firm still writing up press releases every now and then?" I asked.

"I guess," Karyn said, "though personally I haven't written a press release in twenty years."

"You may be right. Maybe the guy likes to keep in shape for the field. I still don't see what the problem is."

Karyn hesitated, and her face kind of twisted in confusion. "What I'm about to say, Sam, falls under the heading of speculation, maybe even innuendo. Don't bother asking me for firm specifics because I can't give any. Okay?"

"Give it to me however you want, Karyn."

"Okay, then." She took a deep breath, held it for a second, then started up again. "On the professional side, Hobart and Howard's operative did fine by Lorie. It took about three weeks before he came up with strong indications that Brian, that's her husband, was indeed having an affair, and another week before he came up with some sort of hard evidence."

"Okay." I wondered if I looked as confused as I felt.

"And one week after they took her on as a client, during her second meeting with the operative, the man asked her out."

I felt a little tightness in my chest. "Do Lorie and, Brian is it, have any kids?"

Karyn gave me a look. "Does that matter?"

"Just trying to get the full lay of the land."

Karyn nodded. "Sorry, you're right. No, they've been married eight years, and about four years ago Lorie had a miscarriage. They, she, haven't really tried since then."

"Okay. When this operative—what's his name by the way?"

"Jacobson. Tom Jacobson. You know him?"

I smiled at her. "Karyn, asking me if I know someone from Hobart is like asking the guy who runs the hamburger shack down on the corner if he knows the chairman of Burger King."

"Sorry. Did I touch a nerve?"

"Not that I'm aware of. When Jacobson asked her out, was there any chance Lorie was confused in some way?"

Karyn gave me a frown, actually more of a scowl. "What's that supposed to mean?"

I held up my hands, palms out. "Come on. You and I are old enough to know several people who've gone through divorces. You're describing a time when both parties' emotions are running wild, and perceptions aren't always at their sharpest."

Karyn sighed and slumped back in her chair. "Sorry. You're right. Either way, it doesn't matter because when Jacobson asked her out, or when Lorie thought he asked her out, she gave him a clear no."

My chest tightened a little more. "Not sure I like where this is going. At the very least, there's about a zillion professional ethics being violated. What happened then?"

"According to Lorie, Jacobson graciously accepted her answer and went about his job, as professional as could be. Within a few more weeks, he finished processing the evidence he'd found, met with her and another of the firm's top people, turnkeyed everything over, and they handed her a final bill."

"Sounds normal enough," I said, "so how's that result in you driving over a hundred miles to see little old me?"

Karyn's face set, almost like granite, and I was pretty sure I knew the answer even before she replied.

"Because," she said, "turns out Jacobson may not have taken her rejection as easily as he let on."

CHAPTER THREE

"What do you mean, didn't take it easily?" I asked. Karyn, usually fairly self-assured, fidgeted.

I made a logical leap.

"He's been stalking her?" I asked.

Karyn shook her head, a notch forming between her eyes. "Not exactly."

"Then what exactly has he been doing?" I asked.

"As far as Lorie can pin down and show any evidence of, nothing."

"Karyn—" I began.

"One day her banking accounts were suddenly emptied of any money for about twenty-four hours. The next day, mysteriously, all her funds reappeared."

"Everything's electronic these days, and stuff like that happens from time to time," I pointed out. "A friend of mine had to go around and around last month with his investment company, who suddenly could find no trace of an account he's had for going on twenty-five years. A couple of hours later, there it suddenly was."

"But all her money gone at once?" Karyn asked.

"Granted that's a bit extreme. What did the bank say?"

Karyn's frown deepened. "Tell you what, Sam. I'll come back to that," she said.

"Okay."

She took a long drink of her coffee. "A few days after the bank thing, her mail, what little a youngster like her actually has delivered these days, was stopped for over a week."

"Post office screwup?" I suggested.

"When she went down to see what the problem was, they pulled up on their screen the form she had filled out online authorizing her mail stoppage."

"Which I'm assuming she claims she didn't fill out."

Karyn glanced at me kind of sharply. I guessed she objected to me using the word "claim."

"Right," she said. "She never filled out a stoppage form."

"She get it going again?" I asked.

"She did, but that's not the point. What I mean is—"

"I get the point, Karyn. Anything else?"

She nodded. "You bet. The worst. A couple of days after the mail thing, she got home, unlocked her door, went to turn the alarm off, and her security code wouldn't work. In no time at all, she was being battered by that ear-splitting wail everyone hates."

"It's not a silent alarm?"

Karyn shook her head. "The house was older when they bought it, and the alarm already there. She and Brian decided to go ahead and keep it, since it was already all installed, and they hooked up with the company. Everything was fine until that day, and her code didn't work."

"How'd she get it to stop?" I asked.

Karyn's eyes hooded over, and a cold knot formed down in my belly. "It just happened that Tom Jacobson pulled up in her driveway."

"Just happened, huh?"

"Yep. According to Lorie, he said he was passing by and heard the noise, and offered to take a look at the control panel."

Okay, now we were edging into creepazoid territory. "She let him in?"

Karyn shrugged. "She didn't really see she had a choice. It was early evening; her alarm was sounding across the whole neighborhood; and she expected the cops to come rolling up any moment loaded for bear."

The two of us stared at each other for a moment, and I almost didn't want to ask.

"Jacobson get it turned off?"

"What do you think?" From anyone less classy than Karyn, the question would have sounded almost like a sneer.

"He was a knight to the rescue," I said.

"I'm not much of a history buff, Quinton. Did the old-time knights first sic the dragon on the maiden before they rescued her?"

I leaned back in my chair and clasped my hands behind my head. "You seem to be implying in a roundabout way that Mrs. Jones thinks Jacobson is behind this spate of problems she's been having."

"You think it's a coincidence he just happened to be driving down her street at the same time she got home and her alarm went wonky?"

"In Providence I could kind of see it as possible," I said. "Not so much in an area the size of KC."

"How about the fact that after he got things quieted down, our helpful private investigator asked her out again?"

I leaned forward, sitting up straight and placing my feet firmly on the floor. "That for sure?"

"Depends," Karyn said, "on if you see any ambiguity in the phrase, 'hey, want to have dinner tomorrow night?'"

I tapped my fingers together for a few minutes as I thought. "Hobart's a pretty well-respected firm," I finally said.

"Of course, they are. That's why I suggested Lorie go there when she decided she needed some ammo for her divorce."

I nodded, hoping I looked like a wise man. "Then you're feeling a little bad about all this, even though you did nothing to feel guilty about?"

"Shouldn't I feel something? I may have had a part in inviting a snake into her life," Karyn said.

"Did she turn him down the second time?" I asked.

"You'd better believe it. Thanked him for his help and somehow managed to scoot him out the door."

"He didn't get physical?"

"Not at all. In fact, from Lorie's description, the guy's a little—uh—I guess you'd say wimpy."

I raised my eyebrows at that. "More brain than brawn?"

"More something than brawn, at least to hear Lorie tell it. Doesn't make sense, does it?"

"How so?"

"Well," Karyn stammered for a moment, "your occupation is rather physical, isn't it? I mean, look at all the scrapes you've been involved in."

"True, but I'm something of a throwback. More and more, it's the brainy guys, and gals, who manage to do the job pretty damned good. And an outfit like Hobart and Howard doesn't usually involve themselves in anything that would result in fistfights or gun battles. That kind of stuff plays hell with workman's comp rates."

"If you say so," Karyn said. "At any rate, when Lorie turned him down the second time, he kind of sulked a bit and asked her if she was sure she wasn't making a mistake."

"Depending on his tone of voice," I said, "there could be a little implication there."

Karyn nodded. "His meaning was clear, and it shook her."

"And this was?" I asked.

"Five days ago."

"She go to the police?" I asked.

"After the last incident, of course."

"And?"

"And that's when she got really freaked," Karyn said. "According to the cops, they can't do anything because there's no real evidence of any kind of harassment. Each individual thing can be explained away."

I thought about it for a minute. "Does kind of make sense. Every one of those could be a screwball type of incident."

"Except for the Jacobson guy showing up at the right place, right time," Karyn pointed out.

"True. Even that's still not enough for the cops to go on."

"They told Lorie they'd look into it . . ." Her voice trailed off.

"So the third incident was last week," I said. "Anything more since then?"

"Not until last night," Karyn said.

That knot in my stomach had grown, and I didn't want to ask the obvious question. "What happened last night?"

Karyn took a deep breath. "Lorie came home from work to find her front door open."

"Okay."

"And on the dining room table, a note had been left for her."

"Which said?"

Karyn looked me straight in the eye. "It said, 'You ready to change your mind yet?'"

CHAPTER FOUR

Karyn and I met up with Lorie Jones about twenty minutes later. Though both women lived in KC, they'd traveled together to Providence, a distance of about a hundred and twenty miles. According to Karyn, when Lorie had unloaded on her about her recent troubles, Karyn had said she had just the person to help her out.

Which would be little ole' me.

They'd taken two rooms at one of our Holiday Inns, located over on the east side of town, and as we entered the lobby and headed toward the elevators, I asked Karyn about that.

"I told her I was going to reach out to you, and she wanted to come along. I don't think she feels safe at home."

"If what she claims is true, can't blame her," I said, "but why not just make a phone call?"

As she punched the elevator button, I could see Karyn tense up.

"Sam, that's the second time you've used the word 'claim' regarding Lorie's story. Why's that"

The doors opened, and we walked in. Karyn pushed the button for the third floor, but as soon as the doors closed, I pressed the Hold button.

I turned to face her. "It's called healthy skepticism. I've learned that, in my line of work, most people lie to some degree or the other. And you said yourself, there's no hard evidence of this beyond Lorie's word. I'm not leaning one way or the other, merely keeping my options open. If she's actually in trouble, from either this Jacobson character or someone else, I'll do what I can. But I'm not in the habit of driving halfway across the state to indulge someone's fantasies."

Maybe saying "fantasies" was a bit over the line, judging from how tightly Karyn compressed her lips, plus the narrowing of her eyes.

"Everybody lies to some degree? Even your clients?"

I pushed the Hold button again, and the car moved on up. "In certain cases, especially clients."

The doors dinged open, and we walked out. Lorie Jones's room was about fifty feet from the elevators, and I'd raised my hand to knock, but hadn't actually made contact with the door, before it swung open.

The woman standing there looked somewhere in her mid-thirties, rather pretty, if not strikingly beautiful, her blonde hair hung down to her shoulders. She had blue eyes and, even at her age, faint frown lines forming parentheses around the mouth and wrinkles under the eyes that shouldn't have been there yet. There was also a tightness to her face, as if the flesh had pinched in on itself.

On Talia Sanderson, one of the deans at our local university, frown lines are sexy as hell. Yet with this woman who, judging by the bagginess of her jeans and droop of her cotton sweater, seemed to have lost a fair amount of weight in a short time, the lines only came off as tense and irritable.

I'd seen the same appearance on others I'd known, both male and female, going through heavy emotional break ups. In particular, she reminded me of how my ex-wife looked around the time she'd finally had enough of my antics.

Lorie Jones gave me the briefest of glances before looking past me to Karyn. "Is this him?"

Karyn nodded, and Lorie stepped aside to let us into her room.

"Mrs. Jones," I said as I entered, "if you're concerned about being the victim of a harassment campaign, why did you fling your door open so randomly?"

Karyn flashed me another look.

Mr. Small Talk: always try to make them feel comfortable.

Lorie Jones walked over to the small desk in the corner of the room and picked up a half-full glass of some brownish liquid. I thought about making a show of glancing at my watch, then decided not to overdo it.

Plus, since I don't wear a watch, the motion would be rather pointless.

"I heard the elevator stop," she said, looking half at her drink and half out the window, "and glanced through the peephole."

I nodded, though it still seemed a bit off.

Then again, seeing as I've never been the victim of a stalking campaign, who was I to judge?

"Lorie Jones, Sam Quinton," Karyn formally introduced us.

I held out my hand, and Lorie looked at it for a moment before reaching out. She gave me the quickest of shakes, then in almost the same instant retracted her hand. Something must have shown on my face because she shook her head and went over to sit down on the edge of the bed.

Feeling a bit uncomfortable at her obvious discomfort, I looked around the room.

There wasn't much to see. The room held two queen-size beds, along with the standard desk, easy chair, mini fridge, and microwave positioned under the 20-inch TV. One floor lamp was positioned behind the chair, and two nightstands were close to the beds.

Economical—it was not the kind of place where you'd expect to find a PR executive staying.

Then again, divorce often does a job on the finances.

"Sorry," she said, for the first time looking straight at me, "but I'm a little leery around men right now, especially ones who look intimidating like you do."

I really hadn't been going for intimidating . . . cuddly, maybe, but you take what you can get.

I pulled the chair away from the small desk and moved it in Karyn's direction.

"Understandable," I said, "if what Karyn tells me is true."

"What do you mean?" Lorie's voice had a bit of a snap in it.

I held out my hands, palms outward. "No offense meant, Mrs. Jones. I got the basic idea, but I need to hear it from you personally."

She roved her gaze up and down me, her eyes narrowed into slits. "Karyn says you're a private detective."

"That's right."

"The last detective I hired is causing me some problems."

"So I hear," I said. "Why don't you tell me about it?"

She gave a quick glance in Karyn's direction. "Didn't she explain it to you?"

"She did," I repeated, "but I want to hear it from you as well."

Lorie looked down and rubbed her hands along her thighs. "She says you may be able to help me."

I was beginning to feel a little light-headed from all this running in place with no progress. "I may be able to, Mrs. Jones. But I need to know exactly what is going on. Far as that goes," now I looked over at Karyn, "there must be something Miss Roberts didn't tell me that would explain why the two of you are hiding out in a hotel room in Providence instead of taking all of this to the KC cops."

Now it was Karyn's turn to look away while Lorie finally faced me square on. I felt a lump in my gut as things began clicking into place.

"Did Jacobson get physical with you, Mrs. Jones?"

"Not exactly, though the last time we spoke he made it clear that he was done 'playing games' as he said."

"That was the night when he helped turn off your alarm?" Karyn hadn't mentioned that part to me.

"That's right."

"But when the cops came, the night of the alarm, they checked it out and found nothing?"

Her face twisted into something rather foreign for a second. "No trace of anything 'irregular' they called it. No evidence of anything happening."

"Anything on your end to give them?" I asked.

Lorie started to shake her head, then paused. "One of my neighbors was there the night the alarm went off."

"She heard it?"

Lorie Jones nodded, a bit too vigorously, I thought. "She was with me outside when he pulled up and offered to help."

"She say or do anything at the time?" I asked.

Her shoulders slumped even lower, something I hadn't thought possible. "I don't remember. I do know the cops talked to her but didn't do anything after that."

"And you think he also broke into your home and left the note behind?"

Lorie Jones shrugged, though the move had little energy behind it. "Who else?"

"And you didn't call the cops then?"

"Why? To give them a chance to tell me again there was nothing for them to do?"

"You still have the note?" I asked.

Lorie shook her head. "It's missing."

"Come again?"

"I put it aside, intending to bring it to show you today, even though there's nothing special about it."

"What do you mean nothing special?"

"I mean it was just printed off from a computer, all caps. Still, I don't know a whole lot about this stuff, so I set it aside on my coffee table to bring to show you today."

"And?"

"And when I got up this morning to get ready to go, it was gone."

"Hear anything last night?" I asked.

"Nothing."

"Nothing on your house alarm." Got to do the dance even though you know how it turns out.

"No indication anyone had been in my house," she said.

"Too bad," I said. "If you still had it, it could be evidence of some sort."

"The way the cops have acted, they'd probably say I printed it out myself."

That was a possibility, though one I'd hoped hadn't occurred to her.

"You're saying they blew the whole thing off," I said.

"Sam," Karyn spoke up, "you kind of plowed your own course. Tell me, though, what's the traditional way someone gets into working as a private investigator?"

That spot in my gut hardened even more. "The guy's a former cop?"

Lorie Jones nodded, and for the first time her eyes showed a little fire. "A friend of one of the secretaries at work is on the force. She asked around about him."

"And?"

"He was a cop in KC for over a decade," Lorie said.

I looked at Karyn, who nodded in agreement. "Ten years," she said. "Can you imagine, in a town that size, how many contacts he has squirreled away?"

"That complicates things a bit," I said.

CHAPTER FIVE

"Hobart and Howard?" Josh Nichols said the next morning. "What's up, Blondie? You thinking of opening a franchise or something?"

Nichols is a detective sergeant on the Providence force, second in command of the detectives' section. He and I go a ways back. All the way, in fact, to the old days in St. Louis, when I was one of the stars of the Midwest Wrestling League and he was a young patrolman, supplementing his public salary by doing security work at MWL events.

Eventually, we both found our way back to Providence, and since he and I have some history, he's one of the few people I don't growl at when he calls me Blondie, a shortened form of my old wrestling name, The Blond Bomber.

"Not looking for a franchise," I said. "Just interested in any stray bits of information."

We were in the squad room at the main Providence station, Nichols sitting behind his desk, because of his position in the squad located right next to the lieutenant's closed-off office, scanning his computer for overnight reports and me sitting in a chair to the side. As I answered, he looked up from his monitor.

"Information? You mean like looking into them for a client?"

"Something like that."

Nichols whistled, turned away from his computer monitor to face me head on.

"Let me get this straight," he said, "you're investigating an outfit like Hobart and Howard?"

"Zipped lips for a while?" I asked.

"This have anything to do with anything going on around here?"

"Not as far as I know."

"Okay, then," Nichols said, "consider the lips duly zipped."

"I'm not looking into the firm," I said, "but into one of their people. All purely speculative at the moment."

"I'm not so sure John Howard will see that as much of a distinction."

Now it was my turn to be surprised. "You know him?"

Nichols leaned back in his chair. "I met him once, back when I was still working in St. Louis. The department sent me to a conference in KC, and he was one of the speakers. I forget what his topic was. He stayed around afterwards for anyone who wanted an informal Q&A. We ended up talking for quite a while."

I narrowed my eyes. Nichols is in his mid-thirties, and he'd been a detective in Providence for some time now, long enough to climb up the ranks to second in command.

"You were still in uniform back then?" I asked.

Nichols nodded.

"Means this must have been some time ago," I said.

"I'd say so. Don't remember the exact year, but I was pretty much a kid still."

"And John Howard was already a big name in investigative circles."

Nichols nodded. "He's actually second generation, I think. Maybe third. Someone in his family started the agency some ways back."

"Is Howard still alive and kicking?" I asked.

Nichols narrowed his eyes at me for a moment before answering. "I guess so. Honestly, though, I don't really know all that much about the company. It's not like out here in the sticks we ever have much to do with anyone from the big city."

I thought for a moment as I drummed my fingers on the arm of my chair. "Could you sniff around a bit for me?" I finally asked.

Nichols's eyes narrowed even more, till they were barely slits in his face. "What exactly are you after, Blondie? Anything that can throw back in our faces?"

"Josh, I only want to know if there's any sort of scandal or bad news associated with the firm. If there's not, fine. If there is, I'd appreciate it if you could sniff it out for me."

"If you're looking for public information, you could find out as easy as I could."

"True. Thing is, though, I'm interested in things not so public. Don't you know some people on the KC force?"

Nichols leaned back in his chair, his gaze fixed on me. "I do. As well as some in Kansas City, Kansas and Overland Park. Far as that goes, Lieutenant Santiago probably has some connections with the brass out there. So what?"

I threw on one of my patented smiles, the kind I used to use back in my wrestling days with kids coming up to the merch table for an autograph. "So how about in the possible interest of friendship you ask a few questions here and there?"

"Friendship?" Nichols snorted. "Between who and whom?"

"Come on, Josh."

"Come on nothing, Sam. If you hadn't noticed," he made a sweeping gesture with his arm which covered his entire desk, "I've got more than enough of my own work to do without taking time out to handle your stray jobs. And as far as the lieutenant goes, you're even less popular with him than you are with me."

I couldn't help but cock a grin, remembering a favor I'd done the lieutenant a while back. "You sure about that?"

Nichols grimaced. "Okay, yeah, he owes you for the whole thing with the Mosby case. Even so, I seriously doubt that's going to cut it with him when you start asking his detectives to do your legwork for you."

"What do you mean start?" I said. "It's not like this is the first favor I've asked you for."

"True." Nichols's grimace became more severe. "But it's the first time you've happened to come around since the new city budget got passed. In case you haven't noticed, buddy, tax revenues are down quite a bit the last year or so."

"Couldn't tell it by me," I said. "My taxes are higher than ever. What say I get some kind of service for the extra I'm paying?"

Nichols slumped back in his chair, as I'd known he eventually would. "Christ. At the very least, how about giving me some parameters. What exactly is it you're looking for?"

I did my best to hide my grin. "Two areas. Anything kind of shady that has to do with the company itself that wouldn't be known to the general public."

"Uh huh. Kind of obvious. What else?"

"Guy name of Tom Jacobson."

"What about him?"

"He's an operative of theirs. Was a cop for quite a while before that."

Nichols sat up straight and fixed me with a somewhat evil eye. "Hold on there, Blondie. Are you telling me you want me to investigate a fellow cop?"

"Former cop," I said. "And not investigate him. Only inquire."

"Uh huh. And what do you think's going to happen as soon as I go about doing all of this inquiring?"

"Well," I said, "offhand I'd say the guy will probably get a little upset, at least if he finds out about it."

"How long was he a cop?" Nichols asked.

"From what I gather, ten years, give or take."

"What rank did he get to?"

"I don't know. Only that he quit whatever force he was working on and moved on to the private sector."

Nichols picked up a pencil and flipped it back and forth a couple of times. "Happens all the time, buddy. Where do you think most of you types come from?"

"I know," I said. "But something feels off about it."

"Off how?"

"Well, according to my information, he only joined Howard's company a couple of years ago, yet he's already one of their top people."

Nichols tapped the pencil on his desk. "So?"

"So how'd he get so high so quick? That's one question. The

other is, what's an executive type doing going out on fieldwork, especially something as mundane as a divorce case?"

Nichols dropped the pencil, interlaced his fingers, and cracked his knuckles. "Hell, Blondie, maybe they've got somebody out sick, or having to testify in court, or maybe he just needed some exercise."

"Maybe," I said, "but I'd like to be able to dot those particular i's if I could."

"You mean you want me to dot them for you?"

I grinned. "I just want to know a little bit about the guy in case I have to take him on."

Nichols glanced over his shoulder to the lieutenant's closed office. "This may take quite a few favors being called in, Sam. You sure it's worth all that?"

I thought back to the talk I'd had earlier with Lorie Jones and the anxiety and nervousness I'd seen in her eyes and mannerisms. Of course, I had my doubts that Tom Jacobson, or Hobart and Howard in general, had anything to do with the nuttiness that had descended on her life. For all I knew, her soon-to-be-ex-husband could have very well instigated it.

But something had spooked the woman, spooked her bad, and whatever it was had to be rooted out.

Plus, Karyn Roberts had vouched for her.

"Yeah, Josh," I said. "I've got a pretty darned good reason."

CHAPTER SIX

"So is Karyn your client?" Talia Sanderson asked me later that evening.

We were sitting at my dining room table, a mess of takeout from El Pollo Isquierdo spread in front of us. The restaurant, one of innumerable Mexican restaurants dotting the Providence landscape like toadstools after a spring rain, ranked as Talia's favorite. I thought it was okay, though I had others I liked better.

I tried once to turn her off the place by pointing out the name meant, in English, The Left Chicken, but if anything my little attempt backfired and she advocated for Isquierdo more vehemently than before.

Good thing I'm so tough and manly, or some of my old buddies from my St. Louis wrestling days would tag me as being whipped.

"No," I said, cutting a quesadilla in half and sliding one portion onto Talia's plate, "Mrs. Jones is my client. Karyn came along for the ride, so to speak."

"She does this thing a lot, doesn't she?" Talia asked.

I took a moment and stared at her. Like me, she's edging pretty close to fifty. Unlike me, she carries it off a hell of a lot better. Like Karyn, she's got nice blonde hair which has only a little gray in it and bright green eyes. And I have it on first-hand observation she keeps herself in great shape.

"What sort of thing?" I said before taking a bite from my portion of the quesadilla.

"Seeking out wayward causes."

I grinned as I finished chewing. "Don't know how wayward. You have to admit Amendment V does some good work."

Talia blushed and looked down at her plate. "Okay, I'm being a little bitchy. She referred this Lorie Jones woman to you, right?"

"Uh huh." I reached over to spear a chicken enchilada. "The lady's in some kind of trouble and needs some help. My kind of help."

"But also the kind of help a lot of other people can provide. I mean, KC must be crawling with detectives, right? Why come all the way out here?"

"Two reasons," I said, "one you can probably guess."

"You mean that you and Karyn Roberts have a little history, and she trusts your professionalism?"

"That's one. Though I'm wondering if that 'history' comment is more antagonism."

She sighed and pushed her food away.

"Talia—"

"I'm sorry, Sam. I don't quite get all of this. You've talked about Karyn before. The two of you met on a case once."

"Right. Before I met you."

"And there wasn't anything between you, then or after."

I shook my head. "Maybe a lingering glance or two, nothing more. It was a fairly intense time."

"This was the Hampton deal, right?"

"Uh huh. After the case was basically over, Karyn spent a few weeks commuting back and forth, helping the lawyers sew up all the loose ends."

"Bernie was in on that one too, right?" Bernie Lyman, my attorney, sometimes helps to throw work my way.

"Right."

"And you and Karyn?"

I shrugged. "Had dinner a couple of times, took in a few movies on nights when, for some reason, she had to stay over. Not much more than that."

"Okay, there's nothing solid between the two of you except she values your professionalism. Again, though, if this Lorie woman needs to hire someone, why not the scads of detectives back home?"

"According to her, she already did that once," I said, "and that's what's put her in a jam."

"This Jacobson fellow, the one she says is stalking her."

I scooped a little pollo con queso onto my plate, then held the rest up as an offering to her. Talia smiled weakly and took it.

"Right," I said. "Jacobson, if he is the one harassing Lorie, works for one of the premiere investigative agencies in the state. Hell, maybe in the whole the country. And from what I gather, he doesn't just work there but is one of the top executives. Take it all together, and it's probably enough to scare off a lot of local operatives."

Talia's smile broadened a bit. I wasn't sure if it was the chicken in cheese sauce or my natural appeal finally winning her over. "And you wouldn't be scared off so easily, huh?" she asked.

"I'm not a local operative, at least not too local. Plus, I'm a small enough fish, especially coming in from out of town, I may be able to fly under the radar for a while."

"And while you're doing everything you can to help your client, how safe is she?"

"I suggested she stay at her hotel here until I got something nailed down one way or the other."

"And?" Talia asked.

"And she wasn't too thrilled with that idea. I then suggested she get a hotel room back home, or stay with a friend, anything to keep from being around her house. She turned that down as well. Said she had a home and she wasn't going to be run out of it"

"But if this man isn't physically dangerous . . ."

"So far," I said. "He hasn't gotten violent to date. Doesn't mean he won't escalate."

"From what I understand, these sorts of people often do."

"True," I said, "but there's a lot about this that feels a little different. Doesn't mean that, if he feels backed into a corner, he won't turn violent at some point."

"Backed into a corner such as finding out she's hired someone else to help her out?" Talia asked.

"Yeah, like that."

"And did you point this out to her?"

"I did."

"What was her response?"

I looked down at my plate for a minute. "Like I said, she doesn't want to be run out of her home."

Talia looked as close to shocked as I've ever seen her. "By her own admission, she believes this man is stalking her, can somehow come and go as he pleases in her place, and can exert almost total control over her life, and she's staying in her house?"

"That's about it," I said. "I did my best to talk her out of it, but she was adamant. Can't really figure it."

"I think I can," Talia said.

"Oh?"

"You've been divorced, right?" Because Talia knew this for a fact, I figured she was setting up some sort of theory, so I let it go.

"Once. A long, long time ago."

"How did you handle it?" she asked.

"Handle what?"

"The pain. The feeling of loss."

"Mainly, I hit the guys in the ring a little harder. Got to a point for a while there where hardly anyone wanted to perform with me."

Talia nodded. "You went outside, in a way. Focused on your physicality instead of your heart."

"I also drank more than I should have during that time."

Talia shook her head. "Don't screw up my perfect argument here, bucko. You know how we academics hate that. The point is you had another angle, another area of your life, that you could latch on to until things got better for you."

"The point?"

She grinned at me. "Oh, big boy, you can be kind of slow sometimes. You were already independent, more or less. Sounds like your Mrs. Jones isn't so much."

"You're saying her independence is what she's latching on to. And if it's the main thing she's got . . ."

"Then she'll be damned if she'll let anyone take it away from her."

By silent assent, we both resumed eating for a few minutes. "I guess that explains it," I said, "but I didn't think psychology was your field."

"It's not. Being a woman in the modern world is."

"Still, not going to make my job any easier if she's insisting on being easy to find. I can't bodyguard and detect at the same time."

"Of course, you can't." Talia nibbled a bit of rice. "What will your first step be?"

"Simple, find out whether or not what she says is happening actually is."

Talia gave a little jerk. "Wait a minute. Let me get this straight. Don't you believe her?"

I took a breath, hoping Talia would understand better than Karyn had. "Let's just say this wouldn't be the first time someone going through a bad time has invented a scene that makes them the victim."

"In other words," Talia said, "you don't believe her."

I shook my head. "It's not a matter of believing or not. It's a matter of covering all the ground, making sure there aren't any landmines waiting for me out there."

"Why would she not be truthful about this? What's in it for her?"

"A number of possible things," I said. "Could be looking for extra sympathy, could be some sort of ploy in the legal proceedings, could be looking down the line to sue the detective firm."

Talia mused for a moment. "That's extremely cynical," she said.

"I'm not saying it's true, or even likely. Most reports of stalking and such turn out to be true, but it is something I have to check into before I start bulling around on foreign turf."

"Let's say you do determine she's on the level," Talia said. "What then?"

"I figure after a couple of preliminary moves, getting the lay of the land so to speak, I'll probably pop in and talk to Jacobson's employer."

Talia's eyes widened, and for a second there I thought she was going to choke. "One more time, please. You're coming in from outside so you can dig around under the radar."

"Correct."

"And one of the first things you're going to do is go to the man's place of employment and talk to his boss?"

"Right again."

"Sam," a sudden, slightly-condescending tone entered her voice, "are you sure you know what under the radar means?"

"Pretty sure. What do you think of my plan?"

My lady put her fork down, steepled her hands together, and gave me a searching look. "Actually, I'm starting to think that back in your wrestling days you may have been dumped on your head a few too many times."

CHAPTER SEVEN

Duke Prowder was the old-time St. Louis detective who'd given me my start in the business. When I met him, I was an ex-jock at the end of the line, having recently blown out the same knee for the third time. That pretty much ended my time in the pro wrestling ring, and while I'd worked briefly for one of the major national promotions, most of my career had been spent as a fairly big fish in a small local pond.

All of which left me approaching middle age with a bum knee and no immediate prospects for employment. My wife had also recently left me, so I was feeling pretty much peachy all the way around.

The one thing I did have, in my grizzled late thirties, was a still-fearsome physical appearance. I picked up some gigs here and there, bouncing in various bars and nightclubs, and at one of those jobs caught Duke's attention. He came up to me and offered to buy a beer, which I had to decline because I was on the clock. We talked a bit, and somehow or other before too long I found myself working as a part-time operative for an actual, real-life private eye.

I learned the craft from a master, picked up more than enough investigatory hours to qualify for a state license, and even had the required number of people willing to vouch for me on my application.

About the same time, an old friend from my wrestling days had decided to retire and sell a gym he'd been running in Providence, which meant I went from shortly before having no career prospects to owning two businesses.

One item Duke had given me a few years back was a genuine, actual old little black book filled with contact info he'd acquired over his decades as a PI. Most of the names, numbers, and addresses the book contained were from the eastern side of the state, of course, though quite a few of them extended across to the western edge of Missouri and into Illinois and Kansas as well.

The night before, I'd sat down for a couple of hours with Duke's black book and my laptop, and after a quick phone call to Josh Nichols, who basically confirmed some of what I'd already found out, I woke up refreshed and ready to dig into the Lorie Jones matter. I put on my least faded pair of Lee jeans and white polo shirt and grabbed a lightweight gray sport coat in case I had to dress up anywhere.

The night before, I'd packed a small suitcase with enough essentials to get me by a few days without driving back and forth. Right before nodding off, I'd gone online and booked a room at a Hampton Inn in downtown Kansas City, Missouri.

I grabbed the suitcase, which also held equipment somewhat necessary to my trade, and headed out.

I stopped by a little café on the northern edge of downtown, had a sausage and cheese omelette with extra toast and three cups of coffee, and by nine o'clock was back in my cashmere pearl Jeep Cherokee and headed west.

The drive from Providence to Kansas City is a straight shot, right across I-70 you go. When you actually arrive is a little harder to pin down.

I-70, at least the part I'm most familiar with, could really use some work. It's four-lane across the entire state. Around midnight on a Sunday night, returning home from catching a ball game say, that's no problem. But get more than four vehicles on the road, and make at least one of them a tractor trailer, and time almost comes to a stop.

It amazes me how few people understand the concept of passing, rather than dawdling, in the inside lane. Add a couple of trucks side by side that simultaneously decide to go about fifteen miles under the speed limit, and what the Eisenhower presidency considered their crowning achievement can result in gnashing teeth and clenching jaws.

At least it's a straight-line drive, no mountains to wend through or anything, about the only geographical interest on the way being the Missouri River winding its way just to the west of town. Once you've passed the river, it's a direct shot to KC with not much to see except for convenience stores, billboards, a scattering of outlet malls, and the occasional road construction crew.

At least this time of year the trees that mass up and down the highway, some growing on small cliffs that crowd against the road, make the drive fairly pleasant.

To folks in most of the country, "Kansas City" means a city located in Missouri, butting right up against the Kansas border. In truth, though, KC is a fairly sprawling metropolitan area, covering parts of both states. While the city itself has around half a million residents, the entire metro area is home to well over two million people and sprawls across fourteen counties. The metro contains, of course, tons of businesses, hospitals, higher educational institutions, museums, and on and on.

So it's a little difficult, despite all the various exit signs that pop up on the interstate, to know when you've actually arrived at KC itself. At the moment, though, even if I were a stranger to the area, I didn't have to worry about that, seeing as my first stop of the morning was over on the Kansas side of the sprawl.

I passed a scattering of small towns along the way, zoomed past the turnoff for a military school, and whizzed my way past Arrowhead Stadium where the Chiefs play.

Eventually, I looped off of I-70 and onto I-435, heading southwest. A few minutes of negotiating ordinary mid-morning traffic brought me over the Kansas state line and into the town of Overland Park.

Overland Park is the center of Johnson County, one of the richest counties in the country and far and away the richest in Kansas. As I came off the interstate and began negotiating the ordinary roads and streets, the proportion of high-end cars, Porsches, Mercedes, Lancias, Ferrari's and even a MacLaren or two, gradually increased.

A little bit of juggling with the Cherokee's GPS, and a few misconnections and turnarounds eventually brought me onto Antioch Rd. Another couple of blocks, and I pulled up a block and a half away from the one-story building housing both the Overland Park City offices and the police department.

Making my way inside, I consulted a directory for a moment to get my bearings, then headed to the lower level, eventually finding both the police department itself and the investigation division in particular.

A couple of questions to a few people up front, and in no time I was seated in a black canvas chair in front of the desk of Detective Michael Sloan. Good thing I'm as tall as I am, or I'd have had a hard time making eye contact with the man over the piles of paper barricading his desk.

I thought again, as I often have, that whether in the dingiest of inner cities or the fanciest suburbs, detective squad rooms and the desks that fill them all look the same.

Sloan was pretty much a contradiction of the popular image of a weary, seen-it-all police detective. Instead of the sagging paunch, messed-up and graying hair, and bloodshot eyes, he was short and slim, more trim-waisted than any man I'd seen for a while—with bloodshot eyes and messed-up, graying hair.

He was wearing a light gray shirt with the sleeves rolled up to the elbow and a solid maroon tie with the knot canted to the side.

After a couple of hellos, he asked to look over my investigator's license, which I handed over. He read it for a moment, then handed it back.

"Providence," he said. "A little out of your area, aren't you?"

I gave a mild shrug. "Hundred miles or so. Not all that far."

"Depends on which direction you're looking. May be only a hundred miles away, but it's also across state lines."

"And?" I said, though I could guess where he was going.

"And I'd have to doublecheck the statutes, but I'm pretty sure our two states don't have reciprocity when it comes to paper like yours."

"You don't have to bother checking, Detective. They don't."

The cop settled a little lower in his chair. "In that case, mind telling me what you're doing here?"

I lowered myself a bit too. "I'm looking into something for a friend."

"Doing someone a favor?" Sloan asked.

"Yep."

"Which means you're not taking any pay for this favor?"

"Not for any part of it I do this side of the state line," I said.

Sloan took a random sheet of paper off his desk, wadded it into a ball, and sent it sailing into a trash basket about ten feet away. "Our little patchwork around here does make it difficult in some ways," he said. "Did you know if someone works here but lives in Missouri, even five minutes away, they have to pay income tax to both states?"

"Like I said, favor for a friend and not going to charge for anything I do this side of the line."

Sloan grinned. "But pad the bill for anything that takes place in Missouri?"

I shrugged.

"In that case," Sloan said, "what the hell. What can I do for you?"

"Lorie Jones," I said.

He took about ten seconds to think it over, then nodded. "Young gal, right? Her and her husband going through divorce."

"That's the one."

"Supposedly been having some trouble with some weirdo harassing her."

Although I caught on to the "supposedly," I let it go for the moment. "According to Mrs. Jones, you're the detective of record for the various incidents."

"I am," Sloan said. "Gimme a minute."

Turning his chair a quarter to the right, he bent down and rummaged through a black, waist-high filing cabinet. I waited patiently until he gave a grunt, then straightened back up with a half-inch thick folder in his hand.

"Don't you believe in those things," I said, pointing to the computer on the left side of his desk.

Sloan grinned. "Sometimes, but even at my advanced age, I find actual physical paper's a little more conducive to my memory."

"Me too. What's your paper tell you about Lorie Jones?'

"About what I remembered," Sloan said. "She's been in here a couple of times complaining about various acts of harassment."

"Such as?" I asked.

Sloan peered at me. "You don't know? Thought she was your client?"

"Just want to see if the story you got is the same one she gave me."

Sloan bent even closer over his desk, his eyes so slitted I could barely make out their color. "You have a reason for disbelieving her, Quinton?"

I spread my hands out. "Just being thorough, Detective."

"You know, I could decide you're wasting my time and remind you again that your license doesn't carry any weight this side of the state line."

"You could," I said. "Another option would be to make a phone call to Providence and check me out."

"Anybody in particular I should talk to?" Sloan asked.

"Best bet would be Detective Sgt. Josh Nichols."

Sloan leaned back, a new look in his eye. "I know Nichols. Ran into him a couple of times at technical seminars."

"He ever mention my name?" I asked.

"Nope."

"Only because he doesn't like to name drop famous people."

"Or maybe he's embarrassed to be connected with the likes of you." Sloan's voice was flat and neutral, though I caught a little gleam in his eye.

"Could be that," I conceded.

The cop chuckled and looked down at the file in front of him. "Mrs. Lorie Jones filed three complaints with us. One concerning a screwup at her bank, one about her mail being messed with, and the last one about the alarm in her home being jacked around some."

So Lorie hadn't reported the latest invasion of her home. Maybe she was tired of running to them and getting nothing accomplished, but when I considered the last intrusion and threatening note had happened before Karyn Roberts had suggested coming to me, my stomach fluttered a bit.

"Not exactly the kind of stuff you go to local cops for," I said. "No offense."

Sloan grunted. "None taken, mainly because you're right. And actually, she didn't initially bother us with the first two incidents."

I nodded. "It was the third went over the top for her."

"Yeah." Sloan closed the file. "Which kind of fits because messing around with someone's home is cop business. The rest of it lies with the post office and the banking people."

"So what did you do?"

"About what?" Sloan looked up at me.

I sighed and managed to keep myself from shaking my head. And here we'd been getting along so well. "Did you look into her allegations?"

"These would be the allegations that a respected employee of a respected firm in the city was screwing around with her mind and emotions."

"No," I said, dropping my voice an octave or so. "Those would be the allegations a licensed private investigator, an ex-cop at that, was harassing and intimidating his own client."

"You implying somehow we slow walked this because the guy she mentioned used to be a cop?"

"No. I'm saying that I'm interested in what you did regarding the complaint so I don't have to retrace anyone's steps. At least on this side of the state line."

Sloan nodded and looked back down at his folder. "I guess you could put it that way. I suppose next you're going to ask me about my procedure."

"Seems like a natural question," I said.

Sloan grinned. "Yeah, I guess it does at that. First thing I did was verify the stuff about the mail and the bank."

"It check out?"

The cop glanced up at me. "You didn't check up on your own client's story yet?"

"That's what I'm doing now," I said.

"Uh huh." Sloan shook his head at me. "Get ready for this. No, it didn't check out."

Even though I'd known that already from Lorie's account, it always helps to confirm information. "Come again?"

"No trace of any issues with her bank account, or any of her financial stuff. We had the bank go through all of their records, and don't believe it wasn't a job to convince them to do that, and found nothing."

I thought that one over for a second and didn't really like what I was thinking. "What about the mail?"

"You ever try to get a straight answer out of the postal people, Quinton?"

"Not during this century."

"Well, I have," Sloan said, "more than a couple of times. All things considered, I'd rather deal with the IRS than the USPS."

"Not impressed you're a detective?" I asked.

"Hell, barely impressed I'm a citizen."

"But with your dogged dedication to justice..."

"Yeah, yeah," Sloan interrupted me. "Took forever and a day, or maybe just two days, till I finally got through to the right person."

"Let me guess," I said, "they showed you the documentation she filled out to stop her mail. Documentation she claims she never filled out."

"Gee, mister. You should be a detective."

"Only if the main requirement is basic common sense, plus the ability to see a pattern when it's in front of you. So you have no evidence of anything going on in the first two instances?"

"None at all."

"According to Mrs. Jones, there was a witness to the third incident, the alarm fiasco."

Sloan narrowed his eyes at me. "What's going on here, bubba? If you know the whole story, why are you bothering me?"

I held up my hands in a friendly gesture. "Sorry, Detective. I've learned never to take everything a client tells me at face value."

His eyes narrowed even more. "You think she's lying to you, to us?"

"Not necessarily. But sometimes people don't recall things clearly when their emotions get jacked up. Surely you've had that happen to you."

Sloan grunted and looked back down at the file. "The witness would be one Irene Lacosta, age seventy-seven, who lives next door to the Jones's."

"Talked to her?" I asked.

"Twice. The day of the incident one of the uniforms got her story, and then after I found those other two dead ends I went and spoke to the old gal myself."

I blinked at that, impressed. A lot of cops I know would have shelved the whole thing by then. "What'd she say?"

"She confirmed Mrs. Jones was acting hysterically that day out on her lawn."

"And?"

"And that's all she had to say."

"She hear the alarm going off?" I asked.

"She did. That's what brought her outside."

"And she saw Jacobson pull up outside," I said.

Sloan glanced up at me, an odd look on his face, then glanced down at the file again. "According to her, no," he said.

"Hmm. You sure about that?"

"I interviewed her myself on the second go-round. She was adamant she heard the alarm and everything, but your Mrs. Jones told her everything was fine, and she went back inside."

"I assume when they arrived the uniforms went inside?"

"They did. And found nothing out of order," Sloan said. "And no one else anywhere around, no signs of forced entry, and nothing seemingly disturbed."

"Not to cast any more doubt, Detective. They followed full procedure?"

He closed the folder, set it on his desk, then leaned over, his arms crossed on the desk. "You've got to get the picture, Quinton. The patrol car pulled up to see a hysterical younger woman on the lawn and a frightened older woman trying to calm her down."

"So the hysteria was their primary worry," I said.

The cop nodded. "Correct. By the time they got her taken care of and managed to go inside, everything seemed pretty much normal. Including no alarm shrieking."

"And with no evidence of any intruder and Mrs. Jones obviously knowing the code to her own alarm. . ."

Sloan opened his arms and leaned back in his chair. "You see our problem."

"Yeah, I do."

"Follow it up at all even so?" I asked.

Sloan nodded. "We did the usual checks. Obviously, talked to the husband right off."

"Even though Lorie didn't implicate him in any way?"

"Even though," Sloan said. "SOP in this kind of thing. No matter what the alleged victim claims, you take a look at the spouse. Plus, it caught our attention that he's an accountant. After all, we were looking for someone who could pull fancy moves with bank accounts and computers and such."

I caught the "alleged" marker but once again didn't comment. "Almost made him a natural suspect," I said.

"Almost."

"Dig anything up?"

Sloan gave me a look. "Unhappy marriage, a few hints of flat out discord, and a personal bank balance that could fit in my niece's piggy bank."

"I didn't know kids kept piggy banks anymore," I said.

Sloan shrugged. "Niece's folks are the old-fashioned type when it comes to money."

"In other words, you didn't find anything you didn't expect to find."

"That's about the size of it. Which left us, assuming the woman's on the level, with the man she identified as hanging around her."

"Who happens to be an ex-cop and has impeccable credentials as a private investigator," I said.

"You got it."

"I'm guessing you questioned Jacobson anyway," I suggested.

Sloan leaned back in his chair. "Like I said a minute ago. You know so much about this stuff, you should join a force somewhere."

"Wouldn't know what to do with the pay bump," I said. "What'd he have to say?"

"You know his background? Cop for ten years on the KC force, decided to look for something with better hours, and he's been in the private sector for a couple of years now."

"And from what I hear doing pretty good there," I said.

Sloan grimaced and slumped a bit in his chair. "Way I hear it, he is. Kind of surprising, though."

I pricked up a bit. "You ever run into him? I know it's different forces, but considering the area..."

"Naw," Sloan said. "I heard his name now and then, but I've been in plainclothes for a long time now, and he was patrol when he was on the job."

I sat up straight, feeling my skin prickle. Something about what Sloan had just said bothered me, though at the moment I couldn't figure what. "Even though he's a big shot now," I said, "I still get the feeling you at least talked to him. What'd he say?"

"What would you guess?"

I tapped my fingers on the arm of my chair for a moment while I thought it over. "My guess would be he was completely perplexed by the allegations and had no idea Mrs. Jones bore him any ill will."

"Come to think of it," Sloan said, "maybe you wouldn't work out as a cop. Who the hell says ill will?"

I grinned. "Sue me. I lived for a long time in St. Louis. A lot of funny talkers there."

"I know," Sloan said, "I used to go out that way every now and then. Caught you wrestling a couple of times."

"A fan?" I asked.

The cop shook his head. "Actually, I kind of wondered why it took you so long before you decided to hang it up."

"So not a fan. How about back to business?"

Sloan sighed and leaned back even further in his chair. "What can I tell you, Quinton? The lady says he's bothering her; he says he's not. As of now, there's not a lick of evidence he, or anyone else for that matter, is up to something."

"Could be a string of coincidences," I said, "but could be something else as well."

"Sure. If what she says happened happened, easy to see somebody's fucking around with the woman. Problem is, even if her story's entirely true, last time I checked driving down the road and stopping to offer assistance to someone in distress isn't a crime in our fair town."

If there had been a time to mention the most recent home invasion Lorie had described, now would have been it. But since that story, at least as far as I could tell, was as vague as everything else, I decided not to risk what credibility the cop seemed to be extending me.

"Keeping the file open?" I asked.

"As open as possible. Something else for her to report, I'm ready to sniff it down. Beyond that, what can I say?"

"Got to admit, I'm impressed," I said. "I'd half expected you to just brush this off as a woman going slightly nuts and looking for attention."

Sloan grinned. "Who knows? Maybe thirty years ago I would have, had I been around back then. We try to think we're rather progressive these days, but don't be fooled. When it comes right down to it, we've got to have some evidence of something one way or the other. Otherwise, what's the point?"

Knowing the man was right, I stood up and held out my hand.

"You get anything I can run with, give me a call," Sloan said.

Again, I thought of the note I still hadn't seen that had supposedly vanished from Lorie's house.

"It matter how I get it?"

The cop gave me the kind of stern look he probably reserved

for four-year-olds jaywalking across the street. "Of course, it's got to be legal."

"Of course," I said as I turned to go.

"And if it isn't legal at first, try to make it look it. Okay?"

Without looking back, I waved my hand and headed on out.

CHAPTER EIGHT

My next stop was to see my client. When I left the Overland Park police building, it was getting on to eleven o'clock. No problem, though, as Lorie Jones had assured me she would stay home until things got resolved, somehow or other.

Lorie and I hadn't gotten into the reasons for her divorce, though from the fact she had felt forced to hire a detective I could pretty much guess either money or fooling around, or perhaps both, had something to do with it, but an address in Overland Park, the wealthiest small town in Kansas and one of the richest in the whole country, made me wonder about the couple's finances.

While both she and her husband had white collar jobs, in today's economy that didn't necessarily mean a whole hell of a lot. My best guess was they were both in the "somewhat comfortable as long as nothing goes kablooey" salary range. The fact they didn't have children would help their finances quite a lot.

And even though it's not as if the entire town is loaded solely with the uber rich, living in Overland Park is not in general a low-rent proposition.

When I pulled up at Lorie's address on Newton street, I saw a modest little bungalow, beige in color with a slightly darker tan roof and white shutters tacked to the outside of the windows.

From the street, I could see a detached garage, also beige, on the right side of the house and what looked like a smallish back yard.

No fence anywhere in sight. The Jones's didn't have kids, and with the lack of fencing I could safely assume they didn't have an outside dog for a pet.

The lawn was a little ragged, as if a week or two had passed since it should have been mowed, though with as little moisture as we'd had this spring it could have been longer. This early in the season, the front yard already had a couple of dry, brownish spots scattered here and there.

All in all, it didn't look like much, especially considering it had been the home of two upwardly mobile young professionals with no child expenses, but as they say looks can be deceiving. The way home prices have been the last year or so, even a small house like this could have way overextended the Jones's credit.

I turned off the ignition, climbed out of the Cherokee, and walked up the flagstone walk to the house. The drapes were pulled on the front windows, and the door was down on the garage, preventing me from seeing what kind of car Lorie drove, or even if she was home as she'd said she'd be.

The natural thing would have been to call her to let her know I was coming over, which wouldn't really have told me if she was home at that moment or not; if she had been out when she said she'd stay home, it would have given her time to rush back to greet me as if nothing had happened.

I felt a bit concerned when I realized how little, at the moment, I was taking on face value from my own client.

On the upside, I'd only given the bell one push before the door whipped open.

"Good morning," Lorie said. She was wearing blue jeans with a couple of slits in the knees, a pink polo shirt, and no shoes. Her socks were of a color that almost matched her shirt.

Her face looked as drawn as the day before. Obviously, hiring me had not caused her a huge amount of relief.

She stepped aside and ushered me in. I walked into the type of house I can't get comfortable in. The interior for sure did not match the exterior in any way.

The living room had a black-framed couch with dark leather

cushions and three matched easy chairs opposite it. The blinds on the front windows were some sort of dark wood, and the TV bracketed to the wall over the fireplace looked like a 60-incher. The hardwood floor had a few rich-looking throw rugs scattered on it, and three tall plant stands with some sort of flowering shrubs in them.

Around a bend, I could partially see into the kitchen. Among other things, the kitchen had marble countertops and a crystal chandelier hanging from the ceiling.

I'd seen similar setups before, usually in the homes of younger couples desperate to look successful while skating on the financial edge. It was a showroom, something to impress visitors with rather than a place to live in. Something that, in some hopeful future, they could look back and remark on how nice their first real home was—but it wasn't a place in which to relax and kick off your shoes.

The interesting thing, to me, was the living room looked fully furnished, even down to few bare spots on the walls. A number of different reproductions, mainly of some sorts of modern art; plaques; and bronze adornments decorated the walls.

The house, what I could see of it, looked complete.

Either Lorie had gone on a wild shopping spree or her husband hadn't taken much with him.

Deciding to get to work gathering information right away, I asked her about that.

She shook her head. "No, Brian left most everything behind. After all, the divorce isn't final yet, and from what I gather the place he moved into doesn't have room for much."

She offered me coffee, which I accepted, and went off into the kitchen to make it.

Although she didn't offer, I figured she wouldn't mind, so I sat down on one end of the couch.

"Have you thought about my suggestion?" I called out.

After a moment, her voice came from around the corner. "You mean about moving out for a few days?"

"Yes."

"I'm not moving, Mr. Quinton, not even for a day."

She entered the living room again, carrying a small pot of coffee and two cups on a brass tray, the mugs of some sort of pewter.

Everything within eyeshot screamed a young couple living beyond their means.

Lorie hadn't brought cream or sugar, which I didn't care a whole lot about.

"This is my home," she said as we both sat back with our cups. "I'm not leaving it. No matter what."

The day before, I would have argued with her. After getting a different point of view from Talia over dinner, I let it go.

"Okay, then how about Plan B?" I asked.

"Plan B? What's that?"

"Plan B is hiring a bodyguard while I dig into all this," I said.

Lorie frowned and looked down at the floor for a minute. Having a hunch what she was thinking, I gave her the time.

"Mr. Quinton, I don't have the money for that. Between the divorce, not to mention some debt Brian racked up I didn't know about, and uncertainty about what's coming, I have to be cautious. I can barely afford you."

In my younger, snarkier days I would have made some obvious gaze at all the furnishings in the room, but I let it go.

"Don't worry about that," I said, "this is more a favor to Karyn than anything else."

"No." She shook her head emphatically. "I'm not a charity case. Be sure to keep track of things. I may not be able to pay you right away, but I will pay you."

"Fine. We can talk about that later. I still think you need a bodyguard."

She nibbled her bottom lip for a moment. "Nothing Mr. Jacobson's done up to now has been violent."

"Not yet," I said, not bothering to point out there was no actual proof of Jacobson's involvement yet. I kind of wondered, when and if I met the guy, what he'd end up looking like. "But it has been invasive to say the least, and there's not much of a leap between the two. Often, these things escalate fairly quickly."

What a soothing bedside manner I had. Maybe after this case I could make some real money by becoming a counselor of some sort.

"But it's been a couple of days now," Lorie said. "And I haven't seen him around anywhere."

I stared at her, wondering if the financial aspect was all that concerned her. Sexist dinosaur that I am, I'd never before encountered a woman in some potential danger arguing so hard against the need for actual protection.

"What if I agree to stay in and not do anything at all until you—resolve the issue?" she asked.

"It may take a while. How long can you stay off work?"

A crack of a smile. Not much, though more than I'd yet seen on her. For an instant only, some of the haggardness went away. "I'm on a salary, Mr. Quinton. And I've got plenty of time saved up. Plus, if need be, ninety percent of my job can be done from home."

I thought about pointing out there were plenty of ways someone could get to her in her house, but by this point figured her staying put was the best I could hope for.

"You've got my number," I said. "Anything happens, anything at all, you call me right away."

She nodded, and the sliver of a smile went away. "What are you going to do?" she asked.

I gave her the friendliest look I could and hoped it showed more confidence than I actually felt. "Going to get you out of this, Mrs. Jones, and on with your life."

CHAPTER NINE

The next obvious step in Investigation 101 was to go by Lorie Jones's work place. I needed to see how much she'd told about her problems to the people closest to her. Sometimes, some slight detail comes up in casual conversation.

I also, since I had no proof yet about Tom Jacobson's involvement, had to see if anyone in her immediate orbit could be pegged as a suspect, providing most of her story was true.

Thus, after a quick lunch at a take-out taco stand I passed as I floated through town, I headed to the big mama herself, Kansas City, Missouri.

I'd been faintly familiar with Lewis and Cochran Public Relations for the last couple of years. I knew of them as the firm Karyn Roberts worked for, and I also knew they had a fairly high level of civic responsibility. Shown mainly by the amount of free time they allowed Karyn to pursue her side work with Amendment V, the locally-based outfit which worked to assist people they felt had been wrongly incarcerated.

Beyond that, though, I knew little about them.

In the middle of everything else, I'd called Karyn the night before and asked her to mention me to her boss, hoping it would pave the way for a little cooperation. However, I'd specifically asked her not to reveal to him the nature of my business. Quite often, hitting people out of the blue with something reveals a lot.

Karyn had agreed, though I could hear the skepticism in her voice.

"It's not like I think your boss is some kind of goon," I'd told her, "but there's a small group of individuals people usually clam up to and refuse to say anything, detectives and lawyers being towards the top of the list."

"And you think that's how he'd act?" Karyn had asked.

"I don't know, Karyn, and that's the point. I'd prefer everyone around me to be as blind as possible for as long as possible."

"You start interviewing people in the office and things won't stay secret very long," she'd pointed out.

"Why I said as long as possible, no matter how short that is," I'd replied.

Thus, when I called the firm after leaving Lorie's house, I got an appointment right away with the head guy.

From Overland Park to Kansas City is about a twenty-minute drive, if traffic cooperates on the interstate, looping around the whole area. I made it to Haverford street in about fifteen, which gave me enough time to find a parking garage, then enter the office building that held Lewis & Cochran with a couple of minutes to spare.

KC, despite being a fairly metropolitan area, still has a Midwestern attitude in terms of the size of its downtown buildings. The tallest in town, One Kansas City Place, has only forty-two floors, five of them below ground. It's a decent-sized structure for around here even though someone from Chicago or New York would probably consider it an anthill.

While Lewis & Cochran didn't have their offices in that building, they were only a block away in one almost as tall.

Parking the Cherokee in a nearby garage, I walked a couple of blocks to their building. A quick look at the building directory indicated L&C on the tenth floor, which they shared with an accounting firm. One or the other of the businesses, or perhaps both, had to be doing pretty well for only the two of them to take up the entire floor.

Exiting the elevator on ten, I figured out real quick L&C held the predominant portion of the floor space. I opened a door made either of oak or something very close to it and entered a reception area marked by a lot of dark wood, black leather furniture that reminded me of Lorie Jones's living room, and small framed prints on the walls.

A polite brunette receptionist, well into middle age but still holding herself together, ushered me down a carpeted corridor to a plain wooden door at the end. This one definitely not oak. Knocking, she entered alone for a second, came back out, nodded me inside, and took herself back to the outer portion of the offices.

I walked in.

"Mr. Quinton." Zach Lewis was into his early fifties, not much older than me. He was wearing the pants to a light wool, charcoal-gray suit with the jacket draped over the back of a chair placed in front of a small conference table. A pink, button-down dress shirt straight out of the eighties and a plain maroon silk tie filled out his wardrobe.

As Lewis came around the desk, hand outstretched, I could see he had the build of a veteran tennis player, with maybe a little bit of golf thrown in. His thick hair was an even mixture of salt and pepper, and he had bright blue eyes.

"Good to meet you," he said as we shook. While his hands, like his face, had the kind of tan that usually comes from artificial means, his shake was firm enough to make clear he probably had something besides tennis and golf in his arsenal.

Lewis motioned me to a high-backed, black web chair in front of his desk as he walked back around to sit down.

"Karyn Roberts thinks very highly of you," Lewis said.

I nodded. "She's pretty swell."

Lewis's eyes crinkled just a bit. "Yes, she is. And it's on her recommendation I agreed to give you a few minutes. Though she didn't exactly prepare me to expect someone so—"

"Thuggish?" I suggested.

"How about rough-hewn" Lewis said.

The guy had a way with words—probably a hell of a news release writer back in his day.

"I hope the jeans and polo shirt don't prejudice you against me," I said.

Lewis smiled, the briefest quirk of an expression, before continuing. "But despite Karyn's asking me to see you, I'm not quite sure what you want from me. I've never heard of private investigators needing public relations work."

"Actually, I'm working for one of your employees."

Lewis stared for a second before slowly nodding his head. "That would no doubt be Mrs. Jones, right. I've been filled in on her recent problems."

"Should make things easier," I said.

Another stare, another brief nod. "And you've been hired to look into the matter?"

"I have."

"Why didn't she go to the police?" Lewis asked.

"She did. She feels they've proven somewhat ineffective so far."

Now the PR exec arched his eyebrows at me. "And you believe you can be more effective than them?"

"Doesn't hurt to try," I said. "After all, Karyn does think highly of me."

Lewis chuckled, and I felt an easing of the slight tension that had developed.

"I was made aware this morning that Lorie has called in sick for a few days. You know anything about that? From what I understand none of these—incidents—have involved physical danger."

"Better safe than sorry," I said.

"I try not to deal in clichés, Mr. Quinton. Occupational hazard. But perhaps, if there's danger to her, shouldn't you be there with her?"

"Mr. Lewis, while I could do the job in a pinch, I'm not really a bodyguard. I'm a detective, and the quickest way to remove any possible danger for Mrs. Jones is to get to the bottom of what's going on."

"I guess that makes sense," Lewis said. "But it leaves the very big question of why you're coming to me?"

"Actually, sir, I'm hoping to talk to a whole lot of your workforce before I'm done."

Lewis now gave me a frown that was gone almost as quickly as the smile a moment earlier. "I don't quite understand. From what I've been told, Lorie already knows who her tormentor is."

"Let's say she has a strong suspicion," I said.

"So how does that lead to you coming around here asking about her? Shouldn't you be out tracking the man down?"

I took a deep breath and spent a moment trying to think of the most diplomatic way to proceed. "Mr. Lewis," I said, "you run a public relations firm."

"Of course."

"So I'm guessing, sometimes, your firm's brought in to help some group or company through some sort of crisis situation?"

Lewis steepled his hands together and rested his chin on them. "In some cases, unfortunately yes. Most of our work is in proactive communication, trying to ensure crisis situations don't occur in the first place."

"Makes sense," I said. "But sometimes you have organizations come to you that are in the midst of a full-blown problem."

"Yes, that's correct."

"And in those cases, before you spring into action, do you take the client's word for everything they tell you?"

Lewis unsteepled his hands and leaned back in his chair. "I see your point. I have to say that a few clients, especially those in some sort of turmoil or turbulence, don't always tell us the exact, unvarnished truth."

I smiled at him. "I have no reason to disbelieve what Lorie Jones has told me."

"But she may not be telling you the whole story," Lewis supplied.

"Or at the very least, she may not know the entire story to tell."

Lewis's eyes glimmered. "You know, that makes perfect sense. What do you need from me?"

"A list of the people who work closest, geographically, to Mrs. Jones. Anyone you can think of who she hangs out with outside of work, who she takes lunches or breaks with, anyone at all she may be comfortable enough to confide in."

"I'm not sure I feel comfortable with that. After all, these people are professionals, and I don't want them feeling like suspected criminals."

"Neither do I," I said. "But I need to dig down, and her workplace colleagues is the most logical place to start."

"But why here? Assuming I provide you with the list you want, couldn't you track them down off site?"

"I could, but that would take a lot more time and effort on my part. The more time I take, the more likely the danger to Lorie will grow. If someone's out there looking to mess up her life, the quicker I can nail them down the better."

The glimmer in Lewis's eyes increased. "You sure you don't want to just talk to all of our employees and get it over with?"

"That depends. How many people you got working for you?" I asked.

"At last count, one hundred and seventy-five."

I crossed my hands behind the back of my head and leaned back on my arms. "Nah, I'll go with whoever she seems kind of close to."

"I wouldn't necessarily know who any of those people would be. Sometimes I go whole days without seeing particular employees."

I grinned. "But I'm guessing you run a tight enough ship you could give me more than a few pointers."

"You're a persistent man, Mr. Quinton. No wonder Karyn regards you as she does."

I gave him my "aw shucks" smile, one of the numerous ones I'd perfected back in my wrestling days.

"Could just be she's wowed by the guns."

"Oh, I doubt that," Lewis said as he reached over and pulled a memo pad closer to him. He then dug around in his desk drawer and pulled out a pen. "It takes a lot to impress, Karyn. A lot more than physique."

The conversation, pretty much at my instigation, had taken a turn I didn't feel all that comfortable with. Fortunately, Lewis seemed to catch my discomfort and began scribbling on the memo pad.

"You understand I'm going on both memory and snap impressions here," he said. "I don't make a habit of monitoring my employees' social interactions during the day."

"Unless they get out of hand," I said.

Lewis looked up. "Yes, unless they get out of hand."

"That happen a lot?"

"Probably no more than in any moderate-sized business. Maybe once a year or so."

"Anyone getting out of hand lately?" I asked.

He looked up again, his gaze sharper this time. "What are you implying, Mr. Quinton?"

"I'm a dumb jock, Mr. Lewis. It's kind of above my head to imply much of anything. I am wondering, though, if there's anyone in the company who Lori has been having troubles with."

Lewis put his pen down, leaned back in his chair. "Now you're doing a hell of a lot more than implying, mister. What exactly are you getting at?"

"It's like this, Mr. Lewis. I'm breaking my job down into two phases. One, is something going on with my client? If so, who's behind it? Seems to me my question's fairly straightforward. Is there anyone you perceive as in any way hassling Mrs. Jones?"

"That sounds like an awful lot of work."

I shrugged. "It's what I get paid for."

"Enough?"

"Excuse me?" I asked.

"If we can be candid, I'm somewhat aware of Mrs. Jones's overall financial situation. Going through family law proceedings is never cheap, and as often happens, from what I hear finances may be at least partly responsible for it."

"And of course you know how much she gets paid," I said.

Lewis glimmered a smile my way. "Yes, I do. The standard rate for her position and experience in this part of the country. My point is, I'm wondering how she's able to afford a second investigator."

"Could be a favor for a friend," I said.

"That would be Karyn, and doing that kind of favor is admirable. Regardless, what I'm getting at is would you be interested in me paying your freight?"

"Why would you want to do that?" I asked.

"Would you believe in the furtherance of effective employer/employee relations?" Lewis asked.

"Maybe if I knew what furtherance meant."

Lewis's smile broadened, and I got the feeling he was enjoying himself. Probably quite a break from his regular day of putting out corporate fires. I guessed he didn't often get the chance during business hours to entertain someone from the rougher side of the tracks.

"Then how about this," he continued. "How about I say I feel sorry for Lorie and want to do what I can to help her. Divorce is bad enough. This other thing, no one should have to go through something like that."

It occurred to me I could point out so far there wasn't any actual proof that Lorie had "gone through" anything, but figured that wouldn't put her, or possibly me, in a good light as far as her employer was concerned.

"Let's try this, Mr. Lewis. What say I dig around, see what I can come up with. I've already agreed to work for Mrs. Jones for a couple of days. If it takes longer, to where it becomes obvious it will be a hardship for her financially, I may take you up on that."

"I can live with that," Lewis said. "And as far as that goes, something this moment occurred to me."

He kept his gaze level on mine for another minute or two, then picked up the pen, wrote down another name, and put a mark next to it. He tore the sheet out of the pad and handed it over.

"Those are the names of the folks I know she associates with on a fairly constant basis. You didn't get this list from me."

"Okay," I said.

"Can I assume you'll use the utmost discretion and not bother the flow of the workday too much?"

"I'll do my best," I said, "but if I get out of hand call the cops and have them hustle me off."

Lewis smiled. "I doubt you'll let it come to that, and," he narrowed his eyes a little, "you may want to take notice of the name I put a star next to."

I glanced down at the list, noted he had jotted down eight names, the last one with that small mark to the side.

I stood up and reached out my hand. "Thanks for your help,"

I said. "Since the day's already halfway done, would you mind if I came by tomorrow morning to do my interviews?"

Lewis considered it for a moment, then shook his head. "Not at all. And please let me know if there's anything more I can do for either you or Lorie."

The words were right, but something about his tone made me feel he'd rather my visit was a one and done deal.

Fair enough.

I nodded and left his office.

CHAPTER TEN

I SPENT A COUPLE OF HOURS THE NEXT MORNING roaming up and down the hallways of Lewis & Cochran, chatting up administrative assistants, account coordinators, production workers, and a few people who I had no clue what they did. As a concession to Zach Lewis tolerating my presence and making his staff available, I did my best to be as unobtrusive as possible.

But when you're my height and weight, with almost shoulder-length blond to graying hair, and are wearing faded blue jeans and a royal blue tee-shirt, it's kind of hard to be inconspicuous in the presence of a whole office floor full of business people.

Turns out within thirty minutes of my dropping in probably the entire firm knew a private detective was snooping around, and that it had something to do with Lorie Jones.

"Freaked her out totally. Why wouldn't it?" said Jamie Hodgkins, a young brunette, somewhere around her late twenties with a kind of pixie-ish face who worked for the company as an art director.

She was working away on some sort of graphics program on a Mac when I accosted her.

"Mrs. Jones told you about some of what's been happening to her?"

Jamie Hodgkins nodded without looking up from her screen. "The deal with her bank money. We had lunch a couple of days after it happened, after it had been put back in, but she was still jittery."

"Jittery how?" I asked.

The young woman looked up and took off her blue-lensed glasses as she looked me up and down. "You're not exactly someone who sits behind a desk all day, are you?"

"Not if I can help it," I said. "Jittery how?"

"Tapping her fingers constantly on the table, moving her food around while hardly eating anything, every few minutes looking away from me and scanning the whole area around us. You know. Jittery."

"You ask her what was wrong, or did she volunteer the info?"

"I asked. Didn't take much to get her to spill the whole thing."

I took a deep breath. Of the four people I'd spoken with so far, she was the first to know what the hell I was talking about. "You remember when this was?"

The kid shrugged and half turned back to her work. Obviously, deskbound or not, I wasn't as interesting as whatever she was working on.

If I was of a more delicate nature, there's a chance I would have been offended.

"Hard to say," she said after a moment of staring at her screen. "Maybe about three weeks ago."

The timing was about right, which left me with confirmation that, at the very least, Lorie Jones's story hadn't been made up on the spot.

Although Jamie and I talked a little longer, she didn't have a lot more to add. Another couple of hours of haunting the corridors of Lewis & Cochran gave me more of the same. I met one or two people who Lorie had confided in enough to let me know something had been going on with her.

This didn't make it a sure thing Lorie's story was, in fact, true, but it leant credibility. I could at least eliminate the possibility that she had, for some bizarre reason, made it up on the spur of the moment and sold it to Karyn.

It could still be part of a well-thought-out plot on Lorie's part, but that was kind of stretching probability quite a bit.

From the beginning, considering the lack of tangible evidence,

I'd had to at least consider she had invented the thing whole cloth. There was the faint possibility she was for some reason trying to do harm to her first investigator and had come up with this concoction to do so.

And discounting the notion she'd come up with it all at once also sliced off most of the possibility she had invented the story. It for sure wasn't an emotional reaction of some kind, not with multiple instances now of her telling people snippets of the events over several weeks.

I was feeling a little better about my client now, though not enough to completely blind myself to all the various possibilities in this case. Even so, I considered the morning spent at Lewis & Cochran fairly productive, and it was possibly about to get even more so.

CHAPTER ELEVEN

For the entire morning, I'd deliberately avoided Adam Thornton, the last name on the list and the one that Zach Lewis had put a star next to.

After talking to everyone I could, and doing my best to stay out of their way as all those busy young professionals did busy young professional things, I stayed around long enough to spot him, a thirtyish man of average height with close-cut blond hair, in what he no doubt thought looked like a military cut. Dressed for the office, he was wearing charcoal gray wool slacks, a blue shirt in what Talia Sanderson had once told me was called tone-on-tone, and highly polished oxblood loafers.

The guy was heavy in the chest and shoulders, unnaturally narrow in the waist, and carried himself in such a way as to add half an inch to his height.

Okay, I had his type and knew what he looked like, which was all I needed at the moment. Leaving the building, I took a position on the northeast corner of the block and settled down on a bench to wait.

A little bit of magic on my phone and I had Thornton's address and phone number. Although I didn't plan to use the information, as long as Plan A worked out okay, it never hurt to be prepared with a backup or two.

Zach Lewis hadn't told me anything more than the guy's name, but a quick search of LinkedIn revealed he was an accounts administrator, whatever the heck that meant. Scanning over the material on his page, I got the idea he was a fairly mid-level guy.

Looking at all the small eateries, some parts of large chains and others seemingly independent shops, dotting the street for a couple of blocks in each direction, not to mention a fair number of food trucks hawking hot dogs, pretzels, BBQ, and assorted Asian foods, I figured it a good chance a young, on-the-go guy like Thornton would pop out, grab something for lunch, then head back to his office.

It was a good guess, but of course there were other possibilities, such as he brought his lunch to work, was planning on driving off somewhere, or was a fitness freak who only ate one meal a day.

Since I couldn't cover all those other possibilities, I decided to wait on the corner and see what happened.

About twenty minutes later, wouldn't you know it, Thornton emerged from the front revolving door, took a sharp left turn, and headed towards a little taco stand at the end of a corner.

I left my observation post, jaywalked across the street, and sidled up behind him. Thornton ordered three chinga chicken tacos and a pineapple Jarritos, and when the old guy running the stand turned half away to get his bottle of soda, I moved up closer until my chest rubbed against his back.

Thornton half turned to complain, but when he got a look at me snapped his mouth shut.

"Good idea," I said, "now pay for your food and let's go off a ways and talk. I'll even let you go ahead and eat your lunch while we do."

"Who the hell are you?" Thornton asked.

"Someone who wants to talk to you."

He looked like he was going to protest but instead kept quiet.

I tend to have that effect on some guys, especially if I tower over them by several inches.

Once Thornton had his food, I grabbed his right elbow and steered him to the side. "There's a nice little bench in front of that clothing store there," I said.

"I usually go back to the office," he said.

"Today you'll eat on the bench while we talk."

Thornton took a second to give me a full head-to-toe examination. He must have seen something that convinced him to follow the better course of valor.

"Okay," he said. "After all, it's not like you can hurt me or anything with all these people around."

"Actually," I said, squeezing the elbow a little tighter, "I can hurt you a lot more than you can imagine, Adam, if I really wanted to."

He jerked a little at my use of his first name, then straightened up a bit. "You want to tell me what this is about?"

"I will when we sit down."

We made it to the bench, hopefully managing to look like a couple of friends who'd happened to run into each other, and sat down.

Thornton put his tacos and drink to the side and stared at me.

"Eat up," I said. "Your lunch hour's ticking away, and I don't want to deprive you of nutrition."

"Who are you?" My guess was he'd hoped to exert a strong, untroubled tone, although the words came out as more of a whine than anything else.

Still, it was a fair question. I pulled out the photostat of my license and showed it to him.

Thornton read the license carefully, looked up at me, then back down to the license before I put it away.

"I don't get it," he finally said, "what do you want with me?"

"Lorie Jones," I said. Duke Prowder had always taught me to hit them right between the eyes.

"Lorie," Thornton drawled out the name.

"Jones," I supplied with a helpful smile. I used the same sort of smile I'd used back in my ring days, when I would offer my hand to help a downed opponent up right before I smacked him upside the head. "She works in your company."

Thornton, his time sitting down no doubt adding to his confidence, snorted. "Lots of broads work up there, dude. How am I supposed to know..."

I didn't let him get any farther before I reached out and smacked him open-handed upside the head. I managed to do it in such a way only someone looking close could tell what had happened, meaning it was more a tap than anything. Even so, he reeled back on the bench, about half of his taco staining his blue shirt.

"Adam," I said, keeping my voice low, "don't give me any shit, okay? I don't care how many women, not broads, work in your office. I'm only interested in one, and from what I hear you're kind of interested in her yourself. Explain why I hear wrong."

His left arm half jerked up, no doubt to rub away the pain from the splotch I'd created on his face. At the last instant, his manly instincts took over, and he lowered the arm down.

"Okay," he said. "Now I get it. I heard something about what she's been going through. You think I'm the one that's been hassling her?"

"Are you?" I asked.

Actually, I'd already pretty much decided Adam Boy was a dead end. He was the kind of guy who back in the seventies would have been called a lounge lizard: tough and manly on the outside, a child on the inside.

I'd known far too many dudes like him over the years. The muscles, clothes, and general air of confidence were only a blind for a truth he didn't want to face about himself.

Not that such guys couldn't be dangerous as hell, especially to someone weaker than themselves, but something in the dude's manner told me wouldn't have the energy to do anything as sophisticated as what Lorie Jones had experienced.

Follow her out to her car, sure. Make weird phone calls, back in the day when you could do that, probably. Leave odd little gifts for her, no doubt.

By looking at him, though, despite the business he worked in, he didn't seem to have the flair for the kinds of things Lorie had reported.

"Look, I'll level with you, okay?" Thornton said.

I nodded. "I'd say you don't have much of a choice, but go ahead."

"I made a play for her a while back." Geez, a play? Even his dialogue was from the last century. "I knew she was going through a divorce, so I thought 'easy pickings.' You know?"

I nodded a second time, wondering how long my self-control would last before I said the hell with it and slapped him off the bench. "I'm guessing she didn't exactly go for it?"

"Naw, not even a whiff," Thornton replied. "Pushed me away like she was too good for me. Didn't even give a good reason for the brush off."

"You mean like saying something like she was going through a hard time and needed to keep her priorities clear for the moment? Maybe feeling a little too beat up and fragile to deal with some pesky little irritant coming into her life?"

Thornton started to rear up a bit at my last comment. I gave him another moderately-hard look and he sank back down again.

"No," he mumbled while looking away. "She didn't say nothing like that."

"How'd you take it?" I asked.

Now he glanced back at me, his eyes showing confusion. "Take it?"

"Yeah," I said. "You've got this pretty woman who turned you down flat, brushed you off like you were nothing. How'd you take it?"

Thornton may have been a lot of things, but he wasn't stupid. He didn't rear up again although through his blue dress shirt I saw his shoulders tense. "Wait a minute, mister. Is this going where I think it's going?"

"Where's that?"

He looked around, still a little boy searching for someone to help him out. Apparently not seeing any rescue coming his way, he turned back to me. "You trying to hook me to all that stuff that's been happening to her?"

"You know about it?"

"Hell, I'd say everyone in the office does."

Now it was my turn to feel confused. "One of us has their wires crossed. I've been talking to people all morning, and only found a couple who Mrs. Jones had confided in."

Thornton, no doubt feeling a little more on solid ground discussing office gossip, shrugged. "What can I say? Word gets around. We're in the communication business after all. And people who work in communication like to—you know—communicate."

I noticed he hadn't yet taken a bite of his food. My reading of Thornton had already taken him away from any sort of threat to anyone, except for the possibility of boring someone to death.

"Okay, Adam," I said as I stood up.

"Wait." He looked up at me. "You mean that's it? No more hassle."

"No more hassle, Adam. Except for one thing." I leaned down into him a bit, using my bulk to make the best impression I could. "She's going through a lot of hell right now, so make sure you give Mrs. Jones a wide berth, okay? Don't try any dumb stunts with her at all. If you do, I'll hear about it, and we'll have another little chat. Got it?"

Thornton nodded, and I figured my work here was done. Before I turned to leave, I gave him one more parting piece of advice.

"And Adam, you've got chicken sauce on your shirt."

Then I walked off.

CHAPTER TWELVE

It was the now the afternoon of my second day on the case. Shortly after leaving Adam Thornton behind, I'd called to check in with Lorie. She'd assured me she was okay but already going a little stir crazy and wanted to know what progress I'd made. I'd pointed out that a day and a half isn't enough time to get much of a jump on things.

"Mr. Jacobson made an awful lot of progress just in his first day working for me," she'd said.

I'd considered saying "and look where it got you," then decided to go the virtuous route and not comment. We chatted a few more minutes; she asked me when she could get a report of my movements; I hemmed and hawed to put her off; and she appeared satisfied to leave it at that.

I still didn't know for sure if she was in any trouble but figured it was time to take the next logical step.

I drove about five miles in the direction I wanted to go before pulling into the parking lot of a small strip mall, shifting the Cherokee into Park, and hauling out my phone again. After a couple of rings, a woman who sounded far happier than anyone should in the middle of the work week spoke to me.

"Sterling Financial Services. How may I direct your call?"

I paused a moment, mentally realigning myself. "You're a real person?" I finally asked.

The bright voice chuckled. "Yes, sir. I am. What did you expect?"

"Oh, you know. The standard robot voice with forty-five menu options after the initial one asking if I wanted to continue in Swahili or switch over to English. You know. The way normal businesses answer their phones."

Another chuckle, verging onto a laugh, this time. I figured I was really making her day. "Well, don't be fooled. Even though we are a fairly large company, we also are kind of stuck to some old traditions."

"Traditions, hell. An actual person answering the phone is more like from the Dark Ages. In a good way," I quickly added.

"Good to know," she said. "How may I direct your call?"

"Brian Jones. Is he in?"

"Just a moment please." She put me on hold, and some sort of synthesized classical music began playing in my ear.

I gave it ninety seconds before my teeth started dropping out from sugar overload.

Only a moment later, though, she came back on. "I'm sorry, sir. Mr. Jones isn't in today. Would you like to leave a message?"

"Is he going to be in later, or is he out for the week?" I asked.

Now, the bright voice took on the slightest hint of frostiness.

"I really can't say, sir. Would you like to leave a message or not?"

"No thanks," I said. "I'll catch him somewhere down the line."

I HAD STRIKE ONE, THOUGH NOT YET OUT of the game. Lorie had given me her husband's new address, at least the most recent one she knew of, and about twenty minutes later I pulled up in an older, more residential portion of KC. The houses along this line looked middle-class, if a little weathered by recent inflation, and considering how tight finances usually were for people going through divorce, my guess was Brian Jones was renting his current residence.

Along with the shift in his family fortunes had come a fairly substantial shift in living location. To an outsider, the difference may not be obvious, but moving from Overland Park to the big city itself would be considered, by some image-conscious types, a couple of steps down.

Remembering what Lorie had said about debts she hadn't known about, I wondered if Brian was such an image-conscious person.

The ranch-style home was painted sky blue, peeling in places, with black frame shutters along the windows. An attached garage with enough room for one small car sat to the right. The chain link fencing surrounding the back yard sagged, with the occasional rusted link.

I pulled the Cherokee up to the curb about half a black down from the house. A three-year old gray Mazda sat in the driveway right in front of the garage. Could be Brian had another vehicle stashed away in the garage.

Or it could be that, like a lot of guys I knew, he'd filled the garage with so many tools, lawn implements, excess furniture, and sports gear that he had no room to actually store his car. As a lifelong apartment dweller, I'd managed to avoid such a condition, even if over half of my friends fell into that category.

On the other hand, good ole' Brian might have been spending the day running errands and popped into the house for a bit to do something or other and hadn't bothered to put his car back in yet.

It was equally as likely, and more concerning for me, the car could belong to someone else, and I may be about to barge into more than I wanted to deal with.

Still, sitting around wondering wouldn't do me any good. I got out of the Cherokee, walked up the uneven sidewalk to the cracked driveway, and knocked on the door.

It only took two knocks before the door opened up. "Yes?" the man standing there said.

He matched the description Lorie had given me: six one, blond on blue, hair done in an almost crew cut. He looked as if he'd once been quite the athlete, a tight end possibly, and appeared to still be in fairly good shape. He was wearing faded blue jeans and a black tee-shirt that fit snugly enough to show that most of his upper torso was muscle.

Not exactly dressed like an accountant in the middle of the work week.

"Brian Jones?" I asked.

"Yeah. What do you want?"

For answer, I pulled out the photostat of my license and held it up to him. He had to squint a bit, even in the bright sunlight, leading me to think Mr. Jones needed reading glasses.

Crunching numbers on a computer screen all day can play hell with the eyes.

Once he'd digested the information on the license, he looked back to me. I smiled, letting him know we were all friends here.

"You've got to be kidding me," he said, his voice dropping an octave. Before I could reply, he kept going. "After everything I've been through, you guys are going to hassle me for this? I took a sick day just for the hell of it. Big fucking deal."

"Mr. Jones," I said, "maybe we should talk inside."

"Or maybe we shouldn't. It's my time off, dammit, and I can spend it how I want, no matter what old lady Sterling says."

Okay, now I started to get it. "Mr. Jones, I'm not here for anything to do with your work. Can we just go inside and talk for a bit?"

He peered at me again. I gave him one of my patented smiles from my wrestling days. I had a whole range of smiles I'd used when I wanted opponents to relax their guard, think I was their friend, or not take me too seriously.

"Whether you're working for the company or not, we can talk out here as far as I'm concerned," Jones said.

So okay, I don't get to practice the smiles as much as I used to. "Okay by me," I said. "As long as you're okay with a stray neighbor coming along and wondering why we're talking about you and your soon-to-be-ex-wife."

Jones sighed, the muscles inside his tee-shirt deflating a little, then held the door open and ushered me in. "Five minutes," he said.

I nodded as I walked through the doorway. Inside, the furniture looked as drab and lifeless as I'd expected from the outside. A couple of easy chairs, one in faded green and the other in faded blue; an old, medium-brown coffee table marked with old wet rings and cigarette burns; and a puke-green shag carpet, the kind my mom once had in our house about forty years ago.

What I didn't see were any open alcohol bottles, stray marijuana joints, or wadded up and tossed-to-the-side fast food wrappers, none of the signs of someone slowly unraveling, a point in Jones's favor, far as I was concerned.

I tried to keep my expression blank, but something must have shown.

"This is temporary," Jones said. "Just until I can get back on my feet."

I grunted and looked around some more. Through a doorway, I could see an open laptop on a wobbly kitchen table. I couldn't tell from that angle, though I'd be willing to bet the tabletop was old-time Formica. From what I could see, the kitchen floor was done in black and white squares. "You're doing something on the computer?" I asked.

"What's it to you? What do you want anyway?"

"And you said you'd called in sick today. Would I be far off in guessing you're double dipping in some way?"

It was a shot in the dark, more an attempt to get the guy off balance than anything else, but as soon as I saw the dark look on his face I knew I'd screwed up, and he wasted no time confirming my suspicion.

"Let me guess," he said. "You're working for my wife, right? What the hell, the first guy didn't do me enough damage? She had to go out and find a second bullshitter to beat me down? You going to threaten to get me in trouble with the firm if I don't fork over even more when settlement time comes?"

The last few words were in a louder volume than he'd started with. Jones may have kept a fairly neat house, all things considered, but the anger was there, palpable.

I had to keep my thoughts in check. One reason I don't do divorce work, other than the fact I'm not that hard up for money, is that there's always two sides to the story, and quite often each side is just as wrong and just as right as the other.

Suddenly wishing I hadn't tried to rile him up, I held out my hands. "Hold on, Mr. Jones. The answer is yes and no."

"Yes and no? What the fuck does that mean?"

He took a step toward me. If I messed this up any more, I'd have to go a round or two with the guy, and for all sorts of reasons I didn't really want to do that.

"What I mean is your wife hired me, yes. However, not for anything to do with your legal proceedings."

He stopped, almost in mid stride, his right fist half raised, his face twisted into confusion. "I don't get you. What do you mean?"

I took a step back. "How about we sit down, okay? Then we can talk things over."

He moved sideways and took a seat in the blue chair. "Okay, so I think I can guess what this is about. I'll sit, but you stand buddy. Like I said, I'll give you a minute or two, even if at the moment you're not a very welcome guest in my house."

"Fair enough," I said, glad we'd managed to avoid bloodshed, at least for the moment.

I crossed my arms, leaned against the doorjamb that led into the kitchen, and started talking.

CHAPTER THIRTEEN

"Of course, I heard all that," Brian Jones said a couple of minutes later, "but the cops already talked to me about it."

I knew going in that the Overland Park cops had already spoken to Jones, but it never hurts to hit someone a second, or even third time, just in case something new pops out. It's the reason that cops often have multiple teams of detectives interrogate suspects at different times.

I'd begun to run down the whole thing, but got barely two sentences in before the man cut me off.

Even so, I would as much as possible stick to the script.

"You have anything to do with it?" I asked.

Jones tensed up a little more, and I craned myself off the door jamb in case I had to retaliate. He looked at me, I looked at him, and a minute later he relaxed and slumped back into his chair.

"Like I said, the cops already asked me that" he said. "Makes sense, I guess. Isn't it always the husband that's guilty? Or at least presumed to be so?"

"That's murder you're thinking of," I said. "But with something like this, you can see it being an obvious question. At the moment, how's your overall feelings towards your wife?"

"You mean do I miss her and would do anything to get her back, hate her guts, or somewhere in between?" He asked the question with a fairly flat inflection, as if the majority of his emotions, except for the anger, had run dry.

I'd heard the same vocal tones on a couple of male friends of mine who'd gone through similar situations. For a moment, I wondered if, back in the day in St. Louis, I'd ever sounded the same as Pamela and I had gone through our rocky breakup.

"Yeah," I said, "I guess that's what I mean."

"Well," he gestured towards the kitchen and the still-open laptop, "as you pretty much guessed it, this whole thing's left me kind of hard up. I'm pretty much scrambling all day every day."

"You're taking time off from work to pick up jobs on the side?"

"Yep. Just until I get a little more on my feet."

"Considering the circumstances," I said, "it seems you and Lorie should split everything more or less down the middle."

"That's pretty much how it's going," Jones replied, "Except she gets to stay in the house until we sell it. A year ago, hell, three months ago, that sucker would have gone inside of a week for more than we're asking. You may have heard the market's finally starting to slow down."

"I have," I said.

Jones nodded. "Now, between interest rate hikes and the latest jump in property taxes, who knows when the money will come in. Too bad we didn't decide to split six months earlier."

He said the words with almost total sincerity, even if I heard a little bit of self-mockery floating around in there somewhere.

I moved away from the doorway and took the other chair in the room. "You angry about that?"

"Cops already came and talked to me about all this," Jones repeated.

"And?"

"And what, mister? It's nothing to do with me. They asked me about some times and dates, and I filled them in as best I could."

"Alibis," I said.

"Uh huh. You know how it is. Who can remember what they were doing even a few days ago, let alone a few weeks?"

"You talk to a detective named Sloan?" I asked.

"Not at first. First go-round was a couple in uniforms, a guy and a woman. They asked me a bunch of stuff, and I told them what I could."

"Which doesn't sound like much," I said.

Jones shrugged. "I know. But they noted what I said and took off. A few days later, the detective came back and went over the same ground. I gave him the same answers and never heard back, so I figured whatever it was had blown over." He peered at me from across the room. "'Course, since she's hired some new muscle I'm guessing it didn't."

"You didn't answer my original question," I said.

"Which was?"

"The current situation have you pissed off in any way?"

"Meaning have I either been harassing Lorie or maybe having someone do it for me?"

I shrugged. "The thought comes to mind fairly easily."

Jones groaned and slumped even further back into his chair. "Is the divorce a fun experience? Not really. Is it particularly acrimonious? Not that I can see."

"Meaning?"

"Meaning we both decided we weren't really good for each other and decided to call it quits. There's a few snags on the money side of things, but show me a divorce that doesn't have that. Nothing we can't work out. Especially once we sell the damned house."

"So no special problems between you two?"

"How many times do I have to say it man? Nothing that would warrant the kind of stuff they say she's been going through."

"Have you spoken to her since the cops came around?"

He glared for a moment, as if suspecting some trick in the question. "You think I'm stupid? You think after I get interrogated about have I been bothering her the first thing I'm going to do is call her up and ask her how things are going?"

I saw his point, yet at the same time he hadn't actually answered my question. "Then you haven't talked to her since all this started?'

Jones sighed and looked at me like I was the village idiot. "No, I've kept far, far away."

I stared at him for a moment, doing my best to gauge his reaction to my next question. "You seeing anybody in particular right now?"

He sat up straight and gave me a glare to end all glares. "Are you kidding? What do you think this is, some sort of movie? You think I've got a girlfriend who's decided to do Lorie bad? Where do you get that from?"

"It's been known to happen," I pointed out.

"Yeah?" Jones spread his arms out, taking in the entire living room and its shabby furniture. "Then take a closer look, dude. Does it look like I'm in a position to attract any girls at the moment?"

I thought about pointing out lack of resources wasn't exactly a disqualifier but decided not to go there.

"Anyway," Jones continued without me saying anything, "the answer is no. I'm not seeing anyone at all, let alone someone who'd go and do something like that.'"

I took a moment and thought it all through. Easy enough to see how the guy could be lying, but I didn't get that vibe from him at all. Looking around the house again, I actually felt a little sorry for him. Far as I could tell, he was a decent sort, and even with her focus on the detective she'd hired, when Lorie had initially walked me through her problem, she hadn't even raised the question of her husband doing something like what had happened.

He had probably been a little sloppy with his money, and who knew for sure what else had gone wrong between the two of them. Nothing I'd seen or heard indicated any sort of violence in his nature.

I could be wrong, of course, but at the moment I was inclined to put him on the same backburner as Adam Thornton, Lorie's co-worker.

"Okay," I said, "thanks for your time."

Jones jerked back. "That it?"

"Yeah," I said. "That's it. Thanks for giving me the time."

"You're not going to tell Lorie about my moonlighting are you? Bringing up the subject of extra income would probably just stretch things out."

"I'm not working for her attorney," I said. "Don't see any reason to say anything to anyone."

"Well, hell, then, thanks for being decent about it. If you wouldn't mind leaving, I'd like to get back to work."

Not having anything snappy to say in reply, I gave the guy a nod and walked out of his house.

I could no longer avoid my next, and most obvious, step in the case.

CHAPTER FOURTEEN

"I'M NOT SURE," I TOLD TALIA THAT NIGHT. "It kind of feels like I'm punching clouds out here."

I'd spent the evening trying to find ways to keep myself occupied. Some time working out in the hotel's fitness center, a late dinner in a restaurant down the street, and about an hour of mindlessly scanning through the 5,218 channels on the TV, most of which were showing old shows and movies from the '60s and '70s.

A storm had come through in the early evening and decided to hang around for a few hours, allowing me to waste more time staring out the windows and watching the lightning show over the city's skyline.

Finally, a little before ten, I'd called Talia. She'd answered on the second ring and explained that, yes I was interrupting her, but since she'd spent the night catching up on the gazillion e-mails she accumulated at work each day, she didn't mind a bit.

"Punching clouds how?" she asked me.

"There's no concrete evidence anything is actually going on, short of possibly Lorie Jones being a hypersensitive scatterbrain. After I got done with her husband, I spent a little time on the phone and online with her bank and the local post office. Then I checked with the company that operates her home alarm system."

"And?"

"And everything's normal. The alarm people did note that on the day she mentioned her alarm went off. According to them several minutes later it shut off, and she called to confirm it was an accidental trigger."

"Which pretty much lines up with her story to you, doesn't it?" Talia asked.

"It does. The problem is it still doesn't prove anyone's hassling her."

"So after two days you still have her word and her word only that something's up."

"You've got it," I said. "I even bothered a guy at her work that was a possible candidate for squeeze of the year, and he came up fairly clean."

"The husband?"

"The same," I said. "No evidence he's pulled anything, though he may have the skill set for the banking deal. But he comes off clean as possible."

"So you've gone over everything the Overland Park cops did and found the same thing?"

"Well, there is one thing I haven't done yet," I said.

"Which would be talking to her original investigator?"

"Yep, and I've got a feeling I'm going to hit the same zilch there as anywhere. I'm almost asking myself what's the point."

"Except it has to be done," Talia pointed out. "If nothing else, you have to check that box off to assure yourself you've done what you could. How are you going to go about it? Talk to him direct?"

"Nope. Got a feeling that would net me no more than what I already have. I've got an idea. It's kind of out there, but it's not like I'll be breaking any laws or anything."

"The company he works for is a pretty big deal, though, right?" Talia asked.

"In my business, saying Hobart & Howard is a pretty big deal is like saying Amazon sells a couple of books."

There was silence for a moment as Talia digested that. "Could this cause any professional blowback on you?" she asked.

"Maybe if I was a professional of any sort," I said.

"You know what I mean, dammit. Can they come after you in any way?"

"Don't worry about it, hon. If I play my cards right, they'll never even know I was sniffing around."

We talked for a few more minutes until a small yawn on Talia's part told me it was time for her to get some sleep. And maybe myself as well. We said our goodbyes. After she hung up the phone, I held onto mine for a while and fantasized about getting in the car and making the hop to Providence to surprise her in the middle of the night, then decided we were both too old for that and put my phone down.

No sooner had I done so than a particularly massive bolt of lightning lit up the entire eastern sky of Kansas City. The thunder snapped and crackled for several seconds, and afterwards the after image of the bolt flickered in my vision.

I hoped it wasn't an omen of some sort.

CHAPTER FIFTEEN

THE NEXT MORNING, I CALLED LORIE to see how she was doing. She sounded okay, said nothing unusual had happened in the last day or so, and she was coming down with a fairly severe case of cabin fever. I asked her to give me a couple more days, give or take, and while she agreed she didn't sound all that enthusiastic.

I then made use of some of the information from my Duke Prowder notes, made a few phone calls, and climbed into the Cherokee to take a drive. I tooled all the way into the downtown KC area, then hung a couple of turns and before I knew it found myself in one of the city's not-so-good neighborhoods.

KC is smaller than Chicago or LA, and it has all sorts of visitor sites and attractions, but the same as any fair-sized metropolis it has its areas where it's best not to venture after sundown, and not too safe even in bright daylight.

The storm from the night before had left its remnants behind in the form of a steady morning shower. This was good, as even with May temps it allowed me to wear a nylon windbreaker over my usual tee-shirt, allowing me to conceal the snub-nosed gun I carried on my left hip.

Turning a corner, I cut through a small, almost trailer parkish neighborhood, filled with single-level houses straight out of the 1970s, with scabs of paint flaking off, bowed gutters hanging off the sides, and oil-slicked driveways.

Down another block, a tiny, not-quite strip mall showed on

the left. I pulled into the parking lot and parked the Cherokee outside a run-down storefront with a black-lettered sign that read "Smitty's."

I had no idea who Smitty actually was or if he was even still alive. Nor did I care. The lettering on the sign was so faded and peeled that it could have stood there for forty years or more. Yet one of the phone numbers in Duke Prowder's old black book had still been active after all this time, and a brief conversation before leaving the hotel had led me to this particular little business at this particular time of the morning.

The windows had been painted over with black paint, and it must have been done around the same time as the original sign because at a quick glance I saw more peeled spots than paint. Even so, the interior remained dark and hidden away, though a small cardboard sign with curling corners, hanging from the metal doorframe by a couple of loops of twine, read "Open."

I opened the door and stepped into possibly the dingiest dive bar I'd ever seen. A few fluorescent lights ran the length of the ceiling, flickering a dull yellow at best, which combined with the partially blacked-out front windows to make the place more shadow than solid.

I could make out a long, narrow bar top running along the right side with about half a dozen old timers half slumped over their beers. Five circular, somewhat angled tables were scattered in front, and peering into the far back I could make out a few pool tables with hunched figures standing over them.

Everyone in the place sat silently, all wrapped up in their own thoughts.

It caused a bit of a shiver to go down my spine. Was I going to some day end up this way, wrapped up in my own little cocoon and thinking about what was, or maybe what should have been?

The bartender, a gray-haired old man wearing a white long-sleeved shirt and an actual apron, green in color, paused at cleaning some glasses in front of him and looked my way. Before I could say anything, a hoarse voice about four feet to my left spoke up.

"He's with me, Joe."

Joe the bartender stared another minute, then gave a half shrug and went back to cleaning his glasses.

I turned to where the hoarse voice had come from.

"You Quinton?" the man asked. He was sitting at one of the small circular tables, a half empty mug and nearly-full ash tray in front of him. Like most cities these days, KC has a no-smoking ordinance, though in places like this that isn't even considered a suggestion, much less a law.

"I am," I said.

Without standing up, he extended his hand. "Jack Phillips."

We shook, and I sat down. Phillips looked to be barely on the good side of eighty. With him sitting down, not to mention the general murk of the place, it was hard to get a real solid gauge on his figure. The long-sleeved flannel shirt he wore seemed to hang off of him some, and the skin around his face was loose and wobbly, as if he'd recently had a sudden, intense weight loss.

He almost looked like he'd been planted at the table and never stirred. With the poor light in the place, his form seemed to melt down into the table, and from there into the floor below.

The resemblance was probably helped by the fact a fifteen-year old phone number had still worked to track him down; otherwise, I wouldn't have been here in front of him.

We shook, and I sat down. "Thanks for meeting me, Jack."

The geezer waved his hand to the side. "Hell, I ought to be thanking you, kid. Not a lot of people want to spend time with me these days." He coughed a small rasp, grimaced a bit, but made no other motion.

I didn't quite know what to say, so I kept quiet for a minute, letting the old man direct the conversation.

After all, he had more time than I did.

Phillips cocked his head to the side and looked at me at a slant. "So you're the one Duke took under his wing."

"I guess you could say that." I half turned in my chair and caught the bartender's eye, then made a motion that I wanted a beer. The barkeep put down the glass he was currently wiping, picked up one to the side, and began pouring a draft.

"Hell of a guy, Duke," Phillips said. "One of the best there ever was. Even back in our day, he was one of a kind."

I nodded. "He did okay by me. Did you guys ever work together?"

"You mean how did a St. Louis PI have my name and number handy, over here on the other side of the state?"

"Well, yeah," I said. "I did kind of wonder about that. Far as I knew, Duke pretty much had his hands full back east."

"He did, but you may have noticed there's a nice long interstate between the two cities. Lots of stuff, both good and bad, goes back and forth on the road. Probably as much back then as now."

I grinned, but it was cut short when Phillips did another slight cough.

He took a long drink from his mug to recover. "Don't worry, son. I'm not going to spend the day pulling your leg with stories from the good old days. If I did that, you'd end up never leaving here. You've got the look of a man with something on your mind. What's up? Why'd you call on me? Can't be anything to do with Duke, not as long as he's been gone."

The barkeep walked over and put a glass down in front of me. I handed him a couple of bills. Without a word, he turned and walked back behind his bar.

"He doesn't say much, does he?" I asked.

Phillips split another grin. A couple of his teeth were missing. "Place like this, the clientele really doesn't come here to talk. You may notice you and I are the only ones in the place jawing."

"Yeah," I said, "I caught that." I took a drink of my beer, choked it about halfway down, and put the glass back on the table. "Duke used to talk about you a lot, and he left me some info in case I ever needed to track you down."

"The old boy was good at keeping records," Phillips said.

"I need some information," I said.

"Okay."

"Actually, not so much info as pointers, maybe direction."

"It's okay, kid. Whatever you need, just spit it out."

I hesitated. Such a simple thing to ask, yet for some reason I felt bad doing so.

"You've been an investigator in this town for something like the last forty-five years or so," I said.

Phillips chuckled. "Make that forty, son. I finally had to give up and retire about five years back. Which I assume has something to do with what you need? You're not looking into one of my old cases or clients are you?"

"No, not at all. What I meant was, my guess is you know almost everyone there is to know in our profession in this area."

Phillips leaned back in his chair, tipping it back on the rear legs, and peered even closer at me. "You going after another private cop for something?"

"Maybe," I said. "An outside chance. Provided I can get all the i's dotted and t's crossed."

"Uh huh. And who is it you're looking to cross, young man?"

I took a deep breath, knowing the next few moments could go either way. "Tom Jacobson," I said, "he's a former cop who works these days for . . ."

"Hobart and Howard," Phillips finished for me.

I blinked a couple of times. "You know him?" I asked.

Phillips nodded. "I do. You always go after such big fish?"

"He that big?" I asked.

The old man gazed at the wall for a moment before looking back to me. "By himself, naw, not all that much. But with John Howard Jr. backing him up . . ."

"Teacher's pet?" I asked.

"You'd better believe it. Way I hear it, no matter what Jacobson wants, he gets."

"In terms of?"

"Hell, kid," Phillips said. "You name it. Bonuses, new employees, budget requests. Whatever."

"He get a company car?" I asked.

Phillips snorted. "You kidding? The way I hear, if he asked John Jr. for a gold-plated Rolls, the old boy would go out and snag one for him."

"John Howard Jr.'s the boss, right?" I'd done my reading, along with talking to Josh Nichols the night before, but I wanted to have things confirmed from someone who would know.

"He is," Phillips said, "now. His grandfather started the firm with Frank Hobart, back around the middle of the last century. John's all that's left of his family, though."

"Any Hobart's still around?"

Phillips shook his head. "Frank died with no heirs, and not much of an extended family. The company's been run by three generations of Howards, only one of Hobart."

I frowned. Something dammit didn't compute. "Way I hear it, Jacobson spent ten rather undistinguished years as a uniformed cop. How's he suddenly walk into such a golden situation and come out on top?"

Phillips shrugged and finished off his beer. He gestured to the bartender in the green apron, who began pouring another. "Who knows? Maybe he's a long-lost cousin. Which gets back to my original question. Is somebody as big as John Howard the kind you like to tackle?"

"Not usually," I said, "at least not if I can avoid it."

"Uh huh." Phillips took a long, slow drink, then put his glass down quietly on the table. "And I'm guessing this time you figure you can't avoid it?"

"Don't know yet. It may be nothing, or it may be that someone's in trouble," I said.

"This trouble coming from Jacobson?"

"Possibly. While I don't want to tar the guy if he's innocent, it's something I need to nail down one way or the other."

Phillips propped his chair back down on all four legs and folded his arms on the table. "You going after just him? Or the whole company as well?"

"Does it matter?" I asked.

"It may," Phillips said with another crooked grin. "It just goddamned may."

CHAPTER SIXTEEN

Unlike a lot of businesses that boast of being in Kansas City, it turned out Hobart and Howard actually did have their headquarters in the main city itself. Situated a little bit north of downtown, in an area that had been attempting for a couple of decades to succeed in gentrification, they had an address close enough to the main action to be convenient but far enough off the path one could avoid the nightmare of downtown traffic in order to get there.

After chatting some more with Jack Phillips, I spent the rest of the day in my hotel room with my laptop and a pad of paper I'd borrowed from the front desk, working up a handful of plans for how to approach the big boys. Phillips had conveyed enough with his tone of voice and attitude that I felt kind of like I was planning to jump headfirst into a pit of snakes.

By ten thirty that night, I'd come up with four solid plans. By a little before midnight, I'd winnowed those down to two, and when I woke up in the morning, I knew which one I wanted to pursue.

It was a pretty good plan, mainly because it was simple but also because it involved me telling almost the entire truth all the way through.

It would also, if things went right, go completely unnoticed by anyone if it turned out Tom Jacobson was in fact innocent of anything.

After a quick breakfast, a shower, and putting on the nicest clothes I'd brought with me, I climbed into the Cherokee and headed out.

Hobart and Howard occupied all five floors of an old-fashioned red brick building that looked as if the individual materials that comprised it came from excavating old-time school houses. At a quick glance, I'd have guessed it had been constructed sometime back in the fifties, though I had no doubt that inside the décor would more than make up for the severity of the exterior.

At mid-morning of a business day, the parking lot was about half full. Some of the cars were mid-size, mid-range vehicles, the kind no one notices or pays attention to. I figured most of those belonged to the firm's actual field detectives.

Despite what you see on TV and in the movies, the goal of most PI's, with their work running almost entirely to divorce work, civil litigation, subpoena deliveries and such, is to be as inconspicuous as possible. It's the same reason I drive a Jeep Cherokee instead of a classic Corvette.

Well, that plus, with my size, I'd have a hard time squirming in and out of a 'Vette.

I also noticed a scattering of Porsche's, Cadillacs, and even a black Maserati.

I guessed those belonged to clients, which indicated the firm probably charged higher fees than I do.

On the front of the building, five feet above the top door frame, perched a bronze-colored H&H logo.

Thinking of my small office in the back of a gym, I began to feel a little outclassed.

On the up side, I was at least detective enough to find the right building.

Inside was a large, open lobby with a few strategically-placed plants, a polished floor with a pattern of alternating bronze and marble stripes, pewter-colored walls, and an honest-to-God spiral staircase along the right wall leading up to a mezzanine overlooking the lobby.

A plain black counter against the far wall had two receptionists, which is what I guessed you'd call them. Both young blond men were wearing blue blazers, manning a pair of computer monitors.

All sorts of people were coming and going, in and out of elevators, up and down the stairs. Most of them wearing some sort of business clothing. While I saw very few ties, there were a whole lot of tailored suitcoats on the men and trim, form-fitting slacks and jackets on the women.

I looked around and didn't see any sort of directory, which either meant it was well hidden or that I'd have to brace one of the Ken dolls behind the counter.

Probably tell me if I had to ask for someone's office I didn't belong there.

As I walked up to them the Ken on the left glanced up and gave me a smile as plastic as his complexion.

"Yes, sir?"

"Sam Quinton to see John Howard," I said.

The plastic face frowned a little. "Excuse me?"

I took a deep breath and tried to think of smaller words to use. "John Howard," I said. "I'd like to speak with him."

"I'm afraid Mr. Howard is . . ."

Before he could finish telling me Howard was unavailable, I pulled out my license photostat and handed it over. Automatically, he took it, read it, and looked back up at me before handing it back.

I smiled. Well aware of Hobart and Howard's reputation, I'd gussied myself up for the day, wearing my least-faded pair of jeans, a white polo shirt, black sport coat, and new black Nikes.

Hell, I'd even shaved, something I usually only do about once every three days. If I'd have been able to think of something to do with my hair that wouldn't have involved cutting most of it off, I would have done so.

"Mr. Quinton," the young man said, the plastic of his face having completely smoothed out again, "do you have an appointment of any kind?"

"Nope," I said, "but I figured Mr. Howard wouldn't mind taking a couple of minutes to entertain a colleague from out of town."

The young man's lips pursed, and while I got the feeling he wanted to do another obvious up and down take of my wardrobe, he managed to stop himself. "Mr. Howard's very busy," he finally said.

"Aren't we all," I replied as I beamed my smile even brighter. I figured I'd give the smile another thirty seconds to work before pulling him from behind the counter by the neck and using him as a bouncy ball.

His clone to the side glanced our way, probably wondering why Left Ken hadn't run the bum off by now.

Left Ken did his best to stare me down, but I had almost thirty years' life experience on him, and his best effort didn't really cut it.

"Maybe I can contact his secretary and see if he has a minute," he compromised.

"I'd sure appreciate that," I said, putting my most mild tone in my reply.

The kid reached down and picked up from the counter one of those almost-wireless headset thingies, clipped it on his head, whispered into it for a second, glanced back at me, whispered some more, then took the headset off.

"If you go to the elevators and up to the fifth floor, someone will meet you, sir. They believe Mr. Howard can spare a quarter hour."

"Awful nice of him," I said. "Okay if I just take the stairs?"

Ken frowned, as if the idea of mussing ones pants on stairs was a foreign idea, then shook his head. "For visitors, we prefer they use the elevators."

"It's a five-story building," I said, "not much way to get lost in it. Or are you guys harboring state secrets or something?"

"The elevator please," Ken said before turning away from me and down to a small laptop screen in front of him.

As he dismissed me, more of his original tone, the kind of rubberized greeting, came into his voice. I thought again about bouncing him out from behind the counter, as I hadn't had a good workout in a couple of days, then decided such an action would be counterproductive to my mission there.

"Thanks a lot," I said as I turned away to go the elevators.

Maybe on my way out of town I could stop by a toy store and buy a pop-up doll to take out my aggression on.

CHAPTER SEVENTEEN

The elevator dinged, letting me out on the fifth floor. I obviously hadn't seen any of the rest of the building except for the lobby, though I had a hunch all of the floors looked the same.

At the very least, the walls on the fifth looked like the same, old-fashioned brick as the outside, giving me the feeling that I was back in elementary school, waiting to be lined up to go to lunch. A woman waited for me outside the elevator. If I'd expected the female equivalent of the plastic men downstairs, I'd have been really disappointed.

She was either a few years away from or a few years after her fortieth birthday. Copper-colored hair with a slight trace of gray, dark brown eyes that reminded you of the old-growth redwooods in California, and a figure hovering right in the sweet spot between toned and conditioned or slightly plump.

Her color for the day was charcoal gray, with a charcoal skirt hovering close to being a tad too short for business, only slightly lighter colored blazer, and cream-colored blouse.

"Mr. Quinton?" she asked in a flat, neutral tone.

"That's me." I thought of giving her a grin, maybe even one of my better smiles, then figured the effort would be as wasted on her as it would have been downstairs. She gave a brief nod, actually more of a dip of the head, half turned away, and gestured down the hall.

"Mr. Howard can give you fifteen minutes," she said as she began walking ahead of me. "Under ordinary circumstances, such an impromptu appointment would be out of the question, especially on a Friday."

"Why on Fridays?" I asked from behind her.

"He only works half days at the end of the week," she said without even looking back. "However, seeing as how you're some sort of investigator yourself, he decided . . ."

"Hey!" I barked as the woman got about ten feet ahead of me.

She turned back, face still composed, and arched an eyebrow.

"How about introducing yourself?" I asked, deciding for the moment to let the "some sort of" comment slide by.

Although the woman's shoulders tightened a bit, she never lost the cool look. "My name's Regan Harper. I'm Mr. Howard's main assistant. I'm going to take you into his office, introduce you, then depart. Satisfied?"

Her hint of annoyance there at the end was the most emotion I'd seen out of anyone since entering the building. Even though I had no clue what caused it, I decided not to be offended.

I thought about looking down to make sure my shoe laces were tied.

"Absolutely satisfied," I said. "Please lead on."

With a curt nod she turned again and resumed walking down the hall. Considering that we only passed a couple of doors on each side as we walked, I cleverly deduced that the offices behind them were rather large, which would mean they belonged to the top people in the company.

Hah. So much for "some sort" of investigator.

Then I remembered I was on the top floor, which automatically meant it held the top people.

Oh well, maybe before I left I could impress Ms. Harper by finding a lost dog or something.

We stopped at the last door on the left, which like the others we'd passed had no name plaque anywhere I could see. As Ms. Harper opened the door, we entered a fair-sized outer office that held a desk, what looked like an antique oak bookshelf against a wall, and a two-seater couch done up in mahogany-colored leather so dark it was almost black.

She walked right up to the door on the other side, tapped briefly, opened it, and ushered me in.

The inner office was an interesting combination of old times and modernism. The desk that formed the focus of the room looked to be aged oak, massive, and had probably come with the original formation of the company. In front of it sat three chairs, the frames some dark wood and the cushions rich leather.

Two walls of the office held bookshelves, but instead of being filled with impressive-looking, leather covered volumes that had never been read by anyone, most of the shelf space held pictures, sports memorabilia, and assorted knick-knacks, such as a Rubik's cube and an old slinky.

Most of the pictures showed the same man shaking hands or standing in an embrace with a variety of politicians, celebrities, and newspeople.

The desk itself held only an open laptop computer, a couple of manilla folders, and a single yellow legal tablet.

Nothing personal, nothing casual—all that kind of stuff was arranged in the bookshelves, but the desk was purely operational.

It didn't even hold any family pictures, making me wonder if the owner had any kids or spouse.

As I got closer, John Howard stood up from behind his desk and walked over to us, his hand outstretched to me.

Not quite what I expected.

Howard, one of the most noteworthy and successful investigators within four or five states, looked the part of an assured, confident CEO.

He had thick silver hair that gave the appearance of being cut and styled at least once a week. His eyes were a sharp, piercing blue, and he had the kind of tan that indicated lots of time spent under some kind of special equipment.

He stood about five eight, which meant I towered over him by several inches. If I hadn't have looked up his bio ahead of time, I would have guessed him for late fifties or early sixties instead of the seventy-one he actually was.

His suit, of a soft gray and made of silk, was offset by a maroon silk tie and white shirt with cuff links.

All told, not exactly the TV image of a guns-blazing PI.

I was pretty glad I'd worn my new black sneaks. The older pair with scuff marks on the sides would have marked me as working class.

"Mr. Quinton," Howard said as we shook, "nice to meet you."

I said the same, and Howard motioned me to a chair in front of his desk that in fabric and color matched the couch in the outer office. "I'm rather busy this morning, most mornings actually. But when Regan gave me your name, I asked that you be brought up."

"Thanks," I said.

Howard smiled and tilted his head. "No thanks necessary. I recognized your name, of course."

My second stunning moment of the interview. "You did?"

The old man's smile practically beamed. "Young man, I may have possibly needed to retire about a decade ago. Even so I do keep up with the news. The last few years, you've been making quite a name for yourself back in Carson County."

If I hadn't been used to people sucking up to me from back in the days when I was, briefly, a wrestling champion I probably would have blushed. As it is, I gave him a brief nod.

"Even so," Howard continued, "I'm not sure why you'd be coming and calling on us. Were you by chance looking for a change of venue and some new employment?"

"Thanks," I said, "but I'm quite comfortable working for myself."

Howard inclined his head a bit. "In that case, what can I do for you?"

"I'm working on a case," I said, "actually more like a favor to a friend, and it concerns the metro area here."

Howard straightened up his head and frowned a bit. "Forgive me, Mr. Quinton. As capable as I assume you are, why wouldn't your friend seek out a local investigator? Is it a question of money?"

"Not money," I said, "more like familiarity level. But you're actually on point. While I think I'm pretty good at my job, and honestly the case isn't all that tough, I could stand a little local help to kind of get me around the rough edges."

The frown disappeared, and Howard's face beamed in a full smile. "Let me get this straight. Are you asking to hire one of my people?"

Now it was my turn to frown, and I hoped I made it convincing. "Not sure about hiring," I said, "as I'm guessing your rates probably equal my monthly mortgage."

Howard gave his head almost a half shake. "More than likely, though I'm sure for a colleague we could probably work out some sort of discount."

"Discounts are always helpful," I said, "especially as I need to buy a new pair of jeans sometime this month. What I was wondering, though, was if I could borrow a couple of hours of time with one of your more experienced people. Kind of sound them out about a few things around here."

"I don't see why that wouldn't be doable. Did you have anyone in particular in mind?"

I reached into my back jeans pocket and pulled out a piece of paper. The night before I'd spent time on the company website, supplementing what Jack Phillips had told me in Smitty's. Then, I'd gotten on the phone and made some late-night calls to people I knew in Providence, Kansas City, and a few all the way over in Topeka, the Kansas state capital.

Although it had taken a while, eventually I'd assembled the picture I was looking for.

I gave Howard three names. I wanted one specific person, but I didn't want to make things too obvious, especially in front of an old operator like him.

"I was thinking either Ron Bellamy, Tom Jacobson, or Rachel Esperson."

I handed the paper to Howard who looked down at it, then turned slightly and tapped a few keys on the laptop. He frowned for a second, manipulated the keypad a bit more, then leaned back.

"Unfortunately, Mr. Bellamy is out of town, doing something for us in Montana. I could let you have Mr. Jacobson, but he's my second in command around here and is usually hip deep in paperwork. Miss Esperson is in the middle of a field assignment, but she should be free later this evening."

I pretended to mull it over for a second. "I don't see why she wouldn't work. Has she worked for you long enough to be reliable?"

Howard took his own moment to think things over. "Long enough, but her longevity isn't really an issue."

"Oh?" I said.

Howard smiled again. The guy was probably one hell of a salesman. "I'm probably going to come off as conceited here, Mr. Quinton. This firm has enough of a reputation we only hire the best people. If Miss Esperson weren't a competent investigator, she never would have made it in the front door."

Made sense, though his statement left me wondering how Jacobson, a uniformed cop with no distinguishing marks on his record, had made it through that same door.

"So it's okay if I borrow her from you? I don't foresee it taking longer than a couple of hours."

Howard's right hand reached out to his office phone. "Let me have the personnel director reach out to her, and we'll put you in touch."

"I'd appreciate it," I said as I settled down in my chair.

CHAPTER EIGHTEEN

I WAS ABOUT FIFTEEN MINUTES OUT from Howard's office, threading my way through daytime Kansas City traffic with the hopes of getting to my hotel before I started collecting Social Security, when my phone buzzed.

Pulling up to a red light, I pulled the phone out of my pocket and saw the call was coming from Lorie Jones. I engaged the call as it rang a third time.

"Quinton."

"Mr. Quinton, it's Lorie."

"Yes, what's up?"

"I—I had a phone call a couple of minutes ago," she said.

The light in front of me turned green, and myself and about a quarter of the population of Missouri began inching forward. "Yes. Who from?"

"I can't be absolutely certain, but it sounded like Mr. Jacobson."

My pulse kicked up a couple of beats. "What's the incoming number?"

"That's the problem, Mr. Quinton. The call came on our landline."

The car in front of me, a canary-yellow Porsche Carrera, began slipping its gears. Who the heck drives a Porsche in downtown urban traffic?

"Wait a minute," I said to Lorie, "a landline? Really?"

She chuckled, though it sounded rather strained. The first sign of real emotion I think I'd seen or heard out of her. "Sounds old-fashioned, I know. Brian was always using so much tech for his work that he wanted something a little throwback in the house, so we got an old fashioned-type phone."

"Which I'm guessing doesn't indicate the number calling you?" I asked.

"No, as I said really old-fashioned."

In other words, still no firm evidence of anything. As I maneuvered through the intersection, another concern popped into my head.

"Lorie," I said, "how many people know your landline number?"

Silence over the phone for a minute as she considered. "I'm not sure. Honestly, I thought the idea was so antiquated I don't think I ever used it until it rang today. I would guess maybe a couple of Brian's friends, if that."

A suddenly clear stretch of payment opened up, and I goosed the Cherokee a little. "Tell me this," I said, "is the number of the phone written down anywhere near it?"

"Nope. There's just the small stand with the phone in it. I don't even know the number. Again, I guess Brian would. But it definitely wasn't Brian's voice."

Scratch the first thought, that someone who'd broken into her house could have gleaned the number somehow.

On the other hand, someone savvy enough to do all the things that had happened to Lorie wouldn't have much of a problem tracking down something as simple as a phone number.

"Okay," I said, "what did the caller want? What did he say?"

I could hear her take a deep breath before answering. "I'm actually a little surprised I'm acting so calm about this," she said, "because I really should be terrified."

"We all react differently to these things," I told her. "What did he say?"

"He said he only had one question for me."

"Which was?"

"He wanted to know if, on my recent trip out of town, I'd brought something home with me."

"Something," I said.

"Yes. Something like a private detective who looks like a bouncer."

Son of a bitch. The guy was already on to me.

Which, if Lorie wasn't making the whole thing up actually counted as a point for her side.

CHAPTER NINETEEN

I CONSIDERED SWINGING BY LORIE'S HOME and staking it out, gun in hand, hoping for someone to show up. I couldn't help making the connection that her call had come only minutes after I'd shown up at Hobart and Howard. Though I hadn't passed Jacobson, that I knew of, somehow or other, if the call to Lorie had indeed happened, he had glommed onto me.

But sitting around her place waiting for something wouldn't do much to resolve the situation. As far as I could see, I had to keep going and nail things down one way or the other.

"Lorie," I finally said after going through all of this in my head, "call the police and talk to Detective Sloan. Tell him what happened. You've spoken to Jacobson before. Did it sound like his voice?"

"Hard to tell. He has such an average voice it's easy to forget exactly what he sounds like."

Average, again. Ordinary guy. Nothing unusual about him. Although perfect for his line of work, it made it damned hard to get a handle on the guy.

"And even if I call Detective Sloan," Lorie continued, "what can he do? It's still only my word."

"Doesn't matter," I said. "We still need to get it on the record. No way of knowing what'll be helpful down the line."

"I guess," she mumbled. "Is there any way you can come out here and keep an eye on things for a while?"

Because she sounded worried, maybe even verging on frightened, I bit my tongue on my inclination to point out I'd suggested hiring a bodyguard a couple of days ago.

"I can't right now," I told her instead. "I've put something into motion that may help us get a line on this whole thing. If I call it off now, we'll be right back to square one."

Judging solely by her occupation in public relations, Lorie would not have been considered a slow person, and it took her splits of seconds to catch on.

"You mean you've started some kind of plan?" she asked.

"Yes."

"Something to try to get a fix on why he's doing all this?"

"Yes," I said, fearing what would come next.

"When exactly did you do this?" she asked.

In the time we'd been talking, I'd managed to get through the worst of the mid-day traffic and was within a block or two of my hotel.

I glanced at the clock on the Cherokee's dashboard. "About half an hour ago," I said.

There was a pause, long and strained, before Lorie said, "In other words, he called me right after you did whatever it was you did?"

No way to sugarcoat it, no way to make it sound any better at all. "Looks like it. Here's what I need you to do. Lock all your doors, stay off the phone. If someone calls you even if you know who it is, let it go straight to message."

"Unless it's you," Lorie said.

"Right. Unless it's me. Don't go by the number that comes up. Let it go to message until you hear my voice, then answer. I don't care who else it is, I don't give a damn if it's your mother, stay off the phone."

"Can I return calls if they're important?" she asked.

"No. Let's not give this guy, Jacobson or whoever else, any little thread at all to grasp onto."

"I suppose I need to stay off the computer as well?"

"For anything involving internet, damned straight," I said.

"In other words, I'm more of a prisoner now than before."

I didn't really want her to look at it that way, but there really wasn't anther lens to peer through. "Guess so. Hopefully, what I've kicked into play will work and we'll get a handle on this dude. You got plenty of groceries in the house?"

"Sure. I went to the store right before Karyn and I came out to see you, and with only one person here . . ."

She trailed off, and I gave her the moment. I'd gotten into the Hampton's parking lot, turned off the ignition and climbed out of the Cherokee. I began moving to the bank of elevators that would take me up to my floor.

"Lorie," I said, "I don't know what this feels like 'cause I've never gone through it before. Do me a favor. Just hunker down for a few more days until I get you through this."

"Okay." Her voice sounded a little wavery. At the moment, I was willing to take what I could get.

"Call Sloan," I said. "Fill him in, then buckle it down. No visitors, no phone calls, no internet use. Just for a while. Okay?"

"Okay," she repeated, and this time she sounded a little stronger.

Not having anything else to say, I ended the call and went up to my room.

CHAPTER TWENTY

Around five that afternoon I met Rachel Esperson at a little steak house about half a mile from her company's building. John Howard had set up the time to give Esperson time to extricate herself from her current fieldwork.

Five was a little later than I'd have wanted, especially after hearing about the phone call to Lorie Jones, but the old man was graciously allowing me to take a few hours of his employee's time during the middle of the work week, meaning I wasn't about to squabble over when and where.

Actually, considering the little three-card monte game I'd pulled specifically to get face to face with Rachel Esperson, without coming right out and asking for her directly, I hadn't even dreamed of pressing my luck.

As soon as I walked in to Jill's Steaks I for sure wasn't going to grumble about the where.

The tacky exterior of the building, peeling paint and a tattered awning, had led me to expect a darkened interior, gloomy enough to obscure whatever stains had accumulated over decades of use. Before walking in, I almost expected my Nikes to stick to the floor.

Instead, the place was well-lighted, decorated in the expected dark woods and deep maroon leathers, and with a nice, glittering shine coming from assorted racks of glassware. A bar ran down one length of the main room with a slate gray marble top and a row of clean, bright wine glasses arranged overhead.

There were a couple of two-seater tables up front, ones seated for four chairs in the middle, and a cluster of booths at the back.

A young woman in a short black skirt and ruffled white blouse, holding a small note pad, came up to me. "How many, sir?"

"Two," I said. "I'm supposed to be meeting someone but don't know if she's here yet."

The girl cocked her head at me and glanced down at the pad in her hand. "Would that be Rachel you're meeting?"

"Esperson?" I asked, and the girl nodded.

"She's already here and waiting in a booth. This way, please."

I followed the young woman towards the farther back part of the main dining area, noticing a door off to the side that let into a smaller room with three long tables. We stopped at one of the booths, and the hostess smiled and placed a menu down on the table across from the booth's occupant.

I nodded my thanks, asked for a glass of water, and sat down to face my contact.

According to what I'd managed to glean from my research the night before, Rachel Esperson was a former patrol officer for the Kansas City, Kansas, police department who'd pulled the plug some years previously and taken a position at Hobart & Howard.

There was some confusion as to why she'd left the official force, one contact implying she'd simply decided to go for a better opportunity, while a local lawyer friend of mine conceded there was some whiff of rumor around the department at the time she left.

More than that, though, something else that came up when I was backgrounding Howard's people caused me to zero in on her.

Esperson looked in her mid-thirties, with glossy black hair worn shoulder length, dark brown eyes and a faintly Hispanic cast to her features. She wore a turquoise green cotton blouse with the sleeves rolled up to her elbows and had two small diamond earrings in each ear.

"Mr. Quinton," she nodded in greeting as I sat down.

"Miss Esperson." I gave her one of my biggest smiles in return.

Her expression remained neutral.

"John Howard tells me I'm on loan to you for a couple of hours.

If you don't mind, I've had a long day so the quicker we can get to it the better."

She didn't speak with any rancor or rudeness, more of a straight telling of facts.

"Works for me," I said.

Rachel Esperson nodded. "Something about a minor case you're working in the area?"

"Actually, I referred to it as a favor I'm doing for a friend."

"Okay. If you want to use euphemisms, that's fine with me."

"Actually," I said as the waitress brought my glass of water, placed it in front of me, and left, "I'd prefer to talk straight out. Is that a problem for you?"

The neutrality left her face now, replaced by a slight frown. "I don't get you. Is this some kind of setup or something?"

I spread my hands out palms down on the table. "Nothing of the sort, Miss Esperson. I actually am doing a favor for someone, or working a case if you will, and I could really use some local input."

Esperson nodded and opened up her menu. "Fair enough, but do you mind if we order first? I've spent the last ten hours on my feet in a department store, and I could use some nutrition."

"Sure," I said. "What were you doing in the store?"

"Stakeout." She continued scanning the menu. After a moment, she gave a slight nod and closed it up.

"Stakeout?" I asked.

Esperson smiled. "Somebody's lifting a few too many brassieres from the women's department of a local store."

"Don't they have security cameras for that?"

"Of course. It's just that whoever's doing it is very good," she said.

I thought about that for a moment as the waitress began coming over our way. "Inside job?"

The server, a slightly older woman with slumped shoulders and tired eyes, took our orders. Esperson ordered a filet with baked potatoes and salad and I, always seeking the high life, went for a bacon cheeseburger with fries.

"Regular fries or curly?" the waitress asked.

"What the hell?" I said. "Time to live it up. Let's go curly."

The woman nodded, made a few marks on her pad, and went off.

As she walked away, Esperson picked up our conversation. "Yep, far as we can tell, it's someone inside. I've been walking in and out, around and about for three days now trying to spot any little telltale sign I can."

I frowned at that. "Isn't it kind of hard to be inconspicuous if you're hanging around the same department of the same store for days on end?"

Rachel paused as the waitress came back with her salad. After she departed again, Rachel picked up a piece of spinach and nibbled on it. "You're from Providence, right?" she asked.

I nodded.

"Spend much time in our glorious little city here?" she asked.

"A little. Usually long enough to catch a ball game out at Arrowhead."

Rachel shook her head. "No, I mean actually in the city. Right in the thick of it."

I shrugged. "Every now and then. It's been a while."

The big-city operator grinned at the small-town bumpkin. "We've got around half a million right here in the thick of things. Add in the entire metro area, both sides of the state line, and you're talking something close to two and a half million."

"Uh huh," I said, doing my best to appear smart yet silent.

"Just imagine, then, how jampacked some of the stores get, especially at certain times of the day. If I keep moving, going outside to my van every now and then to change clothes, wig, and accessories, it's fairly easy not to be spotted."

"Maybe ten or twenty years ago," I said, "but hasn't online pretty much wiped out the mall stores? I know it has down in my neck of the woods."

Rachel grinned and downed a forkful of her salad. "Depends on how high end the store is. We've still got a couple where the most important thing, especially for the women, is not what you buy but where you're buying it from and who sees you there."

"Sorry to take you away from all that," I said.

"Not a problem. As it is, I have to step out every now and then or it becomes a little too obvious, even with the changes I can make. But enough of my hassles, what's up with your thing?"

I'd debated over this part for quite a while, playing tug of war with myself over how much to reveal without making things too obvious. Although Esperson had a decent background, you don't really know how sharp an investigator is until you see them in action.

"Basically," I said, "what I need is some advice."

She gave me a once over." Okay."

"Let's say I have a client, female, who's going through a divorce."

"I don't usually do divorce work for the firm," Esperson said.

"That's okay. It's not really a divorce question I have. It's more of a 'how would you handle this situation' question."

Her eyes narrowed as if she already smelled a rat. "Go on."

"As I said, she's going through a divorce, and she needs a little extra ammo. You know, wants to make sure she's getting everything she thinks she's entitled to."

"Sounds like every divorce I've ever heard of, on both sides. So she hires a PI?"

"Correct," I said.

Rachel gave me a hard stare. "Is this a Hobart client we're talking about? Because I can't . . ."

"No," I lied through my teeth. "Not one of yours. Another agency here in town."

About then, our server arrived with our food. By unspoken consent, Rachel and I dug in for a while without any more shop talk.

When we were both about half finished, she put her fork down and reengaged. "So your potential client wants a little more support for her divorce claim."

"Right," I said.

"Which leads to her seeking out a detective."

"A male detective." I wasn't sure, but I thought I saw a little flicker of tension cross her face.

Her eyes bored into mine. "Is the gender relevant in some way?"

"Potentially," I said.

Rachel chewed another bite or two before sliding her plate away. "For somebody who wants my advice, Mr. Quinton, you're being awfully coy."

Even though she made the comment in her neutral, casual manner, I could almost see the cogs moving in her brain. For whatever reason Rachel Esperson hadn't worked out on the police force, John Howard had made a good call in hiring her.

"You're right, I apologize. Let me put it this way. Are there any operators in the area who would take advantage of such a situation?"

She laughed and gave me a look. "Such a situation meaning a vulnerable young woman having to reach out for help?"

"Correct."

Another flicker, a little more pronounced this time. "You did hear my little spiel on how big of a city we are, right? There's all sorts working in our profession. You think I know each and every one of them?"

"Good point. I guess I'm used to my little neck of the state where everybody knows everyone else. Let me try it this way. Is there anyone in town you either know or have heard of who has a reputation for something like this?"

Without answering, Rachel returned to her filet, and I dug into what was left of my own meal. In a few minutes, she'd cleaned her plate and looked back up at me.

"How bad is it?"

"The taking advantage of?" I asked.

She nodded.

"Not quite what you would imagine. So far, no heavy breathing over the phone, no dead animals left on her doorstep. If anything, it's a whole lot more subtle than you'd imagine."

"Like how?" Rachel asked.

I hesitated for a second. If I wanted her help, I had to be as straight with her as possible. I'd already lied once, which I hoped wouldn't come back to bite me.

I only hoped she wasn't quite as sharp as she seemed.

I gave her a basic rundown of Lorie's problem, being as specific as possible while leaving out any identifying details. Because of how large Howard's organization was, I wasn't too worried she'd know of or figure out the exact people involved.

When I finished, Rachel leaned back in her chair and stared at me. "Then so far there's no actual evidence of anything nefarious?"

I nodded in agreement.

"But if by chance this woman is on the level, she's probably walking on eggshells by now."

I nodded again.

"Either she's a complete loony bird or she's really in it deep," Rachel said.

"That's about the size of it."

"And since you're not sure which, you're erring on the side of caution."

"You mean acting as if it's all true?" I thought for a second. "Yeah, I guess I am. Though everything I've tracked down so far validates something's up."

Rachel reached out and took a long, solid drink from her ice water. Her shoulder muscles tightened up on her. "Why did you ask for my help on this?"

"It was purely a shot in the dark. I went into Howard's office and asked him if anyone was available. He mentioned a couple of people and . . ."

"Mr. Quinton," Rachel put down her water glass. "Please spare me any more of your bullshit. Somehow or other, you managed to arrange to meet with me personally, so can we just get to whatever's on your mind?"

Maybe I wasn't as smooth and cunning as I'd thought. "Most of what I've said is true," I said. "I've got a client who may have run afoul of a detective supposedly working on her behalf, and she asked for my help in setting things straight."

Rachel stared at me. "Most."

"Excuse me?"

"You said 'most' of what you said was true. Exactly what part wasn't?"

Yep, no doubt about it. A sharp one.

"If you're as smart as you come across," I said, "you'll be able to figure it out."

"Maybe I can," she said. "And maybe I know why you sought me out to help you."

I nodded. "No more deceit," I said. "I think you work with the guy I'm interested in, and I think without my even saying it you can figure out who it is."

CHAPTER TWENTY-ONE

For a minute there, I thought she was going to slug me. Her nostrils flared, and her eyes dilated. Her shoulders tensed up, and the muscles at the side of her neck stretched taut.

Not exactly the reaction I'd hoped for, but one I'd kind of expected.

"Let me explain," I started.

"No!" She cut me off like a knife. "Don't explain anything. Just get up and get the hell out of here or I will."

"Rachel . . ."

"You heard me, mister."

"You're a tough woman," I said.

She blinked a couple of times. "Yeah, so?"

"Tough enough to make it with the cops, tough enough to join a firm like yours and get by."

"Your dialogue's out of date, mister. It's not exactly the 1960s anymore."

"True," I said. I thought of giving her one of my patented smiles, but considered it a good chance she'd slap it right off of me. "Doesn't change my point."

"Which is?"

"I've talked to some people, made a few calls, dug up quite a few interesting things."

"And you came up with me?"

"I came up with a couple of people I could have gone with, but I decided you were my best bet."

"You've been looking into me?" The flaring started all over again, though she was cool enough to keep her voice low so our argument wouldn't reach anyone else.

"No," I said, "not looking into you. Into someone else. And I think you know who."

She picked up her napkin and wrestled it back and forth in her hands. After a few minutes, she dropped it, propped her elbows on the table and cupped her head in her hands. "You've been checking out Thomas," she said, not as a question.

"If by Thomas, you mean Tom Jacobson, that's right."

"No," she said, "Thomas, not Tom. Call him Tom and he'll cut your arm off. You met him yet?"

"Haven't had the pleasure," I said. "But I plan to."

Rachel shook her head, looked around, and beckoned our waitress over. "Could I have a glass of wine?" she asked. "Any kind. Doesn't matter."

The server glanced at both of our plates, took one look at Rachel, and nodded. She took off and came back a minute later with the wine.

Rachel took a deep drink, then put the glass down. "Not my usual habit this early in the evening," she said, "but it's been a long day, and you're not making it any better."

"You sure a shot of whiskey wouldn't have been better?" I asked.

"Most definitely not. A sip or two of hard liquor usually does me right in."

"And you want to keep your head clear while talking to me?" I said.

Rachel's eyes bored into mine. "How about we stop dancing around, Quinton? You're coming to me about Thomas because you know something, right?"

"A little," I admitted, "but you should understand I'm not even remotely thinking of anything that will get you into trouble of some kind."

"Shows you don't really know what you're up to then," she said.

"How's that?"

"Having anything to do with that psycho, no matter how remotely, gets someone into trouble."

I breathed deeply for a few seconds. Her use of the word "psycho" had come off as real, not casual or sarcastic.

"You want to fill me in?" I asked.

"Why should I?"

"Because sometimes the second hand stories aren't accurate; because you've obviously got strong feelings about the man; and because you and I are already sitting here, so why the hell not?"

She mulled that one over while giving me a thousand-yard stare.

"How 'bout you tell me what you found out, and I decide what blanks I want to fill in?" she asked.

"Fair enough."

CHAPTER TWENTY-TWO

"I KNOW YOU STARTED WITH HOBART about eight years ago after a long stint on the Kansas City, Kansas, police force," I said. "Worked your way up to a sergeant in the patrol division."

"Right," Rachel said.

"You were born in KCK, from what I gather, and lived there your whole life."

"Still do, far as that goes."

I nodded. "Then you changed plans and decided to jump for possibly greener pastures in the private sector and accepted an offer from John Howard to join his firm as an investigator."

"All of which you could get from my LinkedIn page," she said.

I nodded. "Which I actually looked at. As far as I can tell from talking to people who know, you've been a model operative for the firm. So much so that a while back you were being eyed for possibly moving into the executive level. Better pay, easier work behind a desk for the most part, and better bennies."

Rachel had settled down a bit, some of the tension leaving her, even if I could still sense the smoldering under the surface.

"And?" she asked.

"And then three years ago, Tom, or Thomas if you want, Jacobson joined the firm in the same slot you began in."

"Again, common knowledge. Get to the point, mister."

Alright, if she wanted to play it tough, we'd play it tough. "Shortly after Jacobson's arrival, your advancement kind of cooled down. You still got good quarterly reports, still cleared the majority of your caseload, yet the dream of a corner office somehow whisked away."

"Bastard!" Rachel hissed, though I wasn't quite sure who she was referring to.

"And in no time at all," I continued, "I believe within a couple of months of joining the firm, Jacobson was moved up to the highest slot in the company below the boss."

"You must have been talking to a lot of people."

"I'm a detective," I said. "I detected. Do I have it right?"

"That's about right," Rachel said.

"Any idea how he pulled it off?"

"There's all kinds of speculation, but any talk is done very quietly, very much on the downlow."

I thought that one over for a second. "How's your working environment today?"

Her eyes snapped at me. "In what way, Mr. Quinton? If you think I'm going to say anything against my employer, you've got another..."

"Word is you had a personal run-in with Jacobson," I interrupted.

"That's none of your business," she said.

Before I could answer, the waitress came back and asked if we wanted to consider desert. We both shook our heads, and I asked for the check.

"Wrong," I said once the waitress had left. "There's a very good chance your problems with him are my client's business."

"This client of yours a woman?" Rachel asked.

I nodded

"And she somehow ran afoul of Thomas," she continued. "Can I guess she was a client of our agency?"

"She was, yes."

"Means you lied to me a minute ago."

"I apologize. I had to get you talking. If I'd told the truth up front, what would you have done?"

"The same thing I should be doing right now. Getting up and walking out."

"Good point," I said, "but I kind of notice you're not doing that."

The waitress, with the same spot on timing she'd displayed all along, picked that moment to bring the check. She placed it on the middle of the table, a bit closer to Rachel than to me. I reached over and snagged it.

I looked at the ticket total and was glad Lorie's boss had offered to cover my freight on this case.

"You realize how many company protocols I'm breaking right about now?" Rachel asked. "By not standing up and walking away?"

"Probably a ton," I said as I pulled my Visa card from my wallet. "Which tells me something about you I'd already figured."

"Howard would kill me if he found out."

I grinned at her, hoping to ease the tension a little. "That's one of the nice things about being a one-man shop. The only protocols I have to worry about are my own."

Rachel flattened her right hand on the table for a moment and stared at it. "True," she finally said, "but operations like yours are pretty much extinct these days."

"Last of the dinosaurs," I said.

"Turnabout's fair play," she said. "When Howard set up this meeting, I spent a couple of minutes looking into your background."

"Probably didn't take much more than that," I said.

"You've got a good rep, but is it enough to pay the bills without your other gig?"

"In other words," I said, "you've got a lot more to lose in this thing than I do, right?"

Rachel finished off her wine. "Tell your client to stay as far away from Thomas as she can," she said.

"Any possibility of violence on his part?"

Rachel twirled the stem of her glass back and forth as she considered that. "I'd say no. While he's an opportunistic little bastard, and professionally speaking you don't want to turn your back on him, he's not exactly the most physical of guys." She gave me a bit of a closer stare. "Not like you."

I thought of swelling my chest out but figured it would come off as too showy. "What exactly was your experience with him?" I asked. "Obviously, what I found was only broad outlines."

Rachel shook her head. "Don't want to go into that. Besides, it's more of an office politics thing than anything else."

"Would you say he's in good with your boss?"

She snickered a bit. "That one's pretty obvious, wouldn't you say?"

"You're right," I said. "Stupid question. Would make it a little tough if someone in the company crossed him, huh?"

That far away stare came back into Rachel's eyes. "Yeah," she said, "It really could."

"I need some help, Rachel. I think he's targeted someone, and I need a way to get close to him."

The distance left her eyes, and she came back to me. "Sorry, Mr. Quinton. I've got my own livelihood and career to think about. I left the cops for something I thought would be better, and I don't have a side gig to fall back on like you do."

I didn't really consider my gym a side gig, but I kept quiet because I saw her point.

"He knows people," she continued. "Lots of people. And he knows how to get things done."

"Then can you at least give me a direction," I asked, "a suggestion for how to proceed?"

"The best suggestion I can give both you and your client," Rachel said as she stood up and pushed her chair back into the table, "is to stay as far away from him as possible."

With that, she walked away, leaving me at the table by myself. I sat there mulling over how much I may have just screwed up.

A minute later, Rachel came back to the table and plopped a business card down on it.

"Personal info's on the back," she said, "but only if you really, really need to reach out."

I thought about things as she began walking away, and in the end decided to let her go.

CHAPTER TWENTY-THREE

The next morning, Saturday, I was working my way through a ham and cheese omelette at an I-Hop down the street from the hotel when two men walked in. They stopped just inside the door, ignoring the hostess, and scanned the room. Locking on me, they brushed past the hostess and headed in my direction.

They walked up to my table and, without being invited, pulled out chairs and sat down.

They were young men, no more than mid-twenties at most. Both white, one with curly blond hair and blue eyes, the other with dark brown, almost black hair, and brown eyes. Their hair was cut short—not quite regulation army crew-cut, though close. Both were about five eleven with muscles that could have been lifted off a Marine recruiting poster.

They wore blue jeans, sneakers, and tee-shirts, the blond wearing navy blue and the brown-haired guy wearing bright red. Both wore their tee-shirts hanging out, and the shirts looked a size or two too big for them.

Usually, if anything, young men with muscles wear their shirts on the small side to show off their builds. Looking at these two, a more cynical person would have wondered if the shirts were extra-sized to conceal weapons holstered to their hips.

"How you doing?" the blond one asked me.

"Up to now, not bad," I said.

The blond man continued, "Like to talk to you if you don't mind."

"And if I do mind?"

The two glanced at each other before turning back to me. "Going to talk to you anyway."

I flicked my head towards the second man. "He have a voice?"

"Let's say I'm the spokesman here, okay?" The blond tensed his arms and chest to show me he was in charge.

"You know," I said, "flexing your muscles doesn't do a whole lot when your shirt's too big. You can either show off the muscles or conceal your weapons, but not both at the same time."

Both men made involuntary hand motions towards their left hips, then caught themselves.

I smiled. "See what I mean?"

"We need to talk," Blond repeated.

"No, you mean you want to talk. Just like I want to sit here and finish enjoying my breakfast, which isn't going to happen if I have to take time to bounce you two bozos out into the street."

"You think you can do that?" the brown-haired guy finally spoke up.

"Not sure," I said. "But if you guys keep bothering me, I'm going to do my best to find out. And whether I succeed or not, it's going to cause a ruckus, which I'm guessing your sergeant isn't going to like too much."

Both of them simultaneously flinched, then recovered almost as quickly.

"Sergeant?" Brown-hair snorted. "Just who do you think we are, buddy?"

I shook my head. "Apart from guys who need to stop watching *Goodfellas* for their dialogue, my best guess is you're a couple of off-duty cops who came in here to roust me because you're doing a favor for an old friend."

That stopped them for a moment. Around us floated all the normal sounds of lots of people enjoying their food—forks scraping, plates shifting, and milk and juice gurgling down throats.

The two continued looking at me.

I looked back at them.

"If you think we're cops," the blond spokesman finally started in, "isn't pissing us off about the dumbest thing you could do."

"Depends," I said.

"On?"

"On where your jurisdiction begins and ends. That's one of the problems with patchwork metro areas. Right now, we're both sitting in Kansas City, Missouri. If you have badges from here, you may have a point. If you pull out shields from KCK, or Blue Springs, or Olathe, I don't think I'm going to worry a whole lot."

"You're kind of dumb, man," Brown-hair said. "All we'd have to do is say we were sitting here minding our own business and saw something that gave us probable cause. What about that?"

I sighed, pushed my plate away, and leaned back in my chair. "No," I told them, "I'm not dumb. Dumb would be coming on to me here in a restaurant full of witnesses; dumb would be brushing right past the hostess up front, making sure she'll remember you; and dumb would be sticking yourselves out like this for someone else."

The two looked at me, and I could almost see the gears whirling in their minds.

"Don't feel bad, boys," I said. "We're all inexperienced at some point in our lives. Whatever force you work for, I'm guessing neither of you is more than a year or two out of the academy. You really think you can roust me in such a way, and make up a story to go along with it, that's going to float right past your higher ups?"

In unison, their shoulders slouched, and their upper bodies moved back an inch or two. The air of cocky superiority they'd rode in on had almost completely dissipated in under a minute.

"So we can do this one of two ways." My mouth was getting dry from being the only one talking, but I didn't want to break my tempo by pausing for a drink of juice. "You can either go ahead and try the silly ass plan you came in here with, which is almost certainly going to blow up in your faces sooner or later, or you can go back to whoever put you up to this and tell him you tried but couldn't find me. One way, you come off as criminals to your superiors and entire force, the other you come off as incompetent to one man. Take your pick."

They looked at each other again, and if I hadn't been watching for it, I would have missed the slight nod that passed between them. They slid their chairs back and stood up.

"This isn't over pal," the blond one said.

"Sure it is," I replied. "All that's left to do is go back to the guy who hired you and tell him you screwed it up, then go about your lives."

I must have wowed them with my simplicity because two seconds later they turned and left.

Rookies.

Greenhorns.

So green, in fact, they didn't even consider the possibility I would watch them through the window as they got to the parking lot and climbed into a late '70s black Trans Am to drive away.

CHAPTER TWENTY-FOUR

"You telling me a hotshot like you didn't even get their names?" Det. Sloan asked me a while later.

It was still Saturday morning, I was still in Kansas City, and my next step was to figure out what the heck to do with my new information. Leaving the restaurant, I'd pulled out my phone and, crossing my fingers, made a call to the Overland Park station.

The crossed fingers did their job because I lucked out and found Sloan working on a weekend.

"I'd like to come by if I could," I'd said.

"Got something to give me on your case?"

"Maybe, maybe not. I'd rather go over it in person."

"You mean like, not on the phone?" Sloan had said. "Hell, Quinton, that's straight out of a 1970s TV show."

"If you say so. Still rather run it down face to face. I think it's more believable that way."

Sloan grumbled for a few more minutes, then told me he'd be around till noon.

When I showed up, he was sitting at his desk, the pile of paperwork looking exactly as high and just as disorganized as it had been on my first visit a few days before.

"You lucked out," he said. "I'm usually not here on the weekends."

"The benefits of seniority?" I asked.

"Naw," Sloan said. "More like the benefits of policing a

community where the median annual income's in the six figures. More white-collar crime, fewer street problems."

"So why the weekend work?" I asked.

Sloan grinned. "Today's the day for family reunion on my wife's side. I couldn't realistically beg off entirely, but managed to sneak half a day past them."

"Good to know you've got your priorities in order," I said.

"Priorities. So what have you got for me?"

I filled him in on what had gone down during breakfast, but he didn't seem all that impressed.

"What makes you think your two rousters were cops?"

"They had the look. Young, in shape, hair cut almost as short as military but not quite."

"Could have been military," Sloan pointed out.

"Could have been. I also slipped in a mention of their sergeant, and they got a little antsy."

"You may not know this, buddy, but they have sergeants in the army."

"True. But when I called them out on being cops they didn't deny it."

Sloan sighed and snagged a small yellow note pad from somewhere in the mound on his desk. "You know how many different police forces are scattered across this area? How much total personnel that accounts for? How am I supposed to even have a hell of a hope of finding two guys?"

"I can describe them."

Sloan gave me a deeper, much more intentional sigh. "Better than nothing. Go for it."

I gave him as complete a description as I could of the two men, and by the time I was done he looked ready to snap his pencil in half. "That's it? Two men, muscular, mid-twenties, one with brown hair and one with blond? That's your hotshot PI description of the two men who accosted you?"

"Well," I said, drawing the word out into a couple of syllables, "I also watched them drive away, could give you some information as to their vehicle."

Sloan sat up a little straighter at that. "Now we're talking. License plate?"

"No plate," I said. "I was sitting in a booth next to the window, but they'd parked about halfway down the lot. Too far for me to see a plate."

The cop peered at me. "You holding something back, Quinton? Going for the big dramatic moment?"

I grinned and decided to relent. "Sorry, Detective. Guess it's just the showman in me from my previous life. Although I didn't get a plate number, they drove away in a fairly distinctive car. Even in a city this size, can't be too many of them like it."

"What was it?" Sloan asked. "A gold-plated Lamborghini?"

"Not quite that distinct, but pretty close. How about a late '70s Pontiac Trans Am?"

Sloan's face tightened, and I got the feeling I'd hit some kind of nerve. "Color?" he asked.

"Black, of course," I said.

"Black," he repeated. "Gold screaming chicken on the hood and everything?"

"The very same," I said.

"Jesus Christ."

CHAPTER TWENTY-FIVE

"They're two of ours," Sloan said.

I didn't answer, deciding to wait and let the man work through it on his own.

"Ed Landru and Frank Davis," he continued after a moment. "Landru is the one with the TA."

"They're not partners, are they?"

"Naw, both of them too young to be a street team. They came out of the academy at the same time, two, maybe two and a half years ago."

I gave him a look. "Town this size has its own academy? Property tax values must be even bigger than I thought."

Sloan grimaced. "Don't be fooled by the tax brackets around here. We have to scrape for nickels like everyone else. We share a county academy with about twenty other towns."

"Makes sense," I said.

"Regardless, Landru and Davis were buddies all the way through and far as I know still buddies today."

"Nice thing about having a small force," I said, "you can ID them right off."

Sloan grinned, kind of a lopsided manner. "Your descriptions were shit, Quinton. But you're right. Not a lot of those old-time Pontiacs still on the streets."

"The ones that are are so rare they must cost quite a bit. Any idea how a uniform patrol officer can afford one of those?"

Sloan waved that away. "From what I hear, and understand I don't know these guys all that well, Landru's a muscle car buff. Even though he's got a decent salary for a guy his age, he still lives with his parents, meaning he can spend most of his disposable income on cars."

"Good thing about all this," I said, "is it clears one thing up for good."

Sloan nodded. "Your client's not a nutjob after all. She really did run afoul of someone, and you poking around is causing them to react."

"And the someone is no doubt Jacobson."

"How do you make that much of a leap?" Sloan asked.

"Because this little counteroffensive didn't start until after I visited the man's offices yesterday."

I proceeded to fill Sloan in on my visit to Hobart and Howard, including my dinner afterward with Rachel Esperson.

"There's some history there," I said. "But she wouldn't really budge all that much on what it was."

"You think she ran to Jacobson and told him you were asking about him?"

I skulled that one for a couple of seconds, then shook my head. "Don't think so. Actually, wouldn't be necessary. He's number two in the whole shebang, probably meets with John Howard on a daily basis to go over company business. Or he may have to approve any expenditures of time or resources."

"In other words, there's half a dozen ways he could have found out you were rummaging around."

"You bet," I agreed, "but while this solves one of my questions, it kind of raises another."

Sloan leaned back in his chair so far it creaked, and laced his hands behind his head. "Are you by chance referring to how, if our premise is right, this Jacobson managed to corrupt two young officers of the law?"

"More or less," I said.

Sloan stared at the ceiling for a minute before speaking up. "If what you're thinking is correct, this fellow has quite the ability, plus opportunity, to mess around in people's lives."

"I'm beginning to believe that."

"Could be something as straightforward as he hired them," Sloan said.

"Any indication they've ever been on the take?"

"Hell, no. Far as that goes, what's the point of patrolmen going on the take? What the hell could they ever do for anyone?"

"Maybe look the other way on certain things," I said.

Sloan kept focused on the ceiling. "If you say so. Seems to me it's a lot better return on investment to have sergeants or lieutenants on your pad."

"Or maybe detectives?" I suggested.

He sat back up straight and focused in on me again. "Wouldn't know about it myself. I've never had any offers come my way."

"Must feel humiliating," I said.

"It does, sometimes. But at least I'm not driving around in a goddamned fifty-year old Pontiac."

"Well, there is that," I said.

"You want me to bring them in? Sweat them a little bit? Try find a connection to your boy Jacobson?"

It took me longer to think that one over before I ended up shaking my head. "Not yet. If you think about it, there's really nothing to hang on them other than my say so. And what good would it do?"

"Hope you realize I may have been asking as a courtesy," Sloan said. "If these guys are out there freelancing, it's not exactly like I can leave them running around loose."

"True, but like I say you don't really have anything on them. If I bust Jacobson, there's a chance you will get the goods. Then it's a win-win."

"Something else I'm wondering if you've taken into account," Sloan said.

"Which is?"

"As we've both noticed, the weird thing about all this is that up to now it's been the most violence-free case of stalking I've ever come across."

"True," I said. "It's been more like a mental chess game than anything else."

"And, up until now, nothing to definitely tie your guy to any of the stuff that happened to Mrs. Jones."

I took in some deep air and gave that one some thought. "Still no actual violence," I pointed out.

"True, though a lot closer to it than before. If you hadn't been able to bluff those two, and had actually left with them, what do you think they would have done?"

"So the violence quotient has inched up a bit," I said.

"I never knew a jock to use the word quotient before," Sloan said.

"Hell, Detective. You'd be surprised. Every now and then I can even read without moving my lips. The point is, if at all possible, I'd like to keep Jacobson in the dark as much as I can."

"Meaning it will be obvious to him right away his boys fucked up, but he won't know for sure if you've connected him with them."

"More or less. He'll probably think the connection's obvious. Since my working for Lorie Jones is the only reason I'm in town, he may not think I'm sharp enough to see it. Far as that goes, if you yank them, he'll probably know about it right away. The dude seems to have wires all over this town."

"In other words, keep your powder dry for as long as possible," Sloan said.

"More like keep him guessing until I can think of a handle to stick him with."

"There's another angle to all of this, you know."

"Yeah," I said, "I'm aware of that."

"Considering his rep, what kind of shop is John Howard running over there?"

I nodded. "And how deep, if at all, is the top guy involved."

"You think there's other clients of his that've been in trouble before?"

"Damned if I know. At first, I thought this was pretty small time for a guy like him. But if it's gotten to the point where street cops are becoming enforcers..."

I could tell Sloan didn't like it. "I'll give you as much leeway as I can, but at some point I've got to get those two yanked off the streets. We can't have a couple of loose guns like them running around."

I stood up. "Understood. As much time as possible is all I can ask for."

Sloan stayed seated at his desk. "So what are you going to do about all this?"

"I don't have the foggiest. If I did, maybe I could up my daily rate."

In truth, as I left the squad room, I didn't feel all that good about what I was going to do next.

CHAPTER TWENTY-SIX

As I drove away from the station, I felt kind of crummy. Sloan had been decent to me, especially considering my status as an out-of-towner. I hated to pull one over on him, but in the end he was a cop and had rules and regulations to follow.

Despite his assurances, I figured it wouldn't be long before he pulled the pin on Landru and Davis, which if they were smart would cause them to lawyer up and shut up. That would be the smart thing to do because, at the moment, all we had was a "he said/they said." Sure, the hostess at the I-Hop could maybe testify they'd been kind of rude to her, if she remembered them out of all the customers she saw each day, but there wasn't any sort of crime in that.

No, if Sloan was even half the cop he made himself out to be, which I figured he was if not more, I gave it till Sunday night, maybe Monday morning, before his qualms got the best of him and he went about doing his duty.

Which, to my way of looking at it, would be okay because I planned to have my business with my two accosters done long before then.

Sloan had screwed up, or maybe he hadn't, when he gave me the two young cops' full names.

I drove back to KC proper, stopping for an early lunch at a BBQ place down on the Plaza. Karyn Roberts and I had had occasional arguments as to where in the state to fine the best BBQ, with Karyn naturally touting the glories of KC restaurants.

The one I tried for lunch, I had to admit, far exceeded my expectations. By the time I'd finished a smoked half chicken with honey chipotle sauce, with fries and potato salad, I was ready to chuck Plan A for the day and go to Plan B, which consisted of heading back to the hotel, sprawling out on the couch, and watching a game on TV.

But I was in town for work, not pleasure, or gluttony for that matter. I did go back to my hotel room after the meal but only to make use of my laptop.

In the old days, PI's were often hired to track down basic information on people: where they lived, net worth, marital status, occupation, that sort of thing. These days, almost anyone halfway familiar with basic computers can get that kind of stuff on their own in under an hour or so.

Ed Landru and Frank Davis, however, were cops, and even at the rookie end of things, it's usually much more difficult to get the lowdown on cops. For obvious reasons, of course. That's why it took most of the afternoon, along with lots of phone calls and computer time, to get what I needed.

By the time I finished, my fingers were sore and my eyes strained.

I left the hotel, climbed back into the Cherokee, and headed once again back to Overland Park. If I had to spend much more time there, I'd probably develop an overwhelming desire to go out and buy a Mercedes.

The truth, though, is not all of the town is quite so ritzy, the area where Lorie Jones lived being an example, and in about thirty minutes I was pulling up to the curb in a neighborhood that, while nice, didn't exactly sport below-ground pools in every back yard.

And if I had any doubts as to the efficiency of my sources, the black Trans Am I spotted about a block down from where I pulled up would have wiped those doubts away.

It was parked in front of a light blue ranch house with a big cottonwood tree in front and an unfenced backyard. Kind of hard to tell from where I sat, but the backyard seemed to kind of wrap around to the front of the house, giving the impression it was about double the size of the front. Black plastic shutters on each side of the three front windows were right out of the 1970s, making them a perfect match for Landru's car.

A detached garage sat off to the side with its door all the way shut, leaving me no way of gauging whether anyone else was in the house or not.

Didn't really matter, as I didn't plan to enter.

I turned off the Cherokee, rolled down the windows, and settled back to rest a bit. I didn't fall asleep, instead went into a light doze where I could recharge the mental batteries my afternoon of research had drained, while at the same time being aware of my surroundings.

I had to be cautious on two fronts. One, I didn't want some vigilant neighbor to notice me sitting doing nothing for very long, and two I had to keep in mind Ed Landru was a cop and could potentially spot me himself.

On the other hand, if my encounter this morning with Landru and his running buddy Davis was any indication of his ability, that second was pretty much a soft worry.

With about an hour to go before sundown, the afternoon had been a typically Midwestern day in May, mild with occasional breezes. I didn't plan to merely sit around all night eyeing a car. It was Saturday evening, and because Landru was a young stud, I figured it wouldn't be long before he'd be hitting the town.

Turned out I was right. Forty-five minutes after I'd settled in, the blond-haired cop exited the house, climbed into his pony car, and fired it up. I expected him to gun the motor a couple of times, but he showed a little more maturity than I'd given him credit for.

He backed out of the drive, gave a restrained screech as he shifted into Drive, then took off.

He was so absorbed with himself he didn't even notice the middle-aged guy in the Cherokee parked down the street who pulled away and began following him.

CHAPTER TWENTY-SEVEN

I HAD NO DOUBT MY PLAN VERGED on the risky side of things. While I hoped things wouldn't get too out of hand, when it came time to renew my investigator's license, a charge for assaulting a police officer would probably be somewhat frowned on.

On the other hand, I'd been in KC for almost a week now and spent the whole time punching at shadows. The lack of progress was beginning to eat away at me, and I wanted to wrap things up and go home.

Hence, I shadowed Landru and his classic Pontiac.

We left Overland Park and entered Lenexa, another in the crazy patchwork of municipalities, buttressed up against Overland Park and still on the Kansas side of the line, that most people around the country regard as Kansas City. Lenexa's of a decent size, around sixty thousand people or so. This leaves it a little smaller than my stomping grounds of Providence but not by much.

I almost felt like I'd gone home.

As I tailed Landru, I used all the tricks Duke Prowder had taught me about how to keep another car in sight without them seeing you even though I kind of wondered if any of it was necessary.

Considering what I'd seen of Landru's competence up to now, I wasn't all that concerned, though it never hurts to be cautious.

After wandering back, forth, and every which way for a while, the Trans-Am pulled into a cramped parking lot that sat squarely between a tattoo parlor and an honest-to-goodness old time pool hall. The east and west wall, respectively, of each business formed the boundaries of the lot, with room for, at a quick glance and in the deepening gloom of the evening, maybe thirty cars. The back wall of a business on the adjacent street formed another boundary, leaving literally only one way in or out of the lot.

The lot was almost full, forcing Landru to park his car almost against the back wall. As early in the night as it was, I assumed most of the vehicles, primarily pickup trucks, represented customers in the pool hall. Most of the time, even on weekends, tat parlors don't really ramp up until just shy of midnight.

The pool hall's windows were blackened, and when Landru pulled in I couldn't spot anyone else on the street, in the lot, or anywhere around. I figured this as my best time, so as he parked his car I zoomed into the lot myself, keeping on a straight course and stopping the Cherokee at right angles to the Trans-Am, effectively blocking him from leaving.

I sincerely hoped nobody wandered along to spot us because with the dimensions of the lot, I'd have to back straight out to leave, and I didn't want to attempt that in any sort of hurry.

Landru wiggled out of his car at the same time I climbed out of the Cherokee. There was hardly any space to move around, which is what I'd counted on. Without a lot of light, I couldn't tell if he recognized me or not.

"What the fuck, man?" he bellowed.

He was wearing straight-legged jeans over black cowboy boots and a yellow tee-shirt, unlike that morning, a size too small for him.

"Want to talk to you, Ed, without your buddy around."

He bent his upper body a little closer, and now I could tell he knew who I was. "I said what do you want? And you'd better make it good or I'll run you in for harassing a police officer." As he spoke, he flexed a little to make clear to me what I was messing with.

"Ed," I said, "no one's around at the moment to be impressed, and there's no partner or anybody to come to your aid. If you don't grow up a little real quick, I'm going to have to spank you and send you home."

The kid drew himself up to his full height and pumped the guns a little more. "You think you can take me, buddy?"

"I'm not your buddy," I said. "And yes, I'm pretty damned sure I can take you."

I'll give the guy this. He held his ground. "You know what happens when you assault a police officer, dude? One, all the other cops anywhere around are going to be on your ass like crazy, and two, you can kiss your cool PI license goodbye."

"Ed," I said, "I'm not here to parley with you all night. I've known a lot of cops in my time, and believe it or not I'm on pretty good relations with almost all of them. Mainly because the ones I usually deal with aren't wiseass punks like you."

He set himself, weight centered, arms down straight at his sides, and hands loosely curled into fists. "Come one step closer, old man, and we'll see who's the wiseass punk around here."

"Works for me," I said as I took a step forward.

He came at me, his right arm arcing out to land a blow. Like most younger men, even those with some training, he looped his punch, flinging it at my head instead of driving it.

Plus, he was pretty slow. Took hardly any effort at all for me to duck down, slide forward another couple of steps, and ram a straight right into his midsection. I did kind of a half spin and ended up slightly behind his right side, out of the way as he went crashing to his knees.

Seriously?

After one punch?

Landru knelt there groaning, his arms wrapped around his abdomen. "Need to work on the abs, kid," I said. "You're not going to be much help to your compatriots if you fold after a single punch."

"Suckered me," the young cop hissed between his teeth.

I shook my head. "That wasn't a sucker, kid. That was straight on, full view, after you started it. Want another?"

He started to shake his head, then flashed his arm up in an attempt to get me in the groin. I sidestepped that one as well and gave him a hammer blow, the edge of my hand with my fist curled, onto the back of his head.

This time, he went all the way down on the pavement.

I took a second to glance around. Fortunately, still no one in sight. My luck couldn't hold for long. Whatever I could get out of him I needed to do soon.

"Had enough?" I asked the back of his head.

Landru rolled halfway over so his right eye could look at me. "You're going down hard, mister. Assaulting a cop's gonna get you..."

"Exactly nothing," I interrupted. "We got no witnesses, making it only your word against mine. I haven't left any of my blood on you and vice versa. Your word against mine, kind of like this morning. You may scuttle off and file a report, but I've already had a talk this afternoon with someone in your department, and there's a good chance IA is going to be giving you a good going over in a day or two. So you see, I'm really not all that worried."

"Whaddaya want?" he asked.

"I want to know who put you up to it."

Landru placed his left hand on the pavement and levered himself half up, allowing him to look at me straight on. "Put me up to what?"

I sighed and curled my hands into half fists. The kid flinched a little and scooted back against the fender well of his car. "Don't be a moron, Ed. You and your buddy Davis didn't randomly decide to drive out of your jurisdiction and go roll a tourist. What were you two supposed to do if I'd walked off with you?"

"Just give you a thumpin' or two, you know. A gentle reminder to pack it up and head home."

"Uh huh. And who was it who wanted you to do this?"

Landru's eyes shifted. I took a couple more steps till I loomed over him and raised my arms up again. "Don't lie to me, kid. No matter how this goes down, it's your word against mine."

"Wasn't going to lie," he muttered. "Just trying to think of a way to tell you you'll believe."

"Believe what?"

"That we're not sure who asked us to do it."

"You're right," I said. "I don't believe you. Better think up a better one before I get angry."

"I'm telling you. He's a guy helped us out a while back. He calls us, not the other way around."

Wild as the story was, I kind of believed it. Rather than press my luck, I reached down and grabbed Landru by the collar and reared him up.

"Let's go doofus," I said.

"Where?" Landru staggered to his feet and didn't resist me tugging him toward the Cherokee.

"We're going to take a little ride," I said.

CHAPTER TWENTY-EIGHT

We left Landru's car behind as we headed out of the parking lot in my Cherokee. The big, bad man was huddled in the passenger's seat staring at me.

"Where we going?" he asked, his voice still kind of soft and muffled.

"We're going to drive around for a while until you make things clear to me," I said. "Then I'll take you back to your car, and you and I can go our separate ways."

"How'd you track me down?"

I didn't want to give Sloan away, mainly because I didn't know his eventual game plan.

"I'm a detective," I said. "Figuring things out and tracking people down is what I do. Didn't you know that before you and your friend tried to roust me?"

"Yeah, but we were told it was no big deal. That you were pretty much just an ex-jock who thought he was tough and needed to be taught a lesson."

"Your information was half right. I am an ex-jock, but I don't think I'm tough. I know it."

"We were only going to rough you up a little," he mumbled in reply.

"Uh huh." My stomach began to curdle. I'd known a lot of cops in my life, and most of them were as decent as they come. I was glad I'd sort of lied to Landru about anything coming down on him.

"Didn't really have a choice," he said.

I glanced over at my passenger. "Excuse me?"

"About taking you on. We really didn't have a choice."

I gripped the wheel tighter. "How come?"

Landru turned and looked out his window, shoulders slumped and head cocked at an angle.

"How come, Ed? When you stop talking is when I pull into the nearest dark alley and we go another round. Time I'm done with you, you won't be in the mental or physical state to make any charges against me. How come?"

A deflating kind of sound came from the kid, and his body jerked all over. "The dude who called had something on us. On Frank and I."

"Which was?"

Now he turned to look at me. "You going to tell anyone?"

"Right at the moment, I'd say that's not your main concern. With gas as high as it is, I'm not inclined to drive around all night. What'd he have on you?"

A moment passed, then another, before Landru started talking. "A couple months after we got out of the academy, Frank and I decided to hit the streets together."

Now he'd confused me. "You mean in uniform?"

"Naw. Plainclothes." I got an image of two little boys playing cops and robbers in the back yard. "It was a night off, and we felt like some action. You know?"

"You went out looking for trouble?" I asked.

Landru shook his head. "We went out to do our job. Unfortunately, we kind of bitched it up."

"In what way?" I asked.

He hesitated and started looking out his window again.

"Ed," I said softly.

He turned back to me. "We came across a drug deal in an alley. One guy selling to another. And we went to bust it up."

Just to make sure, I decided right then to make another contact with Sloan tomorrow. No way in hell could these guys stay on the streets. "And?"

Landru must have decided he was already in too deep because once he began talking again he didn't stop until it all came out. "And the taller one, the bigger one, got away. The dealer. We managed to corner the buyer. He was a little punk, skinny and scared. We chased him to the end of the alley, where it dead-ended."

He stopped for a moment, and I wasn't sure but I thought I heard him sniffle. "Frank pulled out his cuffs, you know, get the perp secured. When the light glinted on them, the perp decided to rabbit again, and he pulled out a knife. Can you believe that? Two of us, easily bigger and taller than him, and he pulls a blade?"

I didn't answer, figuring keeping quiet would be the best way for the story to keep coming. We pulled to a red light, and after another sniffle or two, Landru kept talking. "It got kind of blurry after that, you know? A lot of movement back and forth with nobody really certain what's going on. At some point, the kid tripped and fell out into a little pool of light that came from this one streetlamp on one side of the dead end."

The light turned green, and I moved through the intersection. I was holding my breath, afraid where this was going.

It turned out not to be as bad as I'd feared, though still pretty bad. "Turns out he really was a kid," Landru said. "Couldn't have been more than fourteen years old, if that. When he tripped, he conked his head on the pavement and went down."

I couldn't keep quiet anymore. "So you two heroes administered first aid and got him to a hospital, right?"

Landru shook his head without looking at me. I don't know what he saw in the reflection from the window, but I had a hunch he didn't like it very much.

I knew I didn't.

"We patched him up as much as we could and called an ambulance, then took off."

"Called anonymously?" I asked.

He nodded to the window.

"The kid die?" I asked. By now, I'd done something of a loop and was pulling back onto the block that held the parking lot where I'd confronted Landru.

He half turned my direction, and his posture straightened up a bit. "No," he said. "The kid lived."

"All's well that ends well, huh?" I said.

"Except a couple of days later, Davis got a call. From someone who said he knew what we'd done and had proof. Said he may call on us for help every now and then."

Jacobson, I thought—or maybe, stretching a bit there—John Howard.

I pulled into the lot and maneuvered the Cherokee up till it was abreast of Landru's Trans Am. "How many jobs you done for him?" I asked.

"None, mister. Not until this morning."

We were parked next to his car. Landru wasn't making any move to leave. "And you didn't do a very good job of that, did you?" I asked

"Nope."

Not a cocky tough guy anymore, crouched there in my passenger seat he was more like a scared little kid than anything else.

"Old or young?" I asked.

"Huh?"

"The guy who called you. Back then and today. Did he sound like old or young?"

It was a long shot for a couple of reasons. First, unless at the extreme end of one or the other, it's kind of tough to tell ages over the phone. Second, whoever had contacted them, either Jacobson or Howard, what was to say they hadn't hired someone to make the call.

But there was another reason the question was a long shot that I hadn't considered.

"Dunno," Landru said. "According to Frank, both times it was one of those computer-generated voices. You know, like the ones you see sometimes on YouTube videos."

Great.

Another dead end.

More punching at shadows.

"What are you going to do?" Landru asked.

"About?"

"About us. Me and Frank. We screwed up, sure, but we can still be good cops."

I stared at him, almost unable to believe my ears. "You and your buddy were excluded from being good cops around the time you graduated kindergarten," I said. "Now get the hell out of my car. Go home and wait for whatever comes your way."

Landru's shoulders hunched up, and for a moment I thought he was going to protest, then he slumped again, and mumbled something under his breath. The only word I could make out was "you" and it sounded like it was the second of two words.

Didn't really concern me all that much.

Far as I thought about it, those two were now Sloan's problem. I had something more pressing on my mind.

Namely, I was now firmly convinced Lorie Jones hadn't been delusional or pretending. That someone had actually been working on messing with her mind . . . and she clearly wasn't the only one the dude had been messing with.

CHAPTER TWENTY-NINE

The next day was Sunday. I thought of a couple of avenues I could have gone down concerning the case, but on a Sunday in May, with the projected temps hovering around the mid-seventies and no rain in the forecast, it didn't seem like the thing to do.

I had breakfast in a little café I'd discovered on a previous visit to the city a few years back. Since Zach Lewis had offered to pay for my time on this case, I considered going to town and ordering some of everything on their menu, then decided that would come off as a little piggish.

While eating, I considered hopping in the Cherokee and driving back to Providence to spend the day with Talia. After only one week, I was tired of hotel living, and since I'd been in KC for business hadn't had the opportunity to enjoy myself much.

But as I pulled out my phone to call Talia, it occurred to me there was someone else who was probably feeling the cabin fever even worse than I was.

Thus, after thinking it over for a bit I decided how to spend most of Sunday.

Getting back to my room from breakfast, I got out my phone and placed a call to Lorie Jones. She answered on the first ring, giving some idea of how much she'd probably been climbing the walls for the last week.

"Any news?" was her opening line.

"Somewhat," I said. "There's been some movement along a couple of lines, and I think I'm getting a bead on Jacobson."

"Which means what?" Lorie asked.

"Means just what I said. I'm gathering information, getting a feel for the guy's habits, and I hope to get this wrapped sometime soon."

There was a pause of a few seconds before Lorie resumed speaking. "You believe me then? You're sure he's the one who pulled those stunts on me?"

"If he isn't, then we've got a wild coincidence going on. There's a little more."

"More?" Her voice went up half an octave. "Like what?"

"Tell you what," I said. "This would probably go a lot easier in person, and I'll bet you've had about enough of the four walls of your house."

"Meaning what, Mr. Quinton?"

"Lorie, do not take this wrong in any way, shape, or form, but it's a nice day today, and I feel like taking a drive. Why don't I pick you up, we'll get out and get some air, and I'll explain what's happened so far."

Another dead spot, longer this time, and I began to fear I'd pushed a wrong button. Maybe asking a client frightened of being harassed by a male to take a drive with a guy was pretty stupid, but I'd also thought about how nuts she must be feeling after a week of hanging around her house.

Ten seconds went by, twenty, before Lorie spoke. "Come on by. I'll be waiting."

CHAPTER THIRTY

I PULLED INTO HER DRIVEWAY a few minutes after ten and beeped my horn. She came out wearing a pair of black jeans, white sneakers, and a pink tee-shirt that read "Copywriters Rule." She had a small black purse looped over her shoulder and her hair done back in a ponytail.

She slid into the passenger seat and snicked in her seat belt as I pulled out of the driveway. Glancing sideways, I saw she still wore the drawn, tight look of several days ago; not a surprise, really, seeing as how she'd been cooped up with nothing to do except worry about who was coming after her, but I still didn't like the look on her.

"Thanks," she said. "I don't know if I could have stayed shut up in that house an hour longer. Please tell me you've come up with some way to get me free."

I grinned at her as I took a right at the corner. "Wish I could. All I can say is things are moving somewhat."

"What do you mean by moving?"

Before answering, I made a couple more turns until I was headed in the direction of Interstate-435. My plan was to get on the westbound side of the highway and head up and out of town.

"First," I said after I got going the direction I wanted, "I think we were wise to keep you under wraps for a while."

"Yes?"

"There's definitely something going on with Hobart and Howard, and it more than likely concerns Jacobson."

We were zooming along the Interstate now, and I was keeping an eye out for my next turnoff.

Lorie stayed focused on me. "Did you find any evidence about what he's been doing?" she asked.

"Nothing anyone could take into court, but as soon as I started seriously poking around, a couple of men took a run at me."

"A run?"

The turnoff for Highway 169 came up on my left, and I took it and headed north.

"Couple of guys tried to scare me off," I said, "nothing I couldn't handle." Because I didn't want to shake up my client any more than she had been recently, I left out the part about the two being off duty cops.

Lorie turned from me and stared out the window for a couple of minutes before turning back to me. "Bonner Springs?" she asked.

I grinned. "I figured it was about time for a complete change of scenery."

Bonner Springs is a small Kansas town. With less than ten thousand residents, it's one of those places known for arts, entertainment, and all-around general relaxation.

"Did you have anything in particular in mind?" Lorie asked.

I pondered for a moment. "I hear there's a pretty darned good golf course out that way. You play?"

That got me a slight quirking of the lips.

I'd take it.

"Brian plays," she said, "and every now and then I'd go along with him. Usually, I could barely get the ball off the tee."

"What about putt putt golf?" I asked.

"Is this part of the service, Mr. Quinton? Keeping up the client's spirits? I think I'd do better if we just drive, and you tell me what you have to tell me."

Sighing, I kicked the Cherokee up to seventy and tabbed on the cruise control. "I'm pretty sure there's something hinky about your man Jacobson, but it may go higher than that."

"Higher?"

"Or maybe deeper would be the better word. I think there's

something a little bit off with that agency. Maybe Jacobson, maybe his boss. Something's definitely off there."

We stayed silent for a moment as I drove and she mulled things over.

A moment later, the sign for Bonner Springs showed up on my right. Despite its overall size, in the KC area, nothing is very far away from anything else.

"You're saying even if you do rein Jacobson in, it may not be the end of it?" she finally asked.

"Maybe, maybe not. The point is, I can't really tell until I get some kind of a wedge into the place."

"Can you do that?"

I felt some tension tightening up my shoulders. "I thought I could. I approached one of their people who I had reason to believe would be willing to spill some things. Unfortunately, it didn't work out."

"Then what do we do now? I can't keep hiding in my house forever. At some point, I have to start living. Hell, my divorce isn't even finalized yet."

"There's a chance, of course, that Jacobson or whoever has had his fun and games and is going to leave you alone now," I said.

"You don't really believe that, do you?"

The exit for Bonner Springs showed up, which gave me an excuse not to answer her question.

"Besides," Lorie continued, "I can't keep running up a bill with you. How much do I owe you by now?"

I couldn't remember if Zach Lewis and I had discussed letting Lorie know he would pay the freight. Instead of answering directly, I dodged. "Don't worry about it, Mrs. Jones. I'm doing this more as a favor to Karyn than anything else."

"Don't patronize me, Mr. Quinton. This is your profession, right? What you do for a living? I assume you don't ordinarily work for free."

We pulled up to a light on the outskirts of the town, giving me a chance to face her directly. "Actually, this is more of a sideline. My main occupation is running my gym back home."

Lorie peered at me, and I could only wonder at the things running through her head. "Let's assume your first idea is wrong, and he's not going to leave me alone," she said. "What do we do then?"

I gave her a hearty smile I didn't really feel. "Give me a little more time, okay? One way or another, I'll get the darned thing broken up and get you free."

She swiveled her head as we drove. By this time, we'd made it as far as Morse Avenue, one of the main east/west drags. Despite our long drive, the tension in the car hadn't eased much.

"Mr. Quinton?" Lorie asked.

"Yeah?"

"Thanks for trying to get me out, but I think I want to go back home now. I really don't feel like trying anything fun."

Yeah, dammit.

I knew exactly how she felt.

CHAPTER THIRTY-ONE

After dropping Lorie off back at her house, along with the by-now-familiar instructions about not communicating or going out, I stopped at a nearby sports bar for a late lunch. My plan for the day had been pretty much a bust, mainly due to the fact I hadn't exactly been Mr. Tactful.

I figured I could at least get a decent meal out of the day.

I had a bacon double cheeseburger with all the fixings, plus about three handfuls of French fries which came in a red plastic basket. To ease things down, I indulged in three glasses of beer.

There were five TV's over the bar, but for some reason they were all showing the same program, a soccer game going on somewhere, whether taped or live I couldn't quite tell. Soccer's not exactly my game, same with tennis. When it comes to spectator sports, I prefer those where the score can get up into the double digits. Still, wasn't a bad way to while away the afternoon and early evening.

Another game came on after the first, and I thought what the hell and stayed put, downing another few glasses in the process.

A little over a hundred miles to the east was my apartment, not to mention Talia. Sunday evening she was probably still catching up on paperwork left over from Friday. Whenever I got to thinking I was somewhat ineffectual at my job, I could at least thank God I wasn't a higher education administrator.

I finally left the sports bar, climbed into my car, and began the now familiar loop around I-435 to Kansas City. Early Sunday evening traffic was pretty light, and not quite twenty minutes later I pulled into the Hampton parking lot, climbed out, and made my way through the lobby and to the elevators.

I still didn't have a real plan to go on. I'd considered seeking out Tom Jacobson and inviting him to meet me behind the schoolhouse the next afternoon so we could settle things like men, but he'd probably tap a few buttons on his computer and ruin my credit score, so that was out.

Besides, after nearly a week on this case I still hadn't met the guy and, beyond a generalized picture on the company web site, had no real idea what he looked like.

I figured it wouldn't be too far into next morning before Det. Sloan would start kicking things into gear regarding officers Landru and Davis, and there was a chance something would pop out on that end, though I doubted it. Up to now, Jacobson, provided he was Lorie's harasser, had shown how good he was at covering his tracks.

There was still Rachel Esperson, and while she'd turned me down flat the other day, maybe over time her conscience would work on her.

As a last resort, I could plant myself in the middle of the reception room at Hobart and Howard and yell and scream and throw things till I got some attention.

Which, on second thought, didn't seem all that productive either.

The problem with all of these maneuvers was that, except for the yelling and screaming one, they were passive, forcing me to wait on the sidelines for events to happen, and meanwhile something vague and shadowy was hanging over my client, and maybe over me as well.

This was my mindset, not exactly the happiest of places, when I walked out of the elevator, got to my room, and saw the Do Not Disturb sign that I'd hung on the knob that morning was gone.

CHAPTER THIRTY-TWO

I DIDN'T HAVE MY GUN WITH ME; it was in the room packed in my luggage. I hadn't expected any real issues when I went to take Lorie out. Now, I realized I may have misjudged things.

It could have been someone on the cleaning staff had screwed up and entered the room anyway. Then I remembered that, as was becoming common in these days of tight labor, the hotel only did housekeeping every other day, and mine was slated for tomorrow.

Looking both ways to make sure no one else was in the hallway, I eased up to my door and placed my ear against it. Although not as easy as they make it look in the movies, I couldn't hear anyone moving around in there.

Which didn't eliminate the possibility of someone waiting on the other side, sitting comfortably on the bed and waiting to drill me when I walked in.

I could have called Sloan, asked him to reach out to someone on the KC force and send some uniforms over to escort me inside. But I'd feel rather silly if we opened up to an empty room.

Besides, a second call in one weekend, and he'd probably just hang up on me . . . if not send a squad car out to arrest me for hassling a cop on his day off.

In the end, I couldn't really think of anything to do other than slide the key through the lock, stand to the side, and open the door, which I did.

Nobody charged out to assault me; no bullets whizzed into

the hall; and there were no screams for help. I waited a couple of heartbeats to be sure, then moved off the wall and walked in.

The room was empty, but it hadn't been vacant the entire time I'd been gone.

My suitcase and gym bag, the total amount of my luggage, were neatly placed on the right side of the small couch.

Except that's not where I had left them.

Without moving, I looked all around the room, giving it a full 360-degree examination.

Although my laptop was on the desk on the far side of the room, closed, as I'd left it, it had moved about five inches to the right so it lay exactly under the little desk lamp.

I'm not the neatest of housekeepers, and coming out of the shower that morning I'd tossed my towel onto the back of the chair that set in against the desk.

The towel was still there, though more lined up, straighter than my careless toss had left it.

I went to my luggage and riffled through it. All my clothes and money were there, as was my gun, even the bullets. Nothing seemed to have been disturbed, leaving me with only one conclusion to reach.

Someone had come into my room, and they'd made a few slight changes to things.

They didn't want to search it, so much as let me know they'd been in.

A knock came at the door. I instinctively moved to pick up my weapon, then considered if anyone had meant me harm they would have been waiting inside for me.

I walked over and opened the door.

A man stood there. He looked in his mid to late thirties with dark hair beginning to recede and watery brown eyes. He was a little pudgy, the chin and facial features kind of soft and blurry. He wore tan slacks, a white shirt, and a mud-colored blazer and had thin, steel-framed glasses.

"Sam Quinton?" he asked.

"Yep. What can do for you?"

"My name's Thomas Jacobson. I think we need to talk."

CHAPTER THIRTY-THREE

I STEPPED ASIDE AND USHERED HIM IN.
"Pardon the mess," I said even though, the unmade bed aside, the room wasn't that bad. "But someone's been rummaging around in here."

Jacobson stopped about four feet inside and looked my way. "Oh?"

"Yeah," I said, "and kind of sneaky, too. They did it just sloppily enough to let me know they'd visited."

"I see." Jacobson looked around the room for another second before sitting down on the end of the couch opposite my luggage. "That's rather wild. You have anyone in town you'd consider an enemy?"

I crossed my arms and leaned against the wall, not sure exactly what sort of game we were playing here. "Who knows? You know my profession, right?"

"Of course," Jacobson said. "That's why I came over to speak with you."

"Then you know it's sometimes hard to keep track of who does or doesn't have a problem with you. I had a bit of an issue with the mob a few years back, but that was centered mainly in Providence, though there may be one or two people around here still nursing a grudge."

"Regardless," Jacobson said, "I'm wondering if you could take a few minutes to talk to me."

I cocked my head. "I guess. All I'd planned to do was watch some TV, then zone out for the night. What'd you want to talk to me about?"

"Lorie Jones," Jacobson said.

I thought about acting surprised or confused then decided I wouldn't get anywhere by insulting the guy's intelligence.

"What about her?" I asked.

"I'm afraid you've been led down a path, friend, and one professional to another I'd like to steer you straight."

"It's a little late, but there's a lobby area downstairs. What say we grab some coffee and go over what's on your mind?"

"Fair enough," Jacobson said.

Seemed like a pretty decent guy, all things considered.

I made sure I didn't turn my back to him as we left and headed to the elevator.

CHAPTER THIRTY-FOUR

"I GUESS YOU KNOW WHAT I WANT TO TALK ABOUT," Jacobson said about five minutes later.

We were seated downstairs, a cup of coffee for each of us. Jacobson had spent the last minute giving me a good, hard look over.

"Maybe I do, maybe I don't," I said, feeling childish even as I said it.

He gave me another solid look. Not a hard look, though a solid one. It's hard for someone that squishy to look really hard.

"We're both professionals," he said a moment later.

"True."

"Although, to be honest, there are professionals and then there are professionals."

"Meaning?" I asked.

"Meaning when I found out you were sniffing around me, I did a little checking of my own. To put it bluntly, Mr. Quinton, you're not much more than junior varsity."

"Depends on how you define junior," I said.

Sighing, Jacobson brought his cup to his mouth and drained half of it in one swallow. The coffee was actually a little too hot for me, steaming in fact.

Either the man was tougher than he looked or wanted to give me that impression.

Maybe both.

Unable to think of anything better to do, I waited him out.

"What I mean," he said when he finally came up for air, "is you're kind of outmoded."

"Outmoded?"

"Understand, I don't mean anything personal." I had a hunch this guy never actually meant anything personal. "It's just that this is modern times, and the investigatory business has to be fairly upscale these days."

"Upscale," I said.

"Of course."

"My office is the back room of a gym I own," I said.

"Well..."

"My idea of professional attire is a linen sport coat with a clean pair of blue jeans."

"Mr. Quinton..."

"But I bet I can bench press more than you."

Jacobson gave another sigh, a bit more dramatic this time, and took off his glasses to wipe the lens. "All I meant was..." he began.

"How much weight can you squat?" I asked.

"What I'm saying is the business has changed since the days of Duke Prowder and his sort."

I started at his use of Duke's name.

Jacobson grinned. "I told you I checked you out, Quinton. From what I could tell, if it wasn't for that gym of yours you'd probably need to get an actual job."

"I can curl a hundred pounds," I said. "How about you?"

Jacobson shook his head. "Trust me, you're really not impressing me with the jock talk. I'm well aware you have me outclassed on the physical end of things. What I'm trying to say is physicality is one of the least important dimensions of our work anymore."

"This why you searched my hotel room and introduced yourself?" I asked. "To work on my inferiority complex?"

"No," he said, his voice a little firmer than it had been up to then. "I want to talk about Lorie Jones."

CHAPTER THIRTY-FIVE

"She's kind of nuts, you know," Jacobson said.

If his overall mousiness hadn't already put me off the guy, that comment would have pretty much sealed the deal anyway. Not so much the words but his "man-to-man you know how these girls are" tone.

For some reason, what would have been offensive coming from a drunken neckbeard in a sawdust-floored bar came off as almost obscene coming from him.

I hit him with the most brilliant and cutting reply I could think of at the moment.

"Oh?"

"Of course. Surely you had suspicions yourself. Anyone who's even a halfway competent investigator would have pretty much suspected her story right off."

"Because?"

He gave me another of those looks of his. Too many more of them, and I'd see how many swipes it would take me to wipe them off his face. Then he gave a little nod, more to himself than to me.

"I get it," he said. "You're wanting to get my side of the situation before committing yourself. Not a bad strategy."

"Even a dumb jock can have his moments."

Jacobson peered at me, as if wondering if he should take offense, then passed it by. "I'm sure you've noticed," he said, "there's absolutely no shred of evidence anyone is after Mrs. Jones."

One of the hotel clerks walked into the area, opened a cabinet to check on something, then walked back out.

I waited until she was out of earshot.

"I had noticed that."

"The police went through all of her stories and found nothing."

Again, that hint of snideness, distasteful coming from him, had entered his voice. "If by stories you mean her reports of the various incidents, you're correct again," I said.

"You spoke with Michael Sloan?" Jacobson asked.

"I did."

"And I'm going to assume they found nothing."

"That's more or less what he said."

I scored a small point there. Jacobson jerked his head a bit to the side. "More or less?"

"Yeah." I took a long drink to compose my words as well as I could. "He said they'd found no evidence to back up what she reported, but he was suspicious enough that something was up he's keeping the file open."

Of course, that wasn't exactly what Sloan had told me, but no reason Jacobson needed to know that.

He took a moment to recover before plowing on. "I see. And I'm going to assume you've also spoken with Mrs. Jones's co-workers, neighbors, etc.?"

I'd never known anyone to actually use "etc." in a conversation. If there'd been any space for my dislike of the man to increase, it would have done so. "I did talk to some of those folks," I said. "Even a part-timer like me knows enough to do that. Skipped the neighbor, seeing as she'd been questioned twice by the cops."

"And what was your conclusion after all of this?" he asked.

"So far, there's no hard proof she's been enduring any sort of harassment at all."

"In other words," Jacobson said, "the woman's a liar."

Now it was my turn to jerk my head. "I didn't say that at all," I said.

"Then what are you saying?"

"I'm saying I have not yet found any direct corroboration to her story, only some indirect support."

"Such as?" Jacobson asked.

"Such as a stressed-out woman who gives every indication of walking around on eggshells. Such as two rogue cops who tried to do a street number on me as soon as I started looking into this. And such as the fact that your nice, polite visit here comes right after I get back to see someone's been through my stuff."

"Your room was searched?" Jacobson asked, his eyes as mild and empty as ever.

"Yep. Nothing missing, mainly because I don't think theft was the point."

"Then what was their intention, whoever they were?"

I drilled my gaze into his. The false fronts had fallen by this point. "I think they wanted to let me know they were onto me. Maybe rattle me enough to get me to back off and go home."

"Will you?" Jacobson's voice had gone, if anything, even flatter than before.

I gave him the biggest smile I possibly could. "Nope, I'm sticking by my client. After all, that's what we professionals do."

Those watery brown eyes blinked a couple of times. "I think that would be a mistake on your part," he said.

"My mistake to make, Tom."

Jacobson drained his cup, stood up, and walked out.

CHAPTER THIRTY-SIX

After Jacobson left, I went back up to my room. With evening coming on, and the sun setting over the state line, something didn't feel right.

Actually, a whole lot of things didn't feel right, and I wasn't alone five minutes before one long, dangling loose thread popped into my head.

I took Rachel Esperson's card out of my pocket, checked the number, then pulled out my phone and placed a call. It went to voice mail accompanied by a message telling me her mailbox was full.

Feeling a tightening in my gut, I went back downstairs, out to the parking lot and jumped into the Cherokee. Within seconds I was out of the lot and headed to hop onto I-70 and head to Kansas City, Kansas.

There were all sorts of reasons why she wouldn't be answering her phone. Even on a Sunday evening, she easily could have been in the middle of some work-related task and declined to answer.

Of course, it happens all the time, untold numbers of times a day, all around the world.

But the mailbox being full? Rachel was a professional who worked for one of the most prominent firms in her profession. Especially as often as she'd be out in the field, away from the office, she'd be sure to keep as up to date as possible on her messages.

Granted, she could easily be one of those people whose phone messages and e-mails constitute such a continuous bombardment she'd long since given up on keeping up. I knew a lot of people like that.

Somehow, though, none of this fit my impression of the woman I'd met.

Changing my mind on the fly, I flicked my signal and angled over to where I could pull into a convenience store parking lot. I grabbed my phone again and placed a call, hoping the man would be at work.

"Sloan," he said upon picking up.

Damn, did the guy ever go home? At the moment, though, I was glad he hadn't.

"It's Quinton. You know anyone in the KCK department?"

"One or two."

"Do me a favor and call someone and get them over to this address." I rattled off Rachel's address.

"This a definite emergency?" Sloan asked.

"No, more like a strong feeling. Nothing solid enough to go through 911."

"I'm assuming this relates to the Jones matter?"

"Maybe. Or maybe it's nothing. Can you call someone and have them send a car over there. I'm headed that way now."

"Come on, Quinton. You surely know how this works. I could barely roust up a car from my own department on something that vague."

"Then call in a personal favor, but dammit Sloan get someone over there." Not wanting to haggle any more, I hung up, dropped my phone on the seat, and gunned my way back into the traffic.

The cop was right, and I knew it. Even so, that full mailbox on Rachel's line didn't feel right at all.

CHAPTER THIRTY-SEVEN

It took me thirty minutes to find my way to the apartment complex where Rachel Esperson lived. It was a smallish place, from the front about eight buildings, each no more than two stories tall. I circled around till I found building #7, fairly easy to spot because of the patrol car parked outside.

Climbing out of the Cherokee, I walked around to the back, where Rachel lived on the bottom floor.

As I crossed through the breezeway that led to the back, I passed two uniformed cops, a brunette woman in her thirties and a young, red-headed guy. They gave me the hard cop stare as if wondering what I was doing walking around by myself at night.

The point where we passed, a little more to the rear of the building than the front, was within eyeshot of Rachel's door. She was standing in the doorway, wearing faded blue jeans and a white tee-shirt.

From that distance, she looked a little tired but nothing worse.

As the officers and I passed, they gave me an even closer look, and the woman glanced back to Rachel's still-open door. I wasn't quite sure, but I thought I saw a slight nod pass from Rachel to the female cop.

When I got to her door, Rachel turned her back on me and went back inside her apartment, leaving the door wide open, which I took as a general invitation to come inside.

I did so.

The apartment was decent-sized, though rather average in layout: two bedrooms, from the looks of things, a living room in front with short hallway going down the back. To the side was a kitchen/dining room combo with a small table and three chairs.

The living room held a small couch that would hold three in a pinch, a wooden rocker, and an honest-to-God old time bean bag chair.

Rachel walked over to a mid-sized black coffee table made of some sort of composition material and picked up a can of beer. She half thrust it my way, but I shook my head.

She raised the can to her mouth and began drinking.

Not knowing what else to do, I closed the door and took a seat on her couch.

Still standing, Rachel lowered the can and looked at me. "You have anything to do with that?" she said as she gestured towards the now-closed door.

"You mean calling the cops out here?"

"Yeah."

"I did."

Shaking her head, she raised the can again, finished it off, crumpled it up, and walked into the kitchen to throw it away. Rather than come back into the living room, she folded her arms and leaned against the kitchen doorway.

"Mind telling me why?"

"Not at all," I said. "I had the hunch you might be in danger of some kind."

"Danger?"

"Yep."

She stood away from the door jamb and unfolded her arms. "What made you think that?"

"Tried to call you," I said. "It went to voice mail."

"So?"

"Your mailbox was full."

"Again, so?"

"So you're a busy working woman at the end of the week. You're sharp and on top of things, and I find it hard to believe you'd let your messages fill up."

"Okay, you've checked me out. You can see for yourself I'm hale, hearty, and all in one piece. How about doing me a favor and getting the hell out, huh?"

"Nope," I said.

Her arm and shoulder muscles tensed, and her eyes smoldered at me. "Excuse me?"

"I said nope. Despite how things look, something's not adding up. I'm not leaving until you tell me what."

"It ever occur to you that, big as you are, I may be able to throw you out of here without breaking a sweat?"

"Throw me out? Sure. As an ex-cop you probably know a lot of tricks, plus have field experience. Without breaking a sweat? I wouldn't be so sure of that."

"Oh?"

"Oh," I said, "I know a few tricks myself."

She gave me the glare for another minute, then kind of shook herself and sat down in the rocker. "What the hell? For all I know you're not as dumb as you look, and you may be able to think of something I haven't."

"Fresh pair of eyes never hurts," I said.

"Not eyes, big guy. Ears. Let me get my phone, and I'll play you all the messages that are cluttering it up."

CHAPTER THIRTY-EIGHT

Ten minutes later, I sank back on the couch and stared at the ceiling, replaying in my head everything I'd just heard.

"That was all in the last two days?" I asked.

"Less than that if you time it from when we met for dinner," Rachel said.

"One could have been some kind of glitch," I said. "Two could have been a really bad string of luck. The rest..."

"One of the reasons I've been lying low this weekend. Who knows what else may happen if I even step outside of this place."

In the space of only a few days, and the weekend at that, Rachel Esperson had been informed by her landlord her latest rent check had bounced, was three months overdue on her utility payments and if they didn't receive a check within three days she'd be cut off, had her car and renters insurance cancelled, and notified of pending legal action by three dissatisfied clients, not to mention having received three threats against her life.

"You don't look all that surprised or shocked," Rachel said.

"I'm not. Pretty much because this is the same kind of thing that happened to my client, only more accelerated."

Rachel crossed her arms again, this time almost hugging herself. "The woman who used to be Jacobson's client?"

"That's the one," I said.

"You're saying he's the one doing this to me?"

"What do you think? You have one meal with me, and shortly

after it becomes known I'm working on Mrs. Jones's behalf. About the same time, the same crap that happened to her begins happening to you."

I paused to let that sink in, even though I was pretty sure Rachel had reached a similar conclusion even before I showed up. Sometimes, though, it often helps jolt us into action to have someone else verbalize what we're thinking.

"Only thing I don't get," I said, "is how he manages to do all this, especially on a weekend."

Rachel shook her head. "You don't quite get it, mister. Thomas is John Howard's fair-haired boy."

"Yeah, I got that already."

"And Howard's been moving and shaking across the legal, political, and financial scenes of this town for longer than most people could picture."

"Which means he knows a lot of people," I said.

Rachel nodded. "And has leverage on a lot of people."

"And with Jacobson having the keys to the kingdom..."

"You've got it. Thomas has access to almost anything he would want."

I decided to throw one more log on the fire.

"Jacobson came to see me," I said.

That snapped her up. "Come again?"

"At my hotel. Actually, he showed up before I was there and searched my room, though I'm not sure exactly what he was looking for."

"How do you know he searched it?" Rachel asked.

"Let's say he was in my room. He moved a few things around. No ripped pillow cases or slashed luggage or anything. Only enough stuff slightly out of place to let me know he'd been in there."

"It's not as easy to get into hotel rooms as they make it look in the movies," Rachel said. "Especially nowadays."

"Good point. How 'bout I say he may not have been searching but only wanted to let me know that he could get to me."

"At any other time," Rachel said, "I'd say you sound kind of paranoid. After the last few days..." she gestured at her phone and left the rest of it unsaid.

"You got any plans for how to deal with this?" I asked.

Rachel craned her head back and stared at the ceiling. "I could pack up everything I own, hit the road, and go to work at a Krispy Kreme somewhere far away."

"That's an option."

"Or I could," she continued, still staring at the ceiling, "fly out to Vegas, find some rich high roller, and marry him, starting life as a new woman."

"Another possibility."

She snapped her gaze from the ceiling and back down to me. "The only problem with either of those is the bastard somehow managed to freeze all my bank accounts. When I tried to access them this morning, I got nothing but a wall, and I've got a grand total of thirty-two dollars on hand."

"Tried your debit card yet?" I asked.

Rachel shook her head. "I'm almost afraid to."

"I could loan you some money to get by on," I said.

"I'll consider it if things get really desperate."

"You don't call this desperate?" I asked.

Rachel blinked, and some sort of steel descended into her brown eyes. "Not yet, mainly because of option number three."

"Which is?"

The look she now projected was something beyond steel. I had the feeling deep in my gut Tom Jacobson had seriously miscalculated this particular play.

"Bring the bastard down, no matter what it takes," she said.

"Not a bad option," I said, "but there's one little angle I'm wondering whether you've considered or not."

"Are you talking about the question of how Thomas knew I'd met with you, seeing as there was only one person in the office who should have known."

"That's the angle," I said.

"Yes, I have considered that."

"Which means," I said, "that we've got two dangerous people to look out for. Your co-worker being one."

"And John Howard, my boss, being the other," Rachel finished.

CHAPTER THIRTY-NINE

"Have you ever heard anything about your boss being directly tied to anything shady?" I asked her.

Rachel shrugged. "There's been whispers, sure. Rumors floating around he's involved in shenanigans here and there."

"And that didn't make you wonder?" I asked.

Rachel shook her head. "Hobart and Howard is a major organization. The person who runs it is always going to have rumors swirling around them. It comes with the territory."

"Most people, when they think of big business, don't think of investigative agencies," I said.

"True. But think of it. Especially nowadays, how much are people willing to plunk down for security, for either themselves or their secrets? And when you have the reputation of being the best across four or five states, you're talking some serious bucks."

"Bucks that could afford the best of workers," I said.

"Of course," Rachel replied.

"Then how do you explain Jacobson?"

She cocked her head at me. "What's to explain? Ex-cop decides to skip over to the free enterprise side of the fence to do better. Happens all the time."

"You did it yourself," I pointed out.

"Exactly. So what's the big question?"

"The big question," I said, "is that it doesn't add up in Jacobson's case. I checked out his record. He started out as a uniformed patrolman, and ten years into his career he was still in uniform. Then, out of nowhere, he makes the jump to Hobart as a fully-licensed investigator, and a few months later he's the boss's right-hand man. That make sense to you?"

Rachel tapped her foot for a moment. "No," she said, "and it never made sense to a lot of other people. When you met Thomas, what was your impression?"

"In one way, he'd make a hell of a field worker."

"Because?" she asked.

"Because he's such an everyman he'd blend right into any environment, and you'd never know he's there."

Rachel nodded. "But?"

"But unless he's got more than he's showing, I'd hate to depend on him if anything physical started up."

"He lasted ten years as a cop."

"He did," I said. "But in a very undistinguished manner. No real commendations, no big busts I could find. So how's he make such a jump?"

"I don't know," Rachel said.

As if suddenly running out of steam, she sighed and slumped into the chair. "If everything that went down to me the last few days is any indication, waltzing back into work tomorrow morning may not be the smartest thing to do."

"It's okay," I said, standing up. "I think I know someone who can clue me in. How about you sit tight for a while and let me do a little digging?"

"Sounds like a plan, Quinton. But don't take too long, or I may blast my way into Howard's office and ask him what the hell's up."

I had to give the lady credit. I'd never had my whole world crumble around me in the space of forty-eight hours and had no clue how I'd react if I did. She was doing her best to hold it together, and doing a pretty damned good job of it too.

I decided to go about things the old-fashioned way and pulled a business card out of my wallet. She barely looked at it as I placed it on the coffee table.

"Give me the time," I said, "and let me see if I can shake something loose. In the meantime, in case things get too hairy for you."

I tapped the card to make sure she registered it.

Waiting only long enough to get a confirming nod, I headed out.

CHAPTER FORTY

Late Monday morning, I picked up John Howard coming out of his office. I'd made a gamble with myself and gotten lucky. I'd taken a gamble that he'd be the sort to leave the office for lunch, and it paid off.

It occurred to me this was almost the same scenario as had played out a couple of days before with Adam Thornton, though the stakes had gone up some since then.

Howard was accompanied by a middle-aged, balding man in a brown two-piece suit. They came out of the building almost on a mission and turned immediately to the left, headed towards me, the bald man carrying a black leather briefcase.

I didn't know who the other man was and assumed he had some mid-level or higher position in Howard's firm. If he was an accountant or office man of some kind, probably wouldn't be a problem.

But if he was a field operator, there was a good chance he was an ex-cop as Howard's company seemed to employ a lot of them, which could make my having a conversation with his boss a little more difficult.

If he was by chance a bodyguard, things could get even dicier,

When they were about fifty feet away, I half turned so I stood sideways to them. Even though Howard knew me by sight, between the fairly crowded lunchtime sidewalk and the fact he wouldn't be expecting to see me, I figured I could stay hidden until I was ready.

In fact, they walked within three feet of me without Howard

noticing, and as they passed I gave it a count of five before I turned to follow them.

I hoped they were only going a short ways for lunch as I didn't really feel like trundling all across the downtown area.

At the corner stood a building three stories tall that, judging by the signs out front, had an assortment of shops and stores. The ground floor, as I could clearly see from a ways away, held a hot dog diner.

I got lucky.

Howard and his companion headed inside.

I gave them about ten minutes to get their food and get settled before following them in.

Even with the place about two-thirds full, I easily found them in a booth over against the far wall. They both had trays in front of them and were poring over a couple of manilla folders that I guessed had come from the briefcase.

I paused a second to scope out the entire room and, not seeing anything out of the ordinary, headed over to them.

As I approached their booth, both men looked up. They each had a red tray in front of them. Howard's had a single hot dog with relish, while Baldy had three chili cheese dogs with jalapenos and a side order of chili cheese fries.

Made me glad I wasn't planning on kissing him any time soon.

"Help you buddy?" Baldy had a voice that, even almost whispered, sounded like a growl.

"Like a minute with your boss," I said.

Howard looked up from his paperwork. "Mr. Quinton? I didn't expect to see you again. How have you been?"

"Been okay," I said putting a smile on my face. Just one of the guys, we're all friends here. "But I can't say the same for some other people I know."

Howard grinned, though in a kind of puzzled way.

"Mr. Howard," Baldy said, "who is this guy?"

"He's a colleague of ours from out of town."

"Oh yeah?" Baldy replied. "Looks more like a strip club bouncer than an investigator."

"Damn," I said as I pulled a chair from a nearby table and sat up against their booth, "and here I even ironed my jeans today."

Baldy, clearly by now not some accountant type, began to rise out of his seat.

Howard reached over and placed his hand on the man's left forearm. "No, Harris," he said. "No need to start anything."

"Your boss is right, Harris," I said, "mainly because if you do I'll have to end up stuffing you into a trash can."

"Who the hell is this guy, John?" Harris asked.

Howard turned his intense gaze on to me. "He's a gentleman who came to see me the other day with a simple professional request. One I'm starting to think wasn't as simple as it seemed."

"Tell me about it," I said. Sitting sideways to them as I was, I leaned over, placed my elbows on the end of the table and propped my head in my hands.

At the intrusion into their space, Harris scrunched back a bit, then looked ashamed he'd done so.

Howard didn't even flicker an eyelid.

"Did Miss Esperson not help you out with your case?" he asked.

"Don't you know? Don't your employees report to you?"

Harris snickered. "Mr. Howard has over two hundred people on his payroll, mister. How many do you have?"

I grinned in his direction. "Just me."

"Small time," he sneered.

"The smallest," I agreed, "but at least I don't wear brown suits. Keeps me from looking like a giant turd."

When Harris started to rear up again, a glance from Howard lowered him back down.

"Mr. Quinton, we're trying to have lunch and discuss some business matters. If my employee didn't help you out, I'm sorry about that. As I recall, I offered her services as a professional courtesy, so it's not like I can refund your money or anything."

"You're a little off track there, John," I said. "Rachel helped me fine."

"Really?" Howard's brows puckered. "Then what's the problem?"

"Have you spoken with her recently?"

"No. But as Harris here pointed out to you, I have hundreds of people in my offices. Plus, it is only Monday morning. It's not uncommon for me to not . . ."

I stood up, the move causing Harris to flinch. Howard maintained his smooth, even calm. "You may want to call Rachel up and ask her how she's doing," I said. "Better yet, don't call because she's not answering her phone."

A small flinch from Howard. Though slight, enough to show I was getting to him, even if only a little.

"I don't follow you," he said.

"Call her up, John. Or have Harris baby here do it. Ask her how she's been the last few days. And if you can't get ahold of her, why don't you ask Jacobson what's up."

"Jacobson?" Harris's gazed move back and forth between me and his boss. "What does Thomas have to do with anything?"

"That," I answered him while not taking my eyes off of Howard, "is what I'm going to find out."

Considering that a pretty good final line, I turned my back on them and headed out of the diner.

Even so, I knew I didn't actually feel anywhere near a confident as I sounded.

CHAPTER FORTY-ONE

"I**N OTHER WORDS, YOU DON'T KNOW WHAT TO DO**," Talia said to me over the phone.

I was in my hotel room, my shoes kicked off and lying on the bed. On the 42-inch TV across the room, a boxing match played, muted. With the curtains open, I could see the KC skyline outside my window, half-visible and half-muted.

The sunlight had been fading for a while, and it only had another quarter hour to go before vanishing completely.

I'd called Talia because I couldn't think of anything better to do.

"I guess that's one way to put it," I said.

"Is there any other way?"

I thought about it for a minute. "Well, I could go ahead with the simplest possible plan."

"Which is?"

"Say to hell with it, pack my bags, and head home. I could be at your place in two hours tops."

"That's a plan?"

"Yep," I said.

"Even after you've met this Jacobson fellow?" Talia asked.

On the TV one of the boxers, who looked to be taller by a couple of inches than his opponent, had the shorter fellow up against the ropes. The ref was trying to get between them, but not having a lot of luck.

"Met is a pretty mild word for it," I said to Talia. "The guy went about a very subtle way of trying to scare me off."

"Which you, not being that subtle of a guy, didn't catch on to."

I could almost see the laugh lines deepening on her face. "Not exactly. More like I caught on but it had the opposite effect of what he intended."

"And this Rachel woman? What's the connection there?"

"Seems like Jacobson got a little concerned about me poking around, figured Rachel was some piece of the puzzle, and decided to give her a little taste of what to expect if she didn't stay in her lane."

There was a pause on the line. The ref finally got in between the two sluggers and pushed the taller one back. The shorter kid looked winded and a little dazed.

"It's a little frightening," Talia finally said, "to think of a single person having the power to do that much disruption to someone's life in such a short time."

"Sign of the times, babe. Think about it for a minute. If you call up your bank with a complaint, and you've been having a bad day and get a little irritable with the person on the other end of the line, think what they can do to you if they want to."

"I guess we all go through life hoping the worst will never happen," Talia said.

"Some folks try that, but sometimes hard reality gets in the way."

"Is it possible," Talia asked, "you're as down as you are because this whole thing has you a little out of your element?"

The shorter boxer had come roaring out of his corner and engaged his taller opponent. While the kid was swinging for all he was worth, it was obvious, even on TV and across the room, that his legs were starting to wobble.

"How do you mean out of my element?" I asked.

"Think about it, Sam. For all of your life, you've been a fairly physical guy. And most of the times you've been able to solve problems that come up in your work by either direct physicality or just looming imposingly."

"And?"

"And that's worked for you for the most part. Here, you've got someone who takes a different route to his goals, whatever the hell they are. Tell me, have you considered tracking this Jacobson fellow down and beating the crap out of him?"

"I love the way you university types always appeal to our better natures," I said.

"And?" Talia prodded.

"And yeah, I have."

After several seconds of hunching up and taking it, the tall boxer unloaded a combination, left, right, left, that sent the other guy reeling back against the ropes.

"So why haven't you done so?" Talia asked.

"Well, for one thing straight up assault's against the law in most cases."

"I don't think that's the reason at all. Tell me, from everything you know about this man, what would happen if you came at him physically?"

"One, I'd beat the hell out of him without any problem and threaten to do worse if he ever bothered Lorie again."

"Okay," Talia said.

"Two, he'd go to ground and come at me the same way he did with Lorie and Rachel. Only difference is I have less credit to ruin, so he wouldn't have to work as hard at it."

"Good to see you're still keeping your sense of humor," Talia said. "But you're proving my point. So far, you can't approach the problem the way you usually do, which is leaving you feeling inadequate."

"So what the hell do I do? Tuck my tail between my legs and come home?"

"No, Sam, not that. I said you feel inadequate. Not that you are. Is there any way you can play this Jacobson's game? Any way to hit him where he lives?"

I thought about that one for a minute, but nothing came to mind right off. "I'd have to think it over," I said.

"Do it then. And while you're thinking it over, be sure no matter what that you come back in one piece. I miss you and want you back home."

We talked a bit longer, and at some point I realized I'd totally zoned out on the boxing match. By the time I realized that, it was over, and they were on to a new one on the card.

I didn't know what had happened or who had won. Had the taller guy triumphed by his natural skill, or had the shorter one managed to sneak a win?

"Time to go, babe," I said. "I'll skull it around and see if I can come up with something."

"Good enough, just get back to me in one piece. And with your credit rating intact if possible, okay?"

We hung up. I tossed the phone to the side and leaned back against the headboard.

Either find a way to deal with Jacobson on his terms or think of a third avenue. At the moment, nothing really jumped out at me.

As it turned out, I didn't have all that much time to ponder anyway. Barely ten minutes after I'd said goodnight to Talia, my phone buzzed.

"Mr. Quinton?" an unknown female voice queried.

"Yes?"

"My name is Nina Alvarez."

"Okay," I said, not sure if she wanted a response.

"That's Sergeant Nina Alvarez of the KCK police department."

A dull feeling crept over me. "How can I help you, Sergeant?"

"You know a woman named Rachel Esperson? I'm assuming the answer is yes, seeing as how your business card is sitting here on her coffee table."

"Yes, I know Rachel. And can I ask why a cop is over at her place?"

"Why don't you do us all a favor and come on over here, Mr. Quinton? There's something we need to talk about."

CHAPTER FORTY-TWO

I GOT LUCKY WITH TRAFFIC LIGHTS, plus general nighttime traffic, and pulled into the parking lot of Rachel's complex barely twenty minutes after the phone call.

There were two cars parked closer to her apartment, with one of them being a tan, late-model Camaro and the other a standard patrol car. I was a little relieved by what I didn't see, namely an ambulance or two and masses of squad cars and police tapes.

Exiting the Cherokee, I walked up to Rachel's apartment and rapped on the door. I'd barely moved my hand away before the door opened.

I assumed the person who opened it was Sgt. Alvarez. She stood fairly tall, about five nine, with dark black hair and eyes. My best guess put her age somewhere in mid-thirties, with a lean, almost ropy look to her body. She was wearing blue jeans so faded they looked white, a red tee-shirt and, even inside, a light tan poplin jacket.

She and I could have had the same tailor.

"Quinton?" she asked. Behind her, I could see Rachel sitting on her couch and two uniformed cops standing off to the side, both about the same height, five ten or so. Both were white with dark hair with one, even at his young age, beginning to recede quite noticeably.

Both of them looked like they weren't sure what they should be doing.

"That's me."

"Could I see some identification please?"

Pulling my wallet out of my pocket, I showed her the photostat of my license. I figured that was a little more relevant to the situation than my driver's license or insurance card.

Alvarez looked it over, nodded, and stepped aside for me to come in. Three steps in, I got my first full-on look at Rachel perched on her couch.

The lady looked like a discarded punching bag.

Someone had worked her face over pretty good, with the beginnings of three or four bruises almost blending into one. Her left eye was cut open at the brow. She wore a dark blue bathrobe with matching slippers, causing me to worry about something more than a simple assault.

"Rachel?"

She looked up when I spoke and gave me a faint grin, even such a slight motion causing her to wince. She pulled the robe tight around her but not before I could see what sure looked like finger impressions around her throat.

"What happened?" I asked, speaking to the room in general and not really giving a damn who answered.

Alvarez looked Rachel's way, as if to give her the floor. It was a point in the cop's favor.

Rachel shook her head and dropped her gaze downwards.

I began to worry even more about sexual assault.

"Okay, then," Alvarez said as the two uniformed cops continued looking around for something to do. "It seems Miss Esperson here went for a run this evening, and when she got home there were two men waiting inside her place to give her a going over."

As the cop spoke, I kept half an eye on Rachel, who continued looking at the floor.

"How much of a going over?" I asked.

Alvarez shook her head. "Nothing like that. The reason for the bathrobe is her running clothes got pretty bloodied up from the beating. Far as we can tell, they tuned her up pretty good, then left."

Something was off about the vibe in the room, besides the obvious. "Tell me, Sergeant, do you usually speak this harshly in front of victims?"

Alvarez cracked a smile, though one without a lot of humor in it. "I do when they look like she does but refuse medical attention, is a former cop who can't give me a single descriptive detail about her attacks, and just happens to have in her possession the business card of a PI from out of town. Yeah, in these circumstances I do get a little harsh."

I turned to Rachel, who all this time had been looking at the floor. "Well?"

She looked up at me, not the cops. "Like she said, Quinton. I've been cooped up in here for a couple of days and went a little stir crazy. Went for a run to unwind, and when I got back a couple of goomers were waiting for me."

"Inside?" I asked.

"Yep."

"Forget to lock the door?" I asked.

"So she says," Alvarez put in. "Says it slipped her mind. Won't quite say why she's been stuck inside, though."

"Sergeant," I said, "you can tell Miss Esperson's a little rattled. How about saving the hard questions for a day or so?"

Alvarez crossed her arms and gave me her full-on cop stare. "You got anything to contribute here, mister, besides telling me how not to do my job? For what it's worth, I've known Rachel here for a lot longer than you have, and I've seen her rattled. This doesn't even come close."

I glanced over at Rachel, who nodded. "Nina and I came up together on the force. She was only a year or two ahead of me getting out on the streets."

I spread my hands out and gave the sergeant my best "aw shucks" grin. I hadn't used 'aw shucks' for a while, but it's pretty much like riding a bike. "I met Rachel the other day when I stopped in to her office. Since I was in town and had some time on my hands, I figured I'd do a little meet and greet."

"Why?" The cop stare hadn't wavered a millimeter.

"Why do you think? I'm from a smaller town, but you never know when, shall we say, unofficial jurisdictions may overlap. The firm Rachel works for, I figured it wouldn't hurt for them to know my name in case they ever have business out my way."

"Is that so?" By now, the two uniforms looked distinctly uncomfortable.

"It is," I said. "I stopped in, introduced myself to Rachel's boss, and he suggested she and I meet to talk over some basics."

Alvarez shifted her gaze from me to Rachel. "That so, Rachel?"

"Yes," she said, her voice coming out fairly strong.

"And his card being in your possession is a complete fluke, has nothing to do with what happened tonight?"

"Not at all, and to be honest it's kind of embarrassing you called Mr. Quinton over here."

Alvarez's eyes snapped at that, and she turned to the two uniforms. "You guys go ahead and take off," she said.

One of the uniforms frowned. "She needs to be checked out, Sarge. A doc needs to look her over."

"I don't need a doctor," Rachel said.

"You heard the woman," Alvarez said. "She's in one piece and of sound mind. She's officially refusing medical care. And she has no way of identifying her two assailants. Write it up, send it on, and get back on the street."

The two patrolmen glanced at each other, then shook their heads and went out.

When the door closed behind them, Alvarez turned back our way. "I'm not sure what is or isn't going on here, Rachel, but I'm going to cut you a lot of slack 'cause you used to be one of us. However, if anything about tonight comes back to bite me . . ."

"It won't," Rachel said. "I can assure you of that."

Alvarez looked at me, and I couldn't think of anything to do except nod in agreement.

"Okay, then I guess that's it for now. If you change your mind, I'll be taking the call."

Rachel thanked the sergeant. I said goodnight to her, and she left the apartment. As the door closed, I turned to face Rachel.

"What the hell?"

"Sorry," she said. "Wasn't my idea to call you, but Nina's got eyes like a hawk and she spotted your card right off."

"That's not what I meant," I said. "I meant what the hell happened?"

Grimacing, Rachel leaned back on the couch cushion, her robe still clenched around her neck. "Pretty much like Nina described it. I decided to take a run and clear my head, see if I could think of some new angle to try to set things right."

"Did you?"

"Nope. The only thing I got for my trouble was two homeboys waiting for me when I got back."

"They say anything while they were beating on you?"

"Only that I should learn to stay in line. They said that three or four times. Stay in line."

"While you've been hassling with your accounts and stuff, anything you did or said that could have spooked Jacobson?"

"I don't know how. I didn't do anything any other consumer wouldn't. And even if somehow he got word I was trying to fix the mess he caused, so what? Isn't it what he'd expect me to do?"

"Yeah it is," I said. "That's what's weird about this. You didn't go into the office today, right? Haven't called in?"

"Nope. Decided to keep my distance while I tried to get all my stuff straightened out."

"Then what the hell," I said. "Any chance this attack was about something else?"

"Damned if I know," Rachel said. "Other than the department store thing, I'm not working on any active cases,"

"Could this be any sort of blowback from your cop days?" I asked.

"Don't see how. I haven't been on the force for years."

I stood up and began pacing the room. A nasty little thought niggled in the back of my mind. A thought that I really, really didn't want to bring out into the light.

"Besides," Rachel said, "I know the two guys."

I stopped flat, turned, and looked at her. "Come again?"

She grinned, the first show of actual emotion since I'd showed up, though she grimaced right after. "Ouch. I probably shouldn't try smiling for a few days until my mouth heals up."

"You know them?" I asked.

Instead of answering, she got up and went into the back part of her apartment.

A moment later, she came back out carrying a laptop and sat back down on the couch.

"Take a seat, Quinton. This shouldn't take very long."

CHAPTER FORTY-THREE

"Here he is," Rachel said about three minutes later. "Just as I thought."

I sat down on the couch next to her and peered at the laptop screen. The second thing I noticed, after the face that took up most of the screen, was the site she'd landed on.

"Is it acceptable for you to be on an internal police department site?" I asked.

"Depends on your definition of the word acceptable. Is it my fault if they never erased my password access?"

"As you pointed out a minute ago, you've been gone for a long time," I said.

"Is it my fault their system's easy to get into?"

It was nice to see a little bit of humor coming back, so I dropped the matter and read over the information on the screen.

"Jaime Allegro," I said. "This one of the guys?"

Rachel nodded. "I thought he looked familiar. Back in the day, my partner and I busted him during a throwdown in a park. His PD managed to get everything reduced down to reckless endangerment or some such thing. He's been a local bad dude for years. The only question is why he and whoever his running buddy was glommed onto me tonight."

"I'm guessing you can pull up his entire record?" I said.

"Uh huh. But I don't really need to. I wanted to confirm his identity, make sure my mind wasn't playing tricks on me."

"Go ahead and scan through the whole record."

"Why?" Rachel cocked her head at me. "What am I looking for?"

"Any notation of a time when he and Jacobson may have crossed paths."

Rachel frowned, then bent down to the screen. A moment later, she snorted. "I'll be damned. Here it is. About five years ago, Jacobson was part of a patrol contingent that rounded up Allegro and some other members of his gang."

"Taken into custody?" I asked.

Rachel nodded and continued reading. "Suspicion of a drug deal going down, never made it to trial."

I sucked in a breath, then let it out slowly. "Let me guess. Evidence got tainted somehow?"

"Tainted hell. It disappeared out of the evidence locker. They had no choice but to let Allegro and three others go." She lifted her gaze from the screen. "You know something about what happened to me tonight?"

"I think so," I said. "You may want to pick up something disposable and get ready to throw it at me."

"Because?" She drawled the single word out till it formed about five syllables.

"Because I think I may be the one who sicced those two on you."

"Come again?"

"I confronted your boss this afternoon," I said.

"Confronted?" Her tone kind of implied she wouldn't trust me to confront a puppy dog.

"Yeah," I said. "You know, caught up with, talked to, got in the face of."

"Well, dammit, which one was it?"

I grinned sheepishly. "Probably more like got in the face of."

She leaned back and continued giving me the doubtful look. "How'd it go down?"

"I followed him from the office and caught up to him having lunch at this hot dog place."

"Larry's Dogs," she said. "As much as he eats there it's amazing his arteries didn't shut down years ago."

"Yeah, well, he was with a kind of shlebby-looking guy in a really bad suit."

"That would be Harris Cosgove, our office manager."

"Really? From the way he acted, I thought Cosgrove was auditioning for the role of heavy in a Stallone movie."

Rachel smiled, regardless of the pain caused by the movement. "Yeah, Harris tends to kind of glamorize our work."

"Yeah, well, anyway, I kind of hit Howard with the fact you were undergoing some stress, implied that it had to do with Jacobson and left it at that."

Rachel's eyes smoldered a bit and her jaws clenched, though she kept her tone level and clear. "And just what did you hope to accomplish by that?"

"I hoped to nudge something out of the woodwork. You know, get Jacobson to scrambling a bit and see what he'd do."

"Did you at all foresee something as extreme as what happened to me tonight?"

I lowered my eyes and toed the carpet for a moment. "No. Not at all. I expected Howard to reach out to you and maybe at some point rope Jacobson in."

"I haven't heard anything out of John," she said.

"So I gather, which tells us something, doesn't it?"

"It does indeed." She closed the laptop and stood up. "I'll be right back."

She headed back down the hallway.

I almost wandered if she would come out with a firearm and start blasting away, angry at me for putting her in the middle like this.

She came back in a few minutes. The robe was gone, and in its place she had on blue jeans, black canvas shoes, and a long-sleeved tee-shirt untucked.

I wasn't entirely sure, but I had a hunch she had the shirt untucked to conceal a weapon of some sort.

"Let's go," she said, picking up her keys from the coffee table.

CHAPTER FORTY-FOUR

"Mind telling me where we're headed?" I asked as we left her apartment, Rachel locking the door behind her.

"You got a car?" she asked.

"Yep. Right out front. Why?"

"Let's take yours instead of mine. With as much as Jacobson messed up my credit and financial history, I'd hate to think what he may have done in terms of my license plate number."

I directed her towards the Cherokee, and once we were seated and belted I repeated my question.

"Made a quick phone call while I was changing," she said. "Seeing as I barely know Allegro, I wanted some up to date info. A contact told me a place he usually hangs out when he isn't strutting around proving what a man he is."

I glanced her way. The overhead lights from the building put her face half in shadow. "You aren't going to go nuts on me, are you?" I asked.

"No." She kept staring straight ahead. "But I am going to find out why Allegro and his running buddy decided it was the right night to take a swing at me."

"I thought we'd already pretty much figured that out."

"Figuring out isn't the same as proof," Rachel said. She gave me an address in North Kansas City. I plugged it into my phone, and off we went.

Fifteen minutes later, we cruised past the front of a place called Lucky's.

It looked like a typical lower-side watering hole. Despite sounding like a directional area, North KC is its own town, another of the little minnows circling around the great white that is the big city. Or maybe a more apt comparison is that North KC is a minnow that at some point in time was swallowed by the shark, seeing as how over time Kansas City itself has grown enough to practically encircle the smaller town.

As I pulled into a deserted parking lot about half a block down from the fine establishment, I wondered if Lucky, whoever he was, was any relation to Smitty, who owned the bar where I'd met Jack Phillips a few days before.

At least from the outside, the two establishments seemed to share some similar DNA, though judging from the number of vehicles around, at this time of night on a Sunday, Lucky's appeared to be doing better customer wise.

"Think they water down the drinks in there?" I asked.

As the headlights of a passing car washed over the interior of the Cherokee, I saw Rachel's face set into all hard planes and angles, her gaze fixed on Lucky's front door.

"I'm not planning on hanging around long enough to find out," she said.

"We could abort, no harm no foul. You could call up your pal Sgt. Alvarez and lay Allegro's name on her. Eventually, we'd get to the same place."

She kept staring down the street. "We may yet," she said, "but if we're right, my employer set me up for those bozos to take a run at me."

"I don't think it's that simple," I said.

"Maybe, maybe not. What say we find out."

We exited the Cherokee and entered the bar. It was about what I'd expected, another in the long line of run down, smoky, and depressing hangouts. The usual collection of dead enders and almost there's were hanging around, in the dim light seeming to be about sixty/forty male to female.

The noise level didn't go silent when we entered; the clientele didn't all turn our way; and the three bartenders didn't reach under the bar to bring out weapons.

Far as I could tell, no one noticed us at all, despite the fact I seemed to be about twenty-five years past the place's median customer age.

Rachel grabbed my arm and squeezed. When I glanced over, she was staring at two men sitting at a table about ten feet inside the door.

The two were laughing, slapping each other, and downing their beers, paying no attention at all to anything around them.

"That them?" I whispered in Rachel's ear.

She nodded. "Both of them. The taller one is Allegro. They don't look like much, do they?"

Both of the men were around five ten and way, way on the skinny side. They wore greasy tee-shirts with the sleeves cut off and bandannas tied around their necks. Taking a closer look, I figured the bandannas more as a wannabe gesture than affiliation with any particular gang.

"Doesn't take much in the way of toughness to blindside someone from behind," I said.

Rachel nodded and headed over to the table. I followed along.

When we got there, she didn't say anything—merely stood over them for a minute until they noticed her. Allegro's buddy looked up first, frowned for a moment, then moved his chair back a few inches, as if about to stand up.

I walked behind and placed my bulk against the back of his chair, then with a move of my hip shoved him back into the table.

Allegro, too, had started to get up. Before he could, Rachel grabbed a handful of his hair and slammed his head down on the table.

"You know me, right?" Rachel said. Four or five people had glanced our way, then followed the Number One Rule of getting by in dives like Lucky's and turned their backs.

Out of the corner of my eye, I noticed even the bartenders doing their best not to see us.

When Allegro didn't answer, Rachel pushed his face a little deeper into the table. "You know me?"

"Yeah," he muttered, his lips half pressed against the table's unfinished surface.

"You want to tell me why you and numbnuts there attacked me tonight?"

At first, it seemed as if Allegro wasn't going to answer. Then Rachel slipped something out from under her shirt, in the murk of the place I couldn't quite see what, and jabbed it in Allegro's side.

He was not built of strong stuff. "Okay, okay. A guy paid us, alright?"

Rachel eased up on Allegro a little while his buddy flicked his eyes back and forth. Figuring he was considering running, I leaned into him a little more.

He hunched his shoulders, and the eyes stopped flicking.

"I don't know who," Allegro whined. "Guy came in here the other day, asking around for me. Said he had a job for us."

"The job being me?" Rachel asked.

Allegro nodded.

"Did he give you a picture or something," I asked, "or only her address?"

Allegro, his head still planted sideways on the table, did his best to look over my direction. "Who are you?" he asked.

Rachel jabbed him again with whatever she had. "Doesn't matter who he is, answer the question."

"Name, address, and apartment number," Allegro mumbled.

"You didn't recognize my name?" Rachel asked.

The half of Allegro's face I could see looked puzzled. "You mean know that you busted me once? No, not until I saw you. Even then, took me a minute."

"You've been busted so much they all kind of blend together, huh?" Rachel asked.

"That's right," Allegro said.

Obviously, irony wasn't his high point.

"Honest," Allegro continued. "Till we got there, we didn't know you was a cop."

"Ex-cop," Rachel corrected him.

"Okay, ex-cop. We were just hired by a man to rough you up a bit, show you he means business."

Rachel released Allegro and reached into her pocket. She brought out her phone, scrolled around on it a bit, then held it out to me. She'd gone to the company website and pulled up a profile picture of Jacobson.

I nodded in agreement, all while keeping goon number two pressed into the table.

The hip was starting to tire a bit, but I didn't let up.

"This the guy?" Rachel asked, showing Jacobson's picture to Allegro.

The small timer glanced at the phone, then took a closer look before shaking his head. "Huh uh, lady. That's not even close to him."

Rachel and I stared at each other. I imagined I looked as puzzled to her as she did to me.

"Not him?" I asked.

As Rachel worked her phone, Allegro had lifted his head up. He massaged his left side a bit as he answered me. "No, that's not him. The guy who hired us was older."

"That's right," Allegro's buddy chimed in for the first time.

"An older man," I said.

"Yeah," Allegro said. "But classy, you know. Nice suit, good haircut. Almost made you think he was a Mafia guy he looked that good."

"How old?" I asked. "Like me, middle-aged. Or are we talking old-man old?"

As the two goonballs started nodding, Rachel and I walked a little ways away.

"Christ," she said.

"Yep."

"It wasn't Thomas who hired them at all," she said.

"Nope. It was your boss."

CHAPTER FORTY-FIVE

WE GOT IN THE CAR AND HEADED BACK to Rachel's apartment. On the drive back, she'd been a little subdued, hardly saying ten words the whole way. I couldn't blame her, as such, as we both had a lot to think about.

When I pulled into a parking space right in front of her building, she put her hand on the door handle, then paused.

I thought about asking if she wanted me to walk her in but knew that after her experience earlier that night, she had to come to whatever conclusions she had to on her own.

After about thirty seconds of staring at the little breezeway that led back to her apartment, she spoke. "I'm not sure what to do."

"I know."

"I've worked in that place for years, and now it seems as if the whole damned company is conspiring against me."

"Probably not the whole company," I said. "So far, we've only identified two of them."

She nodded in the darkness, but I'm not sure my words reassured her.

"Give it a day or so," I said. "You did good work tonight, and it's pretty certain since this go round failed that they'll lay off for a while."

"But when they come back, won't it be something even worse?" Rachel asked.

"Maybe," I said, "or maybe they'll shift their focus back to me. Either way, we can't exactly charge into John Howard's office and slap the cuffs on him. Not on the word of the two morons we just bopped."

"I'll call in sick," Rachel said. "Tell them I need a few days to get better."

"That'll work. In the meantime, I'll try to scrounge up some more info to use against them. This is getting out of hand. Somehow or other, we need to take Jacobson down."

Rachel nodded, but didn't say anything else as she opened the door, got out, and walked down the breezeway to her apartment. I didn't have any fears that someone would be there lurking for her.

Jacobson, and possibly Howard behind him, would wait to see if their first salvo had any effect. They'd know pretty soon it hadn't, but until they knew there was no reason to come at her again.

I shifted into gear and headed back to the hotel.

I'd always considered myself pretty good at my job, but it turns out that driving back across the metro area that night I hadn't yet even considered the real danger.

CHAPTER FORTY-SIX

I CALLED JOSH NICHOLS ALMOST AS SOON AS I GOT IN MY ROOM. In the spirit of optimism that my buddy had some sort of normal life, I hoped I was waking him up at home instead of catching him at work.

Score one for the good guys.

"Whadda ya want?" Nichols asked in greeting. The words were normal, but something seemed a little off about the tone. "I'm just getting ready to climb into bed."

Since my initial spurt of optimism had gone so well, I decided to double down. "Alone or with some company?" I asked.

"If you knew anything about the average cop's social life," Nichols growled, "you could probably answer that one yourself. Is that all you wanted to know?"

"You know," I said, "if you dressed even half as snappy as Santiago does, you'd have the young ladies flocking around you."

"Shows what you know. Far as anyone can tell, Santiago's love life is even sparser than mine. And why the hell would I take fashion advice from someone who thinks throwing a windbreaker over a wife-beater shirt is dressing up?"

"Remind me never to call you this late again," I said.

Nichols sighed, and I could almost visualize the slump in his shoulders. "Yeah, well, you did call. So what's up?" He sounded odd to me, as if he was holding something inside.

"Know any dirty cops?" I asked.

A pause then, noticeable even if not very long. "What the hell, Blondie? You working for IA now? Things that hard up?"

"Not even close," I said. "And for what it's worth, I'm still in KC. Guess I didn't phrase my question very well."

"Then how about either phrasing it better or getting the hell off the phone and letting me go to sleep."

"Okay, let's try this. Have you ever had any experience with dirty cops? And no, I'm not going to pass this on to your superiors."

"Well, hell," Nichols said. "Even in a town as small as this, it's kind of hard not to know one or two guys that cut corners."

"What about St. Louis," I asked, "when you were back in uniform?"

"Oh, hell, don't even get me started. What do you think is one of the main reasons I pulled up stakes and came back here?"

"Were these mainly uniforms or plainclothes?" I asked.

"That I was familiar with? Naturally, uniforms for the most part. After all, on that force, like on most, like hangs out with like."

"What's the usual motivation?" I asked. "Is it just money like everyone assumes?"

Nichols thought that one over for a moment, and I gave him the time to think. "Lot of the time, it's money," he finally said. "I mean, that's always in there somewhere of course. But there's probably as many reasons for why cops go on the take as there are cops on the take."

"What would some be?" I asked.

"Hell, Blondie. Take your pick. Feeling powerful, wanting to impress someone, even if it's only yourself. Wanting to prove you're smart enough to get away with it. Sometimes just plain old meanness."

"You mean I can show how much of a bad man I am by doing bad things?" I asked.

"Yep."

"You're saying ego can have something to do with it."

"Ego often has a lot to do with it. In cities with strong org crime components, such as St. Louis or where you're hanging out right now, cops are often treated like lower-tier citizens. If they take money from the big boys, it could mean they're up in that rank as well."

I drummed my fingers on my thigh for a moment as I thought things through.

"Enough of a lecture for tonight?" Nichols asked after a few minutes. "Can I go to sleep now?"

"Do most dirty cops stay on the force," I asked. "Or do they quit while they're ahead?"

"Oddly enough, most of them tend to stay on as long as they can, even after it's known what they're like. Human nature, you know. Everyone thinks they can beat the odds."

"Hard to find a good job somewhere else?" I asked.

"What's this about, Sam?" Nichols asked. Again, I heard that kind of catch in his voice. "This about your case out there?"

"Maybe. The guy in question is an ex cop."

"One who was dirty?"

"That's the thing," I said, "I'm not sure he's corrupt so much as just mean spirited, if you know what I mean."

"'Fraid I do." Again, came that odd tone. I thought about asking him if everything was okay, but figured if it was something he wanted me to know about he'd tell me.

"If I give you his name," I said, "could you run a check and see if anything pops up?"

Another pause, a rather heavy one this time. "Couldn't the locals tell you whatever you need?" he finally asked.

"You kidding? Ask them to run a check on one of their own?" As soon as I spoke, I knew I'd crossed a line.

"Oh," Nichols almost barked. "But it's okay to have your good buddy Josh do it, huh? After all, who the hell cares if I get called on doing favors for a civilian, right?"

"It's okay, guy," I said as quickly as I could. "Actually, there's someone out here who seems pretty on the level. I'll go through him."

"Fine." The single word came out almost, but not quite, as a snap. "Anything else?"

"Nothing at all, Josh. How about we get together when I get back in town?"

"Yeah," Nichols muttered. "Let's do that."
Then he hung up.
I sat thinking for a few minutes.
What the hell was that all about?

CHAPTER FORTY-SEVEN

Tuesday morning I whiled away a few hours in my hotel room, mindlessly surfing from channel to channel without really looking at the TV screen. Considering the hotel, as most do these days, was piped into one of those all-inclusive streaming services that offered over a thousand channels, I probably scanned a couple of hundred each of talking news heads, recaps from some game the night before, kids puppet shows, and grade-Z movies from the '70s dubbed into Spanish, Slovakian, Portuguese, and Urdu.

I occupied myself that way till fairly late in the morning, then headed out of the hotel, climbed into the Cherokee and bent my way once more towards the dingier side of town and Smitty's bar.

Walking in, the place didn't seem to have changed in any detail since my last visit. The barman was still dressed the same and still going about his mundane tasks; the assortment of customers ranged along the bar and scattered among the tables looked like the exact same men wearing the exact same clothes; and Jack Phillips was still seated at his table up front.

Phillips was the only one who looked up when I entered, and after peering through the dingy atmosphere for a moment, he nodded his head and waved me over.

"You're still in town," he said as I sat down.

"I am."

"Making any progress on your case?"

"Not that you can tell," I said, "except that the damned thing kind of expanded on me."

Phillips cocked his head and took a sip of his half-drained beer. Out of the corner of my eye, I saw the bartender glance at me and raise a glass up. I shook my head, and he went back to his cleaning.

"Expanding how?" Phillips asked when he put his glass down.

"Last time we spoke, you kind of intimated some stuff about John Howard," I said.

The old man cackled and rubbed his face with his hand. "Intimated, huh? That what you call it? I thought I was warning you."

"Maybe you were, and I was just too deaf to catch on. I'm all ears now."

Phillips took another drink, nearly draining his glass this time. When finished, he set it down carefully and looked me straight in the eye.

"Why don't we do it this way?" he said. "Why don't you ask me questions. See how much old Duke Prowder taught you about following a lead."

"Fair enough. Is John Howard Jr. a crook?"

Another cackle, and the old man shook his head. "That sounds like a straight up yes or no, doesn't it?"

"I kind of thought so," I said.

"But it depends on what you mean by crook." Phillips gazed off in the distance for a second, then snapped back to me. "Sorry, kid. I'm getting up there and sometimes lose the focus. You were asking about John Howard's crookdom?"

"Yep."

"Is he a killer? Would he rob someone at gunpoint? Is he a violent man for no reason? Nope, not that I know of."

"But?"

"But," Phillips said, "back when I knew him he wasn't above padding a client's bill, maybe getting a little sneaky in a card game, even occasionally breaking client confidentiality if it would earn him something."

"So more white collar than anything else?" I asked.

Phillips drummed his fingers on the table. "Yeah, I guess that's how I'd put it. Was he an outright thief? Not as far as I ever knew. Would I have my own lawyer read over something he wanted me to sign before I did so? Absolutely."

Now it was my turn to stare off for a moment.

While I was sorting stuff out, Phillips walked over to the bar, got himself a refill, and came back.

"So what's the verdict?" he asked as he sat down.

"Nothing violent on Howard's end, far as you know."

"No more violent than he had to be as a young man working as a PI."

"You ever hear anything about him flat-out harassing clients, women, anything like that?"

"Nope. Nothing like that. You saying that's what he's up to now?"

"At the least," I said, "he seems to be complicit."

Phillips shook his head. "Doesn't sound like the man I knew."

"Sometimes people change," I said.

"Sometimes something happens that makes them change."

"Which means," I spoke slower than usual, thinking it through, "that I'd have to find out what happened to make him change."

"If he did," Phillips pointed out.

"I'm pretty sure he's changed," I said.

CHAPTER FORTY-EIGHT

When I got back in the car, I took a moment to check my phone for any missed messages. There was one, and the caller surprised me.

Lt. William Santiago, the head of the detective division for the Providence PD and Josh Nichols's boss, rarely reached out to me. And I could never remember him calling me directly.

The fact he was doing so now made a little worm of concern sprout in my gut.

I called him back.

"Hello," Santiago said.

"It's Quinton. You rang?"

"Hold on a sec." Over the next several seconds I heard papers shuffling, chairs scraping, people moving around, and at one point a door slamming shut before Santiago came back on the line.

"Okay, I can talk now," he said.

"Sounds like I interrupted a meeting."

"Never mind that. Where are you right now?"

That little tendril of concern blossomed some more. "Why do you ask?"

"Never mind," Santiago said. "I'm guessing you're still out of town?"

"And you'd guess right, Lieutenant. What the hell's going on?"

"You need to come back, right now."

I took a deep breath. Cordial relationships with the local cops had always been part of my stock in trade, but Santiago was starting to push it a bit.

"Let's get something straight, Lieutenant. First, I'm in the middle of a case. Second, I don't work for you. So unless you have an arrest warrant with my name on it you can just . . ."

"It's Nichols," Santiago interrupted me. "He's in trouble and needs help."

I took a deep breath, then let it out. I glanced at the clock on my dashboard and did a quick calculation. "I'll be there in three hours tops," I said.

"I'll be waiting for you," Santiago said before chiming off.

CHAPTER FORTY-NINE

Even fighting early evening traffic on the Interstate, I beat the estimate I'd given Santiago by about fifteen minutes. Hitting the western edge of Providence, I didn't stop by my apartment but instead took the exit for Arena Avenue, sailed right past my gym without stopping, and hitched on to Main Street. In less than fifteen minutes from the exit, I pulled into one of the city parking garages next to the downtown police station.

I did a brisk walk from my car to the garage exit, and in another five entered the detective squad room. The first thing I noticed upon walking in set my nerves jangling even more.

By now, it was getting on to later afternoon, which meant most of the detective squad should have been gone for the day, with only a sparse skeleton crew hanging around for any calls that came in overnight.

Instead, almost all the desks were occupied by grim-faced plain clothes men and women engaged in some sort of paperwork, and only one or two bothered to look up as I came in.

However, the desk that sat closest to the lieutenant's enclosed office, Josh Nichols's desk, was vacant.

Santiago had his office door open, and when I was halfway there, he looked up and waved me in.

Santiago looked, for him, somewhat bedraggled. The jacket of his navy blue wool suit straddled one of the extra chairs in his office; he had the sleeves rolled up on his pink tone-on-tone silk dress shirt; and his maroon silk tie, which probably cost as much as my utility bill each month, was pulled about an inch down on his chest, his top two shirt buttons open.

Even so, the man looked formidable. Santiago's somewhere in his early forties and stands five ten with a lean, powerful build. He has maybe half the muscle mass that I do, but even sitting at his desk, his pecs and lats knotted and twisted under the pink dress shirt.

"Close the door," he said by way of greeting.

I did as he asked and plopped myself into a black mesh chair in front of his desk. "What's going on, Lieutenant?"

Up close, I could see a tightness in his face that usually wasn't there. Santiago was a cop in Chicago for almost two decades before making the jump to Providence, population somewhat under a hundred and fifty thousand with the colleges in session, and ever since he'd arrived there'd been speculation about why he would have made a somewhat less than lateral move.

When you added in the fact that his workaday wardrobe, on any given day, probably exceeded the combined monthly salaries of at least two of his detectives, there was a lot of talk.

Through all that, every time I'd been around the man he'd exhibited a calm, hard demeanor. He still projected that now, but I felt things kind of crackling around the edges.

He stared at me for another moment before going right for the solar plexus. "Nichols has been suspended."

My breath caught, and for a moment the office rocked around me. "Come again?"

"Suspended," Santiago said, "pursuant to an investigative hearing and possible trial."

The room had settled back on its axis, but I still had to force myself to breathe. "When did all this happen?"

"Came to a head today. Turns out he's been under investigation for a couple of days though."

"A couple of days? You suspend a detective sergeant after a two-day investigation?"

Santiago held up his hands to me, palms forward, in a shushing gesture. "Wasn't me, Quinton. I was as blindsided by this as anyone. Far as that goes, there's a better than even chance that I may join Sergeant Nichols in a day or two."

I frowned, trying to think, to accept this new information into my reality. It didn't fit well at all, and in trying to make it do so, something popped up in my head. "Is Providence even big enough to have an IA section?"

"We do, a small one, but that's not where this originated."

"Sheriff's?" I asked.

Santiago shook his head. "Staties."

"Troopers?" Now I felt like shaking my head. "What'd the state cops pick Nichols up for?"

Santiago looked like he had something he wanted to spit out of his mouth. "Working on an anonymous tip, they got a warrant to search his personal vehicle."

I waited a couple of heartbeats for him to continue, but when he didn't I prodded him. "And?"

Santiago sighed and slumped in his chair. As far as I could remember, it was the first time I'd ever seen him in a slouched state. "Hidden in the spare tire, they found a quart-sized baggie filled with fentanyl tabs."

"A quart?" I asked.

The cop nodded.

"Lieutenant," I said, working to control my heartbeat, "I don't want to tell your brethren at the state level how to do their jobs, but who the hell hauls around quart bags of that crap? That's enough to kill off everybody in the county a couple of times over."

"I know."

"And hidden in the spare tire? Who does that? That's straight out of a bad 1960s TV show."

"You're preaching to the choir, Quinton. And there's lots of other problems with the whole thing too."

I nodded. "Since when is an anonymous tip enough for a full-fledged warrant on a cop with absolutely no marks on his record?"

"My thoughts exactly. I yelled and screamed to whoever I

could and got exactly nowhere. It's like something reached out and sucked Sgt. Nichols in."

"Any help for him?" I asked.

Santiago grimaced. "The union has legal counsel they assign for this kind of thing, but I made a call, at the sergeant's behest, and got Bernie Lyman to represent him. But even Lyman's running into brick walls."

"And the experienced state police investigators don't smell this as a frameup?"

"Not so far," Santiago said.

"Where's Josh now?"

"The arraignment judge cut him some slack and allowed him to be released O.R. but put some pretty strict limits on his movements."

I had the urge to turn my head and look out through the glass walls of Santiago's office. I had the strong feeling that all those cops sitting in there when I showed up were staring at the two of us, attempting to divine our conversation.

"So what do you want from me?" I asked.

Santiago placed his elbows on his desk and steepled his hands, resting his chin in them. "Nichols mentioned a conversation the two of you had the other day, about dirty cops."

"Yeah?"

"Is it possible that whatever you're up to in Kansas City has something to do with all this?" he asked.

"I've been doing my best sitting here not to think about that," I said. "But the scenario you laid out for Josh pretty much fits a pattern I've been running into back there."

"And what exactly is Sgt. Nichols's connection to your case?"

"That's the hell of it, Lieutenant. Far as I can see, his only connection is me."

Santiago unsteepled his hands and leaned back. His chair gave out a slight creak, which sounded like a thunderclap in the stillness of the office. "You mean somebody's trying to send a message to you through him?"

"Would be my guess. Either that or we have to believe Josh has decided to supplement his pension by dealing."

"From here to KC is kind of a stretch distance wise," Santiago pointed out.

"Not really. Let me ask you a question. You worked in Chicago for years. If you wanted to send someone back there a message, could you do it?"

The lieutenant nodded. "I see what you mean. And if you're right, this could be the first of several landmines waiting for Josh, or for anyone else close to you."

"Again, trying not to think that way."

"If I were you, it's all I would think about." The cop pulled a mini legal pad out of his desk drawer and jotted something down. He ripped the top page off and slid it across the desk to me.

"My hands, along with everyone else on this squad, are pretty much tied unless we want to come under the microscope as well."

"Makes sense," I said as I took up the paper and glanced over it. "Who's this?"

"The statie in charge of arresting Nichols."

I nodded, folded the paper, and put it in my pocket. "See you around, Lieutenant," I said as I stood up.

"Let me know how things go," he said.

I winked at him as I left his office.

CHAPTER FIFTY

THE NEXT MORNING, AFTER SPENDING A GLORIOUS NIGHT in my own apartment with Talia as company, I took 63 Highway out of town and headed down to the capital of Jefferson City. I came off the highway, jogged a bit through the eastern edge of downtown and came out on a residential street named Clark Avenue.

A couple of blocks farther down, Clark opened up a bit, and on the right side of the road was the general HQ for the state police.

Despite my years living in Providence, and my side occupation, I'd never had a reason to visit the staties in their home, so I had to spend a few minutes driving back and forth among the cluster of tan colored, official-looking buildings before I spotted the one I thought I wanted.

After a quick detour to visitors parking, and a jog on foot back the other way, I made it to my destination.

Stopping at a desk just inside the front doors, I presented my license to a young uniform manning a desk and asked to see Sergeant Alan Hartman. The officer barely glanced at the license before picking up a phone, muttering a few words, then directing me toward the back of the building and to the left.

Amazingly, considering I'd been dealing with a civil servant, I went to the back of the building and left and found Hartman's office with no trouble and knocked on the opened door. The sergeant, sitting at his desk, looked up and waved me in.

"I know you showed it to Janey out front, but could I see some paper please," he said.

I handed over my license again, waited for the guy to read it through, then took it back from him.

Hartman looked an inch or two taller than me, but he probably weighed about forty pounds less. Even sitting behind a desk, he was a lean, rangy looking guy. His face was pale, and his light red hair was beginning to thin on him in places.

Harman gestured me towards one of three surplus, red vinyl chairs in front of his desk.

"What can I do for you?" he asked.

I sat down. The vinyl creaked and popped under my weight. "Tell me about a bust you made the other day," I said.

The state cop frowned. "And why should I tell you anything about an arrest?"

"Because there's a chance it's involved in a case I'm working on in KC."

Hartman frowned even harder. "Your license gives your address as Carson County," he pointed out.

"Yes, but it's good for the entire state."

"I don't see how a case of mine here has anything to do with the big city," he said.

"Wouldn't it be wise to know which case I'm talking about before making that decision?"

The state cop sighed and pushed himself a couple of inches away from his desk. "I can guess which case it is, smartass. I've been stationed in this area for a couple of years now, and I either know or know about most of the players around."

"Good to know the players, I guess. But what's your point?"

"The point is it's common knowledge around and about that you and Josh Nichols are tight, but that doesn't really cut anything. Your bubba's dirty, and I got the goods on him."

"How?" I asked.

"Come again?" Hartman's eyes crossed a little.

"How'd you catch Josh? What made you go and dig into a city detective with nothing on his record?"

"We got a tip," Hartman said.

"From?"

"Get real, Quinton. I know you're used to things being kind of loose in Providence, but you're not walking into a state posting and getting inside information about a pending case. Your license doesn't entitle you to anything like that."

I took a deep breath, working to calm my nerves, which had started to jitter. "No, but it does entitle me to investigate any crimes, major or minor, within the borders of this state."

Hartman leaned forward, his forearms resting on his desk. "And just what does that mean, private?"

"It means that I'm smelling something here, and I'm going to dig it up."

"You're not recording this, are you?" Hartman asked, his eyes twitching even more.

"No."

"Good, so whether you are or not, with that admission nothing I say now can come back to me."

"Ready to confess?" I asked.

"Like hell," Hartman said. "More like ready to kick your ass right out of here. I made a righteous bust, and it's going to stay righteous."

"You and Nichols know each other, by chance?" I asked.

"No, and what would that have to do with anything anyway." Again, his eyes flickered.

I was getting an odd vibe off the guy.

"I was just wondering if there were some personal animosity between the two of you."

"Animosity. I'll give you animosity if you try fouling up my case."

"You got a tip that Nichols was carrying, right?"

For an instant, Hartman looked like he was going to clam up, but then he relented. "That's what I said. And I'm not giving anything away here, as it's going to be in the court filings anyway. Yeah, I got a tip that he was dirty."

"From who?"

"Confidential informant," Hartman said.

"Ahh. Good old CI himself. You know, Sergeant, I hear tell that some cops make up CI's if they know someone's dirty and want to bust them."

Hartman's face reddened a bit around the edges, but I noticed that even in his anger he didn't quite manage to look at me straight on. "You start implying corruption about me, buddy, and you're going to end up losing that paper of yours."

"I'm not talking corruption," I said. "I'm only talking about a cop making up a source, getting a warrant on illicit grounds, searching a fellow cop's property, and securing planted evidence."

Hartman stood up so violently that his desk wobbled a bit.

"That's enough, mister. If you've got any more accusations, you know where you can take them. You're out of here. Now!"

He clenched his fists, maybe to stop his arms from shaking at his sides, but wasn't all that successful.

I could have made a point of sticking around and really riling him up but decided that getting thrown in the clink myself wouldn't do anything to help either Josh Nichols or the larger issue. Something was off about Hartman's attitude, off just enough that I got the sneaking feeling of him putting on an act.

And if he was the actor, I already could give a pretty good guess as to who the director was.

I stood without another word and left his office.

CHAPTER FIFTY-ONE

I DROVE ABOUT HALF A BLOCK OUT of the trooper complex until I was back in the little residential section just to the north on Clark. I was betting that, whenever Hartman would leave, it would be this way. But since that direction was the simplest way to get to either Jeff City's downtown or the main highway, it seemed a pretty good bet.

With it still only mid-morning, I didn't know for sure that Hartman would be taking off any time soon. But I hoped that I'd pushed him enough to want to make some kind of move, and he didn't strike me as the kind of guy dumb enough to reach out, even on his personal phone, from inside the station.

Leaving me to sit there on a pleasant little side street on a nice May morning and wait him out.

And even if he was as cool as they came, and was planning on working out the rest of his shift, hell, even if he'd already forgotten about our little talk, I figured I had nothing better to do than sit for as long as it took to see what developed.

I thought of making a quick call to Lieutenant Santiago but decided not to for two reasons. For one, I really didn't have anything to report yet. But more importantly, if Santiago had felt comfortable being drug any more into this than he already was, he would have made that clear to me the day before.

Barely twenty minutes after I'd left his office, a bright red SUV came down the street, headed from the direction of the trooper station, and as it went past I could see Hartman at the wheel.

Score one for the good guys. I gave it a count of five so he could get far enough ahead without being able to look back and see my face, then pulled onto the street to follow.

I kept about a block behind him as we went up Clark, then angled over to head east, and in no time at all were going north on the highway.

Trailing a trained observer like a cop, especially with only one car, without being discovered is almost impossible. But it was made a lot easier in this instance. 63 is such a commonly-used route, with only a couple of minor places to get off between the two main cities, that it's just about the most common thing in the world to drive thirty miles or so seeing the same vehicle behind you.

Thus, as long as Hartman was headed toward Providence, or even further north, I didn't have to worry much about pulling all the assorted tricks to try to disguise a tail.

In short, I could settle back in my seat, listen to the radio, keep him in sight with only a little effort, and relax a bit until I saw exactly where we were going.

CHAPTER FIFTY-TWO

As it turned out, Hartman didn't have all that far to go. About fifteen minutes after our little journey began, he turned off the highway into Greenview.

Once its own little town, over the last decade or so Greenview has grown until it's almost, but not quite, a bedroom community of Providence. I've never seen any exact figures, but an eyeball guess from driving around is that the population has probably tripled in the last decade.

Which still only leaves it with around five thousand residents.

Turning onto Main Street, I hung back farther than I had been and let four or five cars get between me and Hartman. It would be tougher now not to get noticed, and I hoped the state cop wasn't going far. If he had a house somewhere in the central area of the town, I could possibly still escape his notice, especially if we weren't going far.

But within a couple of blocks in any direction the route would lead off into flat country, and keeping concealed would be next to impossible.

Once again, though, I lucked out. Hartman made it all of two blocks before turning south, angling past a Pizza Hut and into a tiny residential neighborhood.

I didn't turn with him, instead scooting past the restaurant another block before making my own turn and circling back around to come in the opposite direction.

I made it to the far corner of the previous block in time to see Hartman pull into a smallish, tan ranch house with a slightly unkempt yard surrounded by a chain link fence. I coasted to a parking space about a block away and watched him go inside.

I waited for a while, both trying to figure out what to do next and checking for signs that anyone other than Hartman lived there. I didn't really want anything to go down with the guy in front of wife or kids.

Far as that went, I really wasn't looking forward to confronting a state cop in general, but at the moment wasn't sure what else to do.

Josh Nichols was on the hook, as far as I could tell, for nothing more nefarious than being associated with me. And while we could all just sit back and wait for Bernie Lyman to do his attorney magic, that would take some time. I had enough faith in Lyman that he could get Josh off, but getting him off wouldn't be enough.

His name had to be totally cleared, and the key to doing so had walked into that tan house about half an hour before.

About a quarter hour after I'd coasted to a stop, my phone buzzed.

"Quinton," I answered.

"It's me," Santiago said in greeting.

"Good morning, Lieutenant."

"Any progress?"

Any other time, I would have been irritated at someone birddogging me like that. But I shrugged it off to the top cop being worried about one of his guys. "Not yet," I said. "Though I'm hoping to track something down soon."

"This may help," Santiago said. "I did a little digging into the arresting officer, this Hartman fellow."

"Uh huh," I said, not bothering to tell Santiago I was camped out in front of the sergeant's house.

"Turns out he's a fairly recent transplant to our little corner of the state. He was transferred down this way just a couple of years ago."

A little tickle started in my brain. "He did kind of imply he was fairly new in these parts," I said.

"Want to take three guesses where he transferred from?" Santiago asked.

"Do the first two count?"

"Nope."

"Let me guess," I said. "Troop A?"

"If by Troop A you mean the Kansas City area, you'd be correct."

"Son of a gun," I said. "Lieutenant, I think we have ourselves a clue here."

"Be nice to it," Santiago said as he signed off, "we can use all the ones we can get."

After Santiago hung up, I sat in my Cherokee and mulled things over. The fact that Hartman was originally from the west side of the state could be coincidence. After all, it wasn't unheard of for cops to transfer around to various duties and divisions. But such a clear-cut connection to my current case was stretching the concept of coincidence.

As I waited, my mind took another veer. Why exactly had Tom Jacobson, and I had no doubt he was behind all this malarkey, gone after Nichols? His beef was with me, not a sergeant on the Providence force a hundred miles away from his home base. Unless he was just going full Dr. Evil psycho on anyone connected with me, what was the point?

I sat in the Cherokee and mulled that over. So far, no sign of any other habitants. True, it wasn't even yet noon, and the area schools were still in session, but the longer I sat the more I felt that Hartman lived alone.

Which would make bracing him a little easier, if not still unhealthy for the long-term prospects of my PI license.

Besides which, as small as Greenview is, any time now someone would notice a strange car parked in this quiet little block.

My mind flipped again, going back to the why of it all. Why take on Nichols, someone completely unknown to Jacobson? Why set up, as I was sure he had, a cop he'd never even met? If there'd been any actual connection between the two, I was sure that Josh would have mentioned it when I first brought up Jacobson's name to him.

So what was in it for John Howard's second in command to take an action like this?

What did it get him?

An instant later, as Hartman's house stayed motionless and the neighborhood around stayed quiet, the answer hit me.

What all this with Nichols got Jacobson was me out of KC, out of his hair. It got me half the state away.

Allowing him to do what?

Hell, as dumb as I felt, maybe Jacobson shouldn't have worried about me.

But he had, and he'd found a way to sucker me out of the way.

Again, for what reason? Just to make things a little easier on him?

My phone buzzed, and I grabbed it from the passenger seat.

"Yeah?"

"Sam," Karyn Robert's voice sounded on edge, a bit frantic. "Where are you?"

Not wanting to get into a long-winded explanation, I evaded the question. "What's up, Karyn?"

She plowed on, obviously not noticing my ducking. "Have you been in contact with Lorie?"

"Not for a while now, why?"

A pause, almost a dramatic one except Karyn wasn't a drama queen of any kind. "I think she's missing."

Bile began to curdle in my gut as the clouds began to part. "Why so?"

"I've been trying to call her for hours and not getting anything. And just now I drove by her house."

"And?"

"No answer to my knock, but the door was unlocked."

I took in a deep breath, willing my hands not to shake as I continued staring at Hartman's house.

Son of a bitch.

"Did you look around?" I asked.

"A little, but I didn't touch anything."

"Anything disturbed? Out of place?" I asked.

"Nothing obvious, but I've never been in her house before, so I couldn't really tell. Are you nearby?"

Deep breaths. In and out. Lower the damned heart rate.

"You there now?" I asked.

"Yes, but . . ."

"Call the Overland Park cops and wait outside for them. The department itself, don't call 911. When you get through, ask for Detective Sloan and tell him what you've just told me. Do whatever he says."

"Are you close by? Can you come over?" Karyn asked.

"Not right now. I'm a ways away and tracking something down. Call Sloan, and I'll swing by as soon as I can."

I hung up and reached into the Cherokee's glove compartment for my gun.

The original plan had been to sit on Hartman for as long as possible, follow him wherever he went, see who he talked or met up with, and try to get some kind of angle on him.

But now that I had a pretty damned good idea why Josh had been targeted, I didn't have time for that.

I had to pop the man as quick and hard as possible and hope I could shake something out of him.

I opened my car door and got out.

CHAPTER FIFTY-THREE

Moving up the short walkway to Hartman's front door, I considered pulling out my phone and making a call to Santiago. My license from the state permits me to investigate crimes both major and minor and to provide personal protection for clients.

It doesn't allow me to browbeat presumably innocent citizens in their homes, and it for damned sure doesn't permit rousting law enforcement officials, even if I personally believe there's something bent about them.

Had this been an ordinary case, I would have done the smart thing and hightailed it right out of there.

But this case wasn't ordinary, and I had this mental image of a spider's web, with all of us merely flies dancing around on the various strands while Tom Jacobson, for whatever reason, crouched in the middle of the web, every now and then plucking a strand to make someone dance a certain way.

I felt a queasiness in my gut as I began imagining just what was going on back in KC right about now.

Again, though, I couldn't worry about that just yet.

In the hopes of wrapping things up as peaceably as possible, I didn't kick in the door, or bang it down with my shoulder. Instead, I gave a couple of fairly mild knocks and waited.

I knew Hartman was in there, unless he'd for some reason climbed out a back window or something. I was reasonably sure no one else was in the house, so if things had to get rough, the situation could hopefully be somewhat contained.

After a couple of seconds, I knocked again and this time heard a faint shuffling on the other side of the door. I set myself, just in case, and waited.

A moment later, the door opened up.

Hartman stood there, still in the clothes he'd worn at the station, but the tie was half hung off his collar, the sleeves were rolled up, and at some point he'd ditched his belt.

Away from his desk, he looked a little flabby, a little middle-manager-ish, and I got the odd impression looking at him of a man who'd risen as far as he would in life.

In his right hand, instead of a weapon of some sort, he held a beer can, the droplets beading the can showing that he'd just taken it out of the refrigerator, but the looseness of his expression indicated, even in the short time I'd staked out his car, the can in his hand probably wasn't the first.

"Quinton," he said, his voice low and kind of mumbled, "what are you doing here?"

"Want to come in and talk some more," I said, keeping my voice low and even so there'd be no suggestion of a threat.

Hartman frowned, his entire face contracting in the move. His right hand made a stray gesture to his hip before he must have realized he wasn't wearing his service weapon.

I didn't want to think about how many guns a cop might have in his house. I knew for sure that Josh Nichols had at least three, not counting his department-issued piece.

"We don't have anything more to talk about," Hartman said.

"We do, and I think it's important that we do it here, away from the station. Don't you?"

The state cop's face scrunched in again. "I don't get what you . . ."

"It's like this," I interrupted. "Do you want us in your office, at headquarters, talking about how you allowed yourself to be corrupted? Even with the door closed, I could talk loud enough that somebody walking by would be able to hear and wonder what the heck was going on. And if they asked, I guess I'd just have to tell them, wouldn't I?"

His expression flattened out now, and through the fog of however many beers he'd had, a hard look smoldered in his eyes. "You don't know what you're talking about, Quinton. Now get the hell out of here before one of us gets hurt."

"Won't be me," I said, and Hartman took a swing at me.

It was a lousy punch, fueled by alcohol and whatever else was eating at the guy. Standing in the doorway as he was didn't help.

It started at his side and looped around in a complete 180 until it finally got somewhat close to me.

An alert ten-year old could have avoided the move. I ducked under the punch, slid forward instead of back, and smashed the flat of my hand against Hartman's chest, moving him back several steps before he fell on the floor.

In for a penny, I thought. I'd already assaulted a peace officer so might as well go all the way. I stepped into the house, shut the door behind me, pulled out my gun, and faced Hartman.

He sat on the floor, his face still looking kind of scrunched, and stared at me.

"Here's what I'm guessing," I said. "At some point in the past, maybe some years ago, you did something or other that caught someone's attention. I'm guessing that it's something that happened back when you were assigned to Troop A."

Hartman finally found his voice, though a rather scratchy, gravelly voice. "You're finished, mister. You just stepped over the line. You're losing your license and going to have charges filed against you."

"Don't think so," I said. Looking around, I walked over and sat down in a green cloth recliner. Rather than standing up, Hartman eased himself around on the floor to keep me in sight.

My punch hadn't been all that hard, but I'd seen this before from men in some sort of authority in their daily lives. He was a little in shock that someone had actually laid hands on him. That shock would wear off soon, so I had to get said what I had to say as quickly as possible.

"It went like this. Whatever you did, you screwed up enough so that someone had a hold over you, had a marker, if you will."

"Assaulting a cop," Hartman said, the voice losing a little of the gravel. "You're not walking away from this, Quinton."

"I'm pretty sure I am," I said, "but to continue. Some time went by, maybe a couple of years, until whoever has your marker decided to call it in."

"Fuck you."

"He called it in the other day."

Hartman had started to get to his knees, but froze at that. He shook his head, a little flick, as if trying to get a fly to leave him alone.

"And what he wanted was for you to frame Josh Nichols, get him in some major hot water."

The state cop opened his mouth as if to say something, then closed it.

"What puzzled me at first," I said, "was the why of it all. The frame's lousy, even you've got to know that. It's going to fall apart as soon as a good lawyer gets ahold of it, and trust me, Nichols has a good lawyer on his side. And yet you went ahead with it. But as I sat outside your house for a while here, the why came to me."

"I ain't saying anything," Hartman finally mumbled.

"Fine by me, I'm more than glad to keep talking for both of us. See, the why of it all isn't to get Josh in trouble. It was to get me out here, away from KC, away from the case I'm working on out there."

"If you say so smart guy."

"I do say so," I said, "even if lately I haven't been feeling all that smart. You were supposed to do something so ridiculously over the top to Nichols that I wouldn't have a choice but to come running back home. Question now is, what do we do about this?"

"How about you walk out that door and we call it a draw?" Hartman asked, his voice a little squishy.

"Can't do that," I said. "I started pulling on a thread, and I'm going to keep pulling until everything unravels. Even without me, your frame against Nichols isn't going to hold, and when it comes apart you'll be down for the count. So how about having the good guys score one, huh?"

Hartman glared for a moment, then nodded.

"What was your original sin?" I asked.

"Couple years back, when I was working Troop A, my youngest sister got sick and died."

"And?" I asked.

"And she left four kids. The scumbag husband had taken off long ago, and the kids got shipped off to my other sister, their aunt, to live."

"Best of a bad situation," I said.

Hartman shrugged. "Whatever. Problem was Annie, my kid sis, didn't leave much in the way of life insurance, or anything else for that matter."

The light began to shine a bit. "You needed money to set them up," I said.

Hartman nodded.

"How'd you get it?" I asked.

"How do you think?"

"You're right, dumb question. I'm guessing you looked the other way on something."

Hartman nodded. "The one time. Only once. But somehow that bastard found out about it."

"What bastard?" I asked. I had a strong hunch, of course, but was anxious for another piece of the puzzle to fall into place.

But Hartman shook his head. "Don't know. A voice on the phone is all. About four months after it happened. He said to get ready because someday he'd be calling me for real."

Once again, Jacobson covering his tracks too damned well. I felt a headache coming on. Every time I thought I had a line on the guy, I found myself outmatched.

Maybe I should just say the hell with it and go back to running my gym.

I couldn't do that, yet, though. I had to keep at this until somehow I brought the guy down.

"That's why you transferred out here," I said. " To try to get away from him."

Hartman squeezed his eyes shut. If I'd been a little more perceptive, I would have thought the tough old cop was weeping.

"I had to take a step down for the transfer," Hartman said, "but I figured it was worth it. I'd tried every way possible to track whoever it was down, but nothing worked. Only thing I could think to do was move away, and hope he wouldn't think I was worth the trouble."

"Obviously he did," I said.

Hartman shook his head.

"And now, you're doing the same thing to another cop. And for a much worse reason."

"Meaning what?" Hartman's tone was a strange combination of strangle and gurgle. Somewhere down the line, I'd feel sorry for the guy who'd made a mistake, for the best of reasons, and had thought he'd lived it down, only to find himself sucked into the whirlpool all over again.

Despite all the evidence, I had a hunch there was a decent cop somewhere in there, so I laid it out for him—all of it. Up to and including the call I'd gotten from Karyn before entering his house.

"Jesus," he said when I'd finished, "what a complete fucking mess."

"No doubt, but you can help clean up a little of it. Can you think of any reason he'd kidnap my client except to do her in?"

Hartman shook his head without looking at me.

"Then help me clean it up," I said. "You need to make a clean sweep of it all."

He started to cringe backwards, but only made it an inch or so before relenting. "There's no clean way out of this for me, is there?" he asked.

"You're asking me? You're the law enforcement professional. What do you think?"

His silence gave his answer.

"But there's possibly a less dirty way of going," I said.

"Which is?"

I could tell by the look in his eyes that his question had been moot at best. He was done, and knew it, with no easy way out of the mess he'd fallen into.

I pulled out my phone, made a quick call, and waited through three rings before it was picked up.

"Lieutenant," I said in greeting, still keeping my eyes and gun on Hartman, though he clearly hadn't the will to try anything. "I've got someone who wants to talk to you."

CHAPTER FIFTY-FOUR

I MANAGED TO HIT THE KC AREA RIGHT AROUND FIVE, perfect rush-hour time on a weekday, but even so by a little before six I was seated with Sloan in a booth at an Overland Park coffee shop.

"I requested a patrol car to run by there as soon as your friend called me," Sloan said. "Middle of the day, all the lights in the house were on and the front door unlocked. Uniforms walked right in."

"And probably found everything except for the resident of the house," I said.

"You've got that right."

"So what now?" I asked.

"Now, we officially have a missing person on our hands and we're doing everything possible to find her."

"Look for Jacobson," I said.

"We have been. So far zip, zilch."

We both stayed silent for a moment and stared down at our full cups. Neither of us was drinking our coffee, but we'd bought the two cups as a concession to taking up the booth.

Finally, Sloan spoke up. "This is our baby now, Quinton. Time for you to step aside."

I nodded, though I didn't exactly feel like agreeing. "You talked to Howard yet?" I asked.

"We spoke with him, in terms of his missing employer, yes."

"You feel that was good enough?"

"Doesn't matter what I feel, buddy. We have a book we go by, and we're going by it."

"So what do you want me to do?"

"Take a guess," Sloan said.

I hunched my shoulders as I looked up at him. "My guess would be to go back to my hotel, lay low, and wait for word from you."

Sloan smiled, though the expression didn't have a lot of mirth behind it. "That's exactly what we need you to do."

"You've got my number," I said.

"We do."

I stood up and tossed a couple of bills, I'm not sure how many, onto the table. "It's on me," I said before I walked out of the diner.

CHAPTER FIFTY-FIVE

By the next morning, I hadn't heard anything back from Sloan, so I said the hell with it, and a little before nine, I came out of the elevator on the fifth floor and headed straight for Howard's office. One or two sharp-looking young men, dressed like accountants, made a move in my direction. I threw them a look and they backed off.

Boy, Humphrey Bogart where are you. They sure don't make PI's like they used to.

I made my way to Howards's secretary's desk. She glanced up, no doubt recognized me, and proved she was made of harder stuff than the men employed by the company.

"I'm sorry, Mr. Quinton." Knew she remembered me. "But Mr. Howard is occupied at the moment and can't be disturbed."

"Good to know," I said as I breezed on past her and entered the head man's office.

Howard was sitting behind his desk staring at his laptop screen. He looked the same as he had the first time I'd been in this office. Hell, far as I could tell he was wearing the same outfit.

As he looked up, frowning, I heard the secretary come in behind me. "I'm sorry, Mr. . ."

"Get her out of here, Howard. Just you and me or you'll have more trouble than even you can handle."

Howard flicked his eyebrows, which must have meant something to the secretary because a second later I heard the door close. Without a word to me, Howard got up and went over to the sideboard to make himself a drink.

I don't know hardly anything about hard liquor, but I'm pretty sure he mixed himself a bourbon and water.

At nine in the morning?

"Have a seat Mr. Quinton," he said as he sat back down behind his desk.

I didn't want to sit down. I wanted to tear his office apart. However, the initial mad that had taken me all the way into his office had boiled down to a low simmer and my thinking mind was beginning to get itself together.

I sat.

"I assume you think there's something I can do for you," Howard said. "Something you believe I'd better do for you."

"Lorie Jones," I said.

"Who?"

"Knock it off, Howard. You're no innocent in this. You know goddamned well who I mean."

He took a long pull at his drink, then set the glass down. He leaned forward, elbows on his desk, and steepled his hands together.

His fingers looked a little white, as if he wasn't quite as calm and collected as he made out to be.

"You're talking about a young woman who I believe was a former client of ours," he said.

I shook my head. "That's one way of putting it."

"And what would be another way?"

"That she's the victim of a predatory son of a bitch whose salary you pay."

Howard's eyes narrowed. "Are you saying the lady's life is in danger of some kind?"

"That depends," I said.

"On?"

"On whether a seasoned, experienced investigator like you, unlike a cretin such as myself, considers it suspicious she's not at home, can't be reached by phone, and the cops can't track her down."

Howard sighed, released his hands, and slumped back in his chair. "Believe it or not, Mr. Quinton, I do respect your record in our profession. And I don't for a moment think of you as a mere cretin."

"Good to know," I said. "So how about getting on the phone to your boy and . . ."

"I can't do that, for a couple of reasons."

My stomach tightened up. "Give me the most important one first."

Howard chuckled, though the sound came off as raspy, almost dead. "Both are equally important to me, but probably only one is crucial to you."

"Which is?" I asked, my gut tightening.

"Jacobson didn't show up for work the last two days. He called night before last and said he had some personal business to take care of and probably wouldn't be in for a couple of days."

I sat silent, assuming there was more.

"And this morning he hasn't been answering his phone," Howard said.

CHAPTER FIFTY-SIX

After leaving Howard's office, I wasn't sure what to do. Sloan had been right in that it should have been out of my hands. As he'd said, let the professionals handle it. I kept going back to those first few days when I hadn't entirely believed Lorie and spent time making sure her version of events was true.

If I hadn't wasted so much time then, would things have ended up as they were now? I didn't know one way or the other, and the fact I didn't left me feeling at odds.

Like a good little boy, though, after initially breaking orders and confronting Howard, I went back to the hotel and moped through the day. Ordering food in felt better than going out to eat, and staring out the window at a bright, sunny May day with only a few gray clouds far off on the horizon felt better than doing anything.

Around six, Sloan gave me a call. "You didn't stay put like I told you to," he said.

"I'm guessing you interviewed John Howard at some point today."

"I did. And he says you paid him a visit."

"True."

"Said you acted like a real asshole."

"I tend to think not, but could be true. Found her yet?"

"No. Jacobson neither. We've got alerts out throughout the metro area. Something will pop sooner or later."

"You're forgetting how good he is when it comes to messing with records and such. Not to mention the last few days we've gotten a small taste of the type of network he may have been developing over the last several years."

"I heard about Howard's other detective, the woman he had attacked."

"Add those yahoos to Landru and Davis on your force, and it's anyone's guess who else he has in his pocket."

"You're forgetting one thing," Sloan said.

"Which is?"

"All this crap he pulled with the Jones woman, and with you and the other gal, were done under the radar. Now that we know about him, it'll be a lot harder for him to hide."

"Under the radar," I said.

"Huh?"

"What you said made me think. How?"

"How what?" Sloan asked.

"How any of it. As a cop, wouldn't you say Jacobson was pretty much marginal at best? Ten years on the force and still in a patrol car?"

"So what? Lots of guys, that's the path their careers take."

"True. On the other hand, lots of guys who go that way don't end up with a cushy white-collar job that allows them to harass the hell out of innocent people and get away with it. This has been bugging me for days now. How did he?"

"Damned if I know," Sloan said. "You thinking that's important right now? We've got a missing woman out there somewhere who's been the target of a stalker."

"A stalker who seems to be edging more to the violent side," I pointed out.

"My point," Sloan said. "We'll figure out how he went about doing this crap after we track him down."

"If you say so."

"I do, and note the emphasis on 'we' meaning the cops. I can understand your frustration and going out to see his boss this morning. Problem is, Howard is one well-connected dude, so everyone has to back off of him until we get this all worked out. You got me?"

"I do," I said. "You want me to stay right here and don't stir until I hear back from you, right?"

"That's exactly what I want," Sloan said. "I want to be very clear that I don't want you leaving your hotel, don't want you running around town at all, and for damned sure I don't want you paying any more visits to John Howard Jr. No matter what. Clear?"

I hesitated a moment, in case he had anything else to add. When he didn't, I said, "Crystal clear, Detective. I'm staying right here no matter what."

"Good," Sloan said and hung up the phone.

Yep, his message was clear as could be.

CHAPTER FIFTY-SEVEN

About an hour later, I stepped off the elevator and headed down the hall to Howard's office for what I hoped to be the last time.

Even though it was late enough that most of the building was deserted, I had a hunch the head man himself would still be around. Looking down the hall, I saw light seeping out from only one office, and it was the right one.

Howard was sitting at his desk, same as he'd been at our first meeting four days before. However, he in no way looked like the same man.

His silvery hair, instead of being neatly combed and set, was fraying around the edges. Those clear blue eyes were now weak and watery, except for the color reminding me of Jacobson's eyes. There was a stoop to his shoulders, and he had wrinkles in his shirt, with the sleeves rolled up halfway to his elbows.

Even from across the office, and in the half-light provided by the single desk lamp, I could see lines in his face that hadn't been there even that morning.

He looked like a man beaten down by some unbearable burden that had finally crushed him.

All of which meant nothing when compared to the 9mm automatic he held in his hand.

Despite the change he'd undergone, the hand holding the gun looked firm and steady.

"Is that for me" I asked, "or someone else?"

Howard peered at me. "Does it really matter?"

"It would matter for my peace of mind, sure."

"You've really screwed a lot up, Quinton."

"I screwed it up?" I said. "Seems to me it was screwed for a while before I got here."

"No way. I had him under control."

"The hell you did, John." If he rankled at my use of his first name, he didn't show it. "You've been scrambling back and forth for how long now, trying to keep your boy in line? A lot of men would have given it up by now."

"You talk as if I have a choice in the matter."

"Don't you?" I asked.

Leaning back in his chair, Howard propped his elbow on the desk and supported his gun with both hands.

Most people have no clue how exhausting it can be to hold a loaded gun steady for any length of time.

"I guess you could say I had a choice," he replied. "Do my best to keep a leash on him or watch my entire life and reputation, not to mention that of my company, go down the tubes."

Not saying anything in response, I walked on over and sat down in one of the big chairs in front of his desk.

Doing so, I'd moved out of the line of fire, but Howard didn't adjust his weapon at all.

"I guess I'm not the one you're afraid of," I said.

Howard shook his head.

"Kind of poetic justice though, don't you think?" I said.

"How so?"

"You spend a career sending out tentacles in every direction, increasing your power and knowledge of people's secrets to enrich yourself, and now you're hiding in your office, shivering in terror of someone who learned all the lessons from you."

"I never intended this," Howard said.

I shook my head at the man's naivete. "What did you think was going to happen when you took him in?"

"Not that it's any of your goddamned business, mister, I didn't take anyone into anything. The son of a bitch wormed his way in, and before I knew it . . ."

I almost wanted to laugh. "He took you over, didn't he? How long have you been the big man in town, making other people dance to your tune, while all the time Jacobson was pulling your strings?"

"You're mixing metaphors, Mr. Quinton."

"Can't argue with that," I said, "mainly because I've never been too sure what a metaphor is. I just think it's kind of funny both you and your boy have pointed out to me how out of synch I am at the same time he's pulled it over on you pretty good."

Howard didn't respond. He stayed in the same position at his desk, one eye on the doorway and one on me.

The pose would have been laughable if not for the fixated look in his eyes.

"I seriously doubt he's coming here to get you, Howard. Why don't you put the gun away?"

"You've really screwed things up, Quinton, you know that? You call yourself a detective? You couldn't hold a candle to the men I knew back in my day."

Sighing, I decided if Howard was going to shoot me he would have done it by now. "I never made any such claims," I said, "and after seeing how you professionals carry on, I'm pretty glad to be just a gym rat with a strong-arm side gig."

"Fine!" Howard snapped. "You've had your say, now why don't you get the hell out?"

"And what are you going to do, John?"

"I'm going to wait right here for Thomas to come through that door."

"And blow him away when he does?"

Howard's cheeks were clenched tight enough I wondered if he was going to break a tooth. "If I have to."

"Probably won't come to that," I said.

He canted his head slightly to the side to give me a better look. "Why not?"

"Because someone else is already on their way. An Overland Park detective named Sloan," I said.

"Why?" Howard snapped.

"Why the hell do you think? You think I'm going to uncover everything I have the last few days about Jacobson and sit on it? In case you haven't forgotten, bubba, I still have a client I'm representing."

"Doesn't matter," Howard said. "Your cop will be out of his jurisdiction and won't be able to do anything to me."

"Gee, you think it's possible a cop who's worked this metro area his whole life won't realize that? You think he won't bring a couple of KC cops along for the ride."

All this time, I'd been watching Howard's forearms. They would be the telltale if he decided to make a move of some kind.

"You stay like this," I said, "and it's a good chance that instead of your boy you'll gun down an innocent cop or two when they come through that door."

That caused him to blink a couple of times and use his left hand to wipe a thin sheen of sweat off his forehead before resuming his former position.

Not knowing how long before Sloan and his people would arrive, I couldn't go off and leave the guy like this, not unless I wanted the gunshot death of some innocent cleaning person on my hands. Somehow, I had to snap Howard out of it. If I had to, I'd take a jump at him and wish for the best, though I'd much rather talk him down than wrestle him to the floor.

I cudgeled my brain for any possible gambit to try, and only one came to mind.

"Why?" I asked him after a couple of minutes of silence.

Howard's head did no more than a quarter turn in my direction. "What?"

"I said why. Why go through this? Why do any of it? Why let a nobody like Jacobson run all over you?"

"He's a good operator and an effective executive," Howard said.

"Maybe, but there's no way you could have known that when you hired him. He'd been on the cops a decade and never made it out of patrol. So what the hell could you have seen in him? Far as that goes, how did the two of you meet up anyway?"

Howard's hands trembled, causing my tension to ratchet up a degree or two. Part of me really didn't expect him to answer my question, but at the moment hope was about all I had to latch on to.

"How do you think I met Thomas?" Howard finally asked.

"Damned if I know, unless he crashed the local Dick Tracy Crime Busters convention."

Howard's expression cracked a bit though whether from humor or anger I couldn't quite tell. "Hardly," he said. "Truth is, I ran into him during the regular course of his duties."

"As a cop?"

Howard nodded.

I thought for a moment. "But I'm guessing not in the regular course of your business, right? I can't imagine a street officer and the head of the largest investigative agency in the state would have much to do with each other."

"And your guess would be correct."

The hands began to tremble a bit more. While Howard had the experience, of course, and was in damned good shape for his age, I wondered how long it had been since he'd had to hold a fully-loaded weapon for so long.

"You met him while he was working, right?" I asked. "During his shift?"

Howard started to nod again but stopped himself. "An overindulgence on my part. I usually can control myself better. But we'd just landed a big account with an annual retainer in the seven figures, and I wanted to celebrate a bit."

I went with the law of averages on this one. "By celebrate you mean get hammered?"

Though Howard didn't move or speak, from the set of his shoulders I knew I'd gotten it in one guess.

"What happened, John? What got you in Jacobson's clutches?"

He mumbled something too low for me to get.

"Come again?" I asked.

"I said a wrong turn." Louder this time, though still not the volume he'd been using before. "Heading home. Place I've lived for thirty years. You think I didn't know the route by heart? Blindfolded?

Yet I made a wrong turn, all because of the new client with the big retainer."

Something dark and nasty was flicking around the back of my mind. I really didn't want to bring it out, but I also had to keep him talking. "How wrong?"

More tension in the shoulders now, and his head jerked up and down a couple of times.

"You aren't wearing a wire of some sort, are you Quinton?"

I shook my head. "You're kind of dating yourself, John. Hardly anybody needs to wear wires anymore. All you have to do is set your cell phone to record. Mine's not set. This is only between the two of us."

He looked a little relieved at that. "There was a girl," he said.

"A girl."

A nod while his gaze stayed fixed on the doorway. By now, God only knew who or what he expected to come through there. "A streetwalker, for Christ's sakes. In a neighborhood like that. Out where she didn't belong."

I gave him some time, worried that if I rushed it he'd clam up.

And I still had to get the gun away from him.

"And?'

"And I was going too fast and she wasn't paying enough attention."

Comes the light.

"Jacobson responded to the call?" I asked.

"Yes—no—I don't know who the hell all answered the call. He was one of them I guess."

The sudden uncertainty filled in the rest of the blanks for me, and I now saw the whole story between the two men. "You left the scene before they got there," I said.

Howard clenched his jaws even tighter for a second before relenting. "Yes, wasn't anything else to do. Fast as I was going, hard as I hit her, I was sure she died on the spot."

At the moment, I wanted to look for the nearest trash basket to throw up in. "But you didn't know for sure if she was dead. You couldn't have known for absolute sure."

"Doesn't matter now," Howard said.

"And you took off anyway."

"Only for about ten blocks. I panicked, of course. Eventually, though, I calmed down enough to pull my car into the curb and consider going back."

"Consider."

"Yes." Howard gripped the gun even tighter, if possible, while his hands trembled even more.

Not a good combination.

"Three years later," he continued, "it's hard to tell for sure. But I'm positive that, given enough time to control myself, I would have gone back. I didn't get the time."

"Because he found you."

Howard nodded. "He found me. Parked along the side of the road, crying like a baby. Took one look at the front of my car and knew what had happened."

I took in a deep breath. Howard's eyes had taken on a far-away look, gazing back in time to the ruination of his life.

"He made you an offer, and you had to take it," I said.

Howard nodded. "He recognized me, of course. And no matter what else you can say about Thomas, he's not a stupid man. He must have seen in an instant the opportunity he'd been looking for his whole life and jumped at it."

"He keeps quiet about your guilt, allows you to scoot off home, and you give him a job."

Howard turned and looked fully at me for the first time since I'd entered his office. His forearms began to twitch. "That's right," he said. "What else could I do but go along with him? I was five blocks from my home, for God's sake. Five damned blocks away, and my whole life turned upside down."

"You could have taken your lumps," I said.

Howard snickered. "Easy for you to say, Quinton. If your life got scrambled to pieces, how would you know the difference?"

I didn't give him the satisfaction, if that's what he wanted, of taking offense.

"Moving on then," I said. "I've got another why."

Howard half turned away, as if my desires were of no more importance to him.

"So he extorted you to allow him to leave the cops and get a good job."

"Yes."

"One that paid him more than he would have ever made on the force, even if he became chief somehow?"

Howard's face scrunched a bit, and for a moment I got the idea he was going to lie, or at least fib. "I pay my employees well," he said.

"Especially if they can put you behind bars for homicide, right?"

Howard shook his head at my comment.

"So if he got what he wanted including, it would appear, actual if not official control of your company, what's with all the games?"

"Games?"

"Yeah, John. Games. Jacobson has a better life than he could ever have hoped for while riding around on patrol all those years. Why jeopardize that by going after your clients?"

Howard chuckled, kind of. The sound actually came out more like a rasp than anything else. "You've been big your whole life, right Quinton? Physically big, I mean?"

"Pretty much. So what?"

"Thomas Jacobson was never big, never imposing in any way. Until he found a way to become so."

"By using his clout with you to do whatever he wanted," I said.

Howard nodded.

"And now he's flexing the kind of muscles most people never have," I said.

Howard nodded again but didn't take his gaze from the door. "At first, I figured he only wanted a job. Turned out the notion of using pressure to get something he wanted, I'm guessing an experience he'd never had before, only left him wanting more."

I changed to another topic. "What about Lorie Jones?"

"What about her?"

"How did she factor into all this?"

Howard gave me a bit of a sneer. I gathered his estimation of my intellect was dropping like a rock. "The same way a lot of other women got in trouble since I took him on. She walked through the door one day."

A lump formed in my stomach. That was it. No hidden connection, no super weird obsession, nothing really special to set Lorie Jones apart from anyone else on the planet.

One day, she happened to walk through the doors of Hobart and Howard and into the web of a creep.

"So what do we do now John?" I asked.

He didn't even glance at me, his stare one hundred percent focused on the door. "I don't know what you're going to do, mister. And I really don't care. I'm going to wait here until Thomas comes to see me, and I'm going to finish him once and for all."

"You sure he'll come here?" I asked.

"At some point he has to. Now you've outed him, I'm one of the last dangling threads to be tied up."

If I'd known for a fact it would be Jacobson who would cross Howard's gun sights, I maybe would have gotten up and walked out.

But I couldn't be sure of that, so I had to settle the issue. "I don't think so. I can't leave you like this."

"I don't really see how you can prevent me." As he said the words, his forearms tightened up more rigidly than they had yet, and I moved.

I flung myself straight out of the chair and onto his desk, reaching out for him. Both my hands grasped both of his so that we had three layers: my hands, his, then the gun.

I squeezed his fingers as hard as I could to keep him from being able to fire. Although the weapon was pointed away from me, you never want one going off if you can avoid it.

Howard squealed and tried slamming his arms up and down. I was straddled across his desk, but with half my weight pinning him in his chair he couldn't get any leeway into the move. His breath hissed into my face, and his eyes bugged out.

A small, very small, part of me felt like hell about dominating a gray-haired old man, but it was either that or take the risk of someone getting killed at some point.

Taking a deep breath, I squeezed my hands even harder, and he uttered a short cry of pain before I felt his grip weaken. Releasing my grip, the pistol plunked onto the desktop.

I grabbed it up, scuttled off the desk, and backpedaled away.

Howard hung half out of his chair, kind of slumped down on one side. Instead of looking at me he gazed down at the floor, and in the next minute began crying.

I wasn't sure if he was crying for himself, for his wreck of a life, or finally letting it out for the woman he accidentally killed years before.

But at the moment it didn't really matter a whole hell of a lot.

CHAPTER FIFTY-EIGHT

"Damned if I know what to do," I said to Karyn over the phone.

It took me half an hour from leaving Howard's office to get back to my hotel room, and the first thing I'd done, once I'd given myself time to think it all through, was call Karyn.

I figured I'd get in trouble with the cops for not waiting around for them, but at the moment had more pressing concerns.

Though maybe not the most productive use of time, I'd kind of lost track of keeping Karyn in the loop, which wasn't fair.

"You're not the only one," she said. "The police were in our offices almost all day long, interviewing everyone they could think of."

"Waste of time," I said. "The culprit isn't in your office."

"No, but I guess they have to do it."

"Of course, they do. They've got a missing woman in potential danger. Hell, the guy could have taken her anywhere. For all we know, by now they could be out of the country."

"Why do you think he went full tilt?" Karyn asked. "Everything he did to her up to now was kind of, what, passive? Now, he's suddenly Mr. Violence? Doesn't make a lot of sense, does it?"

"Kind of," I said. "He sent a couple of muscle guys after me, and some hoods after another woman at his firm. He's been slowly building to something here, which may explain why he abducted Lorie."

"Are you thinking that Lorie calling you into this is what caused him to go off?"

"Possibly, though I can't say for sure."

"So what now?" Karyn asked.

"Damned if I know. The big question for the last twenty-four hours has been where. Where the hell did he take her? I was trying to focus on how he did all this stuff, but I got my answers about an hour ago. Now I simply need to see in a crystal ball and find out where . . ."

I stopped in mid-sentence, little bits and pieces coming together in my brain. "Sorry, Karyn, got to go."

I hung up before she could say anything, almost simultaneously tapping my phone and calling Josh Nichols back in Providence. There was suddenly something I had to know, and I had to know it right away. While Sloan could get me the info, provided he was still talking to me after bolting out of Howard's office, I knew instinctively it would be better, in a save-your-career way, for me to get it from an out of towner.

And as far as I knew, Josh was already out from under suspicion for the bogus charges Hartman had thrown his way.

"Josh," I said when he picked up, "it's me. I need to know an address, and I need to know it now. No questions, please. I'll explain all when I get back home. Will you do it?"

I waited a couple of seconds while Josh worked at coming to the decision I knew he would.

"What do you need?" he asked.

"An address. One that's going to be kind of hard to track down."

CHAPTER FIFTY-NINE

About an hour later, I pulled up outside John Howard's home in an exclusive suburb of Kansas City.

It was nice, though not quite millionaire level. On my brief visits to Howard's office, I hadn't noticed any personal family photos anywhere, so I was going on the assumption the man was unmarried, possibly widowed, any kids or grandkids probably far away.

The house was single story, though fairly large. Looking from the outside it probably held at least ten rooms, if not more. The outside was done up in a southwestern motif, constructed with adobe instead of brick or wood. A small black wrought iron gate led one into a tiny brick courtyard, at the end of which was the main door.

I approached the house, gun in hand.

I made it past the gate and across the courtyard to the front door.

Which, for some reason, was unlocked. With all the lights off, the only illumination came from street lamps and stars outside. I swiveled my head left and right, silently begging my night vision to amp up.

A faint groan came from the left, and I looked over that way. Howard lay there, flopping his left hand in what could remotely have been considered a "come here" motion.

Either I hadn't incapacitated him enough in his office or the cops had been late getting there, but he clearly hadn't waited around for them.

And the old boy, no slouch as a detective, must have come to the same conclusion I had.

Not hearing anything or anyone else close by, I sidled over his way and crouched down beside him, my almost-fifty-year old knees creaking as I did so.

The guy was in bad shape. Even in the murk, I could see the paleness of his face, and his limbs were twitching uncontrollably.

"He here?" I whispered.

Howard nodded. His lips wiggled a couple of times. It was obviously too much effort for him to actually speak.

"Mrs. Jones?" I asked.

Another nod, this one with less energy behind it than the last.

I looked Howard over as closely as I could considering the dimness of the light. "You okay?" I whispered.

Howard shook his head, then somehow found the strength to raise his hand and push it against my chest. "Back of the house," he hissed. "He's got her somewhere back in there."

As he spoke, I'd heard the faintest of gurgles, and while I couldn't see for sure, I had the feeling he may have had a punctured lung. I felt the damned seconds ticking away as I tried to decide what to do.

"Phone?" Howard whispered, more as a question than anything.

I nodded and dug my phone out of my pocket and handed it to him, at the same time wondering why he didn't have one on him.

"Smashed mine when I fell down," the old man must also have been a mind reader. "Tried to pull it out, but it was all shattered. Kind of like me right now."

He coughed, and a little dark stream of blood came out of his mouth. I realized why I hadn't seen any obvious wounds, from either gun or bullet, on his body. Peering closer, I could see his face already beginning to puff.

"Jacobson beat you up?" I asked.

The old man nodded, arched his back for a moment, then slumped down again. "Toadied for him all this time, whatever he wanted," he said. "Practically gave him the keys to the company, and he does this to me."

I stood up, knowing I had to track Lorie and Jacobson down. At the same time, a raw anger began building inside of me.

"Bullshit." It's hard to hiss quietly, but somehow I managed it. "You let that bastard run wild for too long, all the while knowing exactly what he was. Don't try going for too much pity now, mister."

Howard gave about a quarter nod and somehow managed to slump even lower to the ground than he had been. "Back of the house," he repeated, "he's waiting with her back there."

I nodded, paused long enough to see Howard begin dialing the phone I'd given him, then gripped my weapon tighter and headed down the hallway and to the far side of the house.

CHAPTER SIXTY

I FOUND THEM IN THE KITCHEN. Next to a large, walk-in refrigerator, I could barely make them out. Two shadowy forms, one crouched down and the other hunched over her.

"Stay right there," Jacobson's voice called out, though with a bit of a crack to it.

I froze in place, my weapon half leveled.

"Drop the gun," he said.

"Don't think so."

The two shadows faintly shifted position.

"You don't have any choice, Quinton. All the light's behind you, so you're backlighted fine for me."

"Maybe I can see you as well." When in doubt, bluff the hell out of them.

"Huh uh. Doesn't work that way. I've got the vision and you don't."

Or at least try to bluff them.

"I drop the gun," I said, "what's to stop you from blowing me away?"

The more upright shadow snickered. "Nothing. It's a chance you have to take. I can tell you right now, you don't drop it and I'm blowing Little Miss Sweetum's head right off."

"How do I know you won't kill her once I've dropped the gun, then take me out as well?"

Another snicker . . . I never knew in real life bad guys actually did that.

"You don't, Quinton. Seeing as how you blundered in here like this, I don't really see you having much of a choice. Guess you really are as dumb as you look."

He had me there. If I dropped my weapon, there was more than a fifty-fifty chance both Lorie and I would be dead in a few minutes. If I didn't drop it, I figured it about a hundred percent Lorie would die soon.

I dropped the gun.

"Now kick it over my way," Jacobson said.

"You've seen too many cop shows, Jacobson."

Another snicker. "You forget I used to be a cop, hotshot. Unlike you, I'm not some overweight jock who thinks flexing his muscles is impressive. I've got a brain, and I use it."

Not able at the moment to find much of a flaw in his assessment, I figured what the hell and kicked the gun about ten feet off to the side.

Although I obviously couldn't see him in the dark, I could imagine Jacobson's nostrils flaring.

"I said kick it my way," he snapped.

"You know how it is with us dumb jocks," I said. "We never can get past words of one syllable."

Jacobson brushed his elbow on the wall, and the lights snapped on.

He was wearing tan slacks, navy blazer, and a white tone on tone open at the neck. The slacks were wrinkled, and his black loafers had a dull sheen to them.

I assumed he hadn't been hiding out in Howard's kitchen this whole time, and more than likely had been moving from place to place, looking for a safe spot.

Why he'd chosen Howard's home as the safe spot, only Jacobson could say.

Lorie, crouched half in front of him and half to the side, had on a pink dress with one shoulder ripped and a black pump on her left foot but not on the right.

"Howard's had me over here lots of times," Jacobson said, "enough to be familiar with the entire layout of the place. Don't try to fuck with me again, Quinton."

So far, Lorie hadn't moved or spoken, and I wouldn't even have been sure she was breathing if I hadn't heard an occasional rasp from her.

"So what do we do Tommy?" I asked. "Stand here and glare at each other till one of us dies of boredom?"

Jacobson's eyes narrowed, and his face flushed a bit at my use of his name. "The name's Thomas, not Tommy."

I shrugged. "What's in a name? You're probably planning on blowing me away right here and now, so you won't be bothered by me anymore. Right?'

"That's right." His voice was back in full snark mode now. "But it's even better than that. Too bad you won't be around to see how it plays out."

I was beginning to feel as if ants were crawling up and down my arms and legs, and my own breathing had become a little difficult. Standing unarmed in front of an obsessed man who was armed didn't exactly sound like the best of plans.

"How it's going to turn out?" I said. "Let's see if even I can figure it out. My guess is you're going to blow me away, then Lorie here, and somehow make it look like I'm the one who did it. You'll take me out and be a big hero to everyone."

Jacobson's glower told me I'd hit things just about right.

"Of course," I said, "you may have to work a bit to come up with a logical explanation of how the two of us ended up in this house together."

"I'm sure I can come up with something."

"Okay," I said, "that leaves only one question."

"Which is?"

"If you've got it all worked out, why haven't you already gunned me down?"

Lorie reared her head a bit right then, but only for a nanosecond before slumping down even more than before. But in that instant she'd caught my eye, and an understanding had passed between us.

Jacobson had to shift his stance to accommodate the additional dead weight.

"Maybe you don't have it all figured out," he said. "Maybe I'm still too damned smart for you."

"Could be. Then again, could also be you're too cowardly to pull the trigger, even with me helpless right in front of you."

A slight cackle began to come out of Jacobson's mouth before he stifled it. "A coward? For real, Quinton? Dude, I was a cop for nearly ten years."

"Sure you were," I said. "And you've ridden that experience to the top. Here's the thing, Tommy. I've been in town for a week now, learning about you, talking to people about you. And you know what I've found out about your time in uniform?"

"What?"

"Not much of anything. Didn't hear any big stories, didn't come across anyone who really remembered you. It's like your entire time on the force you were basically a nothing, barely registering on people's radar."

Jacobson's face set, and I tensed myself even more. If he made a move against either me or Lorie, I wanted to be ready for it.

"That's a lot of bullshit, Quinton."

"It's not bullshit," I shot back. "And I'd be willing to bet if I hung around for another month, really dug into your record, looked it all up, I'd find more of the same. Big fat nothing."

Lorie began taking in deep breaths. Though she was a total civilian, I had the impression she knew exactly where I was headed.

"The reason you don't hear much about me," Jacobson said through gritted teeth, "is jealousy."

That one almost made me laugh. "Jealousy?"

"That's right," Jacobson was spitting the words out hard enough I thought he may chip a tooth or two. "I was too damned good at my job. When you can't help but upstage all the simps and morons around you, they fight back by making you look bad. By keeping you down so you don't get promoted."

This time I couldn't hold the laugh back. "That what this is all about, Jacobson? I was such hot shit everyone conspired against me? So now you're going to . . ."

"Not at all," he said. I wondered how much longer he could stay in such a tensed pose. Like with his boss earlier in the night, sooner or later something had to give.

On the other hand, how much longer could I keep my edge up? Physically, I easily could dominate the man, but his mania could possibly give him the upper hand.

And where the hell were the cops Howard was supposed to call?

"It's just," he continued, "that I decided not to let them win. Soon as I got the chance, I left the force behind and went for greener pastures."

"Where you decided to start being a predator," I said.

Jacobson cackled, actually more of a bark, and stood up straight, his hand still entangled in Lorie's hair lifting her up to an almost standing position. "Call it what you want, Quinton, but here in a moment I'm going to be the big man on campus, doing my best to save my employer, not to mention poor Lorie here, from a scumbag like you."

"Naturally, you'll be a few seconds too late," I said.

For the first time, a genuine smile stretched across his entire face. "Naturally. I'll be too late to save them, but not to avenge them."

"Seems like me that's a line from some movie or other," I said, "but there's one little thing you're forgetting."

Jacobson stood up completely straight now, his gun arm leveled at a straight line from his body. "Which is?"

"Simple," I said, my blood practically frigid in my veins, "you're not taking me on alone. Now!"

At my sudden shout, Lorie snapped into action. She reared up on her toes and rammed her left elbow straight back into Jacobson's rib cage. He ooffed but managed to keep himself straight. However, Lorie's action had been enough to make his gun arm waver off line.

I cannoned into them.

I didn't have time to safeguard Lorie and could only hope she wouldn't get too banged up. I had to take Jacobson down all the way, and I had to do it quick. He may not have been the most field-capable cop who ever lived, and I easily outweighed him by fifty pounds at least, but he was desperate, probably a little nuts, and he was armed.

The three of us smashed back into the wall, causing another loud exhalation on Jacobson's part. Lorie squealed a little, and I felt more than saw Jacobson lose his hold on her hair. Grabbing her shoulder with my left hand, I shoved her to the side and down, then went to work.

I gave him a couple of the most solid hits I could. He didn't go down. He hadn't even lost the gun, and as the arm started coming up again I turned sideways and smashed into him with my shoulder.

He grunted at that. Before I could follow up, he swung his left arm, still holding his gun in a kind of looping motion, and the stainless steel automatic collided with the side of my head.

The bastard was stronger than he looked, and I started seeing stars exploding around me.

Jacobson must have liked the effect the blow had on me because he reared his arm back to give it another go. I hunched my shoulder up to deflect his move, at the same time burrowing a hard left hook into his rib cage. He gasped at that one, and staggered back a ways.

But he still hadn't let go of the gun, and as I made another forward move, he managed to level the weapon up at me again.

"Tough luck, loser," he said as a small pop sounded out.

Jacobson stiffened, reared up to his full height, then fell against the wall and slumped into a sitting position. As Lorie whimpered, I turned to look behind me, in the direction from which the shot had come, and saw John Howard had somehow managed to crawl his way in from the front room, stretched out prone on the floor with a .32 automatic clutched in his hand.

"Bastard never thought to search me after he beat me up," the old man said before crumbling all the way to the floor.

CHAPTER SIXTY-ONE

Karyn Roberts and I were having dinner at a new Italian restaurant in Kansas City, and I didn't even attempt to pronounce the name. It sat on the fourteenth floor of a building in the middle of downtown and offered, in nice weather, a sweeping view of the metro area.

The weather was nice this night.

She had arrived a few minutes before me and snagged a table for us right next to a window. We'd already ordered and were waiting on our drinks.

The lights in the room were at half power, no doubt for atmosphere.

"How's Lorie doing?" I asked.

Karyn smiled, just a flicker of the lips. She wore a royal blue silk dress, black pumps, and had her hair partially done up. A couple of pieces of what looked like real gold jangled around her right wrist and neck, and I couldn't shake the feeling she'd dressed up just for me.

That left me feeling good and bad at the same time.

"She's shook up, of course," Karyn replied. "About what you'd expect from someone who's lived a fairly mild life, then has to go through something like that."

"I tried to shield her as much as I could."

"Of course, you did," Karen said. "And she knows that. She'll need a little time."

"And a lot fewer PI's in her life, right?"

Karyn shook her head and took a sip of wine as I wondered what was taking our meal so long.

"How's Mr. Howard?" Karyn asked a moment later.

I shrugged. "Doing about as good as can be expected for a guy his age. His days of field activity are long behind him, so he took those knocks, both mine and Jaccobson's, harder than he would have a few decades ago."

"What do you think possessed him to jump in like that?" she asked.

I picked up my glass of beer, whirled it a moment in my hand, then put it down without drinking. "My guess? That he thought he was responsible for the entire mess, which he was of course. Not only Lorie, but all the rest of it, and decided he had to make things right."

"Couldn't he have sent some of his operatives in? It's not like his company's short on manpower."

I moved my glass back and forth on the table a couple of times and wondered why I was having such a hard time looking across the table.

"It's kind of hard to send people in to take down one of their own," I finally said. "Plus, with Jacobson turning out to be such a bad apple, he may have wondered who he could trust."

"Turned out Lorie could trust you," Karyn said.

I nodded and finally looked at her. Could have been only a reflection from the downtown lights, or the gloom of the restaurant, but her eyes seemed to glisten a little.

"Yeah," I said. "She was my client, meaning she pretty much had to trust me. But she was Jacobson's client before that, and look where that got her."

Our waiter came by and gently placed our plates before us. Karyn looked down at her manicotti but didn't pick up her fork.

"Something wrong?" I asked, though I could half guess what.

"Turns out I could trust you too," she said. "After all, I'm the one who suggested you to Lorie, and you made it come out okay."

"Maybe. I had a lot of help from John Howard, old as he is."

"Still, it was mainly you," she said.

"That's my job."

"Is that all?" I heard a catch in her voice.

"Dammit, Karyn," I tried to growl, but it didn't come off very forcefully. "Things turned out okay for your friend. What more do you want?"

Now she picked up her fork and knife, wedged off a bit of pasta, and ate it.

Gathering her thoughts, maybe.

She put her utensils down, took a drink of her wine, and leaned back in her chair.

"You going back to Providence tonight?" she asked.

I nodded. Who was I to criticize? I hadn't touched my steak yet. "Figure I'll be home by midnight."

"Home to Talia?"

Well, it had taken a while, but we'd finally gotten there. "Pretty much," I said.

Karyn nodded and turned back to her meal. We ate in silence for a few moments.

"She's a lucky woman," she said a few heartbeats later.

"More like I'm a lucky man," I said.

"Luckier than you deserve, don't you think?" A slight lilt had come back in her voice.

"No argument there," I said.

Somehow, and I wasn't quite sure how, the tension had broken. A few minutes later, full of belly, we both sat back in our chairs.

"All in all," Karyn said, "you did pretty good. Lorie's still in one piece; the bad guy's going off to prison; and the old man got to play hero for once."

"All in all," I said.

Karyn toyed a bit with the stem of her wine glass. "All things considered, I'm glad I called you in. Lorie was in a hell of a lot more danger than we even imagined."

"Service is my business," I said.

"And you do it well."

Smiling, I reached out and clasped her hand in mine. "Time for me to leave."

The glisten came back, fainter than before, though still there. "I know. Promise to come back soon?"

I knew I shouldn't have said it, should have picked any words but the ones I did. "You bet."

Now it was time for my eyes to dim and blur a bit.

Or maybe it was the lights of that Kansas City skyline, just outside the windows, tantalizing with unobtainable promise.

Johnson Photography, Columbia, MO.

A RETIRED HIGH-SCHOOL TEACHER AND FORMER COLLEGE instructor, Kevin R. Doyle is the author of five novels in the Sam Quinton mystery series, all published by Camel Press. He's also written four crime thrillers, including *And the Devil Walks Away* and *The Anchor*, and one horror novel, *The Litter*, along with numerous short horror stories published in small magazines over the years. The first Quinton book, *Squatter's Rights*, was nominated for the 2021 Shamus award for Best First PI Novel. A lifelong Midwesterner, Doyle currently resides in Missouri and has loosely based his fictional city of Providence books on Columbia.

Printed in the USA
CPSIA information can be obtained
at www.ICGtesting.com
LVHW030952010724
784217LV00004B/19